D1727473

MAKING
THE
COMMONS
WORK

❧

A publication of the
International Center for Self-Governance

The mission of the International Center for Self-Governance is to encourage men and women in developing countries to achieve the self-governing and entrepreneurial way of life. In addition to publishing the finest academic studies, such as *Making the Commons Work*, ICSG also provides practical materials in a variety of readily accessible formats. In Fall 1993, a complete set of training materials based on the conceptual framework and case studies in this book will be available, including manuals, learning tools, and interactive tasks and games.

For more information on ICSG or its publications, training materials, and videos, please contact:

ICSG
243 Kearny Street
San Francisco, CA 94108 USA
(415) 981-5353

MAKING THE COMMONS WORK

Theory, Practice, and Policy

Daniel W. Bromley
General Editor

Coeditors

David Feeny
Margaret A. McKean
Pauline Peters
Jere L. Gilles
Ronald J. Oakerson
C. Ford Runge
James T. Thomson

 PRESS

Institute for Contemporary Studies
San Francisco, California

This book is a publication of the International Center for Self-Governance, dedicated to promoting the self-governing and entrepreneurial way of life around the world. The Center is affiliated with the Institute for Contemporary Studies, a nonpartisan, nonprofit public policy research organization. The analyses, conclusions, and opinions expressed in ICS Press publications are those of the authors and not necesarily those of the Institute for Contemporary Studies, or of the Institute's officers, directors, or others associated with, or funding, its work.

Publication of this book was funded by the U.S. Agency for International Development.

Some chapters in this book are revised and updated versions of works first presented at the Conference on Common Property Resource Management (1985), which was sponsored by the National Academy of Sciences and the National Research Council.

Inquiries, book orders, and catalog requests should be addressed to ICS Press, 243 Kearny Street, San Francisco, CA 94108. (415) 981-5353. Fax (415) 986-4878. For book orders and catalog requests call toll free in the contiguous United States: **(800) 326-0263**. Distributed to the trade by National Book Network, Lanham, Maryland.

Project editor: Barbara Beidler Kendrick
Copyeditor: J. M. B. Edwards
Proofreader: Barbara Ferenstein
Indexer: Patricia Ruggiero

Library of Congress Cataloging-in-Publication Data

Making the commons work : theory, practice, and policy / Daniel W.
   Bromley, general editor ; coeditors David Feeny . . . [et al.].
      p. cm.
   Includes bibliographical references and index.
   ISBN 1-55815-198-2.—ISBN 1-55815-217-2 (pbk.)
   1. Commons. I. Bromley, Daniel W., 1940– . II. Feeny, David,
1948– .
HD1286.M35   1992
333.2—dc20   92-24880
                                                          CIP

Contents

List of Tables

List of Figures

Foreword

A common historical myth holds that Europe's peasants and yeomen who worked the commons were inefficient cultivators, and that it took the forced enclosure movements of the fifteenth and sixteenth centuries, turning the commons into private property, to bring efficiency and increased productivity to agriculture. Like yesterday's nobility, contemporary social scientists often take a jaundiced view of common-property institutions, again making the commons an object of derision and "reform." Theorists decrying the "tragedy of the commons" rely on the arid reasoning of the "prisoner's dilemma" to demonstrate the impossibility of long-lasting voluntary cooperation or effective collective action.

The contributors to *Making the Commons Work* take a fresh approach, emphasizing not the tragedy but the possibilities of the commons, both in theory and in practice. Drawing on case studies from countries around the world, they develop a new set of constructs to explain how small-scale common-property systems can be successful and durable.

The message this book delivers is especially meaningful for today's public policy debate over natural resources. This debate usually takes for granted that natural resources should be owned either privately or by the state. The former promises us efficiency, but often at the cost of community and democratic values. The latter claims to address these values, but often at the cost of efficiency, as bureaucracy takes its inevitable toll, destroying community and self-governing values.

Making the Commons Work gives us a third path to consider: common-property ownership by self-governing associations of local users. The studies in this book illustrate the utility of governing resources as common property—from forests to fisheries, grazing land to shared irrigation systems—around the globe. The theoretical implications gleaned from these examples carry important lessons for all areas of the world, both developing and developed.

Most important, this book shows that people on the local level can handle complex social and economic issues successfully and equitably, sometimes for hundreds of years. Often, economic aid to developing countries has ignored these small-scale but effective local institutions, mistakenly relying instead on privatization or state ownership to solve development and natural resource problems. Even in the developed world, political and economic "progress" too often seems to result in stripping creativity, power, and initiative from average citizens. The evidence and arguments presented in this book show that this need not, and should not, happen. Many difficult problems can be ameliorated or solved by empowering those most directly involved with sufficient authority to devise and enforce small-scale, community solutions.

Robert B. Hawkins, Jr.
President
Institute for Contemporary Studies

PART 1

Common Property as an Institution

1

The Commons, Property, and Common-Property Regimes

Daniel W. Bromley

There can be no more important aspect of scholarship than the business of concepts and language. If scholars use the same words or terms to describe fundamentally different situations, ideas, or phenomena, then progress in understanding is impeded rather than advanced. In the literature on natural resources and environmental policy, it would be difficult to find an idea (that is, a concept) as misunderstood as "commons" or "common property." The mischief that arises from the continuing failure to understand common property is perverse in both scholarly discussions and public policy formulation. On the former front, scholars will show no hesitancy to expound on the problems inherent in common property without the benefit of first defining "property," and without betraying any understanding of the historical and contemporary facts surrounding common-property regimes. On the practical side, they will show equal confidence in advising all who will listen about how to "solve" the so-called tragedy of the commons. This mischief is then perpetuated among politicians who, as Keynes put it, are under the thrall of some now-defunct economist. While his language may have been a bit strong, there is cause for serious concern when policy recommendations are predicated upon false definitions of the problem.

The literature is full of casual references to "common-property resources," as if this were a universal and immutable classification—almost, indeed, as if the prevailing institutional form were somehow inherent in a

3

natural resource. Never mind that in one setting trees and fish and range forage are controlled and managed as private property, in another they are controlled and managed as state property, in another they are controlled and managed as common property, and in others they are not controlled or managed at all but are instead used by anyone who so desires to use them. There is no such thing as a common property *resource*; there are only resources controlled and managed as common property, or as state property, or as private property. Or—and this is where confusion persists in the literature—there are resources over which *no property rights* have been recognized. We call these latter "open-access resources" (*res nullius*, which is Latin for "no one's property").

The key concept here is "property." Property is a claim to a benefit (or income) stream, and a property right is a claim to a benefit stream that some higher body—usually the state—will agree to protect through the assignment of duty to others who may covet, or somehow interfere with, the benefit stream. Rights have no meaning without correlated duties, and the management problem with open-access resources is that there are no duties on aspiring users to refrain from use (Bromley 1989a, 1989b, 1991). Property is *not* an object but is rather a social relation that defines the property holder with respect to something of value (the benefit stream) against all others. Property is a triadic social relation involving benefit streams, right holders, and duty bearers (Hallowell 1943) It is for this reason that I urge us to consider the concept of "property regimes." Regimes, after all, are human artifacts reflecting instrumental origins, and a property regime is fundamentally instrumental in nature. That is, property regimes take on their special character by virtue of collective perceptions regarding what is scarce (and hence *possibly* worth protecting with rights), and what is valuable (and hence *certainly* worth protecting with rights). Property is a social instrument, and particular property regimes are chosen for particular social purposes.

The fallacy in traditional approaches to the commons is that writers have failed to understand the concept of property; they have very often treated a particular natural resource as if it had inherent characteristics that suggested it would everywhere be controlled under a particular type of property regime; and they have invariably failed to learn that the world is replete with reasonably successful common-property regimes.[1] By "successful" I mean that the natural resource has not been squandered, that some level of investment in the natural resource has occurred, and that the coowners of the resource are not in a perpetual state of anarchy. In short, common property regimes exist and function very much like private property regimes and state property regimes. Some are not working very well, while others work very well indeed. That is why we have decided to call this book *Making the Commons Work*.

The Plan of This Book

Our purpose in organizing the Panel on Common Property Resource Management in the Developing Countries (under the auspices of the National Research Council of the National Academy of Sciences) was to determine if indeed there were any reasonably successful common-property regimes operating in the world. If we could answer that question in the affirmative, then much conventional wisdom and folklore would be seen to be false.

We first take the reader through some conceptual material (Chapters 2 and 3). In Part 2 (Chapters 4 through 11) we explore a number of actual common-property regimes throughout the world. We end up with a conceptual theme in Part 3 (Chapters 12 and 13), where research and policy implications are explored.

In Chapter 2, C. Ford Runge asks that we understand common-property regimes as often associated with natural resources showing considerable uncertainty. He finds such regimes to be prevalent at the extensive margin where economic surplus is minimal, and hence to be associated with low-income situations. Here we are reminded of one central fallacy in the conventional wisdom about common-property regimes: poverty exists as a direct result of common property. In fact, as Runge reminds us, low-value resources are more likely to be managed under common property for the simple reason that there is insufficient economic surplus to support the more expensive private-property regime. I make this same point elsewhere (Bromley 1989a, 1991).

Runge then calls our attention to the role that game theory can play in understanding common-property regimes. His earlier work (1981, 1984) on the assurance problem represents an important contribution, and he here elaborates it. The classic prisoner's dilemma game is seen as but a special case of joint action, one that can only be understood if one recognizes that the structure of a game—the payoff in each cell—is a function of the institutional environment in which the game is imbedded. Some commentators, Runge argues, have seriously confused cause and effect in the prisoner's dilemma. That is, they have observed the tendency of prisoners to "rat" on their accomplice and have then attributed this behavior to some inherent human tendency toward self-interested individualism. What they take for "inevitable" human tendencies is, rather, an artifact of the way in which the game is set up. If the rules for exacting confessions from apprehended suspects are structured differently, then isolated prisoners have very different optimal strategies and there is no dominance of individual (Pareto-inferior) strategies (Sen 1982, 65). I have called this the "prisoner's dream" (Bromley 1989b, 87).

It is essential to understand that the institutional structure of any game (or life situation) reflects the prior social purpose to be served by the human interaction under consideration. Just as property is an instrumental social artifact, so are the broader institutional arrangements that define patterns of social interaction across a broad array of life experiences. The existing institutional structure reflects, among other things, prevailing cultural and social norms regarding individualism and its relation to collective notions. In that sense we can say that people behave (or choose) in an institutional context—not a very surprising observation really. If the rules (institutions) are designed to be favorable for exacting confessions from isolated suspects, then let us not act surprised when prisoners confess. But also let us not impute to this observed behavior some overarching "truth" about human motivation. On the contrary, if the social context and the associated institutions encourage collective cooperation and collaboration, let us not dismiss this as quaint and primitive— and inconsistent with revealed "truth" from the prisoner's dilemma game.

While Runge has set the theoretical stage, Ronald J. Oakerson, in Chapter 3, offers a more complete picture of the interrelation between the technical and physical base of the society under study and the social organization that evolves to manage and control that infrastructure. Oakerson reminds us of the close relation between the resource base, the social structure, and the belief system out of which will arise decisions about the performance of the complex unit under study. While not using the terminology, Oakerson's framework has similarities to the cultural ecology school of anthropology (Netting 1977; Steward 1955). Oakerson focuses on two performance indicators, efficiency and equity, that will have direct resonance to economists, but he treats them as broader than economists are wont to do.

The Oakerson framework represents the conceptual template against which we asked all authors to study and report on their particular common-property regimes. In that sense it is perhaps the most fundamental chapter in the volume. We have been, in a sense, unfair to Oakerson in that we were reluctant to permit him to revise his chapter substantively in light of all that we have learned since our work began in 1984. Because his chapter was *the* basis for all of the other studies, we thought it important that it stand as it was originally drafted—and as the other authors used it as a guide for the questions they posed. For the most part it stands as written in the earliest phases of our work. It was (and is) an excellent foundation.

We need look no further than Chapter 4, by Margaret McKean, to understand the value of the Oakerson framework. In her chapter the physical and technical basis of the village commons is vividly described. We find a wonderfully detailed account of the decision systems in place over time and see a clear process in place for determining the performance of particular outcomes from prevailing patterns of interaction. She shows us how different incentive systems were in operation, depending upon what was deemed to be scarce, and how the regimes responded—sometimes quickly, sometimes not at all—to new perceptions of scarcity. The responses to both internal and external pressures are nicely documented.

The message from McKean's account of the Japanese commons centers on the evolving concept in Japanese society of the proper decision-making unit. At first it was the (by modern western standards) authoritarian village. Later the "family" came to have more prominence and then, as the centralized state took a greater interest in local affairs, there was a new locus of choice. Many situations in the developing world show similar patterns of evolution, with the exception that few have the structured and orderly state that we know from post-Meiji Japan. Indeed, much of the problem in many developing countries today is that local-level institutional arrangements have been undermined by colonialism and the emerging nation state, while nothing approaching an orderly resource management regime has been put in place by the national government. Local natural resources such as forests and rangelands, having been appropriated by the government as "state property," remain unmanaged and uncontrolled by the national government. As might be expected, the de facto management regime is one of nonproperty, or open access (Bromley 1986, 1989a; Bromley and Chapagain 1984).

In a most interesting historical and contemporary account of common-property regimes, Bruce Campbell and Ricardo A. Godoy (Chapter 5) explore similarities between the medieval common fields in England and the contemporary commons in the Andes. They challenge the idea that common-property regimes were influenced by technology in the form of the heavy mold-board plow. Rather, they argue, social arrangements are influenced (but not determined) by the combination of an economy's ecological and technological attributes. Specifically, it is a reliance on animals rather than plows that seems to explain the parallel evolution of common-property regimes in these two distinct socioeconomic settings. That is, the joint need for forage for animals and fertilizer for crops explains much about institutional arrangements over land, since productivity—and hence the standard of living—depended upon striking a workable balance between the conflicting need on the same unit of land for both livestock feed and manure. Because the same piece of land produced human food and livestock feed at different times of the year, and under very different technical conditions, the instrumental problem for a management regime was obvious. Campbell and Godoy conclude that the disappearance of the English commons and the persistence of the Andean commons may well reflect different social arrangements to prevent ecological destruction. Those inclined to see inevitable resource destruction in common property will not be amused.

Continuing our interest in comparative institutional analysis, James T. Thomson, David Feeny, and Ronald J. Oakerson (Chapter 6) analyze resource-use patterns in Niger and Thailand. The interest here is the tension between and changes in the balance between local-level management arrangements and those at the center (the national government). The intriguing aspect of this work is that it highlights the role of local learning and innovation in management regimes. This feedback is the recursive element in the Oakerson framework. We are reminded in very clear terms that a successful common-property regime implies an effective local capacity to experiment with and learn from various management (and institutional) forms. Equally important, success is enhanced to the extent that the political and economic costs of collective action can be kept "low." As we already learned from Runge's chapter, the ecological base of many areas is not of sufficient inherent productivity to support an elaborate (and costly) managerial structure. If institutional innovation can hold these costs low—given the constrained income prospect from the resource— then joint management arrangements such as common property will succeed.

Given that both the Thais and the Hausa are highly "individualistic," it may happen that privatization would reduce the transaction costs of collective action. Indeed the authors find that privatization does make sense, even though equity problems may arise in the long run. They make a point that will be elaborated upon by Robert Wade in Chapter 9: decision makers must perceive that the collective benefits from joint action will contain a sufficiently large private component—which they can appropriate—to compensate for joint action's high transaction costs. When that condition is not met, common-property regimes are in serious jeopardy.

Fragile common-property regimes are prevalent in fisheries the world over. Governments, intent on encouraging "modern" commercial fisheries, will subsidize a variety of technical changes that threaten existing institutional arrangements. Large, powerful trawlers encroach on near-shore artisan fisheries and quickly overfish the stock. We are then told that common property is to blame. Governments will subsidize motors for small fishermen and once again institutional arrangements will be blamed for the ensuing overfishing and change in patterns of interaction that were actually upset by technical change. Interestingly, many will look at these situations and celebrate the technical change as progress, denouncing the prevailing institutional arrangements as primitive or quaint for their failure to change in response to the imposed technology.

This fascination with new techniques and contempt for allegedly rigid institutional arrangements belies a cultural bias on the part of the observer. Who is to say that every new technical device is automatically good and that existing institutional arrangements are somehow bad because they do not automatically adjust? This problem is highlighted in Chapters 7 and 8. In Chapter 7, Fikret Berkes recounts the close relationship between the technological base of a fishery, the decision-making arrangements, and the ensuing patterns of interaction. In the Turkish fisheries under study we see the close relationship between rules from the national government and the local-level rules for controlling access to each fishery. We also see the forces in some fisheries that may account for their successful management, and that may cause problems elsewhere.

The fragility of management regimes is nowhere more apparent than in the account by John Cordell and Margaret McKean of the Brazilian nearshore fishery (Chapter 8). Here we see a property regime that exists very close to the margin of human subsistence. The tight link between fishing as an income source and fishing as extension of the family is everywhere in evidence. Reciprocity and respect are the glue holding this fragile (and flammable) situation in check; the slightest affront on a personal level is immediately translated into economic reprisal in the fishery. Conversely, personal arrangements such as godparenting have their direct rationale in the economic sphere. While anthropologists know these things, economists are likely to require frequent reminders. The threat of violence, barely beneath the surface, attests to the extent to which this social system is without economic slack.

Cordell and McKean remind us that poverty does not result in anarchy but quite the opposite; the low value of the fishery calls into play a most elaborate social structure to regulate patterns of interaction. We also see how the national government has tended to delegitimize the fishery, and how the fishery persists beyond the official recognition of the state. But of course the fishery is at the extreme mercy of the state. As in Chapter 7, if national fishery policy promotes technical change then fisheries such as this are extremely vulnerable. Not only might the fish be exploited, but the economic system here described would be eliminated. Because the community is already outside the government's definition of legitimate activities, there would be no protection forthcoming for the displaced fishermen and their families.

In Chapter 9, by Robert Wade, we move away from rather single-resource accounts of common property and on to a complex of natural resources important to a village economy. Wade argues that successful organization and management in a South Indian village are dependent upon the demand for such regimes rather than on the mere capacity of a group of individuals to supply them. That is, management regimes are demand driven, and individuals will somehow find the mechanisms to accomplish the necessary tasks. He further argues that collective management is a "backstop institution," in the sense that it will be invoked only when individual choice leads to unacceptable social costs.

Wade sees a hierarchy of goals in his villages, in which defense of production is the highest goal, followed by desires to enhance income. Coming in a distant third are efforts to enhance education, nutrition, and health, plus civic improvements. He reminds us of a common theme, namely, that it is better to rely on existing authority systems to perform new functions than it is to create new authority systems. He also alerts us to the dangers of imposing our egalitarian preferences on these management regimes, for if we do this we are likely to create a situation in which the regime will be undermined by local elites. According to Wade, all decision makers need a private reason for collective success. By restricting the decision body to those with a substantial private interest in success, management councils may well approach the minimum coalition where members find it in their private interest to bear transaction costs.

Having said that, he observes that councils concern themselves with those benefits and costs that cannot be privatized, that is, with collective goods and bads. Moreover, village councils will add less vital functions only after the more crucial ones have been routinized and they appear to be operating well.

The Moroccan grazing commons (the *agdal*) is the subject of Jere L. Gilles, Abdellah Hammoudi, and Mohamed Mahdi's analysis of common-property regimes (Chapter 10). They note that isolation and the high costs of individual use can play an important role in keeping pressure on the management regime—and hence the resource—at a reasonable level. Membership in the village is critical for having a right to use the *agdal*, but that membership can be defined in several ways. We see in this chapter a nice account of the overlay of French colonial administration on the management regime in the grazing commons. This exogenous force modified the traditional pattern of tribal conflict, thereby influencing subsequent management regimes and patterns of interaction.

Piers Blaikie, John Harriss, and Adam Pain, like Wade before them, are concerned with south India (Chapter 11). Here, however, the focus is on a wide range of natural resources—water resources, fuelwood, fodder, grazing land, timber, green manure, and minor forest products. We see how private interests have encroached on the commons, how increased marginalization has increased pressure to encroach on the commons, and how an intervention such as irrigation can take pressure off of some parts of the commons but increase it elsewhere.

Part 3 returns us to rather more conceptual material. David Feeny (Chapter 12) offers an insightful treatment of the lessons to be learned from the material in the book, and he suggests avenues for fruitful research. He asks us to reflect on the methods used in our inquiries concerning the commons. The essays in Part 2 are representative of the valuable contributions that can be made by using the comparative case-study approach. Complementary experimental approaches have the potential to make further contributions to analytical developments, field studies, and more effective policy formulation. An overview of this material would be either inadequate or repetitive and the reader is urged to study this chapter carefully.

The same holds for Elinor Ostrom's Chapter 13. She pursues an important notion, mentioned previously: the extent to which language and concepts ought to dominate our task of theory building. Ostrom brings her considerable experience, and an interesting conceptual approach, to bear on this problem in a most constructive fashion. She urges that we begin to think of "common-pool resources"—an idea that blends nicely with my urging that we then talk of common-property regimes, state-property regimes, or private-property regimes over those common-pool resources. She reminds us that the stock of a common-pool resource may be used jointly, but that the services to flow from that stock are individually consumed. She lists a number of variables that will contribute to the success of a management regime concerned with common-pool resources. Among these are a common understanding of the management problem, a common understanding of the alternatives for cooperation, a common perception of mutual trust and reciprocity, and a shared perception that decision-making costs are less than the benefits from joint action. As with Feeny's chapter, an overview cannot do justice to the richness of the ideas presented.

Concluding Observations

There is a critical difference between "open-access resources" and "common-property resources," a difference that turns on the very concept of property. Property is a secure claim on a future benefit stream. There is no property in an open-access situation, only the opportunity to use something. Many of us see situations of open access and improperly regard them as situations of common property. At the same time, most of us have seen common-property regimes at work without recognizing them as such. Irrigation systems represent the essence of a common property regime. There is a well-defined group whose membership is restricted; an asset to be managed (the physical distribution system); an annual stream of benefits (the water that constitutes a valuable agricultural input); and a need for group management of both the capital stock and the annual flow (necessary maintenance of the system and a process for allocating the water among members of the group of irrigators), to make sure that the system continues to yield benefits to the group.[2] There could not be a clearer illustration of a common-property regime than irrigation systems, despite the fact that they do not always work as well as they ought to.

An equally serious mistake is made in identifying the specific problem to be addressed. We will usually suggest that the problem is one of poor range condition, or a lack of water, or undernourished livestock, or a lack of fuelwood for cooking. Unfortunately, these are not problems but are rather symptoms of problems. Development assistance projects to fix symptoms do not fix problems.

The real problem is, in many of these instances, the absence of effective group management regimes necessary to allow the sustained use of the resource base over time. That is, an earlier situation of common property has deteriorated into one of open access. These resource regimes must not only bear the brunt of their own indigenous population growth, but often must also absorb those individuals displaced from other areas who can freely migrate. Because the migrants cannot, by definition, settle on private lands, there is no other option open to them. Even if they go to urban areas they must be supplied with fuelwood or charcoal, and these come from the public domain.

An important question remains: Why don't common-property regimes always adapt to changing conditions in a way that will protect the natural resource? A corollary question, therefore, is why should such management regimes be supported through project interventions? The answer is quite obvious. To install or to support a particular property regime on the basis of its ability to resist external pressure is the wrong approach—especially when that pressure arises in a manner that is quite unrelated to the nature of the property regime itself. Collectives select property regimes on the basis of their suitability for the resource in question—its variability, its productivity, and so on. Our development interventions will be successful if we approach the support of particular property regimes with the same idea in mind.

Any property regime is the legally and socially sanctioned ability to exclude, and so the fortunate owner(s) can force others to go elsewhere. Common-property regimes, because they often are predicated on large groups, are less successful at excluding individuals in order to keep total resource demands in line with sustainable use. Private-property regimes, on the other hand, have a longer history—and a social expectation—of excluding redundant individuals. If exclusion is thought to be unacceptable, private-property regimes appear to avoid the problem by a tradition of partible inheritance, where plots are successively divided among heirs. The outcome of this process, however, is an ownership structure in which individual plots are too small to be viable economic units. Common-property regimes do not become atomized, but rather seek ways to accommodate the increased population. It is not legitimate to ask of common-property regimes that they not only manage highly variable and low-productivity resources but also adapt and adjust to severe internal and external pressures—particularly when much of the external pressure arises from the existence of private property regimes elsewhere in the polity from which individuals are excluded.

Private-property regimes appear to be stable and adaptive because they have the social and legal sanction to exclude people—to slough off excess population. Under private-property regimes with primogeniture, the eviction of younger sons (to say nothing of *all* daughters) is regarded as a costless social process and therefore it looks as though private property is robust and adaptable; it seems to "work." Private property in such a setting "works" for the oldest son; but those with no rights in the estate may wish to challenge this.

Thus we often find ourselves facing a situation in which private property is not a viable institutional alternative, and common-property regimes have deteriorated. If we can reestablish, in those instances where open access prevails, a successful common-property regime, then we have already done a great deal. The standard approach is to expect development projects to improve incomes, to enhance equity, and to sustain the resource base. Perhaps we should not worry overly much about improving incomes; after all, it is quite enough to be successful in preventing incomes from continuing to decline because of resource degradation. Perhaps if a project in the public domain can merely prevent further resource degradation and hence stabilize incomes, that is doing a great deal.

Moreover, perhaps we should worry less about the equity implications of public-domain projects. Or, we should worry about a different dimension of equity. The pressing issue, I suggest, is less one of equity within public-domain projects than it is of equity across all development projects. Because the very poorest members of society obtain an overwhelming share of their sustenance from the public domain, good projects there address an important dimension of equity. In other words, we clearly work *against equity* when we favor commercial agricultural projects on private lands and avoid projects on public-domain lands that will improve the lot of the poorest. If we can enhance the sustainability of the livelihood systems we know as common-property regimes, that is indeed to work in the interest of equity.

We should not expect too much from projects in the public domain whose purpose is to rehabilitate degraded common-property regimes and their natural resources. Part of the success of such projects must be seen to lie in our ability to provide alternative means of livelihood for those who have moved into these resource regimes and so increased the pressure on the natural resource base. It is in this sense that conventional agricultural projects must be seen as important adjuncts to projects in the public domain. Through such an integrated and coordinated approach we can have a greater chance to bring lasting benefit to developing countries.

NOTES

1. Though it would take us beyond the domain of natural resources to explore the topic further, it must be understood here that private clubs are common-property regimes. Such clubs, whether "country clubs" or more restricted collectives, are joint management regimes controlling assets and allocating use rights among coowners or members.

2. The observations made here, by Ostrom in Chapter 13, and by others in this book are underscored by other recent works on the commons including Berkes 1989, Berkes et al. 1989, Feeny et al. 1990, McCay and Acheson 1987, Pinkerton 1989, Stevenson 1991, and Wade 1987.

REFERENCES

Berkes, Fikret, ed. 1989. *Common Property Resources: Ecology and Community-Based Sustainable Development*. London: Belhaven Press.

Berkes, Fikret, David Feeny, Bonnie McCay, and James M. Acheson. 1989. "The Benefits of the Commons." *Nature* 340:91–93.

Bromley, Daniel W. 1986. "Natural Resources and Agricultural Development in the Tropics: Is Conflict Inevitable?" In *Agriculture in a Turbulent World Economy*, ed. Allen Maunder and Ulf Renborg, 319–27. Oxford: Gower.

———. 1989a. "Property Relations and Economic Development: The Other Land Reform." *World Development* 17 (6):867–77.

———. 1989b. *Economic Interests and Institutions: The Conceptual Foundations of Public Policy*. Oxford: Blackwell.

———. 1991. *Environment and Economy: Property Rights and Public Policy*. Oxford: Blackwell.

Bromley, Daniel W., and Devendra P. Chapagain. 1984. "The Village Against the Center: Resource Depletion in South Asia." *American Journal of Agricultural Economics* 66:868–73.

Feeny, David, Fikret Berkes, Bonnie J. McCay, and James M. Acheson. 1990. "The Tragedy of the Commons: Twenty-Two Years Later." *Human Ecology* 18, no. 1:1–19.

Hallowell, A. Irving. 1943. "The Nature and Function of Property as a Social Institution." *Journal of Legal and Political Sociology* 1:115–38.

Hardin, Garrett. 1968. "The Tragedy of the Commons." *Science* 162:1243–48.

McCay, Bonnie, and James M. Acheson. 1987. *The Question of the Commons: The Culture and Ecology of Communal Resources*. Tucson: University of Arizona Press.

Netting, Robert. 1977. *Cultural Ecology*. Menlo Park, Calif.: Cummings.

Pinkerton, E., ed. 1989. *Cooperative Management of Local Fisheries*. Vancouver: University of British Columbia Press.

Runge, C. Ford. 1981. "Common Property Externalities: Isolation, Assurance, and Resource Depletion in a Traditional Grazing Context." *American Journal of Agricultural Economics* 63:595–607.

———. 1984. "Institutions and the Free Rider: The Assurance Problem in Collective Action." *Journal of Politics* 46:154–81.

Sen, A. K. 1982. *Choice, Welfare, and Measurement*. Oxford: Blackwell.

Stevenson, Glenn G. 1991. *Common Property Economics: A General Theory and Land Use Applications*. Cambridge: Cambridge University Press.

Steward, Julian. 1955. *Theory of Culture Change*. Urbana: University of Illinois Press.

Wade, Robert. 1987. *Village Republics*. Cambridge: Cambridge University Press.

2

Common Property and Collective Action in Economic Development

C. Ford Runge

In much of the developing world, common property provides a complex system of norms and conventions for regulating individual rights to use a variety of natural resources, including forests, range, and water. These arrangements closely resemble the ones that dominated the early stages of European economic development, where institutional rules specifying joint use by a village or other well-defined group prevailed as a form of resource management for at least a thousand years. With the forced enclosure movements of the fifteenth and sixteenth centuries, the common property typical of early Western Europe declined, although it did not disappear. Many localities still maintain complex arrangements of joint tenancy. Common-property institutions continue to be observed, for example, on Swiss grazing lands and elsewhere in Europe (Netting 1978; Rhodes and Thompson 1975).

The European experience with enclosure provides a rich background for this study. Its immediate purpose, however, is to explore contemporary problems of common-property resource management in developing countries. Although common property has proved a stable form of resource management in some traditional societies, the combination of population growth, technological change, climate, and political forces has destabilized many existing property institutions.[1] A fundamental issue in much of the developing world is the degree to which resource mismanagement has actually been caused by common-property arrangements. In the Sahel and southern Africa, for example, serious misuse of resources has been alleged to be the direct result of traditional common-property institutions (see Hitchcock 1980; Picardi and Seifert 1976; Glantz 1977). In response, Western economic consultants and planners have called for the imposition of private-property rights (Johnson 1972; Picardi 1974).

Similarly motivated private-property schemes have been attempted throughout the developing world. Many, perhaps most, have failed to stop overuse, and in many cases may have contributed to even more rapid degradation of resources and to increased inequality in already unequal distributions of wealth. Not unlike European lands that were enclosed, areas formerly held in common are often transferred to individuals (such as high-ranking government bureaucrats) who can exercise influence in the allocation of use rights. These individuals then fail to manage these resources effectively.

Despite this record, such policies are often supported by those who argue on theoretical grounds that individual incentives must always lead common property to be mismanaged. Modern economists often refer to this as the "free-rider problem." When applied to resource management, the free-rider problem leads to the conclusion that common property is not a viable institutional alternative.

This chapter presents an alternative perspective. It describes a number of reasons why common property may be as viable as private property on grounds of both efficiency and equity. Rather than representing an atavistic arrangement of rights that inevitably results in inefficient resource use, common-property institutions may actually contain much that is valuable, and new institutional arrangements with common-property characteristics may also be worthwhile. In many cases, these institutions may play a key role in the effective management of scarce natural resources, complementing and combining with private rights. What follows is thus neither an attack on private property nor a wholesale endorsement of common property. It is an argument in favor of institutions that are well adapted to the particular resource constraints facing villages and groups in developing countries. In this sense, it stems from the work on institutional constraints and innovation developed by Y. Hayami and V. W. Ruttan (1985).

As an institution, common property is to be distinguished from free and open access, where there are no rules regulating individual use rights (Ciriacy-Wantrup and Bishop 1975). Often, what appears to the outside observer to be open access may involve tacit cooperation by individual users according to a complex set of rules specifying rights of joint use. This is common property. Empirically, it is crucial to distinguish between open access and common property if appropriate policy is to be formulated. Problems of open access arise from unrestricted entry, whereas problems of common property result from tensions in the structure of joint use rights adopted by a particular village or group. These tensions may arise from a variety of complex causes, including population pressure, changes in technology, climate, or political forces. The thesis is that too often these causes have been confused and the problem ascribed simply to the "tragedy of the commons" (G. Hardin 1968), in which the misuse of resources is attributed to the institution of common property itself. The problems with this view, and an alternative hypothesis, are investigated below.

Common Property and the Village Economy

To appreciate the traditional role of common-property resource management, three stylized characteristics of village life in less-developed economies must be understood. The first, which follows almost from the definition "less-developed," is relative poverty. Low incomes and levels of living are obvious enough evidence of poverty conditions. What is less obvious is that this poverty, by imposing a strict budget constraint, also eliminates myriad opportunities for many villagers acting alone and many villages acting collectively. These limitations can make joint-use rights a necessity, not simply a virtuous bit of cooperation. In particular, the transaction costs of well-defined and enforced private property typical of the West may simply be too great for a subsistence economy to bear.

Consider the capacity for enforceable claims of private property, a capacity that is crucial to the flexibility and acceptance of such a system. Private rights—individual rights to exclude others— must be based on clear definition and assignment in connection with the thing owned, together with a mechanism to adjudicate disputes when they arise. The more things for which exclusive rights are assigned and defined, the greater must be the social investment in assignment, definition, and adjudication. If common property—the individual right to joint use—is the norm, comparatively fewer claims must be assigned and defined. Less clarity in the assignment of rights (at least by Western standards) may also result. However, this is balanced against reduced social costs of assignment and definition. Naturally, some enforcement and adjudication of even these claims is necessary.

In developed economies of the West, the substantial social overhead necessary for a system of private rights is often hidden from view, except when one faces court costs or becomes directly involved in titling or litigation. Even then, the social overhead required in order to assign, define, and make transferable private property rights, and the capacity to support this superstructure through legal fees and taxes, often goes unrecognized. This capacity is difficult to maintain without an expensive support structure capable of effectively recording, administering, and adjudicating local disputes over these claims.

In a poor, developing economy, a malfunctioning approximation to a Western bureaucratic system would likely be based on incipient titles promulgated by a centralized authority that is only dimly aware of local conditions. Such a situation may be worse than continued dependence on local-level common-property rules. The fair enforcement of formalized private rights and duties may be prohibitively costly compared with customary arrangements. These customary arrangements may involve some private rights that are enforced locally, as well as common rights and a wide variety of "mixed" arrangements. To suppose that these results of poverty are in fact its cause is a heroic claim, although one that has been made in studies of privatization (North and Thomas 1977).

A second characteristic of life in a village economy is that it is critically dependent on local agriculture and natural resources. That a majority of the work force moves away from direct dependence on this base is indeed a mark of development; as this happens, higher value-added goods are produced with inputs from points removed from the local economy, and become the primary outputs of the society (see Johnston and Mellor 1961). Because the distribution of basic natural resources such as soil or water (including rainfall) is often quite random over both time and space, the assignment of exclusive use rights to a given land area can yield an inherently unfair distribution of resources, in contrast to the more equitable results of assigning joint rights of access to these resources. Such distributions may tend to become further skewed as individuals with an advantageous initial endowment acquire more resources over time. The increasing inequality that results may have dynamic destabilizing effects that are ultimately very costly to efficient local resource use.

A third characteristic of life in a developing economy is a consequence of the first two. Poverty, together with a dependence on low value-added outputs and relatively randomly distributed natural resources, results in a high degree of uncertainty with respect to income streams. Poverty eliminates the cushion against adversity represented by accumulated wealth. The random element in natural resource allocation introduces additional uncertainty for those whose income depends on the rain's falling or the hunt's succeeding. In contrast, much more of the randomness of nature is under control in a developed economy, whether through irrigated crop production, feedlot livestock operations, or a highly developed food distribution chain, so that local risks can be shared and uncertainty reduced.

In the face of the uncertainty characteristic of life in a developing economy, no individual can be assured that he or she will be spared failure. Given the intimate connection between basic resources and subsistence, unpredictable events such as floods or drought may bring disease or death. In the face of this environmental uncertainty, common-property institutions may be created; rather than emphasizing the right to exclude some, these institutions provide instead for the right of many to be equally included as a hedge against uncertainty. The expectation is that when one is in need, aid will be forthcoming from others in return for a like commitment—a more agreeable prospect than "going it alone" in the face of nature.[2] This "insurance" against environmental uncertainties complements the relative efficiency of common property, especially in pastoral situations where rainfall, rather than land, is a scarce resource.

Poverty, natural resource dependency, and resulting uncertainties thus create an incentive structure that may make common property a comparatively rational solution to certain problems of resource management. In what follows, I will call this a solution to the "assurance problem," one in a class of coordination problems in which individuals organize their behavior by reference to a particular rule or norm. Sometimes, this rule may be based on joint use. Before developing the argument for common-property institutions along these lines, however, it is necessary to examine current approaches to common-property institutions and their limitations. Although it does capture certain truths in the history of resource management, much current literature leads to the false conclusion that common property is universally mismanaged. This conclusion is not always valid, suggesting the need for a more complete explanation of incentives and choices in resource management.

The Free-Rider Problem

The free-rider problem results when an individual shirks responsibility to the community or group. It is often argued that the incentive for this behavior is logical from the point of view of narrow self-interest. Such narrow logic leads to an outcome in which the group as a whole is made worse off. An often-cited parable used to illustrate this behavior is the "tragedy of the commons," in which the private benefit of grazing an additional head of cattle on a common range exceeds the private cost, because the costs of maintaining range quality can be shifted to the group as a whole (G. Hardin 1968). The "tragedy" of overgrazing results from each person's incentive to free ride regardless of the expected actions of others. Even if an agreement is struck that specifies that all will refrain from further grazing, the strict dominance of free-rider strategy makes such a contract unstable.

Some argue that the proper solution for overgrazing a common range is therefore to "internalize" its costs by making the public aspects of the range private. Instituting a scheme of private grazing rights, if they are properly enforced, is argued to be a necessary (though not a sufficient) condition for creating a market for such rights. This approach has led a number of economists to argue that the mere existence of common-property rights over a scarce resource will lead to a tragedy of the commons (Demsetz 1967; Cheung 1970; Furubotn and Pejovich 1972; North and Thomas 1977).

As noted above, this position ignores considerable historical and empirical evidence to the contrary, and is due in part to a lack of familiarity with common property in practice and to the associated failure to distinguish problems of free and open access from those of common property.[3] However, the fundamental problem is that free-rider behavior is assumed to be a dominant motive, against which the group is defense-less.[4]

This motive is often described by reference to the "prisoner's dilemma," a simple game in which collective decisions produce outcomes harmful to the group as a whole without intervention by some higher authority. The two-person prisoner's dilemma is illustrated in Table 2.1. "Cooperate" and "defect" represent the choices (or strategies) open to each of two prisoners. The ordered pairs indicate the payoffs that will result from a particular coincidence of choices by each person; the first number represents the payoff to the first person, the second number to the second person. Imagine that the prisoners are interrogated separately. Both know that if they cooperate with each other and neither confesses, they will receive suspended sentences (1, 1). If one prisoner defects and turns state's evidence, that one will be paid and released, and the other will receive a heavy prison term (2, −2) (−2, 2). If both defect, each gets a prison sentence (−1, −1). Given mutually disinterested motivation, the course of action represented by the pair (1, 1) is not an equilibrium. For self-

TABLE 2.1
The Prisoner's Dilemma

	Second person	
First person	Cooperate	Defect
Cooperate	(1, 1)	(−2, 2)
Defect	(2, −2)	(−1, −1)

SOURCE: Author.

protection, if not self-interest, each has a sufficient reason to defect whatever the other does. "Rational" decisions by each prisoner individually make both worse off. Even if communication between the individuals results in an agreement to cooperate, both have an incentive to break it. Therefore, the noncooperative pair $(-1, -1)$ is an inferior equilibrium.

Now imagine a village of n individuals who must graze cattle on a common range of fixed size. Each individual must choose to do one of two things. One is "stinting," or cooperative grazing on the commons. The second is grazing at a level that, while advantageous to the individual, ultimately results in exploitative overuse of the commons. This defection strategy is the free-rider option. The cost of grazing to each individual is a function of the grazing decisions of all n individuals. If all cooperate, then the common range is preserved and cattle remain healthy. But if the logic of the prisoner's dilemma accurately portrays the incentives of the village, no one will have an incentive to cooperate and all will defect. The result will be overgrazing.

This analysis of overgrazing may be generalized as a "binary choice with externalities," of which the multiperson prisoner's dilemma (MPD) is one example (Schelling 1973; Runge 1985). The decision whether to cooperate with others in observing a stinting rule, or to defect, is binary when the choice is between cooperation and defection (C and D), and it has external effects when it alters consumption of the resource by other agents. (In trivial cases, the resource is so abundant that no negative external consumption effect occurs.) If agents derive payoffs from cooperation or defection based on the number of other agents who also choose either C or D, then among $n + 1$ individuals there are 2^n possible configurations of choice, depending on how many choose C or D. The decisions of all agents result in a particular physical product of the resource (for example, "total forage availability") from which each agent derives positive utility.

I will first consider this binary choice in terms of a uniform MPD, then extend the analysis to include multiple equilibria and the absence of dominant strategies, which I have argued elsewhere may better approximate actual decisions on common-property resources (Runge 1981, 1984a). This approach provides a theoretical basis for empirical testing of complex incentive structures in various resource regimes.

The Multiperson Prisoner's Dilemma (MPD)

The MPD is characterized by n agents, each with the same binary choice and the same payoffs. As noted above, each agent has a dominant choice, whatever others do, which is dominant for all n agents. Each also has a dominant preference for the others' choices. These preferences go in opposite directions: each prefers to defect while all others cooperate; so defection strictly dominates cooperation, leading to a unique, inferior equilibrium. However, there is some number, $k > 1$, such that if k individuals cooperate and the rest defect, those who cooperate are still better off than if they had all defected. If we explicitly assume the uniformity of agents, k is independent of the particular agents who cooperate or defect, eliminating the possibility (at this level of analysis) of leadership. Below, this assumption will be relaxed. For now, the number k represents the minimum coalition that can make positive gains by cooperating with the rule even though others do not. Where $k = n$, no one gains from cooperation unless cooperation is universal and there are no free riders (that is, unless there is a coalition of the whole). Where $k < n$, some free riders $(n - k)$ can be tolerated while the k cooperators gain, although the $n - k$ free riders benefit more than do the cooperators.

Consider Figure 2.1, in which two linear payoff curves are drawn for a village population of $n + 1$, reflecting the benefits of cooperation and defection in an interdependent decision framework to the $(n + 1)$th agent, where n equals the number of other resource users. The upper curve, D, corresponds to the dominant choice of defection. Its left end is labeled O, for the open-access equilibrium, in which no agents cooperate and rents

FIGURE 2.1
Relationships between Benefits and Cooperation

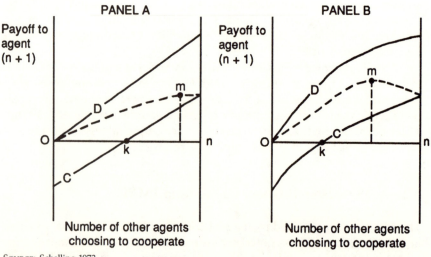

SOURCE: Schelling 1973.

are driven to zero. The D curve rises monotonically to the right. Below it is the dominated cooperation strategy C, which also begins at the open-access equilibrium O, rises monotonically, and crosses the axis at point k, where positive gains to cooperation begin. The number choosing to cooperate with the proposed rule in Figure 2.1 is denoted by the distance along the horizontal axis.

The vertical axis of Figure 2.1 shows the payoff to cooperation by agent $(n + 1)$ when a certain number of others choose to cooperate and the remainder defect. At $k = n/2$ in panel A of Figure 2.1, for example, positive gains are made by cooperators whenever at least half of the other agents cooperate by stinting. Because D lies everywhere above C, it is a strictly dominant strategy. Monotonicity of both curves in the same direction implies that cooperation leads to uniformly positive externalities and defection to uniformly negative externalities. The C curve is higher on the right than the D curve on the left, reflecting the Pareto inefficiency of the dominant defection strategy. The dotted lines show total (or average) values corresponding to the number of agents choosing the two strategies, and point m represents the maximum collective payoff for the group. The slope of these schedules may be interpreted as the marginal payoff to defection and cooperation.

In Figure 2.1, panel A, D rises more rapidly than does C, indicating that the more agents who join the cooperative coalition, the greater is the advantage of defecting. The collective maximum at point m is achieved with some agents choosing D and some C. Point m falls to the right of k on the horizontal axis. This implies that collective gains are greater when there are more than k cooperators, and that these gains reach a maximum at point m and diminish thereafter.

In Figure 2.1, panel B, the slopes of the C and D functions reflect an alternative incentive structure: the proposed rule achieves most of its benefits after about half of the population participates, after which benefits grow at a decreasing rate and ultimately decline after reaching a maximum of m. The collective maximum occurs at about two-thirds participation, with room for gains to cooperators from point k to point m along the horizontal axis. Panels A and B represent two of an infinite number of possible variations on the MPD theme, a distinguishing feature of which is that defection strictly dominates, making some form of coercion necessary to solve the problem of collective action. Restrictive rules and the level of coercion accompanying them alter the payoffs of the C and D schedules, and thus their level and shape.

In the MPD model of common property, each individual has an incentive to free ride and graze heavily in the near term, thereby overexploiting the range. Each expects to receive a higher payoff from defecting rather than from cooperating. The incentive structure is such that it does not matter which strategy the others choose. Therefore, defecting or free riding strictly dominates cooperative stinting for each individual. Hardin, in his original article on the tragedy of the commons, wrote:

> The rational herdsman concludes that the only sensible course for him to pursue is to add another animal to his herd. And another. . . . But this is the conclusion reached by each and every rational herdsman sharing the commons. Therein is the tragedy. Each man is locked into a system that compels him to increase his herd without limit—in a world which is limited. [Hardin 1968, 1244]

The main features of this view of common property are:

• *Inferior outcome.* Each individual will choose "rationally" to defect and graze at an exploitative level, leading to a situation in which all are made worse off. All are led toward this noncooperative equilibrium.

• *Strict dominance of individual free-rider strategy.* The result of overgrazing arises independently of the expectations of each individual regarding the actions of others. Because the choices of each are unaffected by the choices of the others, defecting is a dominant strategy, and uncertainty with respect to the behavior of others does not pose a problem.

• *Need for enforcement.* Even if an agreement is struck that specifies that all will stint on the range, the strict dominance of individual strategy makes such cooperation unstable. Without compulsory enforcement imposed by an outside authority, any such agreement is unstable because each prefers that the others stint while he or she defects and grazes exploitatively (Sen 1967).

In the MPD framework, individuals may attempt to develop cooperative common-property rules to enforce stinting, but they cannot resolve their problem because no one has an incentive to keep such agreements. As a result, an enforceable rule must be imposed from outside. In this sense, property institutions are viewed as exogenous. Private property rights, it is argued, are consistent with this formulation because they can be imposed from outside, as were systems of enclosure. Because this approach starts from the presupposition that individuals pursue strategies regardless of the expected actions of others, the appropriate decision unit is the private individual user. A somewhat contradictory result, especially when the argument is used to support privatization, is that the strict dominance of individual free-rider strategy is argued to be accompanied by rational individuals who will husband and conserve their own private range area at a rate more consistent with the preferences of society as a whole. If this formulation is correct, then only by imposing private property rules from outside can the group optimize its grazing. Any other alternatives are unstable because of the strict dominance of defecting behavior.

Three key difficulties with this model render it unreasonable on empirical grounds. First, its assumption of dominant free-rider behavior leaves no place for cooperative rules unless they are imposed and enforced from outside. Second, the dominant strategy mechanism, by ruling out the importance of changing expectations of others' behavior, fails to capture the interdependence of decisions in a village economy. Third, by sidestepping the importance of mutual expectations in the formulation of individual strategy, the mechanism fails to deal explicitly with the problem of uncertainty regarding the actions of others (Runge 1981).

These objections raise questions over this theoretical approach, which is founded on the restrictive view that free riding is a dominant strategy, that private property is uniquely suited to optimal resource allocation, and that common-property rules cannot be solutions to problems of resource use in developing economies. By restricting our view of the institutional opportunity set, the approach fails to consider a variety of institutional alternatives.

The Assurance Problem and Common Property

The view of common property outlined above, with its underlying premise of dominant free-rider behavior, has been widely used to explain overgrazing, deforestation, and other abuses of natural resources. What is striking is the extent to which resulting policies of privatization have been driven by the unproven premise that free-rider behavior dominates, and by the accompanying view that the expected behavior of others is irrelevant to this choice. Where there are no dominant strategies, a variety of alternative outcomes are possible, depending on the structure of mutual expectation and the resulting patterns of strategic choice. This situation seems to fit most closely with empirical studies of common property. Several authors have argued that it may fit public goods and collective choice situations in general (Kimber 1981; Wagner 1983; Runge 1984a).

The very nature of village-level decisions makes it implausible that free riding will dominate. Such decision making involves interdependent choices in which not only are the benefits and costs of resource use a function of the total actions of the group, but decisions to use (or overuse) resources will be affected by the expected decisions of others. If the use of common resources is conditional on these expectations, this interdependence places a premium on mechanisms that coordinate community decisions. The key observation that bears emphasis is that such mechanisms tend to arise from many different rules, customs, or conventions, of which private exclusive property is only one example.

Consider the more complex and arguably more realistic case in which neither C nor D represents a strictly dominant strategy. Figure 2.2 shows a situation in which a linear D curve dominates a linear curve C until point y, after which C dominates D. The absence of a dominant strategy raises the problem of coordinating the expectations of a "critical mass" of agents around a particular rule change. In Figure 2.2, there are two equilibria, one at O and one at z. The problem of coordination is to achieve the Pareto-superior equilibrium at z. In cases such as these, the coalition must move beyond k to the switch point y; otherwise, defection will dominate and lead to the Pareto-inferior equilibrium at O. Unlike the MPD, in which defection dominates at all levels of participation, implying a continual need for outside coercion, this situation rests on the contingent strategies of agents. If enough people in a village are assured that others will cooperate, then z will emerge as the equilibrium. However, if a Pareto-inferior open-access equilibrium has become established, no agent will decide to join a coalition subscribing to a restrictive rule unless he or she expects a sufficient number of others to do so. Achieving a Pareto-superior solution will require an organized change in behavior leading a critical mass to cooperate with the rule.

FIGURE 2.2
Number of Agents Choosing to Cooperate

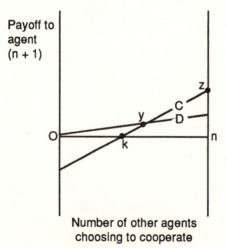

SOURCE: Schelling 1973.

Achieving this level of cooperation probably will require some kind of enforcement mechanism. If the situation resembles Figure 2.2, however, relatively little enforcement may be necessary to organize a change in behavior. Voluntary cooperation with rule restrictions may even be sufficient to organize this change. As F. A. Hayek (1948) has argued, spontaneous recognition of the need for organized collective action in many cases occurs on the part of the affected group simply because the payoff to such organization is substantial.

In the case of a village economy, the structure of incentives may well be of this sort, and villagers will seek a rule coordinating the resource use of all villagers. This search for "coordination norms," to use a phrase of T. Schelling (1960), is an endogenous adaptive response to the demand for scarce information about the likely behavior of others. By providing the assurance that others will not misuse common resources, common-property institutions can make it rational for the individual to respect them. Although expectations of widespread free-rider behavior may be quite likely to provoke a corresponding response, leading to a downward spiral of overuse, the multiple possible outcomes suggest that careful attention also be given to institutions that promote a critical mass of resource-conserving behavior.[5] There is no reason to suppose that these do not include institutions of joint use.

This problem may be described in terms of an alternative to the MPD game, the "assurance problem" (Sen 1967), which is one in a class of "coordination problems" (Schelling 1960). The problem shown in Figure 2.2, where cooperation continues to refer to stinting together, and defection to overgrazing, leads to an ordering of alternatives in which a villager $(n + 1)$ benefits most when everyone stints, but also benefits when a critical mass cooperates with a stinting rule, even though everyone does not. It is precisely the role of village-level conventions, including common-property institutions, to reinforce expectations of collective behavior leading a critical mass of individuals to adopt such a solution as a cooperative strategy (see R. Hardin 1982). If they function optimally, common-property institutions can lead to equilibrium outcomes in which each individual, being assured that a critical mass of others will cooperate, will have an incentive to do so too. This is in marked contrast to the MPD, in which no one would contribute even if everyone else did. Of course, common-property institutions do not always provide this assurance. The approach developed here, like other more formal approaches, emphasizes that the village can get locked into an equilibrium in which the range is overexploited, because a requisite level of assurance is not achieved.[6] The model says that the free-rider problem *can* be solved, not that it *will* be solved.

When elaborated to describe problems of resource management, this model provides an intuitively appealing way of looking at common property as a solution to coordination problems. First, coordinated strategies can evolve inside the structure of the game, rather than always being imposed from without. In this sense, such strategies model innovative, endogenous property rules initiated by a village or group. Property institutions, by providing security of expectation, are responses to the uncertainty of social and economic interaction (see Schotter 1981; Johnson and Libecap 1982). Second, the model places central emphasis on two factors: the interdependence associated with group decision making; and the multiple outcomes possible when agents are engaged in a search for rules of coordination if there are no dominant strategies. In other words, it allows for either cooperation or free riding, rather than saying that free riding will dominate. Third, it emphasizes the key obstacle of uncertainty, emphasizing the fact that opportunity costs must be paid in order to develop support for new rules or norms of coordination.

Approaching common property in this way provides some interesting perspectives in both analytical and policy terms. In contrast to the results of the MPD, the strict dominance of the free-rider strategy no longer holds. Rather, expectations of others' choices must be entered as a formal part of the determination of one's own choice. No individual can decide on a preferred strategy until it is known whether a sufficiently large group of others will cooperate. An inferior outcome is no longer inevitable; if everyone is assured that a critical mass of others will obey a common property agreement, then it is in each person's individual interest to do likewise, since this outcome is preferred.

In the more complex cases faced in actual situations of resource management, the lack of a dominant strategy for each individual means that the particular outcome will depend on an individual's bargaining power, the initial endowment of resources, the culture, climate, and so on. Thus, the assumption that individuals are identical and face identical constraints must be relaxed. R. Sugden (1984) has argued that the more homogeneous a community, the more likely are optimal outcomes; the more heterogeneous, the more difficult coordination becomes. As the heterogeneity of the group increases, and as the resource constraints facing it become more severe, common-property rules (indeed, any rules) may become increasingly difficult to maintain (see Johnson and Libecap 1982). Given a heterogeneous community, however, coordination norms, once established, offer their own incentive to be kept. Naturally, some enforcement of these agreements is likely to be necessary. However, this enforcement may readily emerge from inside the group, as well as be imposed from outside it. The key element that determines the success or failure of institutions is therefore the extent to which the institutions foster coordinated expectations in relation to a particular physical and social environment (Ullman-Margalit 1977).

In this framework, it is easier to see how internal group incentives to maintain and enforce common-property rights may be as strong, if not stronger, than those restricted to private exclusive use. Suppose that tradition—the result of longstanding agreement—is such that each grazer on a common range is expected to stint at an arbitrary level. The result of this property rule is to formalize the expected actions of others. If each expects all others to graze at this level, there is an incentive to do the same, since the rule extends the set of superior allocations available to the group by preserving the range. Because the communication and transactions needed to achieve common-property rules are not costless, agreement on the particular rule for grazing provides a further incentive for it to be retained as tradition. The social overhead costs required to maintain common-property rules may be substantially lower when they are already a part of the customary structure of rights and duties. In a village economy, the benefits possible from free riding in the short term may be more than offset by costs imposed on those who break the rules. Recognized interdependence makes the costs of reputation loss high, much like losing one's credit rating in a developed economy. Other, more severe sanctions may be imposed by the village on its own noncooperative members. These costs, coupled with reductions in overall free riding if such antisocial behavior sets a trend for others, plus the opportunity costs of implementing innovative rules, may well exceed the cost of continuing to observe the common-property rule.[7]

Moreover, where the resource endowment of the group or village is nearly randomly distributed, additional incentives may exist to adopt a rule of joint use. In the Kalahari Desert of Botswana, for example, rainfall is both scarce and highly variable. Rather than demarcating and privatizing the range, and then hoping that rain will fall on one's own private parcel, the appeal of traditional common-property institutions is reinforced by the ecological imperative to move from one area to another. The relative access afforded to scarce resources under this arrangement is both more efficient and a better form of insurance against adverse individual outcomes than a system in which a few are blessed by rain while the majority face drought-like conditions (Peters 1983).

Finally, the fairness implicit in joint access may prove a highly assuring feature of common-property agreements, even if the relative benefits accruing to individual members of the group on average are somewhat less than under a system of exclusive use rights. The expropriation of common property, as P. S. Dasgupta and G. M. Heal note, "while blessed at the altar of efficiency [,] can have disastrous distributional consequences" (1979, 77). Since these consequences may in turn give rise to instability and lead to breakdowns in efficient use, questions of equity, efficiency, and assurance are closely connected in practice over time.

This is not to deny that enforcement from outside may help achieve improvements in the institutions, if the costs of such enforcement are affordable. Where local-level rule making has broken down, such interventions may be necessary. In many cases, local interests may request assistance in enforcing property rights, including private rights, that local authorities alone cannot guarantee. The lesson of the assurance problem is, rather than starting with enforcement mechanisms from outside, simply to let individuals have full freedom first to create self-binding property rules that best serve their needs. Outside enforcement, if needed, can then follow. Property rules will be better suited to these needs and more likely to succeed if they are based on this premise. Such rules may come in many shapes and forms, including various agreements to use resources under some type of common-property arrangement.

Furthermore, enforcement of private property rights from outside the group or village is not a sufficient condition for optimal resource utilization. Not only are the costs of such "top-down" enforcement likely to be high; they also may lead to attempts to impose patterns of land use incompatible with local needs, causing lands to be brought into or taken out of production based on criteria developed by higher authorities rather than at the village level (see Bromley and Chapagain 1984). This may be especially true when control over land use is in the hands of those with fewer incentives for efficient and equitable local management, such as absentee owners. Any enforcement mechanism that operates from outside and above village level institutions and that is designed to coerce local action is thus likely to involve high costs and uncertain benefits.

In summary, the analysis above suggests that common-property institutions may be well adapted to problems of resource management in developing economies. Its major implication is that inferior outcomes, such as overgrazing, do not necessarily arise from the strict dominance of the free-rider strategy (although resource misuse may still occur) but from the inability of interdependent individuals to coordinate and enforce actions in situations of strategic interdependence (see Runge 1984b). Successful responses to these situations may be made even more difficult if property institutions developed for conditions in the West are imposed on the village economies of the developing world.

Common-Property Management

If a variety of responses to problems of resource management are possible, the incentives leading to a particular institutional choice must result from the physical and social environment in which this choice is made. The arguments of the preceding sections may be brought together with the three characteristics of village life in a less-developed economy already identified under "Common Property and the Village Economy." Each suggests a reason for the comparative institutional advantage of joint-use rights. First, low levels of income imply that formalized private-property institutions involving high transactions and enforcement costs are often outside the village-level budget for resource management. Even if a system of private-use rights is affordable, common-property alternatives can be relatively less costly to maintain and enforce and better adapted to local conditions. Since common-property rules are generally enforced locally, abuses of authority, if they occur, may be less widespread than under a centralized program of privatization.

A second reason for the survival and utility of common property is that close dependence on natural resources makes survival more subject to a variety of unpredictable natural events that are likely to fall unequally in both time and space on the local population. If this inequality is threatening to a sufficiently large proportion of the group, incentives may exist to guarantee access to certain resources held in common rather than to restrict access through exclusive use. By institutionalizing a degree of fairness in the face of random allocation, common-use rights may contribute to social stability at the same time that they promote efficient adaptation to changing resource availability.

Common property may be an appropriate institutional adaptation to resource management at the village level for a third reason: the right to be included in a group provides a hedge against individual failure. This hedge will be likely to grow in significance as the overall level of risk to group members increases. In this sense, the combination of relatively high levels of poverty, relatively high levels of randomness in allocation of natural resources, and resulting uncertainty in individual levels of welfare are all mutually reinforcing explanations for the appropriateness of common-property institutions.

A more general reason for continued common-property management is that the opportunity costs associated with changing established practices are high. Despite attempts to break down traditional common-property institutions, these rules are tenacious. As Malinowski observed:

> [W]hile it may seem easy to replace a custom here and there or transform a technical device, such a change of detail very often upsets an institution without reforming it, because . . . beliefs, ideas and practices are welded into bigger systems. [(1945) 1961, 52]

The tenacity of traditional institutions cannot be explained simply as the manifestation of "backwardness" or "irrationality." A more logical explanation is that rational individuals are not inclined to relinquish institutional arrangements that have promoted survival, even if survival has not been especially comfortable. It follows that efforts at economic development should not only attempt to break down belief in and observance of old rules, but should also promote institutions that are consistent with the physical and social environment in which resource management is to occur. In some cases, this will involve the development and promotion of private, exclusive use rights. But in many cases it will involve elaborations of common or joint use. The sooner these possibilities are recognized, the sooner problems of resource management can be addressed in a fashion consistent with the incentives of village-level decision making.

The Need for Empirical Research

The abstract observations made in the previous sections require examination and empirical testing in specific settings. While a number of recent analyses have pointed to the erroneous conclusions resulting from applications of the "tragedy of the commons" model, only a few well-documented studies of modern common-property management have entered the literature until quite recently. These include examples reported by J. L. Gilles and K. Jamtgaard (1981) and by others of pasture management in Peru (see Browman 1974; Orlove 1977, 1980); African grazing and forest management (see Legesse 1973; Horowitz 1979; Thomson 1980; Hitchcock 1980; Peters 1983); Japanese forestry (McKean 1982); and the aforementioned case of Swiss grazing (Rhodes and Thompson 1975; Netting 1978).

In the historical literature, recent research on the common-field systems replaced by eighteenth-century enclosures continues to break down the conventional wisdom that enclosure was a prerequisite to the adoption of advanced agricultural methods. "Open-field" farmers in fact adopted modern practices without changes in property rights (Yelling 1977). Recent empirical research by Allen (1982, 950) concludes that "the major economic consequence of the enclosure of open field arable in the eighteenth century was to redistribute the existing agricultural income, not to create additional income by increasing efficiency." Much more attention in research needs to be given, however, to the rich variety of contemporary resource management strategies that result from alternative environmental conditions and constraints.

The case studies in Part 2 of this book, dealing not only with range resources but with forestry, agricultural lands, fisheries, and water, can begin a much more detailed process of investigation focused on specific common-property issues. In this way, a priori theorizing can give way to empirical investigations of whether certain resources (for example, water or forests) are more or less likely to be successfully managed as common property, private property, or some combination.

The discussion in this chapter, while essentially theoretical, directs attention to the specific resource constraints faced by groups at the local level. Rather than invoking the general superiority of one type of property institution, this analysis suggests that different institutions are responses to different local environments in which institutional innovation takes place. Such innovations are likely to range along a continuum of property rights, from pure rights of exclusion to pure rights of inclusion, depending on the nature of the resource management problems (Runge 1984b).

Institutional innovation, like technological innovation, is responsive to the relative abundance of different factors, and the resulting costs and benefits of alternative strategies (Hayami and Ruttan 1985). As A. Randall states:

> The fact that different configurations of property rights have different impacts on both allocation and distribution illustrates the need for understanding the impact of specific configurations of rights. Collective decision making procedures must select appropriate configurations of rights, not only specifying rights in complete and nonattenuated form but also selecting that particular bundle of rights which will provide the correct incentive structure to achieve the collective goal. [1974, 53–54]

The task of identifying the appropriate configuration of rights begins with a recognition that private, exclusive property is not always comparatively advantageous in the villages of less-developed economies. The search for appropriate institutional responses must respect both the traditions and the constraints of local needs in specific choice environments. There are no universal prescriptions for efficient and equitable resource management.

NOTES

1. Useful historical perspective on current privatization efforts in other parts of the world is offered by the English case. Cromwell's success at rallying popular support early in the English Civil War was based in part on the strenuous objections of commoners to the enclosure of wetlands or "fens" that provided rich hunting and fishing resources. The king had financed groups, called "adventurers," to enclose and drain these open meadows, in return for which one-quarter to one-half of the lands was granted as private preserves. The result was to provoke riots, which Cromwell exploited in organizing a base of opposition to royal

authority. This pattern was repeated throughout the English enclosure movement. A similar process of land acquisition in the North of England and in Ireland can be seen as a partial cause of the "Irish problem" (see Darby 1940; Albright 1955; Fraser 1973, 73–77). A recent comparison of the English experience with that of herders in the Andes of South America is provided by Campbell and Godoy in Chapter 5 of this book.

2. This is the argument described by Rawls (1971) in his analysis of the "original position," in which players in a game of decision making under uncertainty must formulate rules about the distribution of primary resources. The result of a high level of risk aversion is that equality is favored, together with a stipulation (the "difference principle") that inequality must favor those who find themselves worst off. This logic is also the foundation for a variety of real-world voluntary associations, including volunteer fire departments, in which the possibility that one agent might face disaster is mitigated by a joint contract of mutual aid. In addition, there are numerous historical examples from seventh- to twelfth-century Europe of feudal institutional arrangements driven by what Duby (1974) terms *les générosités nécessaires*.

3. North and Thomas, for example, describe the economic state of traditional societies as one in which "[t]he natural resources, whether the animals to be hunted or vegetation to be gathered, were initially held as common property. This type of property right implies free access by all to the resource" (1977, 234).

4. The logic underlying this argument in the "tragedy of the commons" parable (G. Hardin 1968) is formally explicated by Muhsam (1977). The errors, logical and otherwise, of the parable are increasingly recognized by economists. Dasgupta, in an examination of its impact on resource management, observes that "it would be difficult to locate another passage of comparable length and fame containing as many errors" (1982, 13).

5. Axelrod (1984), Taylor (1976), and R. Hardin (1982) have shown that cooperation is consistent with self-interested behavior, even inside the MPD framework, if repeated plays are allowed. Repeating the game opens the door to expectations of others' behavior. The conditions for cooperation then turn on whether the players are sufficiently forward-looking to formulate a "tit-for-tat" rule, motivated by expectations of others' cooperation and fear of retaliation in the case of noncooperation. Similarly, Sugden (1982, 1984) has noted that a "principle of reciprocity" may operate in actual situations of collective choice. This principle does not say that one must *always* contribute or cooperate, but that one must not free ride while others are contributing. The individual villager has obligations to the group from whose efforts he derives benefits. The model of reciprocity that Sugden develops is based on commitment to a rule of behavior, conditional on the expectation that a sufficiently large group of others also will adhere to it. This is the same concept as the "critical mass" discussed earlier.

6. Sugden (1984) and Runge (1981) emphasize that (1) equilibrium exists, (2) it is not unique, (3) one equilibrium is Pareto-efficient, and (4) other equilibria involve undersupply of the collective good.

7. Maintaining rules or norms such as common property may generate second-order collective-action problems. However, the rewards and punishments underlying property institutions, once in place, may be less susceptible to defection because the costs of sanction are small in relation to the benefits of maintaining the rule. Naturally, these rules can, and do, break down.

REFERENCES

Albright, M. 1955. *The Entrepreneurs of Fen Draining in England under James I and Charles I: An Illustration of the Uses of Influence.* Explorations in Entrepreneurial History, vol. 8. Cambridge, Mass.: Harvard University Press.

Allen, R. C. 1982. "The Efficiency and Distributional Implications of 18th Century Enclosures. *Economic Journal* 92:937–53.

Axelrod, R. 1984. *The Evolution of Cooperation.* New York: Basic Books.

Bacharach, M. 1977. *Economics and the Theory of Games.* Boulder, Colo.: Westview Press.

Bromley, D. W., and D. P. Chapagain. 1984. "The Village against the Center: Resource Depletion in South Asia." *American Journal of Agricultural Economics* 66:868–73.

Browman, D. L. 1974. "Pastoral Nomadism in the Andes." *Current Anthropology* 15:630–34.

Cheung, S. N. S. 1970. "The Structure of a Contract and the Theory of Nonexclusive Resource." *Journal of Law and Economics* 13:49–70.

Ciriacy-Wantrup, S. V., and R. C. Bishop. 1975. "Common Property as a Concept in Natural Resource Policy." *Natural Resources Journal* 15:713–27.

Darby, H. C. 1940. *The Draining of the Fens.* Cambridge: Cambridge University Press.

Dasgupta, P. S. 1982. *The Control of Resources.* Oxford: Blackwell.

Dasgupta, P. S., and G. M. Heal. 1979. *Economic Theory and Exhaustible Resources.* Cambridge: Cambridge University Press.

Demsetz, H. 1967. "Toward a Theory of Property Rights." *American Economic Review* 57:347–59.

Duby, G. 1974. *The Early Growth of the European Economy: Warriors and Peasants from the Seventh to the Twelfth Century.* Ithaca, N.Y.: Cornell University Press.

Fraser, A. 1973. *Cromwell: The Lord Protector.* New York: Dell.

Furubotn, E., and S. Pejovich. 1972. "Property Rights and Economic Theory: A Survey of Recent Literature." *Journal of Economic Literature* 10:1137–62.

Gilles, J. L., and K. Jamtgaard. 1981. "Overgrazing in Pastoral Areas: The Commons Reconsidered." *Sociologia Ruralis* 21:129–41.

Glantz, M. H., ed. 1977. *Desertification: Environmental Degradation in and around Arid Lands.* Boulder, Colo.: Westview Press.

Hardin, G. 1968. "The Tragedy of the Commons." *Science* 162:1243–48.

Hardin, G., and J. Baden, eds. 1977. *Managing the Commons.* San Francisco: Freeman.

Hardin, R. 1982. *Collective Action.* Baltimore: Johns Hopkins University Press.

Hayami, Y., and V. W. Ruttan. 1985. *Agricultural Development: A Global Perspective.* Baltimore: Johns Hopkins University Press.

Hayek, F. A. 1948. *Individualism and Economic Order.* Chicago: University of Chicago Press.

Hitchcock, R. K. 1980. "Tradition, Social Justice, and Land Reform in Central Botswana." *Journal of African Law* 24 (Spring):1–34.

Horowitz, M. M. 1979. *The Sociology of Pastoralism and African Livestock Projects.* U.S. Agency for International Development Program Evaluation, no. 6. Washington, D.C.: The Agency.

Johnson, O. E. G. 1972. "Economic Analysis, the Legal Framework and Land Tenure Systems." *Journal of Law and Economics* 15:259–76.

Johnson, R. N., and G. Libecap. 1982. "Contracting Problems and Regulation: The Case of the Fishery." *American Economic Review* 72:1005–22.

Johnston, B., and J. Mellor. 1961. "The Role of Agriculture in Economic Development." *American Economic Review* 51:566–93.

Kimber, R. 1981. "Collective Action and the Fallacy of the Liberal Fallacy." *World Politics* 33:178–96.

Legesse, A. 1973. *Gada: Three Approaches to the Study of African Society.* London: Collier Macmillan.

Malinowski, B. 1961. *The Dynamics of Culture Change.* New Haven, Conn.: Yale University Press. First published in 1945.

McKean, M. A. 1982. "The Japanese Experience with Scarcity: Management of Traditional Common Lands." Paper presented at the Conference on Critical Issues in Environmental History, January 1–3, at the University of California, Irvine.

Muhsam, H. V. 1977. "An Algebraic Theory of the Commons." In *Managing the Commons,* ed. G. Hardin and J. Baden, 34–37. San Francisco: Freeman.

Netting, R. M. 1978. "Of Men and Meadows: Strategies of Alpine Land Use." *Anthropology Quarterly* 45:123–44.

North, D. C., and R. P. Thomas. 1977. "The First Economic Revolution." *Economic History Review* 30:229–41.

Orlove, B. S. 1977. *Alpaca, Sheep and Men.* New York: Academic Press.

———. 1980. *Pastoralism in the Southern Sierra.* Andean Peasant Economics and Pastoralism, publication no. 1, Small Ruminants CRSP. Columbia: Department of Rural Sociology, University of Missouri. Mimeo.

Peters, P. 1983. "Cattlemen, Borehole Syndicates and Privatization in the Kgatleng District of Botswana." Ph.D. diss., Boston University.

Picardi, A. C. 1974. "A Systems Analysis of Pastoralism in the West African Sahel." Framework for Evaluation, Long-Term Strategies for the Development of the Sahel-Sudan. Annex 5, Center for Policy Alternatives, Massachusetts Institute of Technology, Cambridge, Mass. Mimeo.

Picardi, A. C., and W. W. Seifert. 1976. "A Tragedy of the Commons in the Sahel." *Technology Review* 78:42–51.

Randall, A. 1974. "Coasean Externality Theory in a Policy Context." *Natural Resources Journal* 14:35–54.

Rawls, J. 1971. *A Theory of Justice.* Oxford: Clarendon Press.

Rhodes, R. E., and S. J. Thompson. 1975. "Adaptive Strategies in Alpine Environments: Beyond Ecological Particularism." *American Ethnologist* 2:535–51.

Runge, C. F. 1981. "Common Property Externalities: Isolation, Assurance and Resource Depletion in a Traditional Grazing Context." *American Journal of Agricultural Economics* 63:595–606.

————. 1984a. "Institutions and the Free Rider: The Assurance Problem in Collective Action." *Journal of Politics* 46:154–81.

————. 1984b. "Strategic Interdependence in Models of Property Rights." *American Journal of Agricultural Economics* 66:807–13.

————. 1985. "The Innovation of Rules and the Structure of Incentives in Open Access Resources." *American Journal of Agricultural Economics* 67:368–72.

Schelling, T. 1960. *The Strategy of Conflict.* Cambridge, Mass.: Harvard University Press.

————. 1973. "Hockey Helmets, Concealed Weapons and Daylight Savings: A Study of Binary Choice with Externalities." *Journal of Conflict Resolution* 17:381–428.

Schotter, A. 1981. *The Economic Theory of Social Institutions.* Cambridge: Cambridge University Press.

Sen, A. K. 1967. "Isolation, Assurance and the Social Rate of Discount." *Quarterly Journal of Economics* 81:112–24.

Sugden, R. 1982. "On the Economics of Philanthropy." *Economic Journal* 92:341–50.

————. 1984. "Reciprocity: The Supply of Public Goods through Voluntary Contributions." *Economic Journal* 94:772–87.

Taylor, M. 1976. *Anarchy and Cooperation.* New York: Wiley.

Thomson, J. T. 1980. "Peasant Perceptions of Problems and Possibilities for Local-Level Management of Trees in Niger and Upper Volta." Paper presented at the Twenty-third African Studies Association Annual Meeting, October 15–18, at Philadelphia, Pennsylvania.

Ullman-Margalit, E. 1977. "Coordination Norms and Social Choice." *Erkenntnis* 11:143–55.

Wagner, R. H. 1983. "The Theory of Games and the Problem of International Cooperation." *American Political Science Review* 77:330–46.

Yelling, J. A. 1977. *Common Field and Enclosure in England, 1450–1859.* Hamden, Conn.: Archon Books.

3

Analyzing the Commons:
A Framework

Ronald J. Oakerson

My subject can be stated as a riddle: How are forests, fishing grounds, pastures, parks, groundwater supplies, and public highways all alike? Answer: Each one is typically a commons, a natural resource (or a durable facility of human design and construction) that is shared by a community of producers or consumers. The list of shared resources and facilities is both long and diverse. The commons can have a fixed location (like a woodlot) or it can occur as a "fugitive" resource (like fish and wildlife). The commons can be renewable (grasslands), or not (oil pools). Some cases (oceans, the atmosphere) are indivisible over large areas, so that they cannot feasibly be divided and organized as separate parcels of private property; other cases (small pastures) are organized as commons by social preference. While patterns of organization vary across continents and cultures, the key problem remains the same: how to coordinate use by numerous individuals in order to obtain an optimal rate of production or consumption overall.[1]

The commons can be distinguished from both public goods and private goods, though it shares some attributes of each. Pure public goods can be used by any number of consumers because, like the light from a street lamp, such goods are consumed collectively. Although the street itself can become crowded, the rate of consumption of the lamplight is independent of the number of consumers and of the particular use individuals make of the good (walking, jogging, motoring, or dancing in the streets). By contrast, private goods are individually consumed; what one individual consumes is either used up or becomes (at least temporarily)

41

unavailable to others. Like pure public goods, the commons is shared, and unlike private goods, it either cannot be or is not (for any of a number of reasons) divided among separate consumers. Yet like the use of private goods, the use of the commons is characterized by individual consumers who appropriate a portion of the flow of benefits (farmers pump water, cows eat grass) and make that portion unavailable to others. In the case of a resource commons, individuals actually extract private goods from the resource. Unlike pure public goods, the commons cannot be shared without limit.

The commons is like a factory that produces, not a series of differentiated products, but a stream or pool of undifferentiated "product" from which individuals take a portion for their use—hence the term "common-pool resource," preferred by some analysts and equivalent to "the commons." Unlike what goes on in a factory, however, appropriation here affects production, or more precisely, the rate at which individuals appropriate affects the rate at which the resource can produce or replenish a supply. Without coordination, individuals may in the aggregate use too much too fast, causing the rate of production to fall. Sharing without collective consumption—the commons situation—requires restraint, which in turn depends on coordination among users. Otherwise, individuals continue to consume without regard to the diminishing marginal product of the commons as a whole.

Even if aggregate use is suboptimal, difficulties are often not noticed until there is some significant change in the pattern or level of use, and declining yields begin to reduce the size of the shares available to individuals. If a community of users is unable to work through existing arrangements to respond appropriately to changes, destructive competition or conflict may follow. Resource depletion (or degradation of facilities) results—the outcome characterized by Garrett Hardin (1968) as the "tragedy of the commons." In specific cases, the consequences may be soil erosion, overgrazing, diminishing fish harvests, disappearing species, shrinking forests, or impassable roads.

In this chapter, I present a conceptual framework that can be used to collect information about the commons and analyze it across a variety of resources and facilities. Such a framework must be specific enough to offer guidance in the field, yet general enough to permit application to widely variable situations. The trick is to develop concepts that identify key attributes shared broadly by the commons in its many manifestations and that take on different values from one circumstance to another. This allows a systematic approach to the study of a phenomenon that has great variation. Relationships among variables need to be specified in ways that allow one to diagnose what is wrong and why in particular situations. On such a basis, potential solutions can be offered.

Four Types of Attributes

The framework distinguishes four sets of attributes or variables that can be used to describe a commons: (1) the physical attributes of the specific resource or facility and the technology used to appropriate its yield; (2) the decision-making arrangements (organization and rules) that govern relationships among users, as well as relevant others; (3) the mutual choice of strategies and consequent patterns of interaction among decision makers; and (4) outcomes or consequences (V. Ostrom 1974, 55; Oakerson 1981, 81). Each set of attributes is related systematically to the others. The plan of discussion is, first, to introduce each of the four types of attributes and examine the relationships in the framework among them. I will then suggest ways of applying the framework for both diagnostic and prescriptive purposes, as well as for applying it iteratively to understand the impact of technological and institutional change and adaptation.

The framework is no more than a bare-bones representation of the commons in its essentials.[2] It is intended to identify four types of factors, related in specifiable, limited ways, that can be assumed always to operate with respect to the commons. It should not be construed as a fully specified causal model that includes all relevant variables and relationships in every case. Although not a model to feed data into and crank out predictions from, the framework is a heuristic tool for thinking through the logic of a situation and considering alternative possibilities. It can be elaborated in particular cases to whatever level of complexity and completeness may be desired.

Physical and Technical Attributes

Problems of the commons are rooted in constraints given in nature or inherent in available technology. The analytic interest in physical resource properties and technology stems mainly from three considerations: (1) the relative capacity of the resource base to support multiple users at the same time without one interfering with another or diminishing the aggregate level of benefit (the yield of a resource) available to the group; (2) the degree to which (or relative ease with which) the commons permits exclusion of individual users, limiting access to the resource or facility; and (3) the physical boundaries of the commons, which determine the minimal scale on which effective coordination can occur. Each of these concerns is addressed below by introducing a relevant economic concept.

Jointness. The concept of jointness was originally introduced to define a "pure public good" (Samuelson 1954). Jointness means that one person's use does not subtract from the use of others. The opposite case is one in which a single individual fully consumes (and destroys) a good. As a variable, jointness refers to degrees of nonsubtractability (V. Ostrom and E. Ostrom 1978), that is, the degree to which more than a single consumer can make use of the same good. The idea ordinarily refers to simultaneous use, but can also include serial use. "Impure" public goods are those in which jointness is limited by congestion. Once a threshold is crossed, individual users begin to subtract from one another's beneficial use.

The idea of subtractability can be applied to the commons in two ways. First, any user of the commons subtracts from a flow of benefits; what one appropriates, whether gallons of water or blades of grass, is unavailable to others. Second, cumulative use by many individuals will eventually subtract from the total yield of the commons over time—from the rate at which a groundwater basin produces water or a pasture produces fodder. It is the second type of subtractability, which reduces the capacity of a resource to generate benefits, that gives rise to the distinctive problem of the commons. In this sense, the commons exhibits partial subtractability, and the threshold at which use becomes subtractive varies from one situation to another. Each individual user is potentially capable of subtracting from the welfare of other users; but, within limits, all users can derive benefits jointly.

The analysis of a commons, therefore, should specify as precisely as possible the "limiting conditions" that pertain to natural replenishment or maintenance of the resource. Physical limits established by nature or technology provide critical information for devising rules to maintain jointly beneficial use, such as grazing limits in a common pasture, trapping limits in a lobstery, and weight limits on a highway. By having reference to such legal rules, it is possible to introduce a modified concept of jointness, so that one person's *lawful* use does not subtract from the *lawful* use of others (Oakerson 1981). Thus, resource sharing can be efficient even in the absence of collective consumption (that is, of physical nonsubtractability), provided that rules based on limiting conditions inherent in the nature of the resource are implemented.

Exclusion. The "exclusion principle," also used by economists to differentiate private goods from public goods (Musgrave 1959), ordinarily refers to the ability of sellers to exclude potential buyers from goods and services unless they pay a stipulated price. The concept can be broadened somewhat to include the question of access to any type of good, including the commons. The opposite of exclusion is complete openness—unlimited access. Although an organized commons need not be characterized by open access (Runge 1981), the commons always has an access-control problem to some degree. As a variable, the degree of exclusion (or access control) attainable depends on both the physical nature of a resource (or design of a facility) and available technology. Historically, for example, open range was difficult and expensive to fence, but the development of barbed wire to a great extent overcame this limitation.

At this point in the analysis, one is interested not in an exclusion or nonexclusion policy, but rather in excludability, that is, the limiting conditions that apply to the possibility of exclusion as established by nature or technology. Two types of exclusion can be distinguished: (1) access may be fully regulated on an individual basis, or (2) it may be partially regulated and applied only to those outside the immediate community. This distinction is related to the potential exposure of the commons to increases in demand. Within a definite community of users, increases in aggregate demand derive mainly from expanded operations. If there is open access, however, increases in the number of users can also contribute to an increase in total demand on the resource.

Indivisibility. Is the commons divisible? Could the physical resource or facility feasibly be divided among private property holders? What would be the costs of doing so? If the commons is not divisible, what boundary conditions apply to its regulation? On what scale would regulation have to occur to be effective? The relative indivisibility of a commons is mainly a question of scale, determined by specifying the physical boundaries within which the commons cannot be divided without significantly impairing its management potential or production value.

Physical boundaries having to do with divisibility of the resource derive from nature or technology and should not be confused with legal boundaries, that is, boundaries imposed by rule. Consider the example of a groundwater basin. Groundwater occurs in underground aquifers that have fairly definite physical boundaries. The legal boundaries of a jurisdictional unit formed to deal with a groundwater problem may or may not correspond to the physical boundaries of the resource. Other types of the commons may have less definite physical boundaries; nonetheless, it still may be possible to assign geographic boundaries based on physical or technical attributes. The western range in the United States, for example, might superficially be viewed as a single resource; but variations in weather and soil conditions prompt the "division" or partitioning of the range into much smaller units for management purposes.

An analysis of the commons must posit some set of boundary conditions, even if the physical boundaries are somewhat ambiguous. If the boundaries chosen for the purposes of analysis are too small, then relevant aspects of the problem will be left outside; if the boundaries are too large, then multiple problems may be confounded. Although the precise boundary may be somewhat arbitrary, the relevant question is whether it lies within an acceptable range for the purpose of analysis.

In some cases, the resource is technically divisible into relatively small parcels, and the commons exists by human design alone without reference to natural or technological constraints. Still, there may be underlying economic or cultural reasons for the treatment of a divisible resource as a commons. Other parts of the analysis must take cognizance of these reasons as relevant to the design of decision-making arrangements, including the possibility of converting the commons to private property. There is nothing in this analytic framework, however, to suggest that divisibility necessarily implies that privatization is the wisest solution.

Decision-Making Arrangements

The second set of attributes in the framework consists of rules—those rules that structure individual and collective choices with respect to the commons as defined by the first set of attributes. These arrangements may also be thought of as "organizational" or "institutional." The designation used here is intended to convey a very broad set of arrangements that are not confined to any single "organization" or "institution." Daniel W. Bromley (1989) refers to "resource regimes." In such regimes, several discrete institutions or organizations are generally implicated in the management or mismanagement of a commons.

In general, decision-making arrangements are defined by authority relationships that specify *who* decides *what* in relation to *whom*. In the discussion below, decision-making arrangements are sorted into three subsets: (1) "operational rules" that regulate use of the commons; (2) rules that establish "conditions of collective choice" within the group most immediately involved with the commons; and (3) "external arrangements," those decision structures outside the immediate group that impinge on how the commons is organized and used. Operational rules are nested in collective-choice rules, which are nested in external arrangements. At least three different levels of analysis are possible with respect to the organization of the commons.

Operational rules. Various types of rules can serve to limit user behavior in the interest of maintaining the yield of the commons. Alternative patterns of use should be evaluated for the degree to which each subtracts from the flow of the resource. Some uses have the potential to drive other uses out, quickly exhaust the resource, or both. Such highly subtractive behavior may therefore be disallowed. Less subtractive patterns of use can also, cumulatively, diminish the yield of the commons. Limits may therefore be imposed on both duration and type of use, as well as on the amount of the resource flow that can be appropriated during a time period. If more than one use is made of a commons, operational rules need to take into account the relationships among uses. Some types of use may be compatible; others, sharply conflicting. At times a commons is physically partitioned for different uses without being divided into separate parcels of property; the effect is to segregate users while retaining joint use. Use can also be time-partitioned, reflecting conditions of seasonality or potential congestion.

Conditions of collective choice. Operational rules derive from collective choices that are also rule-ordered. Rules that establish conditions of collective choice to allow a group of appropriators to manage their commons can be understood as a"common-property" arrangement. Individuals are no longer entirely free to decide for themselves how to make use of the commons, as in a private property arrangement, but participate in a process of collective choice that sets limits on individual use. In one degree or another, the rights of individual ownership give way to rights of common ownership. Common-property arrangements protect individual shares in the yield of the commons, and thus also provide an institutional foundation for protecting the total yield of the commons.

Four different relationships affect the conditions of collective choice: (1) the capacity of individuals to make decisions solely on the basis of personal discretion in matters of concern to others, perhaps preempting action by others or initiating an action that creates costs of opposition for others; (2) the availability of potential sources of remedy to individuals adversely affected by others; (3) the capacity of an affected population to relax the market rule of willing consent and make a collective decision binding on all relevant individuals; and (4) the presence of potential veto positions in any process of collective decision making—opportunities for any one individual or group to say no.

This portion of the analysis addresses a series of questions: Is coordination purely voluntary? If not, what proportion of the community must agree before a course of action may be adopted? If adopted, is the course of action enforceable? How are enforcement actions undertaken? In what forum can disputes be settled and on what legal grounds? To what extent are collective choice and enforcement dependent on the exercise of authority by more inclusive units of government? Are these more inclusive units local, regional, or national?

In a common-property arrangement, a limited set of individuals has use rights, but ownership is in some sense vested in the group, which thus acquires the power to regulate the commons and to exclude others.[3] "Entry" and "exit" rules (for which see E. Ostrom 1986) are concerned with exclusion and seek to regulate access to the commons. In a broad sense, this set of rules includes qualifications for participation in a community of users (entry) and whether membership in an organization of users is compulsory (exit); it thus affects conditions of collective choice. "Boundary" rules, closely related to entry and exit rules, determine the legal domain of a collective decision-making arrangement. Any organizational arrangement for governing a commons must stipulate a set of jurisdictional boundaries. These boundary rules, however, may or may not be congruent with the underlying boundary conditions determined by the technical and physical nature of the resource.

A number of variations in common-property arrangements can be found. Depending on the particular arrangement and its relationship with more inclusive legal arrangements in the larger community, common property may or may not include the ability of users to transfer ownership and thus derive a joint return on their investment. Alternatively, individuals may have private rights to make use of the commons, and thus to exclude others, but not have the power as a group to regulate the commons, except on the basis of willing consent. Such individuals may, however, be vested with rights that protect them from injury caused by others' use of the commons. Remedies may be available through such "third-party" arrangements as courts. Another possibility is the creation of some form of collective organization in addition to private property rights that endows the group with regulatory authority. This is another way of allowing a community of users to make collective choices, without the willing consent of each party, that establish limits on individual use. Common-property arrangements should be distinguished from general public or government ownership, which vests control of the commons in government agencies rather than in the communities directly affected.

External arrangements. Decision-making arrangements external to the community are also relevant in most cases, but the connection varies widely. Some external arrangements may be mainly constitutional, establishing the capability of the community of users to engage in local collective choice. For example, the State of California has enacted enabling legislation that allows private property owners to form special districts to manage groundwater supplies. At the other extreme, a community may be substantially dependent on external decision makers for the legislation and enforcement of operational rules, replacing common property arrangements with control by external officers. In this case, external arrangements are bureaucratic in nature, characterized by some combination of central rule making and field officer discretion. In addition, third-party arrangements may also be available externally to resolve disputes between users. Courts of law fall into this category, but so do such other arrangements as a bureaucratic hearing officer or a traditional local chief in areas with a tribal history. Finally, market arrangements external to the commons may be relevant in establishing economic parameters within which management of the commons can be undertaken. If there were no market in land, for example, the effect on those who use common land for grazing or agriculture would be different from what it would be if land were also available on the private market.

Patterns of Interaction

Rules, as everyone is aware, do not guarantee the emergence of a particular pattern of behavior. Between rules and observed behaviors lie the unobserved mental calculations of individuals who make choices. Individuals choose strategies for relating to one another and to the commons. Patterns of interaction result directly from the mutual choice of strategies by the members of a group. Given the physical features of the commons and the characteristics of the relevant technology, on the one hand, as well as the decision-making arrangements available to govern its use, on the other, individuals make choices, from which there emerges some pattern of interaction.

Although individual choices can be understood in terms of a comparison of the costs and benefits of alternative actions, these economic concepts remain abstract until related to the particular circumstances of individuals. As experienced by individuals, a "cost" is any perceived *obstacle* to the choice of some alternative (Buchanan 1969). Conversely, a "benefit" is any perceived *inducement* to choose one alternative over another. Individual choices are conditioned by a mental image of obstacles and inducements in a relevant environment. The resulting incentives to act or not to act in various ways may be relatively strong or weak.

Important elements of individual behavior on the commons are interdependent (Runge 1981). How others are expected to behave creates obstacles and inducements for each individual. Several possible strategies are of interest. One is a free-rider strategy. When others propose a course of action, an individual says, "You go ahead, but I'm not interested." If the others do go ahead, the free-rider strategy is successful, at least in the short run. Whether a single free rider can undermine a collective effort depends on the subtractiveness of that individual's use of the commons. Alternatively, an individual may choose a cooperative strategy, continuing to contribute to a joint undertaking as long as others also continue. The mutual choice of cooperative strategies leads to a general pattern of reciprocity.

Reciprocity among group members has an interesting structure. Individuals contribute (through mutual action or mutual forbearance) to one another's welfare, but without an immediate quid pro quo as in exchange relationships (Oakerson 1988; Boulding 1972). On the commons, an individual must practice restraint when the beneficiaries of his or her restraint consist mainly of others. At the same time, each individual draws the larger benefit, not from his or her own act of restraint, but from the restraint practiced by others. Individuals can agree to a pattern of mutual restraint, and mutually enforce such a pattern, but they cannot trade one act of restraint for another the way that individuals exchange commodities. The quid pro quo that regulates an exchange relationship is unavailable to regulate reciprocity. Yet only through a pattern of reciprocity can individuals realize the joint benefit of mutual restraint. Instead of a quid pro quo, reciprocity depends on mutual expectations of future positive performance. While exchange is based on *ex ante* conditions (that is, an exchange does not occur until certain conditions are met on both sides), reciprocity is subject to *ex post* conditions (that is, to conditions that are met following one's contribution to a joint undertaking), as individuals learn what to expect from one another. What is ordinarily called "collective action" can be understood as *n*-person reciprocity—the reciprocal interaction of individuals who jointly contribute to a common effort.

Free-riding behavior erodes reciprocity. Initially, one individual may choose not to contribute with the expectation that others will continue as before. The prospect of "riding free" on the contributions of others can be a substantial inducement. But, as we saw in Chapter 2, an even stronger obstacle to the choice of a cooperative strategy is a lack of assurance that others will do likewise. The organizational challenge is to sustain mutual choices of cooperative strategies among a sufficient number to sustain the yield of the commons.

Collective decision-making arrangements are designed to alter the structure of obstacles and inducements that individuals otherwise would face. However, any assignment of decision-making capabilities simply sets parameters within which individuals choose strategies. While cooperation and noncooperation among users are the first-order strategies of interest, there are also second-order strategies that affect first-order choices. Within the community of users, for example, successful collective action may depend on the degree to which individuals are willing and able to monitor one another's behavior in order to hold each other accountable to shared standards of conduct. If decision-making arrangements provide for the enforcement of rules and application of sanctions, then the choice of enforcement strategies by officials is often critical. A variety of decision makers, from bureaucrats to judges, may play a role.

If reciprocity erodes, and is ultimately abandoned, mutually destructive competition or conflict follows. Users of the commons may try to drive one another out to preclude mutually subtractive use. Or they may engage in a competitive race to exploit the commons without regard to an optimal rate of use. At this stage, the relevant second-order strategies may include concealment, deceit, intimidation, threats, and violence. Range wars observed in the settlement of the western United States are illustrative.

Outcomes

Patterns of interaction produce physical outcomes subject to human evaluation. To supply information for this fourth set of attributes in the framework, the analyst is required to (1) stipulate the use of evaluative criteria and (2) search for consequences that affect users of the commons (and others involved) in accordance with these criteria. The study of consequences is necessarily value laden. To distinguish relevant consequences, the analyst must draw on evaluative criteria such as, most commonly, conceptions of efficiency and equity. But these abstractions have to be converted into operational measures of value in order to be used to appraise specific outcomes.

Considerations of efficiency in the use of commons have to do with the overall rate of use. Technical and physical attributes of the commons indicate some optimal rate. Aggregate overuse, such as placing too many animals on a common pasture or withdrawing too much water from a groundwater basin, eventually reduces the total yield, leaving each user with a smaller share. Accelerating overuse can deplete resources or destroy facilities, leaving everyone with a zero share. Inefficiency is also present, however, if the resource or facility is underutilized: a closed commons can be inefficient, just as can an open commons. A plan of regulation should be evaluated in terms of the value of uses foregone compared to the value of uses retained.

To conclude that there is inefficiency in the use of the commons, in principle one can apply the test of Pareto optimality: If at least one person could be made better off, and no one worse off, by a modification in the use of the commons, then present outcomes are inefficient; conversely, the proposed change is efficient. Often, however, it is not possible to do the precise technical and economic calculations necessary to determine whether aggregate use of the commons is optimal (that is, whether no further improvement is possible). Less information is needed to determine whether the current resource yield is being maintained with a given level of extraction than whether the current yield could be economically increased. Furthermore, some degree of suboptimal use may actually be efficient when the costs of obtaining collective action are taken into account. An emphasis can be placed on identifying Pareto-efficient changes, that is, improvements in efficiency, rather than on identifying a Pareto-optimal condition from which no further improvement is possible. Information requirements—and perhaps the costs of obtaining collective action—are somewhat reduced by seeking amelioration rather than optimization per se.

Inefficiency on the commons is apt to be closely associated with inequity. The basic equity issue is distributive, not redistributive: Are individuals getting a reasonable and fair return on their contribution to a collective undertaking that regulates behavior? The presence of inequities may lead to the collapse of reciprocity, resulting in less efficient use. Equity problems are apt to be aggravated by asymmetries among users, which create opportunities for some to benefit at others' expense. This, in turn, can lead to costly conflict where all parties lose. Such situations may still admit of Pareto-efficient change. In any event, Pareto-efficient changes satisfy a minimal standard of fairness: they do no harm. Measuring equity, however, is even more difficult than measuring efficiency, often compelling a reliance on rough-and-ready indicators, such as whether most members of the commons community seem to be relatively satisfied with existing arrangements. Other questions that arise from considerations of equity include the possibility of arbitrary exclusion from the commons, and selective enforcement of rules. Corruption and abuse of authority may also contribute to inequities.

Relationships

All instances of the commons have characteristics that can be sorted among the four types of attributes considered above: (1) physical attributes and technology, (2) decision-making arrangements, (3) patterns of interaction, and (4) outcomes. The purpose of dissecting the commons in this manner is to examine relationships among these four bundles of variables. Having collected and sorted the data, these relationships become the principal focus of study.

Figure 3.1 depicts the framework, showing how each set of attributes relates to the others. Both physical and technological attributes of the commons and the decision-making arrangements affect patterns of interaction, which combine with physical and technological attributes to produce outcomes. Solid lines *a* and *b* represent weak causal connections, weak in the sense that individual behavior is constrained, but not determined, by either the physical world or by rules. Solid lines *c* and *d* represent stronger causal relationships because human discretion is not involved as a dependent variable.

The technical and physical characteristics of the commons affect outcomes in two ways. One path leads through patterns of interaction. The other affects outcomes directly, independently of human choice. Physical and technological attributes are "hard" constraints. If ignored in

FIGURE 3.1
A Framework for Analyzing the Commons

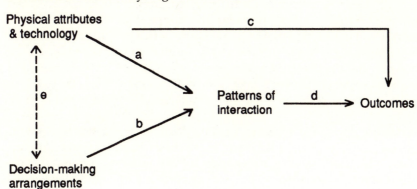

SOURCE: Author.

the process of choice, physical and technical constraints still affect outcomes. Decision-making arrangements, on the other hand, have no effect on outcomes independently of human choice and interaction. Institutions are "soft" constraints, made operative only through human knowledge, choice, and action. Rules exist in the realm of language, whether written or unwritten. Decision-making arrangements, therefore, need to be comprehended as commonly understood and applied by the relevant community of decision makers.

A good example that highlights the way in which the physical nature of a resource affects individual strategies and social interaction is found in the case of Maine inshore lobster fisheries (Acheson 1975; Wilson 1977). Unlike schooling fish, the sedentary lobster inhabits small inshore areas. Thus, the fishing area is easily accessible and can be monitored daily by the community of fishermen. Lobster traps are marked by each fisherman in distinctive colors, so small communities of fishermen can define and monitor exclusive fishing areas. Fishermen from outside the community may lose their gear, but within the community mutual forbearance allows "locals" to leave their gear safely. This pattern of interaction allows the community to control access to the commons. Decision-making arrangements within the community are entirely voluntary. Those outside the community have no effective recourse to gain access. The physical nature of the resource sets the relatively small set of boundaries that defines each inshore area and makes it possible to exclude individual fishermen. Joint use is feasible as long as fishermen are willing to act with mutual forbearance.

The use of public roads for hauling coal from mine to rail in eastern Kentucky (Oakerson 1981) provides an example that highlights how the distribution of decision-making capabilities between local officials and (in this case) state officials can affect the mutual choice of strategies. Although usually considered public goods when they are publicly provided, roads have the characteristics of the commons once provision has been made. Organizing the joint use and maintenance of roads is like organizing the use of a groundwater supply or any other commons. In the case of roads, excessive use includes hauling loads that exceed the weight-bearing capacity of the road surface and base. Rural highway development, provision, and maintenance in Kentucky is largely a state government responsibility; but the application of criminal sanctions against violators of state-prescribed weight limits is in the hands of locally elected judges in each county. Local judges have allowed coal haulers and mine operators to sustain noncompliant, free-rider strategies, hauling loads that often destroy state highways. The efforts of the state highway department to induce cooperation from local judges by withholding maintenance from all coalfield highways in eastern Kentucky proved not to be a politically feasible strategy because ordinary users were affected jointly with coal haulers. State highway officials, nevertheless, were able to reduce maintenance efforts on selected coal-haul routes as an economy measure. This strategy sometimes induced limited maintenance of public roads by mine operators, but did not affect the basic choice of strategy by coal haulers to carry overweight loads. The overall result was a system of public coal-haul roads subject to a combination of overuse and undermaintenance.

To use the framework as a diagnostic tool, an analyst works *backward* through the relationships. Initial inquiry focuses on outcomes: What is happening to the commons and to its community of users? Are individuals investing more and obtaining less from the commons? Are yields declining as effort is increasing? If so, the next question is *why*. A first-order answer can be obtained by examining patterns of interaction among resource users. Are members of the community competing with one another to maximize their individual "take" from the commons? Are there asymmetries among users that allow some to "raid" the resource and then move on? The inquiry cannot stop, however, with patterns of interaction. The question of why recurs. Second-order answers depend on how physical and technical properties of the commons, together with decision-making arrangements, jointly affect patterns of interaction. What constraints and opportunities are inherent in the physical nature of the resource and the technology available to appropriate its yield? What opportunities do the operational rules attempt to foreclose? What are the incentives of users to comply with, and of officials to enforce, operational rules? Do collective-choice rules allow the consideration of alternative operational rules? Do external arrangements allow for modifying the rules that define conditions of collective choice?

Outcomes disclose the *effect* of a difficulty that is manifested behaviorally in patterns of interaction. The *source* of the difficulty, however, lies in a lack of congruence between the first two sets of attributes: a mismatch between the technical and physical nature of a commons and the decision-making arrangements used to govern its use. This is the relationship labeled *e* in Figure 3.1. The dashed line is used to represent a noncausal association that exists, if at all, by human design. The lack of a good "fit" between these two elements in the framework creates the potential for a perverse structure of incentives—obstacles and inducements—leading individuals into counterproductive patterns of interaction that generate undesirable outcomes.

Incongruence between the first two sets of attributes—between the physical world and the institutional world—may first show itself in a lack of fit between operational rules and the corresponding technical and physical attributes of the commons. Use rules should closely match the limiting conditions that bear on maintaining the yield of the commons; entry and exit rules must be related to excludability, that is, to the limiting conditions of exclusion; boundary rules ought to reflect those limiting conditions that bear on the appropriate geographic domain of regulation. If efforts to adapt operational rules to technical and physical attributes have failed, and there is a general understanding in the relevant community of the relationships between attributes of the commons and specific operational rules, the problem may lie with the rules that define conditions of collective choice. Further, if efforts to adjust the conditions of collective choice in the community have failed, the difficulty may lie with external arrangements.

Having diagnosed problematic conditions by working backward through the framework, one can turn to questions of design: how to modify patterns of interaction by adjusting decision-making arrangements to better fit the particular nature of the commons. Design requires an analyst to work prospectively, forward through the framework. What do key features of the technical and physical attributes require of operational rules and conditions of collective choice? What adjustments might be made in external decision-making arrangements? How would these institutional changes affect the structure of incentives that face decision makers? What choice of strategies, and resultant patterns of interaction, would the analyst anticipate? How would anticipated patterns of interaction affect users of the commons and others?

Dynamic Applications

In the short-run analysis undertaken for a diagnostic purpose, both the physical-technical attributes of the commons and decision-making arrangements are assumed to be unchanging. A prescriptive or long-run analysis, however, must allow for change in both sets of variables. One way to introduce a longer time horizon into the analysis is to apply the framework iteratively. The framework is used to record and describe changes at successive points in time. This approach treats institutional change as exogenous; the aim is simply to understand how a series of changes in technology or decision-making arrangements affects patterns of interaction and outcomes. Viewing change as exogenous, however, does not help to explain how change comes about. The effort to understand institutional change raises new issues. What incentives promote investment in technology? What opportunities are present for learning the consequences of actions?

In order to aid in understanding institutional change, the framework can be modified by adding a set of long-term relationships, shown by the broken lines in Figure 3.2.[4] Outcomes can affect patterns of interaction insofar as a process of learning occurs, causing individuals to modify their strategies. Instead of continuing to produce outcomes on the basis of

FIGURE 3.2
A Dynamic Framework

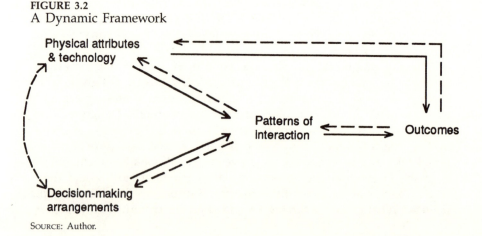

SOURCE: Author.

decision-making arrangements as given, individuals may attempt to modify those arrangements to produce better outcomes. Similarly, individuals may invest in technological innovation that would change the technical and physical attributes of the commons. The latter may also change over time as an indirect result of strategies pursued in securing outcomes; this is easily seen if prevailing patterns of interaction result eventually in the destruction of a resource.

Conclusion

The purpose of the framework presented here is to aid in the collection and assimilation of case-by-case analyses. The ability to observe regularities across many different cases depends on the use of a consistent framework. Some method is needed to array information into meaningful sets in order to examine relevant relationships in a particular case. Use of a consistent method by a community of scholars enhances the comparability of separate case studies. As scholars use and apply a framework, and share ideas, the framework, too, becomes the subject of change— elaboration or modification—in view of experience.

This book is a first step in that direction. The framework was adopted by the Panel on Common Property Resource Management, organized by the Board on Science and Technology for International Development (BOSTID) at the National Research Council, and used to organize the presentation of twenty case studies at an international conference held at Annapolis, Maryland, in 1985 (National Research Council 1986). The cases in the present volume, selected from those presented at the Annapolis conference, represent applications of the framework from which one might learn something about its limits and possibilities, as well as something about the commons. Others have used the framework, or a related version, in studies undertaken since the conference (Blaikie and Brookfield 1987; Tang 1992).

A great deal more work remains to be done. It is important that the collection of cases begun in Annapolis go forward in ways that permit systematic comparisons. There is much more to be learned about the varieties of collective decision-making arrangements, or resource regimes, developed by communities that depend on the commons in one or another form, and, especially, about how these arrangements are nested within the larger set of social and political arrangements found in all societies. Whether communities are to continue managing their commons successfully, or learn how to succeed if they have failed, depends on the base of knowledge we can build.

NOTES

I would like to thank fellow members of the Panel on Common Property Resource Management, National Research Council, as well as the other participants in the Annapolis conference, for the many rounds of discussions and criticism—and editorial work—that contributed to the development and application of the framework presented in this chapter. The conference and its resultant volumes have been products of an extraordinary team effort from start to finish. I am also grateful to Robert Netting, Vincent Ostrom, and Susan Wynne for their helpful comments on one or more drafts. For remaining imperfections, I am fully responsible.

1. It is important to keep distinct the natural production process of the resource system and the production process in which individual users of the commons may be engaged. The product or yield of the commons—grass, water, timber—is often used in the production of a commodity—milk, electric power, lumber. The commodity producers are resource consumers. Sometimes production occurs actually *on* the commons (as with rangelands) and sometimes not (as with groundwater).

2. The generic framework, without specific application to the commons, has been developed in a more elaborate way by Kiser and E. Ostrom (1982).

3. Hardin's "tragedy of the commons" (1968) occurs in a context of unrestricted access and thus may or may not apply to a commons, but it does not in general apply to a common-property arrangement.

4. Since the Annapolis conference I have concluded that a multilevel framework is a better way to represent dynamic relationships, as opposed to the recursive framework shown in Figure 3.2. At least three levels of analysis are needed. First, an operational level of analysis views operational rules as the relevant decision-making arrangements, considers interactions among resource users, and evaluates welfare outcomes. This level is nested within a second level of analysis that treats operational rules as an intermediate outcome and collective choice rules as the relevant decision-making arrangement. Both levels are nested within a third level, this one treating collective-choice rules as an intermediate outcome and more inclusive or external institutions as relevant decision-making arrangements. Institutional change at one level is an outcome of patterns of interaction at another level. (For a related discussion, see Kiser and E. Ostrom 1982.)

REFERENCES

Acheson, J. M. 1975. "The Lobster Fiefs: Economic and Ecological Effects of Territoriality in the Maine Lobster Industry." *Human Ecology* 3:183–207.

Blaikie, Piers, and Harold Brookfield. 1987. "Common Property Resources and Degradation Worldwide." In *Land Degradation and Society*, ed. Piers Blaikie and Harold Brookfield, 186–95. London and New York: Methuen.

Boulding, Kenneth E. 1972. "The Household as Achilles' Heel." *Journal of Consumer Affairs* 6:111–19.

Bromley, Daniel W. 1989. "Property Relations and Economic Development: The Other Land Reform." *World Development* 17 (6):867–77.

Buchanan, James M. 1969. *Cost and Choice.* Chicago: Markham.

Hardin, Garrett. 1968. "The Tragedy of the Commons." *Science* 162:1243–48.

Kiser, Larry L., and Elinor Ostrom. 1982. "The Three Worlds of Action: A Metatheoretical Synthesis of Institutional Approaches." In *Strategies of Political Inquiry,* ed. Elinor Ostrom, 179–222. Beverly Hills: Sage.

Musgrave, Richard A. 1959. *The Theory of Public Finance: A Study in Public Economy.* New York: McGraw-Hill.

National Research Council. 1986. *Proceedings of the Conference on Common Property Resource Management.* Washington, D.C.: National Academy Press.

Oakerson, Ronald J. 1981. "Erosion of Public Goods: The Case of Coal-Haul Roads in Eastern Kentucky." In *Research in Public Policy Analysis and Management,* vol. 2, ed. John P. Crecine, 73–102. Greenwich, Conn.: JAI Press.

———. 1988. "Reciprocity: A Bottom-Up View of Political Development." In *Rethinking Institutional Analysis and Development: Issues, Alternatives, and Choices,* ed. Vincent Ostrom, David Feeny, and Hartmut Picht, 141–58. San Francisco: ICS Press.

Ostrom, Elinor. 1986. "An Agenda for the Study of Institutions." *Public Choice* 48: 3–25.

Ostrom, Vincent. 1974. *The Intellectual Crisis in American Public Administration.* Rev. ed. University, Ala.: University of Alabama Press.

Ostrom, Vincent, and Elinor Ostrom. 1978. "Public Goods and Public Choices." In *Alternatives for Delivering Public Services,* ed. E. S. Savas, 7–49. Boulder, Colo.: Westview Press.

Runge, C. Ford. 1981. "Common Property Externalities: Isolation, Assurance, and Resource Depletion in a Traditional Grazing Context." *American Journal of Agricultural Economics* 63:595–606.

Samuelson, Paul A. 1954. "The Pure Theory of Public Expenditure." *Review of Economics and Statistics* 36:357–59.

Tang, Shui Yan. 1992. *Institutions and Collective Action: Self-Governance in Irrigation.* San Francisco: ICS Press.

Wilson, James A. 1977. "A Test of the Tragedy of the Commons." In *Managing the Commons,* ed. Garrett Hardin and John Baden, 96–111. San Francisco: Freeman.

PART 2

Case Studies of Common-Property Regimes

4

Management of Traditional Common Lands (*Iriaichi*) in Japan

Margaret A. McKean

The centuries-old common lands of traditional Japanese villages are particularly worthy of inclusion in our comparative study of common property, for several reasons. First, they fall squarely into our most pristine definition of common property: they are common lands with identifiable communities of co-owners, as opposed to being vast, open-access public areas used by all and in essence owned by no one. Second, Japanese villages developed elaborate regulations, even written codes, for their commons; even a tiny fraction of the many thousands of traditional villages offers ample variety on most variables of interest. Third, the documentation and historical records allow us to inquire not only into formal rules but also into their operation and enforcement, thus offering more data than we have in other cases of common-property institutions. Fourth, Japanese villages employed threats of ostracism and banishment to control social behavior and as ultimate penalties for abusing the commons; we therefore find a fascinating resemblance between the sanctions they employed and the concept of exclusion that is so important in theories of public goods and property rights used in the study of common property.[1] Fifth, from the mid-seventeenth to the mid-nineteenth century, Japan closed its ports to trade; as a result Japanese society spent two centuries in a conveniently isolated "test tube" uncontaminated by the world economy and living within the limitations imposed by nature and local technology. This fact may limit the applicability of the Japanese experience to less-developed nations today, but it also helps us bring some degree of experimental control to the phenomena we want to examine.

Finally, although economic development and the commercialization of agriculture threatened the Japanese commons as they have commons elsewhere—causing many villages to abandon traditional self-sufficiency in favor of commercial production and even to privatize the commons— thousands of other Japanese villages developed management techniques to protect their common lands for centuries without experiencing the "tragedy of the commons."

As late as the 1950s, there were many expanses of common land in Japan still being managed collectively without ecological destruction. Thus this case offers, in our terms, a successful outcome within the rubric of common property (that is, without privatization). It may tell us much about how what C. Ford Runge, in Chapter 2 of this book, has called the assurance problem can be solved so that cooperation among coowners of a commons is sustained not merely for decades but for centuries, and thus how tragedies of the commons may be averted.

Emergence of the Commons

The common lands that we can trace today came into being gradually, essentially between the thirteenth and sixteenth centuries, though the tradition of the commons may well have begun more than a thousand years earlier.[2] In cultivating arable land, traditional agriculture in Japan relied heavily on the availability of fertilizer, fodder, timber, and other products from uncultivated land. Thus there was a need to manage the uncultivated lands and eventually to define property rights to them also. The great landholders of the medieval period therefore appointed prominent peasants as their officers and agents in each village, empowering them to regulate access to uncultivated forests and grasslands, to summon corvée labor, and to govern the irrigation system upon which wet-rice agriculture depended. At the outset, these rights were presumed to reside in the landholder, and all the villagers had to petition him through his agent for the right to enter the uncultivated lands.

However, as public order deteriorated, especially from the fourteenth century through the sixteenth, villagers became very concerned with communal solidarity to protect themselves from the ravages of war. The self-governing medieval villages found most often in central Japan wrote their own codes to govern common lands, irrigation, and corvée labor (Troost 1985a, 1985b, 1990, 1991). Peasant-cultivators' rights developed more slowly elsewhere, and may not have been secure in many villages until the late sixteenth century when national cadastral surveys were conducted. These surveys assigned most of the rights to arable land that we today consider to be "ownership" to peasants who lived on and cultivated that land (Ishii 1980, 61–63). By 1600, when Tokugawa Ieyasu established the military dictatorship (shogunate) that would control Japan until 1867, most villages had acquired full ownership of large expanses of uncultivated land and clear use rights (perpetual usufruct) to even more land; all of these rights were held in common and shared by all the villagers.

The Physical Attributes of the Commons

Two-thirds of Japan is still occupied by forests and uncultivated mountain plains (about 25 million hectares), and approximately half of this land was still held and managed in common by rural villages at the end of the Tokugawa period in 1867. Even though much of that has been redesignated or sold as public or private property, more than 2.5 million hectares of common land remain in Japan today (Watanabe and Nakao 1975, 45–48; Kawashima 1979).[3] Although Japan now has one of the highest per capita incomes in the world, the infusion of industrial wealth into rural Japan is a very recent development, and in many parts of Japan the commons remained a vital part of the rural economy until the 1950s.

Using the Commons

Communities that retained their common land after the Meiji Restoration in 1868 continued to use their land in the traditional way. But they also developed other methods as their needs changed, especially as subsistence agriculture increasingly gave way to cash crop agriculture and light industry.

The classic type. This type, of course, prevailed during the Tokugawa period and was restricted to activities that left the commons essentially in its natural state. It involved an investment of labor to harvest natural products that were very important in daily life: thatch for roofs, fodder for animals, multipurpose bamboo, firewood, charcoal, underbrush and fallen leaves, compost, wood for furniture and tools, medicinal herbs, fowl and game, and edible wild plants. Those with access rights (whom I shall call "co-owners" of the commons) could enter the commons to obtain these items either as individuals, or by households, or in groups, and either freely or at designated times only, according to the particular set of rules devised by that particular village.

Direct group control. This prohibited access by individuals and was used to harvest the commons for cash income; it has been used for the last century to supplement village treasuries. For instance, a village might develop rice paddies, dry fields, or fruit orchards on the commons and sell the crop for village income. The income earned was either distributed among co-owners or plowed back into the next investment in the commons, or some other village project, as needed.

Divided use. Here, common land is actually divided into pieces for individual co-owners to use as they see fit. This is akin to privatizing the commons, except that co-owners do not own their allotments, must abide by certain limits in their use of the commons (they may not build structures on the land, for instance), and are not free to sell their pieces to anyone else.[4] Pieces are usually assigned by lot, and reassignments are conducted every two or three years to ensure fairness and to prevent the commons from degenerating into private property. This method has obvious appeal to a community in which the collective decision making required in classic or direct group control of the land has become cumbersome or time-consuming, or where individual co-owners of the commons have widely differing needs for timber, cash income, extra paddy land, private vegetable gardens, or natural products. Direct group control and divided use of the commons are known to have appeared occasionally in the management of Tokugawa and even earlier commons in some regions, but these methods of management were probably not widespread until the Meiji period.

Contracted use. The most modern innovation in common land use involves contracts that are written when villages want to hold onto their common land but cannot come up with the labor to maintain it. Here, they retain ownership but grant an exploitation lease to another party.

Most communities that still possess common land combine these methods depending on the activity. In certain areas of Japan, the classic method has persisted until very recently, particularly in impoverished areas that did not attract industry, and where the common lands, often substantial in size and ecological diversity, provided a large share of the local livelihood.

Ownership and Management of Common Land in Three Villages

The summary of management techniques given below is drawn from studies of three villages (Yamanaka, Hirano, and Nagaike, located on the poor volcanic soils north of Mount Fuji in Yamanashi Prefecture) that used the classic method until after World War II (see Figure 4.1).[5] These villages are not necessarily typical, but they have been carefully studied and can therefore serve as a solid starting point for further research. They also

FIGURE 4.1
Iriaichi Surrounding the Communities of Yamanaka, Hirano, and Nagaike

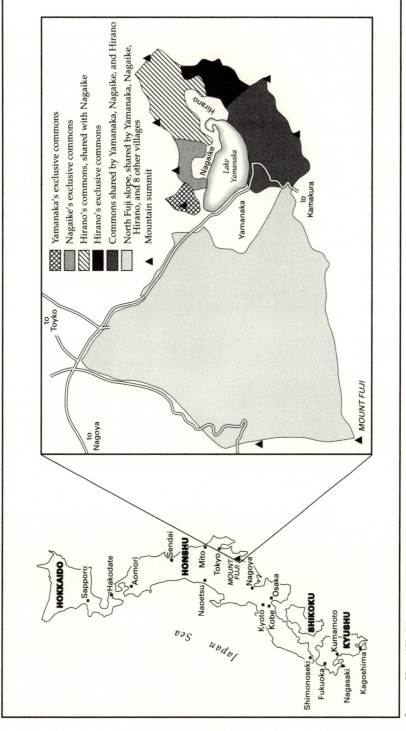

Legend:
- Yamanaka's exclusive commons
- Nagaike's exclusive commons
- Hirano's commons, shared with Nagaike
- Hirano's exclusive commons
- Commons shared by Yamanaka, Nagaike, and Hirano
- North Fuji slope, shared by Yamanaka, Nagaike, Hirano, and 8 other villages
- ▲ Mountain summit

SOURCE: Hōjō 1979, Watanabe and Hōjō 1975, and Kaminura 1979.

vary in ways that are likely to prove interesting and significant in building hypotheses about successful management of the commons.

Yamanaka, Hirano, and Nagaike have diverse common lands: forest and grasslands, large and small expanses of commons, and rich productive lands and relatively poor lands.[6] Moreover, each of these villages possesses some common land of its own, some common land shared with one or both of the other villages, and access rights to the very large expanse of land on Mount Fuji's north slope (Kitafuji) that are shared among a total of eleven villages.

The villages themselves also vary. Hirano is old and wealthy, nestled against verdant mountains, hierarchical in social structure, inegalitarian in income distribution, crusty in traditional values, and intensely concerned with family and reputation. Nagaike is a younger (late Tokugawa), smaller, poorer offshoot of Hirano with very little difference in social standing or wealth among its households. Yamanaka is the largest and most impoverished of the three, located adjacent to the largest but least productive of the commons (the Kitafuji slope), a large village in which horizontal organizations known as kumi are at least as important a focus of loyalty as family. In addition to using the rich historical literature about these villages, I was also able to interview old-timers whose memories of the commons went back to the 1920s.[7]

The ecological health of different parcels of common land in early modern Japan varied enormously, but presumably much land was fragile and vulnerable to degradation if not well managed. Japanese villages obviously altered the commons from its natural state (with such customs as annual burning and occasional clear-cutting), but they also clearly operated their commons according to the principle of sustained yield so as not to degrade the commons as a productive resource. They preserved jointness, then, in Ronald J. Oakerson's sense of the word (see Chapter 3 of this book).

As for the physical and technical possibilities of exclusion, Japanese society during the Tokugawa period relied so heavily on natural materials, and lived at such a generally low standard of living, that fencing was all but economically impossible. The commons often comprised many scattered small parcels of land in any case and could not have been fenced very cheaply, no matter how inexpensive and readily available the fencing materials might have been. The undulating, mountainous topography of rural Japan would also have made fencing a miserable chore. To this day, cultivated land is not fenced in Japan; irrigation dikes in between the rice paddies serve as boundaries, but there are no barriers to trespassers. It was not really possible, then, to exclude (in Oakerson's sense) the ineligible from the commons with physical barriers. Instead, as we shall see, Japanese villages had to substitute rules for physical barriers.

In the same way, just as it was impractical to fence off land for purposes of exclusion, so private ownership of the commons was impractical in traditional villages as long as agricultural practices depended so heavily on the products of the commons. These products were not evenly distributed throughout the common land, and different expanses of land were of many grades and sizes and were used for purposes as varied as timbering and rock quarrying. Given the heterogeneity of the commons, it would have been difficult to divide it equitably.

As C. Ford Runge (1981) notes, common property can provide all its co-owners with entitlement to all the resources of the commons and thus offer some insurance against hard times. As long as participants believed that their investment in maintaining the commons and its rules was a worthwhile use of time and resources, the commons was a sensible and inexpensive form of insurance. Thus we find little privatization of common land until the rise of commercial agriculture in the Tokugawa period. Even then, it often happened that villagers simply stopped using the land (as opposed to selling it); rising agricultural labor costs, levels of technology, and agricultural productivity made farmers unwilling to devote long hours to maintaining and collecting resources from the commons when they could substitute commercial inputs for its products. They did not sell the land to private owners (whether villagers or outsiders) until and unless nonagricultural uses of the land became profitable.

In the three villages involved in this study, most of the common land is still held as a collective asset salable in the future, and most villagers have abandoned farming and instead work in the hotels and leisure facilities that have bought land from the farmers' private holdings. Nagaike alone has sold a portion of its commons to a developer who constructed leisure condominiums with a perfect view of Mount Fuji.

Decision-Making Arrangements Affecting the Commons

External Constraints

In 1600 Tokugawa Ieyasu established an effective military dictatorship and complex administrative structure that gave Japan peace for over 250 years.[8] Japan was divided into nearly 300 administrative units or domains, each governed by a lord. Although these lords had a fairly free hand within their own domains, they were subject to strict constraints designed to prevent the emergence of regional power. They were expected to enforce a body of elaborate laws and decrees from the center within their own domains. The central administration imposed a four-layered class structure and all manner of sumptuary laws to regulate morality, spending habits, and the behavior of the four classes. It also mandated universal registration of all individuals in the country (to track down illegal Christians) and devised complex requirements for licenses and official permission to engage in commerce and even to travel from one domain to another. All of these measures were enforced by a nationwide network of police, spies, and inspection stations at domain borders. A system of magistrates and domainal and shogunal courts handled disputes not solved by conciliation at lower levels.

There is understandable confusion and great controversy among historians over the relationship between this complex, nearly totalitarian administrative structure created by the Tokugawa and the newly assertive and relatively autonomous villages below it. For the most part this controversy does not affect the governing of common lands, which were managed freely and independently by the villagers. But there are three important developments in the Tokugawa period that did influence the management of the commons.

First, an administrative innovation of the Tokugawa regime played a role in enforcing the rules villages devised to govern their common lands: the notorious system of collective responsibility known as *goningumi*— literally, five-man groups, but in fact groups of five to ten households (Yanagida 1957; Smith 1959; Chambliss 1965, 109–12; Henderson 1965, 1975; Befu 1968, 301–14). Villages almost certainly developed this system much earlier than the 1600s and refined it themselves during the era of civil war when they had to provide their own law and order and needed internal spies.

The Tokugawa shogunate and the domains then formalized this preexisting institution to serve their purposes of tax collection and social control. All individuals were members of a five-man group and all were equally responsible and liable for payment of taxes, obedience to the law, and transgressions by fellow members. The heads of all households in a village had to affix their seals to the documents to indicate their comprehension of the rules and to guarantee their own compliance and cooperation with the village officers, who would be considered personally responsible as well for any misdeeds of the villagers. Thus the five-man group system of collective responsibility created an enormous internal incentive for villagers to solve their problems and beg, cajole, bribe, or coerce internal miscreants within the village into conformity. By almost any standard this is a very unpleasant, unjust, but efficient way of frightening people into policing each other, and it seems to produce compliance even when people do not view as legitimate the laws or codes they are expected to obey. There is little doubt that this fairly totalitarian device enhanced the ability of communities to enforce rules governing the commons.

The second important development was that, with the Pax Tokugawa, the new daimyō (feudal lords) who had not already done so tried to acquire more direct control over both their domains and their vassals by replacing fiefs with stipends of rice drawn from their own revenues. Landed vassals became salaried bureaucrats and moved from the lands that had been their fiefs into the cities. This freed the villages from direct interference by a local fief-holder and increased their freedom and independence in the use of all property, including commons. Moreover, it created a system in which private individuals and villages had not only usufruct but ownership, and daimyō had taxation rights but not ownership.

The third noteworthy change was serious deforestation. Widespread civil war in the sixteenth century was followed by peace and the rapid construction of cities and castles throughout Japan in the seventeenth century, which created tremendous demand for timber and caused considerable deforestation (Totman 1982a, 1982b, 1983a, 1983b, 1984, 1989; Osako 1983). The problem was initially most severe in forests owned directly by the Tokugawa family and the various daimyō engaged in the work of reconstruction. Their appetite for timber induced the daimyō to acquire direct control over all prime forest in their domains, so that the best of the existing timbered commons passed from villages to the daimyō. In this way ever-widening areas of Japan were threatened with deforestation.

Eventually, of course, the daimyō recognized that there was only a finite supply of timber available and began experimenting with conservation. Along with the Tokugawa shogunate they created forest magistrates to patrol the daimyō forests, looking for outright theft as well as for violation of rules governing regulated access. The daimyō often granted exclusive access rights on a long-term basis to particular villages, in exchange for the villagers' assurance that they would supervise the forests and keep others out. In effect, then, the daimyō granted these villages increasingly formal entitlement to still more common lands.

They also began to develop principles of management that would not only sustain their own prime forests but later contribute to the reforestation of Japan during the eighteenth and nineteenth centuries. These models also provided the villages with knowledge and experience in designing their own regulations and institutional arrangements, thus lowering the cost of institutional design later. Part of the problem was a conflict of interest between daimyō and peasant as to what type of forest growth to encourage: the daimyō preferred slow-growing conifers for timber, while the peasants preferred broad-leafed deciduous hardwoods whose leaves could be harvested as fertilizer and that offered excellent fuel when finally cut down. Peasants entitled to use the daimyō forests had little interest in protecting the seedlings of trees prized by the daimyō until land-leasing and yield-sharing arrangements were devised to give all of those involved a mutual interest in nurturing slow-growing timber until maturity.

Land leasing was the advance sale of a stand of timber with final payment on delivery years later. Yield sharing was a long-term contract to divide the proceeds of a sale of timber as far as fifty years into the future. These arrangements were adopted variously for all kinds of land—daimyō forest, communal village forest, and private smallholdings—and served not only to promote the notion of "multiple use" but also to encourage afforestation during the eighteenth and nineteenth centuries (Totman 1982a, 1983a, 1984, 1989). We might note that these systems of profit sharing suggest that separation of land rights from tree rights need not be disastrous at all.[9] Rather, the critical factors seem to be whether the rewards for each party create a mutual interest in nurturing a particular kind of tree growth, and whether there is a legal system that will make a fifty-year contract enforceable (the assurance problem). In Japan this tradition did exist, thanks to the development of customary and codified law and of methods of adjudication from a very early period.[10]

The deforestation crisis of the seventeenth century was not limited to privately owned land; it increased environmental pressure on remaining common lands as daimyō commandeered some communal forests and tightened restrictions on lawful use of daimyō forests. However, at this juncture, when theory might predict a tragedy of the commons, neither total environmental destruction nor complete parceling of the commons into private hands occurred. It is not clear that deforestation was worse on common land than on private land, while it is clear that recovery occurred on both without leading inevitably to parceling of the commons (Chiba 1956, 1970; McKean 1988). To be sure, some commons were seriously degraded, and plenty of privatization of commons eventually occurred (Wigen 1985). When daimyō wanted to convert meadows to forests or where villages themselves wanted prime timber to market later, they (the daimyō or the villages) did sometimes arrange to divide the commons into private parcels. These were then sold to families who then reforested the land and profited accordingly years later at the harvest. Other communities devised more stringent rules to govern the commons as its resources became more valuable (Chiba 1970, 153–58). In fact, "deprivatization" to afforest the land also occurred. Dan F. Henderson provides information about a village that decided to create a commonly owned forest from privately owned grassland by buying the land from one of its own residents (Henderson 1975, 76–79).

Frequently the occasion for dividing the commons into private parcels (an event known as *wariyama*, or "dividing the mountain")[11] was the difficulty of managing conflict among co-owners of the commons, and not necessarily the threat of environmental destruction. *Wariyama* was not always perpetual and use rights were not always comprehensive; villages sometimes tried to maintain a future hold on the land or have it revert to the village commons after it was afforested. By and large, the commons that were divided and sold to become privately owned land in perpetuity were shared by more than one village, and it was conflict among different villages rather than among residents of a single village that proved unmanageable. In effect, the transaction costs involved were too high with respect to the benefits from the commons to sustain collective management in this situation.[12] There was a clear trend during the Tokugawa period for the multivillage commons to give way to the single-village commons (Harada 1969).[13] This suggests that whereas one Tokugawa-sized village might have been small enough to manage a commons, several villages were too large, had too many irreconcilable wishes about how to use their resources (conflicts between poor mountain villages and richer lowland ones were especially frequent), and shared no overarching common goals or communal ethic. Such a finding is consistent with the theoretical prediction that normative beliefs or ideology will be crucial in preventing cheating against the commons (R. McKean 1979; North 1981).

For our purposes, the significance of this episode of deforestation during the seventeenth century is threefold: visible deforestation seems to have made many Japanese, both daimyō and villagers, aware of the very real risks of overuse and enabled them to develop and enforce stricter rules for conservation on their own initiative. Rather than destroying the commons, deforestation resulted in increased institutionalization of village rights to common lands. It also promoted the development of literally thousands of highly codified sets of regulations for the conservation of forests and the use of all commons.

Conditions of Collective Choice

Our next task is to examine the circumstances surrounding the development of operational rules for managing the commons, or the "constitution" that governed day-to-day decision making. This requires a look at the structure of the traditional village in Japan.[14] By the early Tokugawa period, each village had a sturdy internal structure and a strong sense of identity. Cadastral surveys identified particular households with particular pieces of land; tax records identified particular property owners; and the family registers attached individuals and families to particular villages. Everyone "belonged" to a particular place, and mobility from place to place was tightly controlled.

The household, not the individual, was the smallest unit of accounting, not just for managing the commons but for all purposes; the household head's name was recorded in documents to represent the entire household. Villages were governed by an assembly of representatives (almost always the family head) from all households with political rights. These could be variously defined as households with cultivation rights in land, or perhaps ownership rights in land as determined by sixteenth- and seventeenth-century cadastres, or perhaps those with taxpaying obligations, or perhaps those who contributed to the maintenance of the local shrine. These four categories were not coterminous, and each village had its own rules for participation.

Villages were usually subdivided into intermediate groupings called *kumi* (literally, "group"), each composed of several households. The *kumi* was a very important unit of accounting and distribution of responsibilities and benefits connected with collective functions: the various *kumi* might not only manage the commons and the irrigation canals, but also occasionally build public works like bridges and roads, take care of the local shrine, hold annual festivals, function as a mutual aid society for destitute villagers, help at funerals, thatch roofs, and organize the transplanting of rice.

Rights to the commons tended to be associated with wealth in private holdings, but wealth did not guarantee access.[15] In some villages, the great majority of households had something akin to ownership rights in land and political representation in the village. In others, however, the proportion of disenfranchised tenants, household servants, and outcastes without rights of access to the commons might exceed 50 percent of the total population. Elsewhere, tenant families who themselves had no political rights or access to the commons might nonetheless use the commons via their landlord's rights (Smith 1959, 24–25; Smith 1968a, 273–74). Some villages apparently gave full rights to tenant families.[16]

On paper, then, villages were democracies in which each household with full participation rights was equal to any other, and officeholders were either elected or selected by some principle of rotation. Obviously, the traditional village assembly was a decision-making unit with some democratic potential, and there is of course a raging debate over whether this potential was ever realized in fact. The conventional view is that the traditional village has always been a bastion of hierarchy, elitism, and authoritarianism. Recently, however, some scholars have argued that, before and perhaps during the Tokugawa period, Japanese villages may have operated as idyllic communal democracies in which horizontal bonds were more important than vertical ones, and in which the young men's association often became a focal point for challenges to village elders.[17] It is quite possible that in villages such as Nagaike, where the distribution of wealth was fairly egalitarian, each household was nearly equal in power. But more frequently a few families held far more land than any of the others, and it is almost certain that the poor deferred to the rich, that the elders tended to make decisions on behalf of the assembly most of the time, and that they themselves came only from the wealthiest families.

That households and not individuals were the unit of accounting, and that villages possessed the power to determine which households were eligible to participate in politics and to extend rights of access to the commons only to such households, are facts of great significance. First, large households had no advantage over small ones—no extra votes in decisions, no extra representation, no enlarged share of benefits from the commons. Indeed, their household benefits were the same as those for smaller households, but had to be apportioned among a larger number of family members. Large households could not obtain advantages by splitting into several households. Permission to form a branch household from the main household had to be obtained from reluctant village authorities, who recognized that creating an additional household would enlarge the number of claimants on the commons without enlarging the commons, and who even viewed creating a branch household as a family's selfish attempt to increase its power over the commons (Smith 1959, 182–83). New households were sometimes grudgingly accommodated but were awarded incomplete political rights—for example, no entitlement to hold village office, or less than one regular household's share of benefits.

Thus, users of the commons did not try to increase their numbers in order to increase their share of the commons, nor did anyone count on the benefits from the commons to bail them out after a period of irresponsible procreation. Villages and total population did grow during the Tokugawa period, to be sure, but slow judicious growth was the rule.[18] It seems eminently clear, not only from these indirect kinds of evidence but also from the contents of village and domain legal codes, that everyone was conscious of a sense of "limits." Records from some villages show that after a certain point—about midway through the Tokugawa period—no new arable land was brought into cultivation and the number of formally constituted (that is, politically participant) households did not increase, because no new households were permitted unless an old one died out for lack of heirs. There is every reason to believe that these villages had "filled up" their legal and topological boundaries and consciously concluded that, given the level of available technology, it simply was not worth trying to bring new lands into cultivation. The commons could produce fertilizer and equipment for cultivating only a certain amount of land, and turning some uncultivated commons into cultivated land would violate that sacred ratio and be useless anyway (until new sources of fertilizer, such as fish meal, appeared).

One final source of information about the unwritten "constitution" governing decision making in the villages is the village codes from the Tokugawa period (Befu 1968, 307–10). These were generated from within the village, and, in contrast with shogunate codes and exhortations that emphasized maximizing production, they focused on resolving disputes. Some codes clearly protected the interest of a village elite, but most empowered the assembly as a whole rather than the village head to enforce the rules. The village codes were streamlined, brief, and clearly based on centuries of knowledge and experience at maximizing the collective good by keeping internal conflict to a minimum. We will now turn to a consideration of the specific rules for managing the commons that were used in Hirano, Nagaike, and Yamanaka to defuse conflict and prevent abuse of the commons.

Rules Governing Rights of Access to the Commons

The villages of Hirano, Nagaike, and Yamanaka relied on the commons as a source of several products. *Kaya* is a grass grown to produce thatch for roofs. When it is still young it is good as horse fodder and for weaving into baskets. After fruiting, it is good for thatch. The dried stalk that remains after winter comes is good for weaving stiffer products, for racks to dry root vegetables, and for certain purposes in sericulture. *Magusa* was a grass used as fodder for draft animals and pack horses. Combined with animal excrement it also made excellent fertilizer. During the growing season each household had to cut a fresh supply daily for its animals. At the end of the growing season an entire winter's supply had to be cut, dried, and preserved so that it could be parceled out to the animals during the winter months. Most households, particularly those with more horses than usual, had to supplement their share of the common supply of winter fodder with grass collected and dried from their own private holdings.

In Nagaike, the animals were allowed to roam within a certain area and pasture at will, but it was more customary for villagers to forbid the use of commons as a pasture and insist instead that people cut the grass and bring it to the horses. This rule may have been devised to eliminate the temptation for a household that relied on common pasturage to acquire more animals than it could supply with fresh-cut fodder and thus to prevent overgrazing. I was told that villagers wanted to make sure that the horses did not eat grass or plants intended for other purposes. In any case, the role of animals in Japanese agriculture was as a precious form of equipment that had work to do each day, and not as a product in itself, so a household's need for animals was limited by the amount of land it had to work. It was not until the late nineteenth and especially early twentieth century that the production of animals became a lucrative activity in itself; families in all three villages began to earn extra income by breeding horses and leasing them as pack animals for transporting freight along the rough mountain roads in the Fuji area. As we shall see, this placed stress on the commons and caused villagers to tighten the rules.

Firewood and charcoal came from two locations. There were patches of forest that villagers could enter at any time as long as they obeyed rules about taking fallen wood first, and cutting only certain kinds of trees—and then only those that were smaller than a certain diameter and only with cutting tools of limited strength. In addition, all three villages conducted a joint annual tree cutting from which each household in each village got an equal-sized stack of wood.

Different villages arrived at different arrangements for guaranteeing an adequate supply of the products from the commons. For items that were needed regularly and that the commons yielded in abundance, a village might allow co-owners free and open entry as long as they abided by certain rules to make sure that a self-sustaining population of mature plants or animals was left behind. To enter the commons, one might need to go to village authorities to obtain an entry permit, carved on a little wooden ticket and marked "entrance permit for one person." The rules would probably restrict the villagers' choice of cutting tools or the size of the sack or container used to collect plants. Everyone would be expected to abide by the village headman's instructions about leaving so much height on a cut plant so that it could regenerate, or taking only a certain portion of a cluster of similar plants to make sure the parent plant could propagate itself, or collecting a certain species only after flowering and fruiting, and so on.

Villagers usually set aside closed reserves for items that had to be left undisturbed until maturity and harvested all at once at just the right time, or that the commons supplied only in adequate, not abundant, amounts. The village headman would be responsible for determining when the time had come to harvest thatch or winter fodder or other products, and would schedule the event, known as *yama no kuchi ake* (literally "mountain mouth-opening"). The rules for mountain-opening day varied with the village and even the product being collected. If the reserve had been closed merely to assure that the plants were allowed to mature but there was more than enough to go round, opening day might simply mark the annual transition from a closed mountain to an open one, allowing individuals and households to enter at will and collect as much as they wanted. If, on the other hand, there was a limited supply of the item, the reserve might be declared open for a brief period of two or three days and households allowed to send in only one able-bodied adult to collect only what could be cut in that time. If the item were in limited supply and had to be collected all at once in a massive effort to prevent spoilage, then the villagers would all enter the reserve together, work until the job was done, and divide the proceeds.

Even among the three villages in this study, there was great variation in the rules applied on mountain-opening days for harvesting different products from closed reserves. In Hirano, for instance, every household had to send one able-bodied adult (two after 1910) and a maximum of one horse to carry what was cut on the day scheduled for opening the closed thatch reserve. Hirano was divided into five *kumi*, each of which was assigned to a particular zone within the thatch reserve.[19] To preserve equality, the *kumi* changed zones according to a fixed rotational sequence each year. Household representatives from each *kumi* gathered in their *kumi* zone in the morning, with the *kumi* chiefs standing guard to make sure no one started cutting prematurely. At the sound of the great temple bell, everyone started cutting. One could cut only in the zone assigned to one's *kumi*, but could keep whatever one cut. After two days, the mountain would be closed again and each household would be required to donate a small fixed quantity of its thatch to the common village reserve used in emergencies. The punishment for entering the thatch reserve before opening day was loss of the right to cut thatch or to receive a share from the *kumi* of the village for that year. These rules appeared to be a judicious combination that rewarded strength and hard work. But they also severely limited the circumstances in which cutting was allowed, and so protected the total supply and prevented any extreme inequality among households in a given year or among *kumi* over time.

The same village used different rules for collective harvesting of winter fodder for the animals from another closed mountain set aside for that type of grass. As with thatch, each *kumi* in Hirano was assigned a zone according to an annual rotation scheme, and each household had to send one, but only one, adult. On the appointed day, each representative reported to the appropriate *kumi* zone in the winter fodder commons and waited for the temple bell as the signal to begin cutting. This grass, however, was cut with large sickles, and since it would be dangerous to have people distributed unevenly around their *kumi* zone swinging sickles in all directions, the individuals in each *kumi* lined up together at one end of their zone and advanced to the other end, whacking in step with each other like a great agricultural drill team. Two or three days later two representatives from each household entered the fodder commons to tie the dried grass into equal bundles. The haul for each *kumi* was grouped together and then divided evenly into one cluster per household. Each household was then assigned its cluster by lottery. This extremely scrupulous division into equal lots per household was done not merely to prevent competitive cutting or to assure an equal amount per household: bundles of grass varied enormously in quality, so they were assigned randomly to eliminate the bad feelings that would result otherwise in households that discovered their bundles to be of poor quality. Random assignment of bundles to households also ensured that household representatives, unsure which bundles would become their own, tried to assemble bundles of equal size and quality.

In Nagaike, the rules for cutting and division of thatch and winter fodder from closed reserves were at one period the reverse of those in Hirano. In Nagaike, households kept for themselves the supply of winter fodder that they managed to cut on mountain-opening day to feed their horses, but thatch was divided equally among the households after cutting. The equal division of thatch may have originated in the fairly egalitarian distribution of income among Nagaike households, meaning that households had dwellings of similar size, and therefore similar needs for thatch. Moreover, because all of the thatch for roofing jobs came from the village reserve, there was little value in amassing a private supply. Nagaike had a highly routinized arrangement for collecting a common reserve of thatch to provide a new roof for an outbuilding or barn for two households per year, and a complete reroofing job for all buildings for two more households per year. By the time the communal system had provided a new roof to all of Nagaike's thirty-eight households, it was time to start all over again. In 1923 the growing population of horses in Nagaike was beginning to create a great deal of competitive pressure for winter fodder on opening day, so Nagaike switched from the "keep-what-you-cut" system to equal division by *kumi* and by household, much like the practice in Hirano. (In fact, there is reason to believe that Hirano, like Nagaike, had originally used the "keep-what-you-cut" system for fodder, and that competitive cutting as well as fear of swinging sickles had produced the change to equal division by *kumi* and household.)

From this brief sketch of the rules for closed reserves in Hirano and Nagaike, one might conclude that the poorer the village or the more dependent on its commons, the greater the likelihood that it would set aside closed reserves and develop stricter rules. However, a review of Yamanaka's practice toward the commons indicates that this was *not* the case.

Yamanaka was the poorest of the three villages, the least endowed with cultivated fields, and the most dependent on day labor, packhorses, and carriage trade to supplement subsistence agriculture. Its common lands were scruffy and dismal compared to those of Hirano and Nagaike. Nonetheless, Yamanaka's own commons combined with the huge Kitafuji slope that it shared with eleven villages made up in quantity for what it lacked in quality. Yamanaka was located immediately adjacent to the Kitafuji slope and could conveniently use it, whereas the other villages that shared in it were located far away and could not easily take advantage of their access rights. Then in 1939 the Japanese government expropriated the Kitafuji slope, and even though the government was supposed to honor the villages' rights of access, the routine conduct of military exercises on the slope damaged the ecosystem and further reduced the productive potential of the Kitafuji commons. Yamanaka therefore grew more heavily dependent on another piece of common land that it held in its own right, and was forced to set aside a portion of that as a closed reserve for horse fodder. Even then, Yamanaka did not need to create a closed reserve for thatch. The supply of thatch on Kitafuji was sufficient, though so sparsely distributed that the same quantity required ten to fifteen times longer to collect than in Hirano.

A more appropriate conclusion, then, would be that as demand for the products of the commons—whether that demand reflected wealth or poverty—approached the maximum sustainable yield, portions of the commons would be set aside as reserves and the rules would be progressively tightened.

Thus far we have examined the benefits that villagers drew from the commons. Equally important, however, is the contribution of labor to the maintenance of the commons. In the classic type of commons villagers did not till the soil or sow seeds, but they often engaged in a systematic program of harvesting and weeding in order to increase the natural production of the plants they wanted.

One very dramatic technique of this sort was the annual spring burning of the grasslands, or *noyaki*; throughout Japan many of the common meadowlands were burned completely clear once a year. The burning undoubtedly altered the ecosystem drastically, but it absorbed the custom, and common lands nevertheless survived. Essentially, the burning converted the previous season's leftover dried grass and this season's early but undesirable grasses and "bad" insects into a layer of ash (rich, desirable fertilizer to nourish the desirable vegetation) without the effort of handweeding or manual redistribution of fertilizer. Somehow the game population was able to escape from the fast-moving flames, to return later after delicious new shoots of grass had appeared.

There were written rules about the obligation of each household to contribute a share to the collective work of maintaining the commons—to conduct the annual burning, to report to harvest on mountain-opening days, or to do a specific cutting of timber or thatch. Accounts were kept about who contributed what to make sure that no household evaded its responsibilities unnoticed. Only illness, family tragedy, or the non-existence of able-bodied adults whose labor could be spared from routine chores were recognized as excuses for getting out of collective labor. (Temporary absences from the village were not acceptable; all healthy adults had to make themselves available.) In such cases others in the unrepresented family's *kumi* might cut a share of thatch or fodder for the missing family and the accounts would be evened out later. But if no acceptable excuse could be found, punishment was in order.

Patterns of Interaction on the Commons

As we have just seen, villages had elaborate rules to govern both open and closed commons. Abuses were possible: taking too much or taking unallowed items from an open commons, entering a closed commons before mountain-opening day, violating the strict rules for mountain-opening days, and failing to contribute labor. What actually happened? What were the real behavioral responses to rules and circumstance? What do we learn from these responses about both individual and collective agendas for using and abusing the commons?

Enforcement of Rules

One mechanism for enforcement of the rules about the commons, as well as the rules about everything else, was the general atmosphere of mutual dependence and collective responsibility in the village. In economic terms, this arrangement served to internalize within the household most of the costs that a household might otherwise have been able to impose on others. To the extent that the formal system of collective responsibility (the five-man groups already referred to) was effective in a village, all potential violators of rules knew that those near them had strong incentives to advocate compliance as a general rule—or, when persuasion failed, to snitch on one's colleagues rather than be implicated with them. For most people most of the time, obedience to the rules was probably the path of least resistance.

But villages did not rely entirely on formal collective responsibility, or on social pressure from peers, or even on the individual's sense of identification with the welfare of the community to protect the precious commons. Villagers were not so naive as to imagine that there would never be temptations to violate the commons. Accordingly, they created groups of detectives to patrol them. This task might be assigned to the young men's association or to the village fire brigade, which would in turn delegate the job to its members on the basis of annual rotation. The detectives would patrol the commons on horseback every day looking for intruders and in effect enforcing the exclusionary rules.

In Hirano the detectives had to come from families that could spare a
young man's labor and a horse for an entire year. The job was considered
one of the most prestigious and responsible available to a young man. In
Nagaike these positions changed hands more frequently but all eligible
males had to take a turn, so that no family was without its full labor
supply for very long. Nagaike, the smallest, most egalitarian of the three
villages, which also happened to depend completely on the commons for
the thatch and animal fodder that private holdings in the village simply
did not produce, appears to have had virtually no violations of the
commons by Nagaike residents. The detectives there had to deal only
with intruders from villages on the other side of the mountain.

Interestingly, Yamanaka had no system of detectives to patrol its
commons, although it did observe the principle of "citizen's arrest"—
anyone, not merely a designated detective, could report violations.
Yamanaka had no closed reserve until 1939 and fewer rules to enforce on
the open commons. It may also have been too poor to spare the labor of
those who might serve as detectives. In any case, the commons to which
Yamanaka had exclusive access rights (not the Kitafuji slope it shared with
other villages) had been formally registered as property of a Shinto shrine
during the Meiji land reform—one of the few available ruses by which a
village could preserve common land—and the elders among the pa-
rishioners performed functions akin to patrolling.

Violating the rules devised to protect the commons was one of the
most terrible offenses that a villager could commit against his peers, and
the penalties were very serious. Most villages had written codes to govern
the commons. These stipulated specific punishments for specific violations, with a built-in scheme of escalating penalties for noncooperation.
Most violations were handled quietly and simply by the detectives, who
would set the penalty. It was considered perfectly appropriate for the
detectives to demand cash and sake (rice wine) from violators and to use
these as their own entertainment cache. Anyone found violating the rules
of an open commons or illegally entering a closed commons was instantly
deprived of his equipment, his horse, and whatever he had cut. To retrieve
his equipment and horse he would have to pay a fine—usually a bottle or
two of sake—and apologize to the detectives who apprehended him. The
contraband harvest was of course retained by the village. If the offense
were relatively large or the apology unsatisfactory, the head of the culprit's
household, his *kumi*, or his temple priest would have to make the apology
on his behalf and offer a larger fine in his stead. To prevent the stain of
collective responsibility and humiliation from spreading to them, the
culprit's family or *kumi* members would exert powerful pressure on him to
make adequate amends. If the intruder were a resident of another village,
the leaders of his village would have to travel to the village whose

commons had been violated and apologize. Very rarely did a village have to go beyond these first three stages of punishment to obtain satisfaction.

When necessary, though, the village could then threaten to employ its more powerful sanctions: ostracism in increasingly severe stages, followed by banishment. The Japanese term for ostracism, *murahachibu*, signifies that the village cuts off all contact with the offender except for assistance at funerals and fire fighting. In fact, it was usually employed in gradual stages, starting with social contact and only escalating to economic relations if the offender did not express remorse and modify his behavior. To ensure that others would remember to shun and criticize him, the offender might be required to wear unmatched socks or a brightly colored waistband, or be made to sit at village gatherings in a special section reserved for the antisocial (Minzokugaku Kenkyūjo 1951, 472). Ostracism was a horrible punishment for Japanese villagers, not only because it cut them off from society and made daily life unpleasant, but because it actually deprived them of tangible services essential to daily living: village water supplies, irrigation for rice paddies, and, of course, access to the commons. A villager of ordinary means would never jeopardize the survival of his household and his family's reputation for many generations when a simple apology could extinguish the controversy, and when strict obedience to the rules could guarantee that such possibilities would not arise in the first place. Only families of great wealth and pride could afford to risk ostracism, often gambling that their social status would win them enough allies to defeat the established village leadership in a political contest or to secede from the village and form a new one.

Compliance and Violations

It is very difficult to ascertain how well the rules were obeyed, how well the threatened penalties discouraged violations, and how honestly the rules were enforced—especially when, the offender being a resident of the village, the controversy did not go to the local magistrate's office to become a matter of public record. It is not yet possible to arrive at reliable generalizations about Tokugawa villages on the basis of the written record. Moreover, this is a matter about which loyal villagers then and now would be understandably defensive and reticent, and one is forced to be skeptical when the available evidence suggests that all worked well. At the risk of exaggerating dysfunction in the enforcement system, then, I will take special note below of examples of violations of the commons in these three villages that have been so carefully studied.[20]

It would appear that villagers' reluctance to incur the disfavor of their peers was usually enough to keep violations of the commons at a manageable level. Offenses by outsiders were far more numerous than offenses by village residents, and all offenses taken together were usually minor in degree and did not threaten the ecological health of the commons. Moreover, the villagers—certainly village elders and *kumi* chiefs, and probably heads of all households—thoroughly understood the direct relationship between the rules and the preservation of the commons. Every time I asked about the reason for a particular rule, my informants explained the rule in terms of environmental protection and fair treatment of all the villagers. There was always a sophisticated and sensible explanation, never "Well, we've always done it that way." Obedience to the rules was almost certainly based on an appreciation of the value of the rules, and not merely on compliance to avoid penalties.

In these three villages taken together, there has been only one case in which violation against the commons led eventually to ostracism. The original violation was a minor one: entering an open commons to cut fresh grass on an official work holiday (essentially a compulsory vacation to give everyone a rest but to prevent any single family from gaining an advantage over others by working). This would have had no impact on the health of the commons and could have been taken care of quickly with an apology. The violator, however, indignantly argued that, in effect, the rules did not apply to him because he was a village elder and former headman. This claim, of course was a more serious threat to the rule of law in the village than the act itself. The man refused to apologize and rejected his relatives' efforts at mediation. The controversy and punishments escalated to the point where he had to do all of his trading and marketing in distant towns. Finally the village deprived him even of fire-fighting services and assistance at funerals.[21]

Certain violations, however, were almost routine. For instance, in the weeks and days preceding mountain-opening days, impatient households would occasionally enter closed reserves prematurely. The detectives ordinarily collected one bottle of sake per minor violation, but during this "peak season" prior to opening day the young men collected more liquor than even they could drink, and they usually had to give it away.

Similarly, the detectives were young men with predictable weaknesses, and some households intentionally sent their attractive young daughters into the commons to collect grass in violation of the rules of the commons. The detectives might then be disposed to look the other way, or even to ignore repeated offenses in exchange for sexual favors. Except for this single example, there is no evidence of detectives exploiting their position by coopting bits of the commons and concealing their own violations, or by terrorizing suspected offenders against the commons, or even by concealing others' violations in exchange for favors. Certainly, there was an intrinsic pride in the importance of doing one's duty by the commons and in preserving the village's well-being. However, these incentives were augmented by the system of collective responsibility, and the detectives patrolled in teams. Any detective who felt tempted to violate the rules had to answer to his colleagues and risk the possibility that they would rather turn him in than be caught later as coconspirators in an offense. Apparently, not only violations of the rules but abuse of power by the "police" appointed to search out those violations was expected, and correctives were built into the system.[22]

Violations of rules to protect the commons would also increase noticeably in response to certain special circumstances. First, there might be a real challenge to the wisdom of the village chief in, say, setting mountain-opening day too late. In this instance, an entire faction of disgruntled villagers might violate the rules together in an act of civil disobedience; this would clearly be a protest against an error in the leadership rather than any disrespect for the rules to protect the commons. One former detective in Hirano, now a respected village elder, described how he had been patrolling a closed commons one day and came upon not one or two intruders but thirty, including heads of some leading households. It was not yet mountain-opening day, but they had entered the commons en masse to cut a particular type of pole used for building trellises to support garden vegetables raised on private plots. If they could not cut the poles soon enough, they risked losing their entire vegetable crop, and they believed that the village headman had erred in setting opening day later than these crops required. Outclassed in both numbers and status, the detectives were unable to resolve this episode quietly and had to go through channels "all the way to the top." The thirty offenders were ordered to make a donation to the village school.

Second, sudden changes in the economy or in the supply of certain products that increased dependence on the commons as a source of some particular item would increase violations. This seems to have been the case in Yamanaka, which experienced a fairly severe breakdown of the rules during the depression of the 1930s. Almost all the villagers knew that almost all the villagers were breaking the rules: sneaking around the commons at night, cutting trees that were larger than the allowed size, even using wood-cutting tools that were not permitted. This is precisely the behavior that could get a tragedy of the commons started, but that did not happen in Yamanaka.

Instead of regarding the general breakdown of the rules as an opportunity to become full-time free riders and cast caution to the winds, the violators themselves tried to exercise self-discipline out of deference to the preservation of the commons, and stole from the commons only out of desperation. Inspectors or other witnesses who saw violations maintained silence out of sympathy for the violators' desperation and out of confidence that the problem was temporary and could not really hurt the commons. Yamanaka was also fortunate to have ready access to the Kitafuji slope, so that when its own commons was endangered the villagers could switch to its more widely shared commons instead. Finally, I strongly suspect that the rules villages adopted for the commons were very conservative and left wide margins for error, so that the violations that did occur did not often pose a serious threat to the commons. Interestingly, villagers did not question the rules themselves or become more casual about obeying them when they observed that these violations did not damage the commons. The system of rules and values they embodied seems to have been perceived as entirely legitimate and not subject to being challenged as unnecessarily cautious.

However, when villagers felt that the rules were too *lax*, or when they began to fear the environmental consequences of too many violations, they modified their management techniques in the direction of still greater caution in order to save the commons. For instance, when Yamanaka found in 1939 that the Kitafuji slope was no longer very productive, it converted its own commons—from which it had silently conspired to steal earlier that decade—into a closed reserve in order to make enforcement of the rules and identification of violators much easier. Similarly, when Hirano and Nagaike discovered that competitive cutting even on a closed reserve was becoming a problem, they removed the incentives for individuals to race against each other on mountain-opening day by abolishing the keep-what-you-cut system, instituting equal distribution, and assigning the harvest to households by lottery. These measures automatically reduced the frantic pace of cutting and thus the total quantity cut in a season.

Outcomes and Lessons

We have explored the experience of these three villages in governing access to their commons in order to diagnose the factors that help and hinder a community in dealing with common property. I must point out that, in addition to the rules and enforcement schemes, these three villages had other factors—their small size, their very strong community identity, and a sense of mutual interdependence that was reinforced by a formal structure of collective responsibility—that almost certainly enhanced their ability to make *any* regulatory scheme work, even a very badly designed one. Nonetheless, we can extract a few themes and suggestions about the ingredients of successful management of common property, all else being equal, since there was variation among the villages, the types of commons they possessed, their respective risks of producing a tragedy of the commons, and the economic changes they endured over time. Naturally, it is hazardous to generalize from just three villages, as it is to extrapolate from the commons in a closed agrarian society in the historical past to common property problems today. But the tentative conclusions below can serve as hypotheses to be tested and refined in further studies. I will organize these evaluations around four questions suggested by the facts themselves and by Oakerson's analytical framework.

Efficiency of the Use of Common Property

One might handily dismiss the value of the Japanese experience with common property by arguing that the natural environment was never hard-pressed in Tokugawa Japan. In other words, communities never caused tragedy on their commons because they were never very close to any trouble; they would have succeeded at managing the commons no matter what they did because they imposed so little on their common resources. We must remember, however, that in the seventeenth century the Japanese did face the threat of massive deforestation, and there is good reason to believe that within the limits of local preindustrial technology they were actually pressing their natural environment—their agricultural potential—to its limits by the late Tokugawa period. Villagers knew how much forest they had to leave intact to produce the fertilizer they needed for their cultivated plots. It is not clear whether villagers got as much from the commons as the commons could have spared without deterioration, but to extract more from the commons would have required a still greater investment of labor. Villagers resisted shogunal pressures to reclaim more arable land from the forest. Clearly, they viewed the reclamation of additional upland fields (inevitably of poorer quality than what they already had) to be an inefficient use of their labor, especially later in the period when conditions of labor shortage arose.

Villages sensed that they might be pushing the commons too far when they let the rules break down. They did alter the rules to relieve pressure on the commons at various times, a move suggesting that Tokugawa and later peasants were indeed pressing the commons. By extension, it also suggests that managing the commons did require some skill, and that villages did have to be concerned about an efficient use of their commons.

Equity among Co-owners of the Commons

It is quite apparent that Japanese villagers were deeply concerned with some notion of fairness. This can be concluded from the rules, the sanctions for violations of rules, the kinds of disputes over the commons that reached the courts, and the explanations of behavior that are still offered today. Fairness was not synonymous with equality in material possessions; many villages had considerable inequality in holdings of private property and did not seem troubled by this. But there was an overriding sense that access to the commons should be distributed according to some principle of fairness that ignored existing maldistributions in private wealth. Hence the frequent use of random distributions, assignments by lottery, frequent rotations to move the good and the bad around, and scrupulous attention to bookkeeping to keep track of contributions and exchanges and offsetting aid. Such methods provided assurance to each co-owner that the sacrifices and gains of other co-owners would be similar, and offered the additional advantage of removing the competitive impulse (which is very dangerous when it becomes a race to see who can deplete the commons first). Yet laziness was not rewarded, because someone who failed to do his share of the work lost entitlement to a share of the proceeds altogether. Nor did this notion of fairness mean that entitlement was automatic for all comers, the way food stamps or food aid sometimes are for us. A household had to earn its eligibility through some period of established residence in the village, and casual drifters were ignored. The attraction of becoming a casual drifter was thus considerably reduced while everyone's incentive to solve problems rather than run away from them was increased.

Enforceability of the Rules

Violations of the rules and conflicts over use of the commons suggest that any such rules must be designed to have an obvious and direct relationship to the goal of preservation. Co-owners of the commons will not obey regulations that they regard as frivolous or arbitrary. They will obey regulations that are quite clearly based on principles of maximum sustainable yield. They will consent to being deprived of certain products of the commons only if they can be convinced that what they do not extract from the commons is truly needed for its long-term maintenance, and that others will exercise similar self-restraint.

The Japanese experience also demonstrates that no rules are self-enforcing. Japanese villagers had a strong community identity; they were very concerned about social reputation and bonds with the group, and internalized the preservation of the commons as a vital goal. Nevertheless, even these allegedly cooperative and compliant people were vulnerable to the temptation to bend, evade, and violate the rules governing the commons. Thus there had to be a scheme of penalties and these had to be enforced. To make enforcement possible at all, the rules and penalties had to be designed to distinguish handily between good and bad behavior. It was harder to enforce the rules governing open commons without individual inspection of each user's activities. Therefore, as pressure on the commons increased, it became necessary to close it off so that any intruder could be instantly and automatically designated as a violator.

Moreover, villages not only assumed that violations could occur but that even the police or detectives who patrolled the commons would be tempted to steal from it or abuse their privileged position in other ways. Even though traditional Japanese were about as far from being libertarians as anyone might imagine, they too worried about who would watch the watchers. Correctives for this problem were built into the system: the watchers watched each other; collective responsibility applied to the watchers as well as to the watched; and the duty of watching rotated through the body of co-owners, so that everyone got his turn to exercise power, to be suspected of abusing his power, and finally to prove himself innocent by exercising exemplary behavior on duty. All of this also suggests that small intimate communities of co-owners, united not only by their mutual interest in the commons but by other social relationships, were essential. The ever-present anxiety about preservation of the commons and the expectation that violators would harm it seemed in themselves to operate as some sort of deterrent.

Although the system of collective responsibility is not at all attractive to someone who values liberty, we have to admit that it was a very cheap tool for enforcement because it encouraged each village, each *kumi*, and each household to monitor its own recalcitrant members. A somewhat more palatable lesson may be found in the use of a unit other than the individual for calculating contributions to and benefits from the commons. This practice seemed to induce each unit (here, the household) to restrict its own size—and, by extension, to restrain its own demand for products of the commons.

Finally, these villages had an escalating scale of penalties that began with confiscation of the contraband taken from the commons—instantly negating the advantage of violating the rules—and proceeded through gradual stages of exclusion from the commons and eventually from all contact and exchange with other co-owners. This scale of punishments may seem harsh but in fact it operated rather gently, most violators confessing and apologizing quickly rather than having to suffer more severe consequences. Because it was graduated to fit the offense, the scale may have been very important in controlling repeat offenders: the desperate knew that they might be forgiven that once, but the malicious knew that they would suffer severely.

Legitimacy of the Rules

In conclusion, it is also important to point out that the villagers themselves invented the regulations, enforced them, and meted out punishments. It is not necessary, then, for regulation of the commons to be imposed coercively or from the outside. This, along with the fact that villagers could change their own rules through a process of consultation and consensus that was democratic in form if not always in fact, almost certainly increased the legitimacy of the regulations. Although the To-kugawa social order was very oppressive toward *individuals* it classified as "deviant," the village itself was largely self-regulating in this regard, and did not require intervention by an autocratic state to protect the commons.

The implications for democratic processes and individual liberties in societies that face tragedies of the commons are mixed. The apparently important role of a system of collective responsibility that victimizes innocent members of groups containing free riders, and the ability of the village to impose ostracism to the point where life is threatened, are ominous. The importance of uniform and impartial applications of law, the restraint exercised before harsh penalties are employed, and the room for democratic rule making and rule amending are more assuring.

NOTES

I would like to thank David Feeny, Bonnie McCay, Pauline Peters, and Kristina Kade Troost, as well as two anonymous reviewers, for very helpful comments. I am also grateful to the Joint Committee on Japanese Studies of the Social Science Research Council and the American Council of Learned Societies, as well as the Duke University Research Council, for the support that allowed me to gather material for this study.

1. For a summary of the literature on free-rider and public-goods problems, see McMillan 1979. Other major works are G. Hardin 1968; R. Hardin 1982; Olson 1965; Brubaker 1975; Buchanan 1968a, 1968b; Coase 1974; Demsetz 1964; Frohlich et al. 1975; Furubotn and Pejovich 1972; Groves and Ledyard 1977; Sweeney 1973, 1974; Mishan 1971; and Stigler 1974. Buchanan (1975) reaches the unhappy conclusion that exclusion must be used.

2. On the nationalization and decentralization of landholding, see the two studies by Asakawa (1914, 1929a) that are reprinted in Asakawa 1965; and Asakawa

1918; Arnesen 1979; Duus 1969; Hall 1966, 99–295; Hall 1968, 1981; Ishii 1980; Mass 1974; Miyagawa and Kiley 1974; Sato 1974; Smith 1968a, 1968b; Nagahara and Yamamura 1974, 1981; Sansom 1958, 339–89; Totman 1979; Wakita 1982; Wintersteen 1974; and Yamamura 1990.

3. On the attrition of common lands since the Meiji period, see Furushima et al. 1966; Hōjō 1979b; Kainō 1958, 1964; Kawashima et al. 1959–1961; Watanabe 1972.

4. A crucial distinction between owning a share of the commons and owning any other form of property jointly with others is that traditional co-ownership rights to the commons are conferred only on households of long standing in the village, and they cannot be sold to anyone else. Each household possesses one share in the commons and no more; households or persons not invited into the group of co-owners (*iriai shūdan*) are simply not entitled to a share. (For a brief explanation of the current legal status of ownership of common access rights, see Watanabe and Nakao 1975, 67–97.)

5. The most important general work on the history of the evolution of common access rights is Furushima 1955. The major works on the history of the common lands in the particular area studied here—Kitafuji—are Hōjō and Fukushima 1964; Hōjō 1977, 191–433; Hōjō 1978, 1979a; Kamimura 1979; Ōshima 1978; and Watanabe and Hōjō 1975.

6. These three communities were three independent villages or *mura* during the Tokugawa period. I will continue to use the term "village" to refer to the classical village of that period. Since 1868 the Japanese government has encouraged administrative amalgamation of villages. The three villages of Yamanaka, Hirano, and Nagaike have in fact been amalgamated once, so that together they now compose one modern village, called Yamanaka-mura. But they have rejected further amalgamation with additional communities in the area.

7. The following descriptions draw principally on the work of Hōjō Hiroshi, Kamimura Masana, and the interviews that they arranged for me.

8. This structure is sometimes called "centralized feudalism," a bewildering and misleading label for a political system that was at once federalist, authoritarian, highly bureaucratic, and perhaps even totalitarian in the extent to which the state controlled information and monitored individual lives. On the Tokugawa political order, see Duus 1969, Hall and Jansen 1968, Ishii 1980, and Totman 1967. Berry (1982) suggests that Toyotomi Hideyoshi began much of what Tokugawa Ieyasu has been given credit for, and Brown (n.d.) suggests that domain lords began much of what Hideyoshi has been given credit for.

9. For the consequences of such a separation of land rights from ownership in Niger, see Chapter 6 of this book.

10. On the early development of Japanese law, see Asakawa 1929b, Bock 1970, Mass 1979, Grossberg and Kanamoto 1981, and Wigmore 1969.

11. *Wariyama* can mean the parceling of commons into individual private property, but it can also refer to temporary division and allocation of parcels that revert to the community for subsequent rotations.

12. Fenoaltea (1988) argues similarly that collective ownership and use of open fields in England was efficient until commercialization began to give co-owners different and conflicting opinions about the best uses of the commons.

At that point the transaction costs of cooperative decision making outweighed the efficiencies of cooperative production.

13. An interesting exception to this trend is available in Henderson (1975, 66–67), in which two villages that could not agree on the precise location of a boundary between them decided instead to create a joint commons for grass in the area in dispute.

14. On the traditional village, see Asakawa 1909–11; Befu 1968; Smith 1959, 1968a; Nagahara and Yamamura 1974; and Chambliss 1965. For twentieth-century versions of these traditional forms of organization and cooperation, see Embree 1939, Fukutake 1967, Shimpo 1976, and Marshall 1984.

15. Only six of the ten richest families in Chiaraijima had rights to common land (Chambliss 1965, 44–45).

16. In one case, a document creating a commons to be shared between two villages was signed by representatives of tenant families as well as by landowning households (Henderson 1975, 66–67).

17. Tsurumi (1975) summarizes these views of the traditional village. See also Irokawa 1973a; Irokawa 1973b, 508–64; and Gluck 1978.

18. On population and economic growth in Tokugawa Japan, see Hanley and Yamamura 1977; Smith 1977; Kalland and Pedersen 1984; and Kelley and Williamson 1971, 1974.

19. *Kumi* are sometimes considered survivals of the Tokugawa five-man groups. See Embree 1939, 112–57; and Fukutake 1967, 96–104.

20. I have drawn these examples from Kamimura Masana's research and from several interviews with former commons detectives who were remarkably forthcoming about matters that would not ordinarily be revealed to outsiders. I am very grateful to Professor Hōjō Hiroshi for giving me the introductions that allowed these candid discussions to take place.

21. When the ostracized man's children went out to play, other children threw stones at them. When the grandfather of the household drowned in Lake Yamanaka, no one would come to help recover the body. At the funeral, rather than helping to carry the coffin, the village fire brigade actually tried to block the path to the cemetery until prefectural police arrived. Then finally the man's house burned down—it is said that village officials actually started the fire intentionally—and no one came to his assistance. When other villages felt sympathy for the man's perfectly innocent family, village officials pointed out that having any contact with a family that was the target of ostracism would destroy the effectiveness of the sanction and make the contactor subject to ostracism too. The fear of spreading ostracism was so powerful that even though prefectural police arrested some of the onlookers at the fire for negligence (standing idly by was actually a violation of fire laws), no one offered to help extinguish the fire. This episode of ostracism lasted five to six years, and it took four generations for the family to shake off the taint of having been ostracized. (See Kamimura 1979, 219–22).

22. During a drought in the village of Shiwa, farmers at the downstream end of the irrigation system, including the water guards on patrol, were sorely tempted to alter the dikes so as to receive more than their allocated share of water. During such times, the collective response was for all adult males to patrol the dikes all night long in mutual surveillance. (See Shimpo 1976, 9–17.)

REFERENCES

Japanese names place the patronymic first. Hence, for works published in Japanese, no comma is necessary between the patronymic and the given name of the first author listed. For these works, I have also followed the Japanese convention in names of coauthors: thus Watanabe Yozo and Hōjō Hiroshi are cited in the text as "Watanabe and Hōjō." In English-language works, however, the Western convention is followed, as can be seen from the comma after the first author's patronymic.

Arnesen, Peter Judd. 1979. *The Medieval Japanese Daimyo: The Ōuchi Family's Rule of Suo and Nagato.* New Haven, Conn.: Yale University Press.

Asakawa, Kan'ichi. 1909–1911. "Notes on Village Government in Japan after 1600." Parts 1–2, *Journal of the American Oriental Society* 30:259–300; 31:151–216.

————. 1914. "The Origin of Feudal Land Tenure in Japan." *American Historical Review* 21 (1):1–23.

————. 1918. "Some Aspects of Japanese Feudal Institutions." *Transactions of the Asiatic Society of Japan* 46 (1):77–102.

————. 1929a. "The Early *Shō* and the Early Manor: A Comparative Study." *Journal of Economic and Business History* 50 (2):177–207.

————. 1929b. *The Documents of Iriki, Illustrative of the Development of the Feudal Institutions of Japan.* New Haven, Conn.: Yale University Press.

————. 1965. *Land and Society in Medieval Japan.* Tokyo: Japan Society for the Promotion of Science.

Befu, Harumi. 1968. "Village Autonomy and Articulation with the State." In *Studies in the Institutional History of Early Modern Japan*, ed. John Whitney Hall and Marius B. Jansen, 301–14. Princeton, N.J.: Princeton University Press.

Berry, Mary Elizabeth. 1982. *Hideyoshi.* Cambridge, Mass.: Harvard University Press.

Bock, Felicia Gressitt, trans. 1970. *Engishiki: Procedures of the Engi Era.* Tokyo: Sophia University Press.

Bolitho, Harold. 1974. *Treasures among Men: The Fudai Daimyo in Tokugawa Japan.* New Haven, Conn.: Yale University Press.

Brown, Philip C. n.d. *Domain Formation in Early Modern Japan.* Stanford, Calif.: Stanford University Press. In press.

Brubaker, Earl. 1975. "Free Ride, Free Revelation, or Golden Rule?" *Journal of Law and Economics* 18 (1):147–61

Buchanan, James M. 1968a. "Congestion on the Common: A Case for Government Intervention." *Il Politico: Rivista Italiana di Scienze Politiche* 33 (4): 776–78

————. 1968b. *The Demand and Supply of Public Goods.* Chicago: Rand-McNally.

————. 1975. *The Limits of Liberty: Between Anarchy and Leviathan.* Chicago: University of Chicago Press.

Chambliss, William James. 1965. *Chiaraijma Village: Land Tenure, Taxation, and Local Trade 1818–1884.* Tucson: University of Arizona Press.

Chiba Tokuji. 1956. *Hageyama no kenkyū* (Research on bald mountains). Tokyo: Nōrin kyōkai.

————. 1970. *Hageyama no bunka* (The culture of bald mountains). Tokyo: Gakuseisha.

Coase, R. H. 1974. "The Lighthouse in Economics." *Journal of Law and Economics* 17 (2):357–76.

Demsetz, Harold. 1964. "Toward a Theory of Property Rights." *American Economic Review* 54 (3):347–59.

Dore, Ronald P. 1959. *Land Reform in Japan*. London: Oxford University Press.

Duus, Peter. 1969. *Feudalism in Japan*. New York: Knopf.

Elison, George, and Bardwell L. Smith, eds. 1981. *Warlords, Artists, and Commoners: Japan in the Sixteenth Century*. Honolulu: University Press of Hawaii.

Embree, John F. 1939. *Suye Mura: A Japanese Village*. Chicago: University of Chicago Press.

Fenoaltea, Stefano. 1988. "Transaction Costs, Whig History, and the Common Fields." *Politics and Society* 16 (2-3):171–240.

Frohlich, Norman, Thomas Hunt, Joe Oppenheimer, and R. Harrison Wagner. 1975. "Individual Contributions for Collective Goods: Alternative Models." *Journal of Conflict Resolution* 19 (2):310–29.

Fukutake Tadashi. 1967. *Japanese Rural Society*. Ithaca, N.Y.: Cornell University Press.

Furubotn, Eirik G., and Svetozar Pejovich. 1972. "Property Rights and Economic Theory: A Survey of Recent Literature." *Journal of Economic Literature* 10 (4):1137–62.

Furushima Toshio. 1955. *Kinsei iriai seido ron* (On the common access system of the early modern period). Tokyo: Nihon hyōron shin shuppan.

Furushima Toshio, Ushiomi Toshitaka, and Watanabe Yōzō. 1966. *Rin'ya iriaiken no honshitsu to yōsō* (The substance and appearance of forest common access rights). Tokyo: Tokyo University Press.

Gluck, Carol. 1978. "The People in History: Recent Trends in Japanese Historiography." *Journal of Asian Studies* 38 (1):25–50.

Grossberg, Kenneth, and Nobuhisa Kanamoto, trans. 1981. *Laws of the Muramachi Bakufu*. Tokyo: Sophia University Press.

Groves, Theodore, and John Ledyard. 1977. "Optimal Allocation of Public Goods: A Solution of the 'Free Rider' Problem." *Econometrica* 45 (4):783–809.

Hall, John Whitney. 1966. *Government and Local Power in Japan, 500–1700: A Study Based on Bizen Province*. Princeton, N.J.: Princeton University Press.

————. 1968. "Foundations of the Modern Japanese Daimyo." In *Studies in the Institutional History of Early Modern Japan*, ed. John Whitney Hall and Marius B. Jansen, 65–78. Princeton, N.J.: Princeton University Press.

————. 1981. "Japan's Sixteenth-Century Revolution." In *Warlords, Artists, and Commoners: Japan in the Sixteenth Century*, ed. George Elison and Bardwell L. Smith, 7–22. Honolulu: University Press of Hawaii.

————. 1983. "Terms and Concepts in Japanese Medieval History: An Inquiry into the Problems of Translation." *Journal of Japanese Studies* 9 (1):1–32.

Hall, John Whitney, and Marius B. Jansen, eds. 1968. *Studies in the Institutional History of Early Modern Japan*. Princeton, N.J.: Princeton University Press.

Hall, John Whitney, Nagahara Keiji, and Kozo Yamamura, eds. 1981. *Japan before Tokugawa: Political Consolidation and Economic Growth, 1500 to 1650.* Princeton, N.J.: Princeton University Press.

Hall, John Whitney, and Jeffrey P. Mass, eds. 1974. *Medieval Japan: Essays in Institutional History.* New Haven, Conn.: Yale University Press.

Hanley, Susan B., and Kozo Yamamura. 1977. *Economic and Demographic Change in Preindustrial Japan, 1600–1868.* Princeton, N.J.: Princeton University Press.

Harada Toshimaru. 1969. *Kinsei iriai seido keitai katei no kenkyū: yamawari seido no hassei to sono henshitsu* (A study of the process of the dissolution of the early modern common-access system: Genesis and change in the "mountain-division system"). Tokyo: Hanawa shobō.

Hardin, Garrett. 1968. "The Tragedy of the Commons." *Science* 162: 1243–48.

Hardin, Russell. 1982. *Collective Action.* Baltimore: Johns Hopkins University Press for Resources for the Future.

Henderson, Dan Fenno. 1965. *Conciliation and Japanese Law: Tokugawa and Modern.* Vol. 1. Seattle: University of Washington Press.

———. 1975. *Village "Contracts" in Tokugawa Japan: Fifty Specimens with English Translations and Comments.* Seattle: University of Washington Press.

Hōjō Hiroshi. 1977. *Rin'ya iriai no shiteki kenkyū (jō)* (Historical research on common access to forests (volume 1). Tokyo: Ochanomizu shobō.

———. 1978. *Mura to iriai no hyakunen shi: Yamanashi ken sonmin no iriai tōsōshi* (A hundred years' history of a village and its common access: The history of the common-access struggle of the villagers of Yamanashi Prefecture). Tokyo: Ochanomizu shobō.

———. 1979a. *Kinsei ni okeru iriai no shokeitai* (The various forms of common access in the early modern period). Tokyo: Ochanomizu shobō.

———. 1979b. *Rin'ya hōsei no tenkai to sonraku kyōdōtai* (The development of forestry law and village community). Tokyo: Ochanomizu shobō.

Hōjō Hiroshi and Fukushima Masao. 1964. *Meiji 26 nen zenkoku sanrin gen'ya iriai kankō shirō shū: Yamanashi ken* (Collected documents from the Meiji 26 National Survey of Customary Common Access to Virgin Mountain Forests: Yamanashi Prefecture). Tokyo: Rin'yachō.

Irokawa Daikichi. 1973a. "Japan's Grass-Roots Tradition: Current Issues in the Mirror of History." *Japan Quarterly* 21 (1):78–86.

———. 1973b. *Shinpen Meiji seishin shi* (A new spiritual history of the Meiji period). Tokyo: Chūō kōronsha).

Ishii, Ryosuke. 1980. *A History of Political Institutions in Japan.* Tokyo: University of Tokyo Press.

Kainō Michitaka. 1958. *Iriai no kenkyū (A study of common access)* Tokyo: Ichirūsha.

———. 1964. *Kotsunagi jiken: sandai no wataru iriaiken funsō* (The Kotsunagi Incident: A struggle over common access spanning three generations). Tokyo: Iwanami shoten.

Kalland, Arne, and Jon Pedersen. 1984. "Famine and Population in Fukuoka Domain during the Tokugawa Period." *Journal of Japanese Studies* 10:31–72.

Kamimura Masana. 1979. *Sonraku seikatsu no shūzoku, kanshū no shakai kōzō* (The social structure of the folkways and customs of village life). Tokyo: Ochanomizu shobō.

Kawashima Takeyoshi. 1979. "Iriai ken kenkyū no genjō to mondaiten" (The current state and problems in research on common-access rights). *Jūrisuto* 682:70–76; 683:120–27.

Kawashima Takeyoshi, Ushiomi Toshitaka, and Watanabe Yōzō. 1959-1961. *Iriaiken no kaitai* (The dismemberment of common-access rights). 2 vols. Tokyo: Iwanami shoten.

Kelley, Allen C., and Jeffrey G. Williamson. 1971. "Writing History Backwards: Meiji Japan Revisited." *Journal of Economic History* 31 (4):729–76.

———. 1974. *Lessons from Japanese Development: An Analytical Economic History.* Chicago: University of Chicago Press.

Marshall, Robert C. 1984. "Collective Decision Making in Rural Japan" University of Michigan Center for Japanese Studies, Papers in Japanese Studies, no. 11. Ann Arbor, Mich.: University of Michigan Press.

Mass, Jeffrey P. 1974. "*Jitō* Land Possession in the Thirteenth Century: The Case of *Shitaji chūbun.*" In *Medieval Japan: Essays in Institutional History,* ed. John Whitney Hall and Jeffrey P. Mass, 157–83. New Haven, Conn.: Yale University Press.

———. 1979. *The Development of Kamakura Rule, 1180–1250: A History with Documents.* Stanford, Calif.: Stanford University Press.

McKean, Margaret A. 1982. "The Japanese Experience with Scarcity: Management of Traditional Common Lands." *Environmental Review* 6 (2):63–88.

———. 1988. "Collective Action and the Environment in Tokugawa Japan: Success and Failure in Management of the Commons." Paper presented to the Annual Meeting of the Association of Asian Studies, San Francisco. March 25.

McKean, Roland N. 1979. "Economic Aspects of Ethical-Behavioral Codes." *Political Studies* 27 (2):251–65.

McMillan, John 1979. "The Free-Rider Problem: A Survey." *Economic Record* 55 (149):95–107.

Minzokugaku Kenkyūjo (Folklore Research Institute). 1951. *Minzokugaku jiten* (Dictionary of folklore). Tokyo: Tōkyōdō shuppan.

Mishan, E. J. 1971. "The Post-War Literature on Externalities: An Interpretive Essay." *Journal of Economic Literature* 9 (1):1–28.

Miyagawa Mitsuru with Cornelius J. Kiley. 1974. "From *Shōen* to *Chigyō*: Proprietary Lordship and the Structure of Local Power." In *Japan in the Muromachi Age,* ed. John Whitney Hall and Toyoda Takeshi, 89–106. Berkeley and Los Angeles: University of California Press.

Nagahara Keiji. 1975. "Land Ownership under the Shōen-Kokugaryō System." *Journal of Japanese Studies* 1 (2):269–96.

———. 1977. *Chūsei nairanki no shakai to minshū* (Society and people during the medieval civil wars). Tokyo: Yoshikawa kōbunkan.

Nagahara Keiji with Kozo Yamamura. 1974. "Village Communities and Daimyo Power." In *Japan in the Muromachi Age,* ed. John Whitney Hall and Toyoda Takeshi, 107–23. Berkeley and Los Angeles: University of California Press.

———. 1981. "The Sengoku Daimyo and the *Kandaka* System." In *Japan before Tokugawa: Political Consolidation and Economic Growth: 1500–1650,* ed. John Whitney Hall, Nagahara Keiji, and Kozo Yamamura, 27–63. Princeton, N.J.: Princeton University Press.

North, Douglass. 1981. *Structure and Change in Economic History*. New York: Norton.

Olson, Mancur. 1965. *The Logic of Collective Action: Public Goods and the Theory of Groups*. Cambridge, Mass.: Harvard University Press.

Osako, Masako M. 1983. "Forest Preservation in Tokugawa Japan." In *Global Deforestation and the Nineteenth-Century World Economy*, ed. Richard P. Tucker and John F. Richards, 129–45. Durham, N.C.: Duke University Press.

Ōshima Mario. 1978. *Kinsei ni okeru mura to ie no shakai kōzō* (The social structure of village and household in early modern Japan). Tokyo: Ochanomizu shobō.

Runge, Carlisle Ford. 1981. "Common Property Externalities: Isolation, Assurance, and Resource Depletion in a Traditional Grazing Context." *American Journal of Agricultural Economics* 63 (4):595–606.

Sansom, George. 1958. *A History of Japan to 1334*. Stanford, Calif.: Stanford University Press.

Sato, Elizabeth. 1974. "The Early Development of the *Shōen*." In *Medieval Japan: Essays in Institutional History*, ed. John Whitney Hall and Jeffrey P. Mass, 91–108. New Haven, Conn.: Yale University Press.

Shimpo Mitsuru. 1976. *Three Decades in Shiwa: Economic Development and Social Change in a Japanese Farming Community*. Vancouver: University of British Columbia Press.

Smith, Thomas C. 1959. *The Agrarian Origins of Modern Japan*. New York: Atheneum.

———. 1968a. "The Japanese Village in the Seventeenth Century." In *Studies in the Institutional History of Early Modern Japan*, ed. John Whitney Hall and Marius B. Jansen, 238–300. Princeton, N.J.: Princeton University Press.

———. 1968b. "The Land Tax in Tokugawa Japan." In *Studies in the Institutional History of Early Modern Japan*, ed. John Whitney Hall and Marius B. Jansen, 263–82. Princeton, N.J.: Princeton University Press.

———. 1977. *Nakahara: Family Farming and Population in a Japanese Village, 1717–1830*. Stanford, Calif.: Stanford University Press.

Stigler, George J. 1974. "Free Riders and Collective Action; An Appendix to Theories of Economic Regulation." *Bell Journal of Economics and Management Science* 5 (2):359–65.

Sweeney, John W., Jr. 1973. "An Experimental Investigation of the Free-Rider Problem." *Social Science Research* 2 (3):277–92.

———. 1974. "Altruism, the Free-Rider Problem, and Group Size." *Theory and Decision* 4 (3–4):259–75.

Totman, Conrad. 1967. *Politics in the Tokugawa Bakufu 1600–1843*. Cambridge, Mass.: Harvard University Press.

———. 1979. "English-Language Studies of Medieval Japan: An Assessment." *Journal of Asian Studies* 38 (3):541–51.

———. 1982a. "Kinsei Nihon no ringyō ni tsuite no ikkōsatsu" (A perspective on early modern Japanese forestry). *Tokugawa rinseishi kenkyūjo kenkyū kiyō*, 377–99.

———. 1982b. "Forestry in Early Modern Japan, 1650–1850: A Preliminary Survey." *Agricultural History* 56 (2):415–25.

———. 1983a. "The Forests of Tokugawa Japan: A Catastrophe That Was Avoided." *Transactions of the Asiatic Society of Japan*. 3d ser. 18:1–15.

————. 1983b. "Logging the Unloggable: Timber Transport in Early Modern Japan." *Journal of Forest History* 27 (4):190–91.

————. 1984. "Land-Use Patterns and Afforestation in the Edo Period." *Monumenta Nipponica* 39 (1):1–10.

————. 1989. *The Green Archipelago: Forestry in Preindustrial Japan.* Berkeley and Los Angeles: University of California Press.

Troost, Kristina Kade. 1985a. "Common Land in Late Medieval Japan." Paper presented to the Triangle East Asia Colloquium on Common Rights in Land and Water in East Asia, April 13, Durham, N.C.

————. 1985b. "The Medieval Origins of Common Land in Japan." Paper presented at the American Historical Association, December 28, New York.

————. 1990. "Common Property and Community Formation: Self-Governing Villages in Late Medieval Japan, 1300–1600." Ph.D. diss., Department of History, Harvard University.

————. 1991. "Common Property and Community Formation: The Origins of Self-Governing Villages in Late Medieval Japan, 1300–1500." Paper presented at the Washington and Southeast Regional Seminar on Japan, April 27, Williamsburg, Va.

Tsurumi Kazuko. 1975. "Yanagida Kunio's Work as a Model of Endogenous Development." *Japan Quarterly* 22 (3):223–38.

Tucker, Richard P., and John F. Richards, eds. 1983. *Global Deforestation and the Nineteenth Century World Economy.* Durham, N.C.: Duke University Press.

Wakita Osamu. 1982. "The Emergence of the State in Sixteenth-Century Japan: From Oda to Tokugawa." *Journal of Japanese Studies* 8 (2):343–67.

Watanabe Yōzō. 1972. *Iriai to hō* (Common access and the law). Tokyo: Tokyo University Press.

Watanabe Yōzō and Hōjō Hiroshi. 1975. *Rin'ya iriai to sonraku kōzō: Kitafuji sanroku no jirei kenkyū* (Common access to forests and village structure: A case study from the north Fuji slope). Tokyo: Tokyo University Press.

Watanabe Yōzō and Nakao Hidetoshi. 1975. *Nihon no shakai to hō* (Law and society in Japan). Tokyo: Nihon hyōronsha.

Wigen [Lewis], Kären. 1985. "Common Losses: Transformations of Commonland and Peasant Livelihood in Tokugawa Japan, 1603–1868." M.A. thesis, Department of Geography, University of California, Berkeley.

Wigmore, John. 1969–. *Law and Justice in Tokugawa Japan.* Tokyo: University of Tokyo Press. Eventually to comprise ten sections.

Wintersteen, Prescott B., Jr. 1974. "The Muromachi *Shugo* and *Hanzei.*" In *Medieval Japan: Essays in Institutional History*, ed. John Whitney Hall and Jeffrey P. Mass, 209–20. New Haven, Conn.: Yale University Press.

Yamamura, Kozo. 1975. "Introduction." *Journal of Japanese Studies* 1 (2):255–68.

————. ed. 1990. *The Cambridge History of Japan.* Vol. 3, Medieval Japan. Cambridge: Cambridge University Press.

Yanagida Kunio, comp. and ed. 1957. *Japanese Manners and Customs in the Meiji Era.* Tokyo: Obunsha.

5

Commonfield Agriculture:
The Andes and Medieval
England Compared

*Bruce M. S. Campbell and
Ricardo A. Godoy*

Commonfield agriculture is one of the most distinctive and intriguing manifestations of common-property resource management. Distinctive, because of its peculiar blend of private and communal endeavors and its complex patterns of decision making and interaction. Intriguing, because farmland is inherently divisible, there being no technical or physical reason why individual holdings should not be managed on an entirely private basis. That this has not been the case in many parts of the world over remarkably long periods of time is consequently a matter of considerable interest.

Four key attributes define the core dimensions of commonfield agriculture (Thirsk 1964). First, the holdings of individual cultivators comprise many separate parcels scattered among unenclosed commonfields. Second, after the harvest, and usually during fallow years, these commonfields revert from private farmland to communal pasture ground, as all villagers exercise their customary right to graze their animals on the herbage temporarily available on the arable land. In commonfield agrarian regimes, villagers also enjoy the collective right to gather peat, timber, and firewood from common pastures and fallow fields. Finally, regulation and supervision of the entire system is provided by an "assembly of cultivators."

Any of these features may be found in isolation in other farming systems. Many pastoralists, for instance, graze their stock communally. Village councils rule Himalayan, Swiss, Andean, Japanese, and Vietnamese peasant communities (Rhoades and Thompson 1975; Popkin

1979). The simultaneous occurrence of all four traits, however, is rarer; we see it only in selected parts of Europe, colonial New England, the central Andean highlands, Mesoamerica, India, the Middle East, and West Africa.[1] The two- and three-field system of England is probably the best known of these systems and certainly one of the most systematized and regularized. In its case, historians now believe that the four elements noted above coalesced only after a long gestation period, possibly in the tenth and eleventh centuries. Thereafter, the system endured in some parts of the country until well into the nineteenth century.[2]

No single definition is likely to capture all the subtleties of an agrarian system found over so wide a geographical area and so long a period of time. Nor is any one theory likely to explain the causal factors responsible for the emergence of such a complex system in so many geographical areas and sociopolitical environments. What this exploratory essay offers, therefore, is a systematic comparison of the technical and physical attributes, the decision-making arrangements, and the patterns of interaction among users of commonfield systems found in two widely separated parts of the world: the central Andean highlands and medieval England. This comparison is less farfetched than might at first appear for, despite vast differences in the material underpinnings of these two commonfield regimes, they manifest striking similarities in their functional attributes, demographic patterns, and evolutionary trajectories.

Current knowledge and understanding of Andean commonfield systems may be deficient, but, as Marc Bloch once remarked, there are times when synthesis, comparisons, and the formulation of interesting problems contribute more to an understanding of cultural phenomena than further detailed case studies. Accordingly, this essay is offered as a first step in the development of a genuinely cross-cultural understanding of commonfield systems.[3] It also serves the more immediate function of helping to frame questions and rank priorities for further research. Above all, in the wider context of this book, it furnishes two illuminating cases of highly developed and successful common-property management systems.

Historical Background of the Two Systems

English and Andean commonfields are far removed from each other in time and in space. In England, commonfield farming is a thing of the past. Today, only a solitary, consciously preserved, commonfield township survives—at Laxton in Nottinghamshire (Beckett 1989). In contrast, in

Peru and Bolivia, commonfield farming continues to be practiced over an extensive geographical area.

Precisely when and how commonfield farming came into being in England remains a matter of considerable debate. Nevertheless, there is general agreement that the system reached its heyday during the early Middle Ages, from approximately the tenth to the fourteenth centuries. Throughout that period, commonfields were expanding and developing; by its close, approximately two-thirds of England's population lived in commonfield townships (Baker and Butlin 1973; Dodgshon 1980; Campbell 1981a; Rowley 1981). Thereafter, the prevailing trend, with certain exceptions, involved increasing consolidation and enclosure, so that by the close of the seventeenth century England had become a country in which farming in severalty (that is, with land held by an owner in his own right and not jointly or in common with others) predominated (Wordie 1983).[4]

It was at this same time that a fully fledged commonfield system seems to have been crystallizing in the Andes, as native systems of husbandry were transformed under Spanish colonial influence. Almost everything remains to be learned about the history of these commonfields, but fragmentary evidence suggests that it was during the seventeenth and eighteenth centuries that the system became most widespread (Chevallier 1953, 60; Gade 1970; Custred and Orlove 1974; Gade and Escobar 1982; Málaga Medina 1974). Since then, these commonfields have also begun to succumb to alternative methods of land management.[5]

Technical and Physical Attributes of English and Andean Commonfields

Entirely different though their respective chronologies of development may be, both commonfield systems share the same fundamental physical attribute: arable fields made up of myriad unenclosed and intermixed parcels. This is the one abiding feature of all commonfield systems and it is from this that associated decision-making arrangements and patterns of interaction spring. Thus, rights of stubble grazing and the communal regulation of cropping are most satisfactorily interpreted as responses to the problems of farming in subdivided fields (Dahlman, 1980). That being said, subdivided fields could exist independently of such rights and regulations: the latter were not an invariable concomitant of the former.

In Andean and medieval English commonfields, the degree of subdivision was often extreme. The community of Irpa Chico in Bolivia, for instance, possesses six great fields in which W. Carter and M. Mamani

(1982, 26–27) noted some 11,000 separate parcels. These mostly ranged from 1,200 to 3,000 square meters, with some diminutive plots and others as large as 24,000 square meters. In England, the size range of plots was narrower, although some diminutive plots did exist. At Martham, in Norfolk, for example, the land held by the peasantry was divided into at least 2,500 separate plots at the end of the thirteenth century, with an average plot size of 2,000 square meters and a significant number of plots measuring 1,000 square meters or less (Campbell 1980).

There has been much discussion of the reasons for this most distinctive form of field layout. It has recently been suggested that dispersed holdings may represent a strategy of risk minimization. The Andean evidence lends some support to this interpretation, insofar as plot scattering increases with altitude, which is positively linked to higher natural risk factors (McCloskey 1976; Dodgshon 1980, 22–25, 45–46; McPherson 1983; Figueroa 1982, 127, 129, 132; Bentley 1987). Yet, although plot scattering may reduce the risk of wholesale crop failure, there is no unequivocal, empirical evidence to show that it was actually undertaken with this express purpose.[6] Indeed, it may have arisen from entirely different motives. Thus, in England, several studies have demonstrated that piecemeal colonization by groups of cultivators, together with the repeated partitioning of holdings between heirs and the sale and exchange of portions of land between different cultivators, were all capable, over a period of time and under conditions of population growth, of creating subdivided fields from formerly consolidated holdings (Bishop 1935; Baker 1964; Sheppard 1966; Campbell 1980). When the rules governing the transference of land permitted, population growth was likely to lead at one and the same time to an extension of the cultivated area and the fragmentation of established holdings. As population expanded, so holdings proliferated, individual parcels became smaller, and the degree of scattering increased. In this context, it is significant that partible inheritance, whose contribution to the formation of subdivided fields in medieval England is now well established, is still practiced in many Andean commonfield communities today. Other things being equal, such an inheritance system is likely to ensure the persistence of a highly subdivided field layout.[7]

Notwithstanding the high degree of parcellation in both English and Andean commonfields, it would be misleading to represent their physical appearance as at all similar. The shape of the parcels and the way in which they were organized into fields differed due to the contrasting technological and ecological circumstances under which the two systems evolved.

English commonfields were developed for the most part on level or gently undulating terrain and in conjunction with a plow technology and mixed grain and stock economy. Indeed, the plow was arguably the single most formative influence upon the morphology of English commonfields. As J. Langdon has shown (1986), three main types of plow were in use by the thirteenth century: the wheeled, foot, and swing varieties.

Wheeled plows were more likely to be drawn by horses than were the other varieties (on the lightest soils, a team of only two horses would sometimes suffice), and in distribution were confined to the southeastern counties and parts of East Anglia. This pattern is partly a function of soil conditions, but it also reflects social, economic, and institutional factors, insofar as the adoption of horse traction entails a greater emphasis upon the production of fodder crops, notably oats. This, in turn, is associated with higher labor inputs and the kind of intensive cultivation system that, at this date, was found only in conjunction with the more loosely regulated commonfield systems.[8]

Elsewhere in the country, swing and foot plows predominated, the ox was the principal plow beast, and plow teams were often large—usually eight animals, but sometimes ten, or even as many as twelve. Again, this is partly because of physical conditions, as large, slow, ox teams were a necessity on the heavy clay soils of much of lowland England; but it also correlates with lower population densities and cultivation systems that placed greater emphasis upon fallowing, with a corresponding dependence upon natural rather than produced fodder. These conditions obtained in much of those parts of central and southern England where commonfield farming was most strongly developed, so there was a general association between foot and swing plows, large ox teams, and regular commonfield systems. Finally, it was for the simple but obvious reason that these large teams were cumbersome to manage and awkward to turn that individual parcels within the commonfields acquired their characteristically long, sinuous, and strip-like shape (Eyre 1955).

The prevailing plow technology can also be credited with creating the equally characteristic micro-relief pattern known as "ridge and furrow." This resulted from the repeated turning of the sod inwards, toward the center of the strip, which the fixed moldboards (it was the moldboard that turned the sod) of medieval plows made unavoidable. The boundaries between strips thus became marked by furrows, which had the additional advantage on heavy soils of assisting drainage (Beresford 1948; Kerridge 1951). A buildup of soil also resulted at the end of each strip from the action of turning the plow: the resultant "headlands" often became so massive that they may still be identified from aerial photographs, even where the associated strip pattern has long since been plowed out (Hall 1981).

Land hunger during the thirteenth century pushed the cultivated area of most commonfield townships to its physical limit, so that property boundaries became clearly demarcated (double furrows, grass balks, and marker stones and posts were all used for that purpose) and property rights—private as well as communal—became jealously guarded.[9] Odd patches of ground were sometimes left untilled within the commonfields for reasons of shape, accessibility, or soil conditions; these were generally utilized as a valuable supplement to the otherwise meager pasturage resources. For the most part, however, commonfields were very regular and only appeared fragmented and haphazard in areas of broken relief, poor soil, or bad drainage (Elliott 1973). Even then, they still bore little physical resemblance to the commonfields of the Andes.

Andean commonfields occur in high mountains, where the terrain is extremely fractured, and where cattle, and especially plow oxen, have difficulty in adapting to the altitudes. The commonfields are distributed over a very extensive geographical area: they have been found as far north as Huanuco in Peru and as far south as Macha, Department of Potosi, in Bolivia (Orlove and Godoy 1986). Within this zone, they lie at 3,000–4,000 meters above sea level on both the eastern and western flanks of the Andes, including the *altiplano*.

Throughout this area, yoked oxen are employed for plowing only in the lands surrounding Lake Titicaca and on the flatter patches of the Bolivian plateau. Elsewhere, plow animals are precluded by the rugged topography, easily degradable soils, and risk of hypoxic stress (Guillet 1981). For these reasons, and partly because the principal crops are roots and tubers (notably potatoes), the predominant tool of cultivation is not the plow but the digging stick (*chakitaclla*), supplemented by picks, shovels, and scythes for planting and harvesting (Gade and Rios 1976). Individual parcels of land are therefore free to assume every conceivable size and shape, a phenomenon that is encouraged by the steep and broken slopes and stony soils.

In consequence, the typical appearance of Andean commonfields is a mosaic of irregular parcels, many of them Lilliputian in scale. The boundaries between these parcels are often vague; they include natural features, untilled land, marginal pasture grounds, and up-ended sod blocks. The same applies to the commonfields themselves and the boundaries between them, which tend to be zones rather than precise lines and are usually demarcated by small piles of stones (*mojones*) or natural landmarks (Godoy 1985). This endows commonfield agriculture with an element of flexibility, for cultivation can be expanded or contracted as required according to demographic changes and altered land requirements (Mamani 1973, 93). It also produces a different agricultural landscape from the neatly aligned arable strips of lowland England.

Decision-Making Arrangements in
England and the Andes

Pronounced though outward differences may have been, both English and
Andean subdivided fields presented their dependent cultivators with the
same basic problem: how were cropping and grazing to be organized in
fields that were so parcellated? In particular, how was advantage to be
taken of the valuable opportunity that fallow land afforded for feeding
livestock and fertilizing soils? In medieval England, the need to utilize the
fallow grazings was especially acute, for in many townships (especially in
the counties of the East Midlands) the area of arable land had been so
expanded that permanent grassland was scarce (Fox 1984). Yet livestock,
both for traction and manure, remained an indispensable adjunct of
arable production. In the plowless Andes, the need was different. What
was important here was the conservation of soil fertility in a mountain
environment where soils are deficient in nitrogen, phosphate, and po-
tassium, and easily degradable (Eckholm 1976; Crawford, Wishart, and
Campbell 1970; Orlove 1977, 119; Ravines 1978a, 3–74; Thomas 1979; Brush
1980). Indeed, adequate dunging of the soil (usually by flocks of sheep
and llamas), is essential to the successful cultivation of one of the region's
main staples, the potato (LaBarre 1947; Browman n.d.; Winterhalder,
Larsen, and Thomas 1974; Camino, Recharte, and Bidegaray 1981).[10]

It is in the context of these ecological requirements that the adoption
of communal decision-making arrangements must be interpreted. The
precise nature of these arrangements depended upon environmental,
technological, demographic, and sociopolitical circumstances, which is
why England, for example, contained so many different types of commonfield systems (it remains to be established whether the same applied
in the Andes, although it is a priori likely).[11] These systems differed from
one another in both form and function, possessed distinctive geographical
distributions, and followed separate chronologies of development. Apart
from subdivided fields that were devoid of communal decision-making
arrangements, two basic generic types of field systems can be identified:
irregular commonfield systems, and regular commonfield systems.
Within the former category, further distinctions can be drawn among
systems in which there was no regulation of cropping, systems in which
there was some regulation of cropping, and those where, very occasionally, there was complete regulation of cropping. This last feature was,
however, more typical of regular commonfield systems, whose distinctive-
ness lay in the superimposition of communally enforced rotations upon a
regular layout of holdings, with the result that each peasant holding, large
or small, effectively became a microcosm of the entire arable area.[12]
S. Fenoaltea has recently argued that this offers the additional, and in his

view more profound, advantage of optimizing the allocation of village labor to the village land, as though the township were a single village-wide farm, "*without* loss of effort to shirking or supervision, as each household optimizes the allocation of its own labor to its own land" (1988, 191).

Although many different commonfield types existed, it is important to recognize that there have always been some subdivided fields within which individual holdings have been managed without reference to any wider framework of decision making. J. Thirsk believed that attempts to herd and farm in subdivided fields were so prone to conflict that "the community was drawn together by sheer necessity to cooperate in the control of farming practices" (1964, 9). Commonfield agriculture is thus regarded as offering lower transaction costs than the continuance of farming in severalty. In fact, this was by no means necessarily so, as England and the Andes both demonstrate.

Examples may be found in both countries of intensely subdivided fields with little or no communal regulation of cropping and herding. This was particularly the case in environmentally favored areas of relatively high population density and intensive agriculture. A high population means that labor is available for the fencing and policing of individual plots and private tethering, herding, and folding of livestock. At low population densities, as B. C. Field has demonstrated for seventeenth-century New England, such exclusion costs, and especially the costs of fencing, were a major factor promoting communal herding. On the other hand, as Field also observes (1985, 104–7), the tendency of population growth is to push property-rights institutions in the direction of individual tenures. Intensification of cultivation also means that the area left fallow and available for pasturage is usually either small or nonexistent.

The husbandry systems where this occurred in medieval England—notably in parts of Sussex, Kent, and Norfolk—were characterized by the cultivation of fodder crops and associated stall-feeding of livestock, coupled with labor-intensive methods of fertilizing the land. When fallowing occurred, its sole purpose was to cleanse the land of weed growth by means of multiple plowings, a practice that would have been in direct conflict with any attempt to utilize fallows as a source of forage. Wherever these husbandry methods were employed, rights of common grazing on the arable fields were therefore either restricted to the period immediately after the harvest (the one time in the year when the fields were free from standing crops) or absent altogether (Baker 1973; Campbell 1981c, 1983).

In the Andes, the counterparts of these intensive grain-producing districts are the areas of irrigated maize production, at lower altitudes than the main area of commonfields, where a warmer and more stable climate and a more benign topography permit a greater intensity of cultivation and correspondingly higher densities of population. Here, too, the organization of cultivation is largely on an individual basis, as communal supervision of grazing is precluded by the intensity of cropping (Donkin 1979, 120; Guillet 1981; Platt 1982). Cultivators make their own private arrangements for feeding the plow oxen employed in these areas.

The opposite extreme is represented by the classic commonfield system of the English Midlands. Here, demographic, economic, and environmental circumstances were less conducive to the kind of intensification of production outlined above, insofar as this area supported only moderate population densities, was at some distance from major urban markets, and lacked cheap and ready access to external supplies of nutrients for the maintenance of soil fertility. As a result, there were both greater incentives and fewer obstacles to the adoption of collective controls upon agriculture. In fact, communal management of an integrated system of cropping and grazing was taken further in this system than in any other. What made this possible was an artificially regular layout of holdings, whereby an equal amount of land was held in each of the commonfields of the township. This was essential since a regular, and communally enforced, rotation of crops was superimposed upon the entire arable area, effectively transforming the village into a single large farm (Fenoaltea 1988).

The furlong—a bundle of adjacent strips—was the basic unit of cropping, with the result that individual commonfields frequently carried a range of different crops. Nevertheless, when it came to fallowing, the field retained a central place in the whole system of rotation: "Whatever changes in cropping were rung on the furlongs of the sown field or fields, the fallow field remained inviolate" (Fox 1981, 74). Under the two- and three-field system, each field was fallowed either every second or every third year. The basic rotation was either a combination of winter- and spring-sown cereals and legumes followed by fallow, or a season of winter-sown crops, a season of spring-sown crops, and then fallow. The purpose of the fallow was to rest the soil so that it might recuperate its fertility, to allow the land to be fertilized with the dung of grazing livestock and, above all, to supply the livestock with forage, which was in such short supply in many of the townships that followed this system. Since the need to find grazing for the livestock was, ecologically, the raison d'être of the entire system, there was no question of subjecting the fallow to repeated plowings: on the contrary, it was left to sward over with weeds and grasses and only put back under the plow shortly before it was returned to cultivation.

Andean commonfields share many affinities with these English arrangements and display the same association with a moderate density of population and intensity of land use. They, too, employ communal controls to rationalize the distribution of sown and unsown plots, thereby facilitating common grazing of the fallows. On the other hand, the crops involved are very different from those grown in medieval England, as are the functions and organization of fallows. These differences ensure that Andean commonfields possess considerable individuality in their decision-making arrangements and attendant patterns of interaction.

Within the Andes, commonfield lands are generally sown for up to four consecutive years and there is no distinction between winter-sown and spring-sown crops. The normal rotational sequence is: first, potatoes fertilized with llama or sheep dung; second, native chenopods (*guinua* and *cañahua* and the tubers *ocas* and *ullucus*); and then cereals and leguminous crops in the third and fourth years. Having deep roots, the cereals and legumes seek nutrients below the shallow surface layer of the soil, whose fertility is rapidly depleted during the first two years of cropping (Freeman 1980). Thereafter, soil nutrients are allowed to build up because the fields are allowed to rest for as long as thirty years, but the mean fallow duration is three or four years. The length of fallow is never fixed; it varies according to soil conditions and cropping requirements, and this proves the key to the whole system. The higher the altitude, the longer must be the fallow period, because of reduced soil fertility and slower rates of growth (Caballero 1981; Orlove and Godoy 1986).

In very few cases are fields sown for more than five consecutive years or fallows reduced to one year. The exceptions include areas undergoing intensification, or those communities situated on the shores of Lake Titicaca that, thanks to a more benign climate and richer soils, plant on what approaches a continuous basis (Carter 1964; Mamani 1973, 89, 110; Urioste 1977, 43; Lewellen 1978, 16, 49; LeBaron 1979; Godoy 1985). It remains to be established how far such intensifications of production have led to modifications in conventional Andean commonfield arrangements and to what extent they have led to irreversible ecological degradation. Nevertheless, that intensification has occurred at all does demonstrate that commonfield systems are nowhere a direct adaptive response to environmental factors; various nonecological considerations have always been important.

Once a field is designated for cropping, the precise pattern and sequence of crops sown is a matter of individual choice. There is thus no Andean equivalent of the furlongs found in medieval England. The range of crops grown within any field is usually quite wide, as cultivators tend to diversify their pattern of planting as a hedge against environmental hazards and the risk of wholesale harvest failure (Brush 1981, 71). Nevertheless, as far as the decision-making arrangements of these commonfields are concerned, it is not so much what crops are sown that matters, but rather, which fields are to be left fallow and for how long. Such important decisions are taken at a village level. To accommodate the relatively long fallow period required in this high mountain environment, the arable land of each community will usually be divided into at least seven or eight commonfields, and sometimes as many as fifteen. Whenever any of these fields lie fallow, villagers exercise a customary entitlement to pasture their livestock, collect firewood, and cut turf. At the same time, arrangements are made for the systematic dunging of the land by sheep and llamas penned in movable folds. This ensures that all the land is adequately manured before it is eventually returned to cultivation: the dung, urine, and treading of the animals are all highly beneficial to these upland soils. Analogous arrangements occurred in certain English commonfield systems on the light soil of East Anglia, where there was likewise a tendency for fallow periods to be of several years' duration (Postgate 1973; Bailey 1990).

Two aspects of these Andean arrangements require further comment. The first concerns the household's entitlement to common pasturage. In some cases, households have rights to graze only portions of the stubble of the commonfields. When this occurs, the location of this grazing ground is often independent of the distribution of parcels making up the holding. W. E. Carter has described this distinctive arrangement (Carter 1964, 68; see also Platt 1982; Godoy 1983). According to him, the section of the commonfields reserved to each household as pasture for its flocks is known as an *unta* (literally meaning "that which one can see"), which is a prolongation of the houseplot into the commonfields. This *unta* privilege directly overlays the normal rights of cultivation that apply to individual plots in the fields and sometimes applies to such uncultivable land as mountaintops or swamps. Such demarcation of each family's own grazing zone within the village's territory is an Andean peculiarity and reflects a desire for private control of their own animals by individual community members. It finds no counterpart in the commonfield villages of lowland England, with their greater emphasis on arable farming, scarcer pasturage, and much smaller flocks and herds.

A second, much more significant, characteristic of Andean arrangements is that a communally determined system of cropping and fallowing coexists with an irregular layout of holdings. Such a state of affairs carries with it the obvious penalty that each year some households will be obliged to leave a disproportionate amount of their land uncultivated. There is thus an inherent inequity within the system, a deficiency that is avoided in the English midland system by the equal distribution of a holding's strips among all the fields of a township.[13] Such a regular layout of holdings would be of no practical advantage in the Andean situation, where the timing and duration of fallows are, perforce, subject to such flexibility. It is certainly true that (as in those few English instances where there was a similar mismatch between holding layout and rotations) Andean people are sometimes able to use land held outside the common-field system to offset the inequities arising within that system. Thus all commonfield holdings include a houseplot that is held in severalty and capable of intensive cultivation. Although such plots are occasionally quite substantial, most have been much reduced in size through the application of a custom of male partible inheritance (Carter 1964, 65; Heath, Buechler, and Erasmus 1969, 177; Rodríguez-Pastor 1969, 84–86). For the tenants of these diminutive houseplots, the most effective supplements to commonfield land are therefore valley plots. Not only are the latter not subject to communal decisions, they are also environmentally more favored and can consequently be cropped much more intensively than the commonfields (Guillet 1981; Platt 1982).

When houseplots, valley lands, and pasture grounds are all taken into account, it transpires that commonfields generally constitute between 20 and 70 percent of total landholdings, the proportion rising with altitude (Figueroa 1982, 133). Nevertheless, many individuals remain dependent upon the commonfields for the basic staples of daily life. For them, the only solution when they are temporarily disadvantaged by the system is to come to some kind of reciprocal arrangement with those who are temporarily advantaged. It is upon this kind of social exchange between members of the same agricultural community that the commonfield system ultimately depends for its success.

The nearest equivalent in England was the commonfield system of parts of East Anglia, noted above. Here a similar coexistence occurred between common rotations and an irregular layout of holdings. The rotations in question assumed the form of flexible cropping shifts which were capable of variation from plot to plot and year to year. Their object was likewise to concentrate fallow strips for sheep folding. Since this periodically placed certain individuals at a disadvantage, successful operation of the system, as in the Andes, depended upon the establishment of a satisfactory method of compensation. As control of the system was vested in the manorial lord (who, as principal flockmaster, was also usually the major beneficiary of it), a tenant thus placed might receive part of the lord's crop, temporary use of a portion of the lord's demesne, or financial compensation in the form of a cash handout or rent rebate. Even so, this system was particularly prone to conflict, as is testified by the large number of resultant court cases (Allison 1957, 1958; Simpson 1958; Postgate 1973; Bailey 1990). It was also one of the issues that provoked Kett's Rebellion of 1549 (MacCulloch 1979).

On the whole, both English and Andean commonfield systems made good practical sense in a situation where land was cropped with only moderate intensity, and where population levels were such that substantial dividends were to be derived from pooling scarce labor and organizing basic farming tasks in common. Savings in exclusion costs were obviously to be made by eliminating the need for fencing and by appointing a few guards to watch over the field and stock of all the villagers. Moreover, information and transaction costs were reduced when decisions were taken at a village level as to when and where to plant and pasture. Real gains in agricultural labor productivity may consequently have resulted (Fenoaltea 1988).

Such arrangements may also have proved advantageous to subjects faced with heavy labor-tribute liabilities, a relevant point in both a medieval English and an Andean context. In the former, lords were entitled to exact labor services from their tenants through the institution of serfdom; these services characteristically assumed the form of agricultural work on the lord's demesne. In fact, under the conditions of labor scarcity that probably prevailed when serfdom was first instituted, lords would have had a vested interest in promoting the development of a system of husbandry that enabled them to redeploy labor to their own ends. Certainly a general association existed between areas of strong lordship and fully developed commonfield systems.[14]

Likewise in the Andes, the Spanish instituted a system of forced labor to work the silver and mercury mines of Potosi and Huancavelica. This assumed the form of an annual migration of able-bodied males (the *mita*) drawn from a very extensive area. At the end of the sixteenth century, this migration totaled some 13,000 workers per year, some of whom came from so far away that they had to walk for an entire month to reach the mines. As E. Tandeter (1981) has pointed out, a migration on this scale must have had major repercussions for the accumulation and reproduction of the communities that were being exploited, the more so as these heavy labor demands coincided with a prolonged and massive reduction in population.[15] It seems, therefore, that in the Andes too there is a coincidence between the area of heaviest labor-tribute liabilities and the area where commonfield agriculture appears to have attained its most complex form and survived the longest.

Patterns of Interaction

The common denominator of all these commonfield systems is a reversion from private use of the soil for tillage to communal rights for grazing on the herbage of the fallow fields. This communal arrangement places a premium upon the collective management of resources. For instance, since commonfields remain unfenced, individual householders face incentives to steal crops from adjacent plots and encroach upon neighboring lands. This potential threat fosters collective action, as isolated households by themselves would be less effective in opposing interlopers (Gade 1970, 51; Orlove 1976, 213; Albo 1977, 23; Platt 1982, 45). That is why villages appoint guards and other officials. Furthermore, the movement across time and space of different flocks and herds, and the designation of fields to be sown and fallowed, involve complex scheduling problems affecting all villagers.

These logistical problems are therefore frequently decided upon by village assemblies; it is they who determine the date and place of planting, harvesting, and grazing. In the Andes, these village councils, as noted by McBride, constitute the "*de facto* government of a community, though its operation is so silent and its deliberation so carefully guarded that its existence is seldom even suspected" (1921, 9). Much the same is true of similar assemblies in England, whose existence is often barely hinted at in the historical record. Yet although there is a clear association between commonfield agriculture and strongly developed corporate village communities, the precise causal connection between them is enigmatic. At any event, the outward physical expression of the strong corporate character possessed by these commonfield communities in both countries is the nucleated village, in which the dwellings of the cultivators and other inhabitants are concentrated into a single settlement cluster. Such villages are now recognized by archaeologists as having made a relatively late appearance on the rural scene, their arrival coinciding, it would appear, with that of commonfield agriculture in the ninth and tenth centuries (Astill 1988b; Fox 1992). In contrast, more dispersed and more ancient forms of settlement—loosely clustered hamlets, isolated farmsteads, and a mixture of villages and scattered messuages—tend to prevail in areas without a commonfield system.[16]

The Andean evidence demonstrates that the corporate sense of these commonfield communities is usually strong enough to override even quite substantial inequalities of holding size among cultivators.[17] As is to be expected, the larger landholders do tend to exert a disproportionate influence within village assemblies and dominate the principal village offices. On the other hand, all household heads serve as field guards by yearly turns. This rotational incumbency possibly had colonial origins, but it still functions (Rasnake 1988).

These officers, known variously as *pachacas, campos, muyucamas, arariwas, camayoqs,* or *rigidores de varas,* are in charge of supervising fields, preventing animals from straying onto cultivated lands, guarding against crop theft and trespass, punishing and levying fines on miscreant shepherds, and performing rituals to protect crops when hail, drought, and other natural calamities threaten. Their honesty is ensured because they are answerable to the higher-level authority of the village and charged with responsibility for any crops stolen from the fields. In recompense, if the harvest proves successful, they receive the produce of a few furrows from each family, or are allowed to plant in uncultivated plots of the commons.

As B. Thomas observes, this system of incumbency by yearly turns symbolizes total community involvement in the decision-making process of the entire community (Thomas 1979, 161; see also Gade 1970, 12; Degregori and Golte 1973, 42; Preston 1973; Fujii and Tomoeda 1981, 54). Household heads also sponsor village festivals at one or more times in their life cycle. These festivals confer prestige upon those who sponsor them, but are also essential for validating the individual household's rights of access to village assets in the eyes of the community (Platt 1982; Godoy 1983).

The need to establish who belongs to a community and has a stake in its resources is critical: that it is perceived as such is demonstrated by the symbolic reapportionments and public reconfirmations executed under the supervision of *hacienda* officials of a household's rights to land.[18] If anything, the issue of who is entitled to land rights has become more prominent in recent years as expanding populations have brought resources under increasing pressure.

Today, as in the past, a pronounced social stratification is apparent within many of these villages. In Bolivia, the true insiders (*originarios*) tend to have more parcels within the commonfields than do later arrivals (*agregados*). Below these two groups lie the *kantu runas* ("people of the margin"), peasants who settled in the village during the nineteenth century and who obtained indirect access to common land in exchange for services rendered to wealthier households (Platt 1982; Godoy 1983).[19] These divisions tend to be perpetuated by rules that proscribe the renting or selling of commonfield land to outsiders, although they permit cultivators to rent or mortgage their parcels to other members of the community (Guillet 1979; Fujii and Tomoeda 1981, 53; McBride 1921, 14; Metraux 1959; Carter 1964, 68; Godoy 1985; Custred 1974, 258). Such entry and exit rules are enforced by the village council, which, if need be, employs expulsion as the ultimate sanction. That village councils should have acquired such powers is a function of the historic weakness of national power structures in the areas of commonfield agriculture.

In medieval England, the administrative structure and patterns of interaction of these commonfield communities are more difficult to ascertain, filtered as they are through the historical record. Most of what is known is provided by the proceedings of manorial courts (the lowest level of courts with legitimate legal jurisdiction). It was in these courts that commonfield bylaws were enacted and enforced, and their proceedings usually record innumerable boundary disputes and prosecutions for trespass and crop theft (Ault 1965). The election of village officials was also usually enrolled in the courts. Some of these officers, like the "pinder" and "hayward," are close equivalents of the Andean field guards. They watched over the livestock feeding on the commons, and when necessary impounded them and assessed the damage done by cattle and tres- passers, after which a fine was imposed by the manor court on those responsible. Effective operation of these courts was obviously partly a function of the strength of seignorial authority, but it also depended upon the cooperation of the village community. Although a good deal of friction often existed between the villagers and their lord, it is clear that they derived considerable benefits from such ready access to a means of resolving local disputes.

The role of the manor court was important in the operation of the commonfield system, but the prerogative of overseeing the regular routine of commonfield husbandry and ensuring that cultivators conformed to its discipline was probably reserved to informal village assemblies.[20] Effec- tively, all those who owned land in the commonfields had a say in their management and enjoyed an entitlement to the appurtenant common rights that was usually in proportion to the size of their landholding. The only exceptions were various landless but long-established families within the community who sometimes retained a customary claim upon its resources through retention of the ancient houseplot. All those holding such rights were known as "commoners."

On the large Worcestershire manor of Halesowen, there were no less than twelve separate commonfield communities, each of which was represented in the central manor court by two villagers elected by its members, an arrangement implying that they must each have possessed some kind of well-organized self-governing machinery. As in the Andes, these "assemblies" were almost certainly dominated and run by the richer peasants, for it was they who usually fulfilled the majority of manorial offices. Patterns of social and economic interaction reconstructed by Z. Razi from these court records indicate a high incidence of reciprocity between peasants, its precise nature varying according to socioeconomic status. It is his view that in the late thirteenth and early fourteenth centuries the manor of Halesowen was characterized by "a high degree of cohesiveness, cooperation, and solidarity as a result of the requirements of an open-field husbandry, a highly developed corporate organization, and a sustained and active resistance to the seignorial regime" (1981, 16).

Nevertheless, the strong corporate sense manifested by these com- monfield communities should not be mistaken for rural egalitarianism. Nor should commonfields be regarded as an expression of such principles.

Cooperation, a shared identity, and a sense of common purpose at a village level were perfectly compatible with the existence of sharp inequalities between peasants and marked intragroup rivalry. Moreover, in the long term, these internal divisions were potentially disruptive to the commonfield regime, particularly in view of any changes in the wider political or economic context.

Documentation of the long-entrenched social stratification that existed within these rural communities is now becoming increasingly available (Dewindt 1972; Britton 1977; Smith 1979; Razi 1980). Thus, Halesowen village society may have functioned as a community but it was also highly monetized and competitive. From his reading of the evidence, Razi was in no doubt that the well-to-do villages were exploiting the needs of their less well-off neighbors to maximize their profits. Equivalent studies of villages in other parts of England have come to much the same conclusion. There was no question of arable lands being periodically reallotted (all attested cases of reallotment relate to meadowland, a common resource, like most other sources of herbage). From at least the middle of the thirteenth century, it is plain that peasants had attached strong individual ownership rights to their land. According to customary law, even villein land, which theoretically belonged to the lord rather than the tenants who held and worked it, descended according to the prevailing rules of inheritance within the same family; only in default of heirs did it revert to the lord, who might then reallocate it among his tenants. Moreover, an active market in peasant land was already established by this date in much of lowland England. Its effect was generally to encourage the emergence of socioeconomic differences between individual peasant families (Smith 1984b; Harvey 1984). Nevertheless, through the observation of certain commonsense safeguards, this land market proved in no way inimical to the effective operation of the commonfields.

Conclusions

That two commonfield systems with such a strong functional affinity should have developed under such fundamentally different technological conditions is highly significant, for several writers on the origin of English commonfields have placed great stress on the role of technology. F. Seebohm (1883) and the Orwins (1967), for instance, have all attributed the creation of commonfields to the practice of coaration or joint plowing with a heavy mold-board plow (Dodgshon 1980, 30–34). Yet the culture that evolved such similar agricultural arrangements in the Andes was effectively plowless.

Environmentally, too, there was a vast difference in the circumstances under which these two commonfield systems developed. However, despite the obvious physical differences between the high Andes and lowland England, both environments presented cultivators with an analogous problem. In each case, the productivity of the agricultural system rested upon the maintenance of a delicate ecological balance that required the reconciliation, on the same land, of the conflicting requirements of animal and pastoral husbandry. The need to supply forage to the animals and dung to the soil was the link between them. Even so, that the same basic need should have elicited such a similar institutional response says as much about the sociopolitical conditions prevailing when commonfields emerged, as it does about environmental considerations per se.

As has been shown, English and Andean commonfields make complete sense only when viewed in the context of a specific combination of economic, demographic, social, and political circumstances. Field (1988) has emphasized the connection between cultivation practices at one extreme and sociopolitical institutions at the other, although this is difficult to demonstrate empirically. Nevertheless, we believe that it was a real and vital link in both of the cases discussed above. Such a conclusion is not merely of relevance to students of commonfield systems: it also provides a warning against adopting an approach to the whole question of common-property resources that is either too environmentally or too economically deterministic.

These two cases also demonstrate the capacity of common-property resource management systems to take on an existence of their own, independent of the circumstances that may have led to their creation. Commonfield systems were self-perpetuating. This was partly because the system could only be dismantled if the common rights that applied to it were dissolved first, a step that entailed considerable costs because it required a consensus particularly difficult to obtain where there were so many vested interests. The process of parliamentary enclosure in England provides a graphic illustration of this and demonstrates that the intervention of a superior legal authority was sometimes required before long-established common rights could be finally extinguished (Tate 1967; Yelling 1977; Turner 1984).

Strict adherence to the specific agricultural routine imposed upon a community by the commonfield system was a further source of inertia. It was not that progress was impossible—the system could not have survived for so long had this been the case—but rather that substantial changes, such as in the number of rotational courses, were cumbersome to achieve (Havinden 1961; Dahlman 1980, 146–99). Communal consent was required before any deviations could take place from established crop rotations, or before alterations could be made in the existing ratio of pasture to tillage. Radical changes in the techniques and intensity of cultivation were consequently to be avoided. As Fenoaltea observes, where technologies were in flux and the agricultural population poorly educated, "the critical advantage of enclosed farms was that they could introduce advanced techniques without the need to convince a village full of cautious peasants that the new methods were better than the old" (1988, 197). For these various reasons, commonfield systems had a bias toward the maintenance of the economic and demographic status quo, and their dependent communities adopted social and cultural values and demographic strategies that actually retarded population growth and moderated technological change (Homans 1941; Howell 1975; Goody, Thirsk, and Thompson 1976). The resultant symbiosis between commonfield regime and sociodemographic behavior sometimes endured for centuries.

Nevertheless, commonfield systems were by no means immutable, and it would be a mistake to presume that seventeenth- and eighteenth-century commonfields were carbon copies of medieval ones. Over time they furnish much evidence of adaptation to new technologies and socioeconomic circumstances. Parcels have been altered in shape and size, and fields in layout; new crops have been incorporated into rotations, and increases made in the number of rotational courses; livestock stints have been reassessed; and modifications have been made to the management of fallows. Provided that the pace of change has been gradual, it has usually been possible for commonfields to adapt themselves to it.

Problems have, however, arisen when the pace and nature of change have been more revolutionary. In England, for instance, although economic and technological developments rendered commonfield agriculture increasingly anachronistic from the fifteenth century onward, so that enclosure by agreement began to make quiet but steady progress, the final demise of the system did not come until the nineteenth century. Even then, it took powerful economic forces and strong vested interests, combined with the facility of enclosure by Act of Parliament, before the last bastions of the system fell. During this final period, commonfield agriculture was much castigated by agricultural writers so that it became widely regarded as a moribund and inefficient system. This verdict has tended to color contemporary Western attitudes to communally managed resources in general and has been used to support a strong preference for privatized property systems in particular. Yet recent research into the productivity of English agriculture before and after enclosure has begun to challenge this traditional orthodoxy. Thus, R. C. Allen has argued that English commonfield farmers achieved major productivity gains during the seventeenth and eighteenth centuries, and has further argued that the major economic consequence of enclosure was not a gain in productivity, but the redistribution of agricultural income in favour of landlords (1982, 1991).

Yet in the Andes, the question of enclosure remains very much a live issue. Much privatization of former commonfield land has already taken place, by one means or another, in those areas where agriculture has been most strongly exposed to commercial penetration (Heath, Buechler, and Erasmus 1969, 192; Rodríguez-Pastor 1969, 86; Mamani 1973, 87–88; Preston 1974, 247; Mayer 1981, 82; Figueroa 1982, 133). But away from the influence of the Peruvian coastal cities and the chief towns and mining centers of the Bolivian interior, traditional commonfield agriculture continues largely unaffected. Coincidentally, it is in these same areas that the terrain is most rugged and rural poverty greatest, and this poses a major dilemma for those working in development (Eckholm 1976; Thomas 1979; Guillet 1981; Godoy 1983). Should contemporary Andean commonfields be condemned, like their erstwhile English counterparts, as an obstacle to progress and a cause of rural poverty and backwardness? Or should a lesson be drawn from recent reassessments of the English evidence and stress be placed upon the delicate ecological balance that they undoubtedly maintain in this high mountain environment, the moderate rates of technological progress and productivity growth which they are potentially able to sustain, and the sense of corporate identity and solidarity that they nurture in these isolated, materially deprived, and agriculturally dependent communities?

NOTES

1. For the European distribution, see Bloch 1967, 69. For commonfields in New England, see Walcott 1936, 218–52, Bidwell and Falconer 1925, and Field 1985. For Andean commonfields, see Orlove and Godoy 1986. Mesoamerican systems are briefly discussed in Wolf 1966, 20–21. Indian commonfields are described in Chapter 9 of this book. Middle Eastern systems are discussed in Goodell 1976, 60–68; and in Poyck 1962.

2. For an up-to-date review of the literature on English commonfield origins, see Fox 1981, 64–111; and Fenoaltea 1988, 171–240. For a comprehensive treatment of the development of English commonfields, see Baker and Butlin 1973.

3. Pleas for comparative research into commonfield systems have been made by Bloch (1967, 70), Thirsk (1966), and McCloskey (1975, 91).

4. For the late medieval antecedents of the enclosure movement, see Fox 1975, 181–202; and Campbell 1981a.

5. See Godoy 1991 for a consideration of the evolutionary trajectory of Andean commonfield systems.

6. In this context, it should be noted that the main reason that the villagers of Vila Vila, in the north of Potosi, abandoned commonfield tillage was that a frost would kill everyone's potatoes, since all the villagers planted potatoes in the same great commonfield (Mamani 1973, 88).

7. The most usual arrangement is for male coheirs to work a holding as a group: each brother receives the right to work some parcels within each commonfield, and further plot fragmentation is thereby halted (Mamani 1973, 91–92).

8. The complex economics of the changeover from natural to produced fodder, and thus from ox to horse plowing, are discussed in Boserup 1965, 36–39.

9. For agrarian conditions at this time, see Miller and Hatcher 1978.

10. One author has suggested that simple fallowing may not be enough to build up nutrients in the Andes (Yamamoto 1988, 130). For an analysis of the corresponding situation in England see Shiel 1991.

11. These different British field systems are surveyed in Baker and Butlin 1973.

12. For a fuller specification of the diagnostic features of these different commonfield systems, see Campbell 1981b, 112–29.

13. Households will also be faced with a periodic seasonality of agricultural surpluses or deficits, depending upon the amount of land held in the commonfields open to use.

14. This argument is elaborated more fully in Campbell 1981b. On the strength of seignorial power at the time that European commonfields were crystallizing, see Duby 1974. For an illustration of the coincidence between variations in lordship and variations in field systems, see Harley 1958, 8–18; and Roberts 1973, 188–231. For the factors that promoted the institutions of serfdom, see Hatcher 1981, 3–39.

15. The population collapse after the conquest is discussed in Dobyns 1963, 493–515; Smith 1970, 453–64; and Shea 1976, 157–80.

16. For the pattern of rural settlement in Britain, see Roberts 1979 and Astill 1988a.

17. See, for instance, Albo 1977 and Isbell 1978. Earlier echoes of the same theme may be found in the *indigenista* literature, as in Valcarcel 1925 and Castro-Pozo 1936.

18. These reapportionments seem to date from Inca times, when they were used to ensure that all households had the means of meeting tribute obligations to the kings in Cuzco (Murra 1980a, xv). The system was adapted by the Spanish to serve a similar purpose (see Rowe 1957, 182). This practice survives in fossilized form today. The shift from true reallotment to a system of nominal or symbolic reallotment, wherein households continue to use the same parcels year after year, probably reflects a growing shortage of land and concomitant increased specification of individual land rights (Carter 1964, 69; Buechler 1969, 179; Preston 1973, 3).

19. For the existence of unequal holdings among commonfield farmers in Peru, see also Mishkin 1946, 421–22; Soler 1958, 190; Matos Mar 1964, 130–42; and Guillet 1981, 146.

20. For a review of the literature on this subject, see Smith 1984a.

REFERENCES

Alberti, G., and E. Meyer, eds. 1974. *Reciprocidad e intercambio en los Andes peruanos*. Lima: Instituto de Estudios Peruanos.

Albo, X. 1977. *La paradoja aymara*. La Paz: Centro de investigación y promoción del campesinado (CIPCA).

Allen, Robert C. 1982. "The Efficiency and Distributional Consequences of Eighteenth-Century Enclosures." *Economic Journal* 92:937–53.

———. 1991. "The Two English Agricultural Revolutions, 1450–1850." In *Land, Labour and Livestock: Historical Studies in European Agricultural Productivity*, ed. Bruce M. S. Campbell and Mark Overton, 236–54. Manchester: Manchester University Press.

Allison, K. J. 1957. "The Sheep-Corn Husbandry of Norfolk in the Sixteenth and Seventeenth Centuries." *Agricultural History Review* 5:12–30.

———. 1958. "Flock Management in the Sixteenth and Seventeenth Centuries." *Economic History Review*, 2d ser. 11:98–112.

Arguedas, J. M., ed. 1964. *Estudios sobre la cultura actual del Perú*. Lima: Universidad Nacional Mayor de San Marcos.

Astill, Grenville. 1988a. "Rural Settlement: The Toft and Croft." In *The Countryside of Medieval England*, ed. G. Astill and A. Grant, 36–61. Oxford and New York: Blackwell.

———. 1988b. "Fields." In *The Countryside of Medieval England*, ed. G. Astill and A. Grant, 62–85. Oxford and New York: Blackwell.

Ault, W. O. 1965. "Open-Field Husbandry and the Village Community: A Study of Agrarian By-Laws in Medieval England. *Transactions of the American Philosophical Society*, new ser., 55, no. 7.

Bailey, Mark. 1990. "Sand into Gold: The Evolution of the Foldcourse System in West Suffolk, 1200–1600. *Agricultural History Review*, 38:40–57.

Baker, A. R. H. 1964. "Open Fields and Partible Inheritance on a Kent Manor." *Economic History Review*, 2d ser. 17:1–23.

———. 1973. "Field Systems of Southeast England." In *Studies of Field Systems in the British Isles*, ed. A. R. H. Baker and R. A. Butlin, 393–419. Cambridge: Cambridge University Press.

Baker, A. R. H., and R. A. Butlin, eds. 1973. *Studies of Field Systems in the British Isles*. Cambridge: Cambridge University Press.

Baker, A. R. H., and D. Gregory, eds. 1984. *Explorations in Historical Geography: Interpretive Essays*. Cambridge: Cambridge University Press.

Beckett, J. V. 1989. *A History of Laxton*. Oxford: Blackwell.

Bentley, J. W. 1987. "Economic and Ecological Approaches to Land Fragmentation: The Defense of a Much-Maligned Phenomenon." *Annual Review of Anthropology* 16:31–67.

Beresford, M. W. 1948. "Ridge and Furrow and the Open Fields." *Economic History Review*, 2d ser., 1:34–35.

Biddick, K., ed. 1984. *Archaeological Approaches to Medieval Europe*. Kalamazoo, Mich.: Medieval Institute, Western Michigan University.

Bidwell, P., and J. Falconer. 1925. *History of Agriculture in the Northern United States 1620–1860*. New York: Smith.

Bishop, T. A. M. 1935. "Assarting and the Growth of the Open Fields." *Economic History Review* 6:13–29.

Bloch, M. 1967. *Land and Work in Medieval Europe*. Berkeley: University of California Press.

Boserup, E. 1965. *The Conditions of Agricultural Growth: The Economics of Agrarian Change under Population Pressure*. London: Allen and Unwin.

Britton, E. 1977. *The Community of the Vill: A Study in the History of the Family and Village Life in Fourteenth Century England*. Toronto: Macmillan.

Browman, D. L. n.d. "Llama Caravan *Fleteros*, and Their Importance in Production and Distribution." Unpublished manuscript.

Brush, S. 1980. "The Environment and Native Andean Agriculture." *América Indígena* 40:163.

———. 1981. "Estrategías agrícolas tradicionales en las zonas montanosas de América Latina." Seminario internacional sobre producción agropecuaria y forestal en zonas de ladera de America tropical. Informe Téchnico 11. Turrialba, Costa Rica: Centro Agronómico Tropical de Investigación y Ensenanza.

Buechler, H. C. 1969. "Land Reform and Social Revolution in the Northern Altiplano and *Yungas* of Bolivia." In *Land Reform and Social Revolution in Bolivia*, ed. D. Heath, H. Buechler, and C. Erasmus, 179. New York: Praeger.

Caballero, J. M. 1981. *Economía agraria de la sierra peruana*. Lima: Instituto de Estudios Peruanos.

Camino, A., J. Recharte, and P. Bidegaray. 1981. "Flexibilidad calendárica en la agricultura tradicional de las vertientes orientales de los Andes." In *La tecnología en el mundo andino*, ed. H. Lechtman and A. M. Soldi, 169–94. Mexico City: Universidad Nacional Autonoma de México.

Campbell, B. M. S. 1980. "Population Change and the Genesis of Commonfields on a Norfolk Manor." *Economic History Review*, 2d ser., 33:174–92.

———. 1981a. "The Extent and Layout of Commonfields in Eastern Norfolk." *Norfolk Archaeology* 38:5–32.

———. 1981b. "Commonfield Origins—the Regional Dimension." In *The Origins of Open Field Agriculture*, ed. T. Rowley, 112–29. London: Croom Helm.

———. 1981c. "The Regional Uniqueness of English Field Systems? Some Evidence from Eastern Norfolk." *Agricultural History Review* 29:16–28.

———. 1983. "Agricultural Progress in Medieval England: Some Evidence from Eastern Norfolk." *Economic History Review*, 2d ser., 36:26–46.

Carter, W. E. 1964. *Aymará Communities and the Bolivian Agrarian Reform*. Social Science Monograph no. 24. Gainesville: University of Florida.

Carter, W., and M. Mamani. 1982. *Irpa Chico*. La Paz: Juventud.

Castro-Pozo, H. 1936. *Del ayllu al cooperativismo socialista*. Lima: Mejia Baca.

Chambers, J. D., and G. E. Mingay. 1966. *The Agricultural Revolution 1750–1880*. London: Batsford.

Chevallier, F. 1953. *La formation des grands domaines au Mexique: Terre et société XVI–XVII siècles*. Paris: Institut d'Ethnologie, Musée de l'Homme.

122   Bruce Campbell and Ricardo Godoy

Crawford, R. M. M., D. Wishart, and R. M. Campbell. 1970. "A Numerical Analysis of High Altitude Scrub Vegetation in Relation to Soil Erosion in the Eastern Cordilerra." *Journal of Ecology* 58:173–81.

Custred, G. 1974. "Llameros y comercio inter-regional." In *Reciprocidad e intercombio en los Andes peruanos*, ed. G. Alberti and E. Meyer, 252–89. Lima: Instituto de Estudios Peruanos.

Custred, G., and B. Orlove. 1974. "Sectorial Fallowing and Crop Rotation Systems in the Peruvian Highlands." Paper presented at 41st International Congress of Americanists.

Dahlman, C. J. 1980. *The Open Field System and Beyond; A Property Rights Analysis of an Economic Institution*. Cambridge: Cambridge University Press.

Degregori, C., and J. Golte. 1973. *Dependencia y desintegración estructural en la comunidad de Pacaraos*. Lima: Instituto de Estudios Peruanos.

Denevan, W. N., ed. 1976. *The Native Population of the Americas in 1492*. Madison: University of Wisconsin Press.

Dewindt, E. B. 1972. *Land and People in Holywell-cum-Needingworth: Structures of Tenure and Patterns of Social Organization in an East Midlands Village 1252–1457*. Toronto: Pontifical Institute of Mediaeval Studies.

Dobyns, H. 1963. "An Outline of Andean Epidemic History to 1720." *Bulletin of the History of Medicine* 37:493–515.

Dodgshon, R. A. 1980. *The Origin of British Fields Systems: An Interpretation*. London: Academic Press.

———. 1981. "The Interpretation of Subdivided Fields: A Study in Private or Communal Interests?" In *The Origins of Open Field Agriculture*, ed. T. Rowley, 130–44. London: Croom Helm.

Donkin, R. A. 1979. *Agricultural Terracing in the Aboriginal New World*. Tucson: University of Arizona Press.

Duby, G. 1974. *The Early Growth of the European Economy: Warriors and Peasants from the Seventh to the Twelfth Century*. London: Weidenfeld and Nicolson.

Eckholm, E. 1976. *Losing Ground*. New York: Norton.

Elliott, G. 1973. "Field Systems of Northwest England." In *Studies of Field Systems in the British Isles*, ed. A. R. H. Baker and R. A. Butlin, 42–92. Cambridge: Cambridge University Press.

Eyre, S. R. 1955. "The Curving Ploughstrip and its Historical Implications." *Agricultural History Review* 3:80–94.

Fenoaltea, S. 1988. "Transaction Costs, Whig History, and the Common Fields." *Politics and Society* 16, no. 2–3:171–240.

Field, Barry C. 1985. "The Evolution of Individual Property Rights in Massachusetts Agriculture, 17th–19th Centuries." *Northeastern Journal of Agricultural and Resource Economics* 14, no. 2:97–109.

———. 1988. "The Evolution of Property Rights." Department of Agricultural and Resource Economics, University of Massachusetts, Amherst, Mass.

Figueroa, A. 1982. "Production and Market Exchange in Peasant Economies: The Case of the Southern Highlands in Peru." In *Ecology and Exchange in the Andes*, ed. D. Lehmann, 126–56. Cambridge Studies in Social Anthropology no. 41.

Fox, H. S. A. 1975. "The Chronology of Enclosure and Economic Development in Medieval Devon." *Economic History Review*, 2d ser., 28:181–202.

———. 1981. "Approaches to the Adoption of the Midland System." In *The Origins of Open Field Agriculture*, ed. T. Rowley, 64–111. London: Croom Helm.

———. 1984. "Some Ecological Dimensions of Medieval Field Systems." In *Archaeological Approaches to Medieval Europe*, ed. K. Biddick, 119–58. Kalamazoo, Mich.: Medieval Institute, Western Michigan University.

———. 1992. "The Agrarian Context." In *The Origins of the Midland Village*, 36–72. Papers prepared for a discussion session at the Economic History Society's annual conference. Leicester, April.

Freeman, P. 1980. "Ecologically Oriented Agriculture." Unpublished manuscript.

Fujii, T., and H. Tomoeda. 1981. "Chacra, laime y auquénidos." In *Estudios etnográficos del Perú meridional*, ed. S. Masuda, 33–63. Tokyo: Tokyo University.

Gade, D. 1970. "Ecología del robo agrícola en las tierras altas de los Andes centrales." *América Indígena* 30:3–14.

Gade, D., and M. Escobar. 1982. "Village Settlement and the Colonial Legacy in Southern Peru." *Geographical Review* 72:430–49.

Gade, D., and R. Rios. 1976. "La chaquitaclla: herramienta indigena sudamericana." *América Indígena* 36:359–74.

Godoy, R. A. 1983. "From Indian to Miner and Back Again: Small-Scale Mining in the Jukumani Ayllu, Northern Potosi, Bolivia." Ph.D. diss., Columbia University.

———. 1985. "State, Ayllu, and Ethnicity in Northern Potosi." *Anthropos* 80:53–65.

———. 1990. *Mining and Agriculture in Highland Bolivia.* Tucson: University of Arizona Press.

———. 1991. "The Evolution of Common-Field Agriculture in the Andes: A Hypothesis." *Comparative Studies in Society and History* 33, no. 2:395–414.

Goodell, G. 1976. "The Elementary Structures of Political Life." Ph.D. diss., Columbia University.

Goody, J. R., J. Thirsk, and E. P. Thompson, eds. 1976. *Family and Inheritance: Rural Society in Western Europe, 1200–1800.* Cambridge: Cambridge University Press.

Guillet, D. 1979. *Agrarian Reform and Peasant Economy in Southern Peru.* Columbia: University of Missouri Press.

———. 1981. "Land Tenure, Ecological Zone, and Agricultural Regime in the Central Andes." *American Ethnologist* 8:139–56.

Hall, D. 1981. "The Origins of Open-Field Agriculture—the Archaeological Field Evidence." In *The Origins of Open Field Agriculture*, ed. T. Rowley, 23–25. London: Croom Helm.

Harley, J. B. 1958. "Population Trends and Agricultural Developments from the Warwickshire Hundred Rolls of 1279." *Economic History Review*, 2d ser., 11: 8–18.

Harvey, P. D. A., ed. 1984. *The Peasant Land Market in Medieval England.* Oxford: Oxford University Press.

Hatcher, J. 1981. "English Serfdom and Villeinage: Towards a Reassessment." *Past and Present* 90:3–39.

Havinden, M. 1961. "Agricultural Progress in Open-Field Oxfordshire." *Agricultural History Review* 9:73–88.

Heath, D., H. Buechler, and C. Erasmus. 1969. *Land Reform and Social Revolution in Bolivia.* New York: Praeger.

Homans, G. C. 1941. *English Villagers of the Thirteenth Century.* Cambridge, Mass.: Harvard University Press.

Howell, C. 1975. "Stability and Change 1300–1700: The Socio-economic Context of the Self-perpetuating Family Farm in England." *Journal of Peasant Studies* 2:468–82.

Hoyle, B. S., ed. 1974. *Spatial Aspects of Development.* London: Wiley.

Isbell, B. J. 1978. *To Defend Ourselves: Ecology and Ritual in an Andean Village.* Austin: University of Texas Press.

Kerridge, E. 1951. "Ridge and Furrow and Agrarian History." *Economic History Review,* 2d ser., 4:14–36.

Langdon, John. 1986. *Horses, Oxen, and Technological Innovation: The Use of Draught Animals in English Farming from 1066–1500.* Cambridge: Cambridge University Press.

LaBarre, W. 1947. "Potato Taxonomy among the Aymara Indians of Bolivia." *Acta Americana* 6:83–103.

LeBaron, A., et al. 1979. "An Explanation of the Bolivian Highlands Grazing Erosion Syndrome." *Journal of Range Management* 32:201–8.

Lechtman, H., and A. M. Soldi, eds. 1981. *La tecnología en el mundo andino.* Mexico City: Universidad Nacional Autonoma de México.

Lehmann, D., ed. 1982. *Ecology and Exchange in the Andes.* Cambridge Studies in Social Anthropology, no. 41. Cambridge: Cambridge University Press.

Lewellen, T. 1978. *Peasant in Transition: The Changing Economy of the Peruvian Aymara. A General Systems Approach.* Boulder, Colo.: Westview Press.

MacCulloch, Diarmaid. 1979. "Kett's Rebellion in Context." *Past and Present* 84: 36–59.

Málaga Medina, A. 1974. "Las reducciónes en el Perú durante el Virrey Francisco de Toledo." *Anuario de Estudios Americanos* 31:819–42.

Mamani, M. P. 1973. *El rancho de Vila Vila.* La Paz: Consejo Nacional de Reforma Agraria.

Masuda, S., ed. 1981. *Estudios etnográficos del Perú meridional.* Tokyo: Tokyo University.

Matos Mar, J., ed. 1958. *Las actuales comunidades de indígenas: Huarochirí en 1955.* Lima: Instituto de Etnologia y Arqueología.

———. 1964. "La propiedad en la isla de Taquile (Lago Titicaca)." In *Estudios sobre la cultura actual del Peru,* ed. J. M. Arguedas. Lima: Universidad Nacional Mayor de San Marcos.

Mayer, E. 1981. *Uso de la tierra en los Andes: ecología y agricultura en el valle del Mantaro del Perú con referencia especial a la papa.* Lima: Centro Internacional de la Papa.

McBride, G. 1921. *The Agrarian Indian Communities of Highland Bolivia*. New York: Oxford University Press.

McCloskey, D. 1975. "The Persistence of English Common Fields." In *European Peasants and Their Markets*. ed. W. Parker and E. Jones, 73–119. Princeton, N.J.: Princeton University Press.

———. 1976. "English Open Fields as Behaviour toward Risk." *Research in Economic History* 1:124–70.

McPherson, M. F. 1983. "Land Fragmentation in Agriculture: Adverse? Beneficial? and for Whom?" Development and Discussion Paper no. 145. Cambridge, Mass.: Harvard Institute for International Development.

Metraux, A. 1959. "The Social and Economic Structure of the Indian Communities of the Andean Region." *International Labour Review* 74:231.

Miller, E., and J. Hatcher. 1978. *Medieval England—Rural Society and Economic Change 1086–1348*. London: Longman.

Mishkin, B. 1946. "The Contemporary Quechua." In *Handbook of South American Indians*, vol. 2, Bulletin no. 143, ed. J. H. Steward, 411–70. Washington, D.C.: Bureau of Ethnology.

Murra, J. V. 1980a. "Waman Puma, etnógrafo del mundo andino." In J. V. Murra, *El Primer Nueva Coronica y Buen Gobierno*, xiii–xix. Mexico City: Siglo Veintiuno.

———. 1980b. *El Primer Nueva Corónica y Buen Gobierno*. Mexico: Siglo Veintiuno.

Orlove, B. 1976. "The Tragedy of the Commons Revisited: Land Use and Environmental Quality in High-Altitude Andean Grasslands." In *Hill Lands: Proceedings of an International Symposium*, 208–14. Morgantown: West Virginia University Press.

———. 1977. *Alpaca, Sheep, and Men: The Wool Export Economy and Regional Society in Southern Peru*. New York: Academic Press.

Orlove, B., and R. Godoy. 1986. "Andean Sectorial Farming System." *Journal of Ethnobiology* 6:169–204.

Orwin, C. S., and C. S. Orwin. 1967. *The Open Fields*. 3d ed. Oxford: Clarendon Press.

Parker, W., and E. Jones, eds. 1975. *European Peasants and Their Markets*. Princeton, N.J.: Princeton University Press.

Platt, T. 1982. "The Role of the Andean Ayllu in the Reproduction of the Petty Commodity Regime in Northern Potosí (Bolivia)." In *Ecology and Exchange in the Andes*, ed. D. Lehmann, 27–69. Cambridge Studies in Social Anthropology no. 41. Cambridge: Cambridge University Press.

Popkin, S. 1979. *The Rational Peasant*. Berkeley: University of California Press.

Postgate, M. R. 1973. "Field Systems of East Anglia." In *Studies of Field Systems in the British Isles*, ed. A. R. H. Baker and R. A. Butlin, 281–322. Cambridge: Cambridge University Press.

Poyck, A. P. G. 1962. *Farm Studies in Iraq*. Wageningen, Holland: Mededelingen van den Landbouwhogeschool te Wageningen, Nederland 62.

Preston, D. 1973. "Agriculture in a Highland Desert: The Central Altiplano of Bolivia." Department of Geography, Working Paper 18:6. Leeds, England: University of Leeds.

———. 1974. "Land Tenure and Agricultural Development in the Central Altiplano, Bolivia." In *Spatial Aspects of Development*, ed. B. S. Hoyle, 231–51. London: Wiley.

Rasnake, R. 1988. *Domination and Cultural Resistance*. Durham, N. C.: Duke University Press.

Ravines, R. 1978a. "Recursos nasturales de los Andes." In *Tecnología Andina*, ed. R. Ravines. Lima: Instituto de Estudios Peruanos.

———. ed. 1978b. *Tecnología Andina*. Lima: Instituto de Estudios Peruanos.

Razi, Z. 1980. *Life, Marriage, and Death in a Medieval Parish: Economy, Society, and Demography in Halesowen (1270–1400)*. Cambridge: Cambridge University Press.

———. 1981. "Family, Land, and the Village Community in Later Medieval England." *Past and Present* 93:3–36.

Rhoades, R. E., and S. I. Thompson. 1975. "Adaptive Strategies in Alpine Environments: Beyond Ecological Particularism." *American Ethnologist* 2:535–51.

Roberts, B. K. 1973. "Field Systems of the West Midlands." In *Studies of Field Systems in the British Isles*, ed. A. R. H. Baker and R. A. Butlin, 188–231. Cambridge: Cambridge University Press.

———. 1979. *Rural Settlement in Britain*. London: Hutchinson.

Rodríguez-Pastor, H. 1969. "Progresismo y cambios en Llica." In *La Comunidad Andina*, ed. J. R. Sabogal Wiesse, 73–143. Mexico City: Instituto Indigenista Interamericano.

Rowe, J. H. 1957. "The Incas under Spanish Colonial Institutions." *Hispanic American Historical Review* 37:182.

Rowley, T., ed. 1981. *The Origins of Open Field Agriculture*. London: Croom Helm.

Sabogal Wiesse, J. R., ed. 1969. *La Comunidad Andina*. Mexico City: Instituto Indigenista Interamericano.

Seebohm, F. 1883. *The English Village Community*. London: Longmans, Green.

Shea, D. 1976. "A Defense of Small Population Estimates for the Central Andes in 1520." In *The Native Population of the Americas in 1492*, ed. W. N. Denevan, 157–80. Madison: University of Wisconsin Press.

Sheppard, J. A. 1966. "Pre-enclosure Field and Settlement Patterns in an English Township, Wheldrake, Near York." *Georgrafiska Annaler*, ser. B, 48:59–77.

Shiel, Robert S. 1991. "Improving Soil Fertility in the Pre-Fertiliser Era." In *Land, Labour and Livestock: Historical Studies in European Agricultural Productivity*, ed. Bruce M. S. Campbell and Mark Overton, 51–77. Manchester: Manchester University Press.

Simpson, A. 1958. "The East Anglian Foldcourse; Some Queries." *Agricultural History Review* 6:87–96.

Smith, C. T. 1970. "Depopulation of the Central Andes in the 16th Century." *Current Anthropology* 11:453–64.

Smith, R. M. 1979. "Kin and Neighbours in a Thirteenth Century Suffolk Community." *Journal of Family History* 4:219–59.

————. 1984a. "'Modernization' and the Corporate Medieval Village Community in England: Some Skeptical Reflections." In *Explorations in Historical Geography: Interpretive Essays*, ed. A. R. H. Baker and D. Gregory, 140–94. Cambridge: Cambridge University Press.

————, ed. 1984b. *Land, Kinship, and Life-Cycle*. Cambridge: Cambridge University Press.

Soler, E. 1958. "La comunidad de San Pedro de Huancaire." In *Las actuales comunidades de indigenas: Huarochirí en 1955*, ed. J. Matos Mar, 167–257. Lima: Instituto de Etnología y Argueología.

Steward, J. H., ed. 1946. *Handbook of South American Indians*. Vol. 2, Bulletin no. 143. Washington, D.C.: Bureau of Ethnology.

Tandeter, E. 1981. "Forced and Free Labour in Late Colonial Potosi." *Past and Present* 93:98–136.

Tate, W. E. 1967. *The English Village Community and the Enclosure Movements*. London: Gollancz.

Thirsk, J. 1964. "The Common Fields." *Past and Present* 29:3–9.

————. 1966. "The Origins of the Common Fields." *Past and Present* 33:143.

Thomas, B. 1979. "Effects of Change on High Mountain Adaptive Patterns." In *High-Altitude Geoecology*, ed. P. J. Webber, 139–88. Boulder, Colo.: Westview Press.

Turner, M. 1982. "Agricultural Productivity in England in the Eighteenth Century: Evidence from Crop Yields." *Economic History Review*, 2d ser., 35:489–510.

————. 1984. *Enclosures in Britain 1750–1830*. London: Macmillan.

Urioste, M. 1977. *La economía del campesinado altiplánico en 1976*. La Paz: Universidad Católica Boliviana.

Valcarcel, L. 1925. *Del ayllu al imperio*. Lima: Editorial Garcilaso.

Walcott, R. 1936. "Husbandry in Colonial New England." *New England Quarterly* 9:218–52.

Webber, P. J., ed. 1979. *High-Altitude Geoecology*. Boulder, Colo.: Westview Press.

Winterhalder, B., R. Larsen, and B. Thomas. 1974. "Dung as an Essential Resource in a Highland Peruvian Community." *Human Ecology* 2:89–104.

Wolf, E. 1966. *Peasants*. Englewood Cliffs, N.J.: Prentice-Hall.

Wordie, J. R. 1983. "The Chronology of English Enclosure, 1500–1914.": *Economic History Review*, 2d ser., 36:483–505.

Yamamoto, N. 1988. "Papa, llama, y chaquitaclla. Una perspectiva etnobotánica de la cultura andina." In *Recursos Naturales Andinos*, ed. S. Masuda, 111–52. Tokyo: University of Tokyo.

Yelling, J. A. 1977. *Common Field and Enclosure in England, 1450–1850*. London: Macmillan.

6

Institutional Dynamics: The Evolution and Dissolution of Common-Property Resource Management

James T. Thomson, David Feeny, and Ronald J. Oakerson

Institutional arrangements for the management of common-property resources are created in particular settings and evolve as responses to certain combinations of circumstances. A full understanding of the evolution and survival of such arrangements thus requires dynamic analysis of case studies. The framework presented by Oakerson in Chapter 3 of this book may be applied recursively to examine dynamic sequences of change. Thus, responses to exogenous shocks in one period become part of the existing set of institutional arrangements in the next, affecting the subsequent path of institutional evolution.

The dynamic sequences of change in the management of forest resources in Niger (1884–1984) and land resources in Thailand (1850–1990) are the subjects of this chapter. By applying Oakerson's framework iteratively, changes in both individual strategies and decision-making arrangements may be made endogenous. The approach is applied at both the local and the supra-local level.

In both cases exogenous changes in population and market opportunities combined to make the common-property resource more valuable. Utilization of the resource increased to accommodate the subsistence needs of a growing population. The trend was reinforced by expanding market opportunities at the local, national, and international levels. The response to growing scarcity was a search for new arrangements to manage the resource more effectively.

In each case, too, the behavior of the state was important in affecting the choice of new arrangements. In the Niger case, especially in the colonial period, the government's lack of accountability to constituencies of resource users meant that new, socially inefficient arrangements could be gradually imposed. In Thailand, in spite of the general lack of democratic forms of government, indigenous regimes provided new arrangements that better served the interests of the resource users. The key difference between the two cases is, however, not merely the type of regime and degree of its accountability to those whom it governed. Elite Thai decision makers shared in the gains created by the provision of the new property relations. Their interests affected the possibilities of innovation.

Given the existing constitutional structures in each case, basic changes in institutional arrangements relevant to resource management required that the central government take some action. The local arena is, however, also important in shaping the interpretation, enforcement, and operational meaning of the new and existing arrangements. In the Zinder (Niger) woodstock case, arrangements extralegal by national standards, but increasingly legitimate in local eyes, are becoming relevant as well. In the Thai case, traditional patterns of the exploitation of land resources were retained in spite of the lack of official sanction and eventually legal compromises were introduced that served to officially recognize actual practices, and formerly extralegal arrangements. In each case, the changes in institutional arrangements occurred within and were linked to the ongoing evolution in the system of resource exploitation. The evolution of each system will be briefly described.

The Zinder Woodstock Case

During the first half-century of relative abundance (1884–1935), the woodstock was subdivided on a de facto basis into three parts:

- a series of small local common properties around settled areas
- an undifferentiated common-property resource composed of all remaining undeveloped bushland
- a de jure statewide commons for one tree, *Acacia albida*, which is widely valued and protected for its agroforestry properties (Pelisser 1980; Weber and Hoskins 1983, 9–15)

At the beginning of the forty-year period of rough equilibrium (1935–1974), colonial legislation imposed a de jure common-property status on the fifteen most valuable tree species (including *A. albida*). Management authority was centralized for the protected species at the colony level. Colonial foresters created a small force of forest guards, assisted by local informers, to enforce these rules in rural areas. But enforcers were so few as to be relatively ineffectual in those places they did patrol. In other areas, the forest service simply did not make its presence felt. Nonprotected species remained a common-property resource, management of which was left to evolve in light of local concerns. Given extensive undeveloped bushland in the immediate vicinity, few residents of the Zinder area perceived any real scarcity of wood or any real reason for woodstock management.

In the final ten-year stage of relative scarcity (1974–1984), the fifteen-species common property remained a state concern and off limits to unauthorized users. In consequence, rough species were nearly destroyed and pressure, generated by the demands of a growing population, mounted on protected species. An attempt to organize common-property village woodlots failed because the technical forestry package was inadequate, commons regulations remained inchoate, and rules governing management were never specified. Though it is fair to suppose more elaborate management regulations for the common woodstock might have arisen as local people perceived wood shortages, such rules were not developed because the postindependence state maintained the preemption and centralization of management authority. One result has been the recent emergence of individual attempts by peasants to assert personal rights to the trees growing on their own land.

The Thai Land Rights Case

In the nineteenth century, a reliable market developed for surplus paddy production. Subsistence agriculture became increasingly commercialized. As land became more valuable, disputes over commons-land ownership became endemic, inducing a series of innovations in institutional arrangements that resulted in the privatization of arable land in Thailand. Ultimately, in the early twentieth century, national legislation established a land-titling system by cadastral survey.[1] This law was the culmination of successive attempts to reduce or resolve land disputes.

For land rights in Thailand, neither jointness nor excludability posed prohibitive problems, given the fixed, immovable character of land and the technology available for excluding others, as well as for exploiting it. Divisibility posed no theoretical problem. As rice cultivation spread in response to world market demand, however, divisibility was at the heart of efforts to firm up land titles to parts of the original commons.

Institutional Innovation

Pressure for privatization was the result of change, in both the Zinder and the Thai cases. It is probably not coincidental that both cultures are characterized by a high degree of individualistic behavior. It should be stressed, however, that in the Zinder woodstock case, privatization by peasants is far from a foregone conclusion. Effective subdivision of the woodstock commons into discrete, individually controlled units remains legally impossible and highly problematic today. In the Thai case, continued management of land as a common-property resource was improbable, given the combination of factors at work. The world market impact on the local economy during the nineteenth century stimulated the replacement of usufruct cultivation with intensive exploitation of private arable land.

In addition to examining each of the case studies within the Oakerson framework, we will analyze the Thai case explicitly (and the Zinder case implicitly) in terms of a simple supply-and-demand model of institutional change. In the supply-and-demand model, the demand for institutional change arises when some gain cannot be captured under existing institutional arrangements.[2] Changes in relative factor or product prices, changes in the size of markets, changes in technology, and changes in the fundamental decision rules of government are among the important variables that create disequilibria in the existing institutional arrangements. Whether institutional change will occur depends, however, on the supply of institutional change—the willingness and capability of the fundamental institutions of government to provide, permit, or prevent new arrangements. The capability depends in part on the cost of institutional innovation, which in turn depends in part on the stock of existing knowledge about the design and operation of institutions. The willingness to provide new arrangements also depends greatly on the private benefits and costs of change to the agents who are in a position to provide it, namely, the elite decision makers of government. Thus the existing set of institutions and initial distribution of power will have an important impact on the kinds of new institutional arrangements that are supplied.

Institutional change, then, arises through the interactions of the demand for and supply of change in dynamic sequences. The institutional response in one period becomes part of the initial conditions in the next, thus affecting the subsequent path of change.

Institutional innovations in both Zinder and Thailand contrast with those reported in Chapter 4 by McKean in her analysis of Japanese woodlots. In Zinder the French colonial state sought to impose a commons management. Because management was so ineffective, peasants have recently attempted informal privatization. By contrast, in Thailand the state, major landholders, and peasants all pressured for privatization.

In the Japanese case, local village decision-making authority and tradition facilitated continuing effective local management of the village's common woodlot, despite changing circumstances, for more than three centuries. In the Thai and Zinder cases, new rules to exclude potential users of the resource were officially adopted (Thailand) or attempted on a de facto basis (Zinder). In the Japanese woodlot case, the rules governing inclusion in the group of those who had rights to use the commons were instead retained and refined. Thus, although increased scarcity will in general lead to pressures for some change in institutional arrangements, neither privatization nor state control is the inevitable outcome (in addition to Chapters 1 and 13 of this book, see Bromley 1989, Ostrom 1990, Berkes et al. 1989, Feeny et al. 1990).

Woodstock Management in the Sahel

In the arid West African Sahel around Zinder, changing patterns of woodstock management illustrate several rounds of institutional evolution as population pressure mounted, supplies of wood as a renewable resource eroded, and various actors attempted to deal with the problem.

The Zinder region lies in the south-central portion of present-day Niger. Its southern boundary is established by the country's common border with Nigeria. The area centers on Zinder, a regional town some 200 miles north of Kano, the major city of northern Nigeria. A century ago, a Sahelian state, the Sultanate of Damagaram, was expanding rapidly to the south and east from its seat at Zinder.

The dominant ethnic group in the sultanate leadership were Beriberi. They were related to the Kanuri peoples who, a thousand years earlier, had established the Kanem-Bornu Empire at Lake Chad. Damagaram in the late nineteenth century was expanding largely by incorporating the western frontier kingdoms of that empire as it faded (Salifou 1971). The sultanate comprised Beriberi and Hausa agriculturalists, Fulbe transhumant pastoralists, and eventually Twareg pastoralists and their associated slaves. Because these populations, and their major production systems, have persisted largely unchanged during the ensuing century, they will be briefly described to provide a background context for the changing patterns of woodstock use and management.

Both Beriberi and Hausa groups engaged in sedentary agriculture, some of it based on shifting cultivation around small rural villages and towns. Most rural families cultivated millet and sorghum, peanuts, cotton, and tobacco, and kept small herds of goats and some sheep and cows. Peoples in these groups, in addition to destroying marginal

amounts of woodstock when clearing lands for agriculture, used woodstock resources for fuel, construction, fencing, tools, and foods. Their
animals browsed woodstocks around settlements, but did not impede
woodstock regeneration in an era of abundant land and forests. Fields in
that era were fallowed for long periods and not allowed to become
exhausted. Bushes and trees rapidly reestablished themselves on these
lands.

Eighty years later, by 1970, growth of human and livestock populations posed major threats to the woodstock, and continue to do so today.
Agricultural land clearing is clearly the major cause of deforestation in the
Zinder area, as it is throughout the Sahel. In addition, domestic livestock
are permitted to forage freely from November on, during the six-month
dry season following the annual harvest. Particularly in years when
animals are redundant, they browse tree and bushes severely, and often
destroy seedlings.

Damagaram lay astride one of the major nineteenth-century trans-
Saharan trading routes. Control over that trade was a key element in the
Damagaram political economy. To ensure control, the Damagaram leaders
made common cause with their erstwhile enemies, the Berber Kel Owe
Twareg. The latter were desert-edge pastoralists who engaged, depending
on the season and opportunity, in stock raising, warfare, slave raiding,
and long-distance trade in salt, Korans, gold, slaves, and foodstuffs, as
well as in metal working and sedentary agriculture. In return for access to
land, an autonomous judicial system, and rights to a share of the booty
from annual dry-season forays against Hausa, Fulbe, and Kanuri kingdoms to the south and east, the Kel Owe collaborated with Damagaram
expansion strategies, paid nominal taxes, and supplied the state with
indispensable imports from North Africa.

In order to consolidate their control over the area and to develop its
economic potential, both Beriberi and Kel Owe Twareg settled black slaves
taken in war and during raids on frontier lands within the state. In the
contemporary era, Twareg and the Bugaje people, descendants of the
Twareg slaves, continue to live separately from the Hausa and Beriberi.
Many Twareg and Bugaje communities still maintain a distinctive form of
land-use management that allows them to combine forestry, stock raising,
and field crops in the same production system. But population pressure
and the rules of Maliki Muslim inheritance law have combined to fragment
land holdings to the point where traditional agro-silvo-pastoral management systems have ruptured. Like other residents of the Zinder region,
Twareg and Bugaje now contribute to woodstock destruction through
land clearing, shortened fallows, overbrowsing, and lopping of trees and
bushes to meet stock and domestic needs.

In addition to the Beriberi and Hausa sedentary peoples, and the

Twareg and Bugaje, transhumant pastoral Fulbe groups move north and south over the Zinder territory, following the seasons and pastures with their herds of zebu cattle, sheep, and goats. The Fulbe generally frequented the uncultivated areas between settlements. Their demands on the woodstock, in an era of abundance, were limited to browsing bushes and small trees. Over the last two decades, Fulbe herders have become locked in an increasingly bitter struggle with sedentary Hausa and Beriberi groups over access to forage for their animals (Thomson 1985, 232–37). As land clearing has eliminated the last virgin woods and sedentary farmers, caught in a land squeeze, have shortened their fallows, traditional areas and sources of forage for Fulbe herds have been sharply reduced or have disappeared. In consequence, particularly during the dry season, Fulbe have had to exploit woodstock resources ever more fully in order to survive. Between December and May, Fulbe pastoralists now lop large leafy branches from the remaining trees on farmers' fields, often under cover of darkness, in order to provide their herds with vital green protein. These animals, along with sedentary herds, intensify the pressure on tree and bush seedlings. This negative dynamic can be expected to continue until such time as rural people are given the authority to establish and enforce management regulations for local land use. It is probable that with effective local regulation, woodstock productivity could be dramatically increased, and so provide important inputs for all local production systems.

Before woodstock abundance gave way to scarcity in the Zinder area, trees were managed passively. People simply allowed natural regeneration to reclaim fallowed fields. Though their usefulness was recognized, trees were generally taken for granted because supplies more than met demand. Trees on village lands (typically 1 to 2 square miles in all) were apparently dealt with as a common-property resource, but access and use rules were probably very loose given the abundance of wood at that time.

As colonial foresters perceived wood scarcities elsewhere in the French West African empire, an important part of the woodstock was declared by colonial government fiat to be a common-property resource, subject to management at the colony level. This imposed management system has since proven to be largely ineffective, and woodstock capital is under increasingly serious threat. As a consequence of institutional stalemates within the forest service and the national government, some peasants are now moving, often by formally illegal means, to privatize parts of the woodstock. For them, this now appears to be the cheapest option for preserving their own dwindling wood supplies against complete destruction.

On the basis of woodstock supply and demand, the century can be divided into three distinct periods: (1) 1884–1935, or relative abundance; (2) 1935–1974, or equilibrium; (3) 1974–1984, or increasing scarcity.

Relative Abundance, 1884–1935

Resource attributes. The physical attributes of the resource and the techniques for controlling and exploiting it remained roughly constant throughout the three periods. The full description provided here will thus not be repeated for the two later periods. The local woodstock is clearly a renewable resource, composed of all the woody vegetation in the area (Thomson 1983, 167–71). It can be exploited on a sustained-yield basis by various users for different purposes, so long as demand does not cut into woodstock capital and impair the process of effective renewal. The limiting condition here on joint use is set by the productive capacity of a given woodstock. This capacity may be gradually enriched; it may also be impaired by overcutting. Unless patrols are mounted (which they have not been), exclusion is feasible only within an area which can be enclosed by traditional fences. Such areas will usually be of limited size—gardens and residential compounds, for example—because thorn fences require substantial investment of labor. Fields are not generally enclosed.

The Bugaje agro-silvo-pastoral communities are, however, exceptional in this regard: they collectively fenced their lands. Each community was subdivided into a variable number of quarters or sections, organized over time as new groups arrived in a village and took up land. Within each quarter, families resided on their own fields, which were laid out in long, contiguous, parallel strips. Each family managed its land as a separate enterprise. But the residents of each quarter jointly maintained a common fencing system that both enclosed all quarter fields and separated all the quarter's fields from its fallows (Nicolas 1962; Thomson 1976, 261–64).

Decision-making arrangements. Rules and institutions governing woodstock use during this initial period of excess supply were appropriately simple. People planted and owned privately at least two tree species, the baobab (*Adansonia digitata*) and the date palm (*Phoenix dactylifera*), because they produced valued foods. A third species, *Acacia albida* (*gawo* in Hausa, with the plural *gawuna*), was protected by the fiat ruling of Tenimun, sultan of Damagaram from 1851 to 1885. This tree, already mentioned as part of the statewide commons, has long been prized and selectively cultured in many Sahelian arable areas. It fertilizes the soil, recycling leached nutrients. It also fixes nitrogen and facilitates uptake of phosphorus in cereal crops (National Academy of Sciences 1983, 13). Sultan Tenimun reportedly had those who cut the *gawo* put to death (Salifou 1971, 7). All other tree species formed an open-access resource that anyone was at liberty to exploit. Trees were relatively plentiful during that period (Thomson 1983, 169-71). People viewed them more as a nuisance to cultivation than as a valuable good, even though they recognized that leaf litter and wood ashes sharply improved soil fertility.

The woodstock could have been subdivided by allocating discrete portions to individual owners of land where trees grew but this was never done. This would have modified traditional rules, which instead separated land tenure from tree tenure, and permitted overlapping property rights and different systems of effective control of land and woodstock resources within the same piece of real property. As noted, some peasants are now trying, a century later, to effect this change. During the period of relative abundance, however, divisibility remained a moot point because wood was freely available and off-field supplies more than met demand.

Interactions. The interactions that resulted remained largely nonconflictual because different demands for the good were not yet competitive (supply exceeded demand). Indeed, the only time that use rules might have resulted in conflict was when the Zinder sultan ruled by fiat against cutting *A. albida*. It is not clear from available data whether people generally accepted the sultan's assertion of authority in this matter as legitimate. At the end of the period, which came midway through the colonial era (1899–1960), wood was still plentiful; much unexploited bushland still existed in the Zinder area, and people continued to found new hamlets in unsettled regions.

Outcomes. Interactions changed little. The dynamics of wood production and consumption appear to have varied little during the entire period. We have no information about the extent to which cutting of *gawo* seedlings was policed and punished under the precolonial regime. Under the early colonial government, presumably, little would have been done along those lines, since the impact of consistent population growth was yet to be felt. In this case, the supply of forest products generated by passive management of the woodstock in the Zinder area, which consisted of regular fallowing after brief periods of extensive cultivation, plus large areas of uncultivated bush, covered demand. The need for active management of a renewable resource was not yet perceived by local residents.

Equilibrium, 1935–1974

Attributes of the Resource. During the first half of this forty-year period, woodstock users still did not interfere with each other in exploiting the common property. Demand could still be satisfied. Nor did exclusion conditions change: barbed wire appeared in the area only after 1960, and then only in small amounts financed by foreign donors. The woodstock was potentially divisible, but economic considerations militated against it. Demand for wood did not yet justify the investment in fencing or patrols to enforce exclusion. In most of the Zinder hinterland, wood was not sold until well into the 1960s.

Decision-Making Arrangements. Existing legal limits (forestry code rules) and political constraints, which might have hindered subdivision by individuals, were not tested at this point. Somewhat larger units, based on either quarters or villages, might have served as appropriate levels at which to devise common resource management efforts when scarcity became apparent toward the end of the period, if the state-imposed rules that emasculated local organization had been relaxed. As it happened, most villages had lost their power of independent activity as the result, first, of the colonial, and then of the independent regime's efforts to establish controls over major forms of organization in rural areas. Villages (or village quarters) had no authority to enforce sanctions against violators of locally devised use rules. In practice, few such rules appear to have been made.

The year 1935 saw the founding of the French West African forest service, charged with overall responsibility for managing the woodstock. A few French tropical foresters had concluded that deforestation trends then becoming apparent, if unchecked, would threaten and perhaps destroy the resource. In accord with the metropolitan French forestry tradition, which vested in the forestry department relatively extensive controls over the exploitation of the woodstock outside national domain lands, colonial legislation simply arrogated to the colonial regime authority to regulate wood use in the colonies. Because colonial subjects—the vast majority of the population in the Sahelian colonies—had at the time no effective political or legal recourse against these centralizing initiatives, and little power to force colonial officials to take account of local conditions, individual rules included in the French West African imperial forestry code reflected precious little sense of local realities. Small forestry agencies were set up by French administrators in each colony to implement central policies elaborated through a bureaucratic process and imposed through the colonial administrative hierarchy.

This legislation defined far-reaching changes in the regulation of woodstock use. First, it provided for creation of state forests, subject to exclusive forest-service control concerning woodstock and land use. Second, and much more important, it centralized in the forestry service the authority to regulate the exploitation of the fifteen most valuable species of trees outside, as well as inside, the state forests. New regulations prohibited cutting live specimens, or lopping branches above the height of

10 feet without an authorization (provided free by the forestry service if trees were destined for personal use) or a cutting permit (sold to the holder if the wood was to be harvested for sale). Other provisions of the forestry code left intact local customary rights to exploit nonprotected species.

This restructuring of controls on woodstock exploitation amounted, on one level, to a simple broadening of the prerogative to protect valuable trees first asserted in the area by the precolonial sultan Tenimun. Those who wrote the code provisions clearly foresaw the day when wood would become a scarce and valued commodity. They sought to set up rules to reduce consumption, or at least shift demand from valuable to rough tree species.

On another level, however, the French West African imperial forestry code formalized control over the commons. The code removed, or drastically restricted, what had hitherto been fairly broad local-level discretion in dealing with woodstock management. Although little, if anything, had been done along these lines before 1935, because wood was plentiful, the option of developing local management solutions presumably existed before forestry code legislation eliminated the prerogative. As a result of the forestry code, devising new local political solutions to management problems became a much more difficult and expensive process.

Although most regulations outlined above were, at best, sporadically enforced, villagers recognized foresters' authority to control woodstock use. Very few if any attempted to establish alternative controls on access and use. The independent state of Niger inherited and maintained the common-property framework institutionalized in the forestry code imposed by the French.

Interactions. With the creation of the forestry code and the formalized, colony-level commons, a whole new series of interactions gradually arose. Nothing changed until the forestry service managed to patrol an area. Once it did, and forest guards began to impose fines, new patterns of behavior arose. As a result peasants may have left more trees on fields than they otherwise would have. Aware however, that they would not subsequently be allowed to cut protected species without special authorization issued by a forester, they may have done a more systematic job of surreptitiously destroying seedlings.

Enforcement pressure mounted. Foresters regularly blamed and fined landowners for any trees illegally felled on their fields. Those who feared fines for harvesting live trees on their own land cut the wood they needed in remaining areas of bush. Some cut surreptitiously on others' land. Eventually, in the early years after independence, some landowners began to discourage cutting on their property when they found people in the act.

Some simply told cutters to stop. Other landowners said they would reveal violators' names to the forest guards if the latter threatened to fine them for the code violation. But few landowners ever complained to forest guards about illegal cutting, or asked for their help in controlling it.

To assist with identification of code violators, foresters hired local informants. Often these men were traditional policemen attached to canton chiefs. Peasants soon realized they could bribe the informants to steer a touring forester away from a fresh stump. A number of people adopted this strategy, calculating that it would in most cases be far cheaper to bribe than to pay the fine. Here, a new interaction may be noted: peasants who were caught by a forest guard did what they could to reduce the fine. Local people saw this as a process of bribe bargaining. Because almost all were illiterate, few knew details of the forestry code, and few knew what actually became of the money. In any case, receipts were seldom issued by enforcing officers (Thomson 1977, 64–71). Most forest guards probably did profit illegally from their power to fine forestry code violators.

Perceiving no need, people planted very few trees until at least the mid-1960s. At most, some planted shade trees in courtyards or fruit trees—mangoes, guavas, and date palms—in gardens, where they could be protected against animal and human damage. But none planted trees in fields or did very much to preserve natural regeneration there. Because others might cut without permission what field-owners planted or protected, investments in future woodstock supply made little sense. The potential still existed for investments to renew the woodstock once available wood supplies no longer met demand, or perhaps even earlier, when shortages began to appear. But the new rules of the game made investments in augmenting the stock of trees much more problematic.

The outcome is particularly unfortunate when silvo-agriculturalists would willingly preserve certain seedlings on their fields to fertilize soils and improve harvests if they felt confident they could trim, lop, or cut trees as needed. Such is not the case, however. Farmers unwilling to risk that trees may eventually overshadow crops, or attract birds that would destroy ripening millet and sorghum, will simply eradicate seedlings rather than leave themselves with no recourse if they end up with too many trees on their fields. Limited questionnaire data from the area (Thomson 1982) and in-depth interviews during 1971 and 1972 strongly suggest that most landowners accepted the proposition that foresters control the use of trees on lands villagers own and farm. This division of authority over the two resources, which reflects traditional land and tree property rules in some African areas, means that they will not often be managed as an integrated renewable unit.

Outcome. Up until the very end of this intermediate period of relative equilibrium between the supply of and demand for woodstock products, the patterns of resource exploitation and mismanagement that flowed from the structure of decision-making arrangements had little direct effect on peoples' lives in the Zinder area. The price of wood did begin to rise slowly in Zinder, the regional center, and a firewood market developed in some rural settings, supplementing the existing markets in building poles. But shortages did not really appear in the rural area surrounding Zinder. Furthermore, people did not really perceive the woodstock destruction caused by their actions, whether through direct cutting of mature trees or deliberate destruction of seedlings.

Relative Scarcity, 1974–1984

The landscape has changed somewhat since the early 1960s, but few places are totally cleared of trees. Instead, one still finds rather impressive stands of *A. albida* in particular, and, in scattered, interspersed sites, other protected and rough species. Everywhere the scrub bushes *Guira senegalensis* and *Combretum micranthum* appear, apparently indestructible and forever a part of cultivated fields.

Resource Attributes. In general, the limits of joint use, without one person's use imposing a burden on others, have been reached throughout the Zinder area. Few indeed are the places where all can find the wood they need. Instead, each person's harvesting reduces the amount available for other people, increases the time they spend harvesting, and adds to the general overexploitation of the woodstock. Exclusion through fencing remains largely impossible because neither foreign nor adequate local materials are available at reasonable cost. Those who use branches from protected thorn trees (*A. albida*, *A. senegal*, *A. scorpioides*, and others) risk fines at the hands of roving forest guards.

The resource can in fact be subdivided in a few special situations—through garden and compound enclosures, for example. Such plantings have increased recently. Fenced village woodlots have also been created in some communities since 1974 as a matter of state policy, through foreign-financed projects.

Decision-Making Arrangements. The central government and donor organizations introduced common-property village woodlots on a trial basis, beginning in 1974 in the Zinder area. This ever so slightly changed the character of rules governing woodstock exploitation. The new system involved creation of a new set of formal and working rules for the small, 1-to-4 hectare plots fenced with barbed wire and financed by foreign assistance. The land for woodlots was "donated" by villagers. Often the burden fell on the village headman as the individual possessing the most land, and thus best able to bear the loss of cropland or fallow "for the common good."

Formal rules specified by foresters supervising implementation of these projects were minimal: within the project context, village volunteers, in exchange for token wage payments (equivalent to about half the then daily rate for field labor), were to clear land, fence the plot, excavate planting holes, and plant seedlings (mainly exotic neem and eucalyptus, poorly adapted to plantation forestry under local arid conditions). They were then to cultivate peanuts or other leguminous food crops (to insure weeds would not smother the newly planted tree seedlings), and generally watch over the plot. No formal agreement defined the system of distribution. Forest guards who supervised creation of the woodlots asserted that the lots were "for the villagers" and that the wood produced there "belongs to the villagers."

Villagers remained skeptical. Many assumed the woodlots really belonged to the government or to the forest service, which they feared would claim the wood when it wanted to, without further compensation for villagers' efforts (Thomson 1980). As far as the rest of the woodstock is concerned, common-property rules remain unchanged. The forestry code, as interpreted by local forest guards, still provides for centralized control over use of protected species. Remaining rough species are exploited subject to local use regulations, often highly informal in nature.

Interactions. Because villagers conclude that the new woodlots will benefit the government, not them, they try to minimize their inputs. In most cases they kill off seedlings by benign neglect: when the fence collapses, or when animals break through it, they do nothing to protect trees. Most trees die quickly, if not from overbrowsing then from drought. As for protected species, little has changed from earlier periods, although in some villages illegal use of wood growing on others' fields may have increased. In any case, many villagers are beginning to perceive the growing wood shortage.

Some react as usual, allowing the cutting to occur because they feel that the trees do not belong to them. A second class of landowners, frightened about fines, try either to stop illegal cutting on their land or to identify responsible parties so they can escape paying unjust fines by naming the real violators. Finally, some individuals have begun to defend the trees on their fields when they have the chance. They chase off would-be cutters, asserting a personal right to the trees by virtue of ownership of the land on which they grow.[3] This smaller group of individuals is intent on changing the working rules of wood use as previously accepted in the locality. Some take their disputes to village moots or before canton chiefs. To prevent destruction of trees on their fields, others stand up to cutters authorized by the forestry service to harvest wood for commercial use. In neighboring areas, individual field owners have begun to take authorized woodcutters before the arrondissement foresters, to inquire why the latter allow cutters to chop down trees on their fields. The foresters generally reply they never authorize cutting trees on fields, but only in the bush. But the bush has for all practical purposes been destroyed throughout the Zinder area.

Around Zinder, some field owners have begun during this period to make use of the Qur'an, considered for this purpose to be a magical fetish, in order to identify timber poachers and wood stealers and force return of their property. A few even go so far as to place a future Qur'anic prohibition on all unauthorized harvesting of wood on their fields, despite the fact that this conflicts with recent national-level prohibitions on such use of the Qur'an. The village woodlots, as presently organized, are a fatally flawed experiment in commons management. Those who established them failed to address the most fundamental concerns of putative producer-users: they gave no effective guarantees of property rights to the latter, nor did they provide any information about the distribution of trees or wood produced. Users legitimately concluded they would derive no or at best little benefit.

Attempts by individuals to police wood on fields, and thus in effect to establish private-property rights over those trees, represent efforts to parcel out the commons. It is not yet clear what, if anything, these efforts will produce by way of code changes.

Outcomes. State-organized attempts to reforest through a program of village woodlots have demonstrated once again to villagers in the Zinder area that such efforts will not help them, at least as presently organized. They remain highly suspicious of both the technical feasibility of woodlots and the eventual distribution of any wood produced. For villagers, collective woodlots amount to a losing proposition unless they receive pay equivalent to or better than the going rate for field labor for the time they put in.

As for the rest of the woodstock, investment possibilities are stalemated. This leaves everyone worse off, because reduction of the woodstock increases the risk of soil erosion and reduces the likelihood that soil fertility will be reconstituted through natural regeneration. As people press relentlessly on the remaining trees, the costs of fuel and building materials rise rapidly. At the same time, women use more and more animal droppings and crop residues for cooking fuel. The supply of organic matter available to restore soil fertility has dropped off sharply.

Failure to increase wood supplies to keep pace with rising demand in turn translates into a significant lowering of living standards in Zinder rural areas.

Development of Property Rights in Land in Thailand

Among the Western developed nations there is a centuries-old tradition of well-defined and enforceable private property rights in land that allows the owner to exclude others from using the land, pass it on to heirs, pledge it as security against financial liabilities, and within limits (set for instance by zoning regulations) use the land as he or she sees fit. That system of property rights took centuries to develop and is still evolving.

Comparable systems in much of the less-developed world today are usually of more recent origin. In many countries during much of the nineteenth century (and more recently in some cases), the rights to land were usufruct rights. With the rise of commercial agriculture, this system of property rights often proved to be inadequate. Some of the inadequacies were a consequence of the common-property nature of the usufruct land rights. Because in a usufruct system land rights were use rights and did not apply to the stock, the individual users had an incentive to take the flow of services from the use of the renewable resource into account over a shorter planning horizon than they would have if their property rights had extended to the stock, the ownership of the resource itself. Because of the temporal insecurity of land rights, cultivators had an incentive to overuse the resource since, if they took the effects on the future resource-service flow into account, they could not be sure that they would be able to capture the gains from stinting.

Commercial agriculture and more profitable opportunities for the sale of the produce from farming the land were generally associated with a rise in land values and increase in the rate of return on land-clearing and development activities. Because of the development of a reliable market for output in excess of subsistence production, the clearing of additional land and investments in leveling, draining, and otherwise developing the land became more attractive. In order to fully capture the gains from the investments as well as the capital gains from the appreciation in relative land values, the land developer needed a mechanism whereby he could exclude others from using or taking possession. Under a usufruct rights system the ability to exclude was contingent on nearly continuous use. Such use conflicted in some cases with the fallow-rotation system for maintaining soil fertility.[4] The developer might also want to capture some of the gains by using the land as collateral—an unattractive option to a creditor wanting security if the ownership rights were conditional on continued use by the debtor. Because land often became open-access property once it was left idle for a period of time, the common-property aspect of the system created disincentives for a socially optimal level of investment in land development during a period in which, setting aside the prevailing property-rights system, the economic returns on such investment were in fact increasing.

The generalized case described above applies to a number of Asian and African countries during the nineteenth and twentieth centuries. The specific changes in the decision-making arrangements and interactions among the parties that occurred in Thailand will now be described as a case study.

In Thailand the opening of the economy to increased participation in international trade, population growth, and generally favorable terms of trade for agricultural export products led to an appreciation in land prices. For the nineteenth-century period, there are numerous accounts indicating that the expansion of the rice-export economy was accompanied by an appreciation in real land rents and prices (see Feeny 1982). For the twentieth-century period, the qualitative and fragmentary quantitative evidence is supplemented by data on land prices derived from mortgage transactions. The data document the overall appreciation in real land prices.

The increasing value of land in turn led to disputes over land ownership that induced changes in the property-rights system, ultimately culminating in the privatization of land rights (Feeny 1982, 1988a, 1988b, 1988c, 1989). The major changes in the system of land rights are summarized in Table 6.1.

Changes in Land Rights through 1954

Under early nineteenth-century monarchy, the system of property rights in land in Thailand was essentially one of usufruct rights. As long as the cultivator continued to use the land, he (or she) had the right to exclude others from using it, to sell it, to pass it on to heirs, or to use it as collateral to obtain a loan.[5] The maintenance of the rights depended on the payment of land taxes. In addition, if the land was not cultivated for more than three consecutive years, rights were forfeited. Operational rules thus provided for serial joint use.

The provisions created temporal uncertainty in the security of the usufruct land rights in Thailand. Homesteaders were particularly concerned by the insecurity of long-term rights: they wanted to be sure that they could reap the gains of having cleared the land for cultivation. In a

TABLE 6.1
Major Changes in the Thai System of Property Rights in Land,
1800–1982

Period	Institutional change
Early nineteenth century	Usufruct rights, existing system
1811	Survey of land holdings, title deeds based on taxation of land
1836	Removal of tax exemption on rice lands held by nobles
1851–1868	Title deeds issued based on tax receipts on paddy land
1861	Edict clarifying private property rights with provision for monarch's right of eminent domain
1867–1868	Title deeds issued based on the area harvested
1882–1883	Title deeds issued based on the area owned
1880s	Standardized forms and procedures prescribed in an effort to reduce land disputes
1892	Comprehensive land law enacted with provision for title deeds and use of land as collateral
1901	Torrens system of land registration instituted and cadastral surveys conducted
1936	Law of 1901 amended to allow for ownership based on registration with the Land Department of claims on unsurveyed lands
1954	New land law enacted providing for a variety of documents and levels of security of land rights
1972	Use of unrectified aerial photomaps begun to speed issuance of certificates of utilization
1982	Increase in rate of issuance of title deeds is made a priority

SOURCE: Chatthip Nartsupha and Suthy Prasartset, eds., *Socio-Economic Institutions and Cultural Change in Siam, 1851–1910: A Documentary Survey* (Singapore: Institute of Southeast Asian Studies), 1–3; David Feeny, "The Development of Property Rights in Land: A Comparative Study," in *Toward a Political Economy of Development: A Rational Choice Perspective*, ed. Robert H. Bates (Berkeley: University of California Press, 1988), 285–86; David Feeny, "The Demise of Corvée and Slavery in Thailand, 1782–1913," in *Breaking the Chains: Slavery, Bondage, and Emancipation in Africa and Asia*, ed. Martin A. Klein (Madison: University of Wisconsin Press, n.d.); Barend J. Terwiel, *A History of Modern Thailand 1767–1942* (St. Lucia [Brisbane]: University of Queensland Press, 1983), 103–7; Ian P. Williamson, "Cadastral Survey Techniques in Developing Countries—with Particular Reference to Thailand" (Washington, D.C.: World Bank, East Asia and Pacific Projects Department, 1983).

monsoonal rain-fed agricultural system, land use was not always predictable and any lapse in use could be preyed upon by acquisitive neighbors and officials.

The first half of the nineteenth century saw a gradual increase in the degree of commercialization of the Thai economy.[6] As a consequence, jointness became more problematic. During the fourth reign (1851–1868), land rights were made more formal through the issuance of title deeds based on tax receipts from paddy land—a change in operational rules. In 1867–1868 titles were introduced for paddy land, for which the tax was based on the area harvested.

In 1882–1883 titles based on the area owned rather than harvested were introduced for some major rice-producing provinces of the Central Plain. Thus, by paying taxes on land not currently in use, ownership rights could be maintained. Titles could be obtained by presenting to officials the tax receipts for the previous ten years. Documents were also available to give cultivators of newly cleared areas the rights to exclude others from developing the land for three years, at which time rights were forfeited if the area had not been developed.

As land prices continued to appreciate, inadequacies in the property-rights system became apparent. Frequent land disputes occurred. Conflicts over ownership of the same piece of land became endemic. During the 1880s the government responded by issuing standard forms and prescribing standardized procedures. Although the administrative changes represented improvements, the lack of a central place for land records meant that more than one set of titles could be issued for the same piece of land. With increased commercialization disputes became increasingly frequent.

The response was another change in operational rules, namely, the passage of a more comprehensive land law in 1892. It created nine types of land, including land held by religious institutions, royal land, residential land, agricultural land, land used for mining, forest and jungle land, and waterway land. The agricultural land category included three types of orchards and gardens, upland land, two types of paddy land, and garden lands. Provisions were made for transferable title deeds that could be used as collateral, and there were documents and procedures for the registration of such transactions.

Homesteading provisions were included as well as procedures for converting old documents into the newly created ones. The 1892 land law replaced the earlier rather ad hoc system with a more comprehensive one.

However, major deficiencies in the legislation and its administration remained. The continued lack of central land-title offices and precise descriptions of the boundaries of the land in question meant that disputes over ownership could not be easily resolved and land could not be unambiguously identified. These problems became very conspicuous in the Rangsit area (to the northeast of Bangkok, a major commercial rice-exporting region in the Central Plain) during the boom of the 1890s, when a number of very bitter land disputes arose. Conflictual interactions dominated once the limits of jointness had been reached. As a result, the

Royal Survey Department was diverted from its work on mapping and in 1896 began cadastral surveys, initially concentrating on the Rangsit area but later expanding into most of the major rice-exporting areas in the Central Plain.

New operational rules were formally introduced in 1901; the Torrens system of land titling with central land-record offices for each province and cadastral surveys was formally adopted. From 1901 to 1909, eleven land-record offices were established. By the 1909–10 period, 539,069 title deeds had been issued in the Central Plain (637,001 for the whole kingdom), and the area surveyed was 1.605 million hectares (1.671 hectares for the whole kingdom). The work was carried out by Australian and European experts, mainly on loan from the Indian Civil Service, who, in addition to conducting the survey work, also provided training to the Thai staff.[7]

The system was not fully realized. A lack of diligent record keeping and administration reduced the benefits. Not all farmers obtained or were able to obtain the proper documents for land which they held. Cadastral surveys in areas outside the Central Plain were particularly incomplete.[8]

In 1936, the 1901 law was amended to allow for the registration of claims on unsurveyed land.[9] While claims on apparently unclaimed lands were traditionally registered with the village headman, the 1936 law required registration at the Land Department. The 1936 law represented a compromise between the elaborate European cadastral survey system of the 1901 law and the incomplete implementation of that system. The compromise was extended in 1954, when a new comprehensive land law was enacted. It provided for a variety of land documents that gave different levels of security of land rights.

The 1954 code is the basis of the current system of land rights in Thailand. Occupation certificates are issued by village headman and commune leaders; they allow the holder to temporarily exclude others from using land as long as it is being developed. Reserve licenses issued by district officers also give rights for temporary occupation subject to utilization. Exploitation testimonials (again issued by district officers) confirm that utilization of previously reserved land has taken place and confer rights that are transferable and inheritable. Finally, full title deeds issued by cadastral survey and providing for the recording of land transactions are issued by officials in the provincial capital. Greater security in land rights thus comes at the expense of higher transaction cost, both formal and informal. (Under existing law, rights to titled land that has been left idle for more than ten consecutive years may be canceled; for land held under exploitation testimonial the period is more than five consecutive years.)

The Land Rights Situation since 1954

Even within the parameters of the compromise embodied in the 1954 code, the system is still incomplete. James C. Ingram (1971) reports estimates for the late 1960s of the area covered by three types of land documents. Only 12 percent of the area had full title deeds, 4 percent had reserve licenses, 18 percent had exploitation testimonials, and 65 percent had no formal legal documentation at all. Thus documentation of secure land rights applied to approximately 30 percent of the area—the area covered by title deeds and exploitation testimonials.[10]

The incomplete realization of the system of private property rights in Thailand, especially in upland areas, is creating disincentives that hinder efforts to intensify cultivation in the face of a rapidly shrinking land frontier. Recent World Bank and other reports (Anan 1987; Dhira and Suthawan 1988) have pointed to situations in which socially profitable investments in land development are being underexploited in favor of continued extensive cultivation systems, such as swidden (slash-and-burn) agriculture. The reason for the lack of intensification is often not that farmers are unaware of the higher rates of return on more intensive land development but that they lack the means to obtain secure property rights. Thus they make investments in land clearing that have only marginal returns and in the process contribute to soil erosion. During the first few years, however, the marginal returns exceed those initially available with more intensive modes of cultivation that require larger investments in land development. In the long run, the outcome is clearly suboptimal and, because these farmers are generally members of the lower income group in Thailand, equity is also not well served.

The lack of adequate documentation of private-property rights in land in Thailand affects more than the choice between swidden cultivation and more permanent forms of settlement. In many areas outside the Central Plain the degree of documentation of land rights is insufficient for land to be used legally as collateral on loans. Although the risk of eviction in these areas is generally low (unlike the hill areas described above), the lack of full documentation means that farmers in these permanently settled areas have restricted access to credit. Typically they are able to obtain less credit and at more unfavorable terms (Siamwalla et al. 1990). Gershon Feder and coworkers have demonstrated that farmers with adequate documentation of rights farm more intensively, use more capital inputs, and achieve both higher output and productivity (see Feder and Tongroj 1987; Feder 1987; Feder et al. 1988; Feder, Tongroj, and Yongyuth 1988; Yongyuth and Feder 1988; see also Tongroj 1990). The estimates by Feder and his colleagues also indicate that the private and social benefits of the provision of more fully documented rights exceed the costs. Again because the lack of full documentation usually occurs in less commercialized areas, both efficiency and equity can be served through an expansion of land surveying (see also Medhi 1985, 341).

Disputes over conflicting claims to the same piece of land have played an important role in stimulating the Thai government to develop more systematic and elaborate systems of private land rights. The creation and actual operation of that system has also had distributional consequences. Although in general the preexisting rights of cultivators and homesteaders have been formally recognized under the new system, differential access to formal procedures and the ability of powerful government officials to manipulate land records have allowed elites in some cases to obtain ownership of land that under the traditional system would have been controlled by homesteading cultivators. A striking example of this occurred when the Siam Canals, Land and Irrigation Company successfully evicted twenty-nine previous occupants in an area along the east bank of the Nakorn Nayok River to the northeast of the company's Rangsit development scheme. In reviewing the records of the dispute in 1916, Prince Rabi, the then minister of agriculture and former minister of justice, concluded that the courts had incorrectly found in favor of the company and its powerful investors. The previous occupants first brought their grievances before local administrative officials and after obtaining no satisfaction took their case before the court. They provided various certificates of occupancy and land-tax receipts as evidence of their prior rights. The company had, however, been able to use its superior access to government officials and procedures to have the titles for the land issued in the company's name.[11]

Given the high-level political connections of the company and its allies, there was little that could be done in this case to protect the original occupants. Although the outcome was in this case somewhat atypical, the process by which external arrangements and third-party dispute settlement were brought to bear was not. Initially the parties typically approached local administrative officials who attempted to resolve the dispute. As mentioned above, their ability to do so often depended upon the precision and accuracy of the land records; thus the evolution of more precise documentation and record-keeping systems. When disputes could not be settled at the district level because the parties were intractable or the records were incomplete or inaccurate (whether through deliberate manipulation, carelessness, or negligence), the provincial courts were then employed to resolve the dispute.

Today, intrafamilial manipulation of the system has allowed some heirs to gain at the expense of others.[12] The traditional system of equal inheritance by all surviving children is frequently subverted by more literate and knowledgeable siblings, and the result is a clash between the use of the modern system and traditional inheritance practices. The central government through its provincial courts has become increasingly involved in the adjudication of local disputes that in former times would have been settled by local officials.

The trend has two important implications. First, common people can use the court system to inhibit arbitrary behavior on the part of officials. This advantage, however, comes at the expense of a higher level of transaction cost than in the traditional system. The second implication is that differential access by claimants in land disputes to the Thai bureaucracy, an imperfectly competitive political arena, has distributional consequences. We have already seen that, in the early twentieth-century period, elites were sometimes able to successfully manipulate the system. Similarly, today, especially along the mountain slopes in northern Thailand, ethnic Thais are often able to obtain legal claim to lands previously cleared and occupied by non-Thai minorities.[13]

Conflicts in frontier areas today share many characteristics with those of the earlier period. These conflicts have served to focus the attention of the Thai government on providing cadastral surveys. Ian P. Williamson (1983) reports that boundary disputes continue to be more common in undocumented areas (see also Muscat 1990, 24).

In recent years the Thai government and World Bank have responded by increasing the provision of land documentation services. The Fifth National Economic and Social Development Plan (1982–1986) adopted a goal of providing land titles to all legally occupied lands within twenty years (Williamson 1983). Data for the early 1980s indicate that land documentation in the form of title or exploitation testimonial accounts for approximately 39 percent of the area in Thailand (ibid.). While approximately 74 percent of land parcels have secure rights in the form of title deed or exploitation testimonial, 23 percent of parcels remain without documentation. Thus, although the degree of documentation of land rights has improved since the late 1960s, extensive areas remain undocumented.

Tongroj Onchan (1990, 13, 64–66) reports similar data on the incomplete documentation of land rights in Thailand in the mid-1980s. Rights are undocumented for approximately 47 percent of the area held as private agricultural land; reserve licenses have been issued for 4.7 percent, exploitation testimonials cover 36.2 percent, and full title deeds cover 12.2 percent.

Institutional change. In the Thai case, the appreciation of land prices led to an increase in the demand for a more systematic set of procedures for defining property rights in land. The government in fact responded to the demands and gradually a new system of property rights evolved. What factors contributed to the willingness and capability of the government to supply the institutional change?

In part the new system evolved as a practical solution to the land disputes that became so common as land became more valuable.[14] The cost of supplying a new set of institutions was lowered by the availability of European systems and officials—that is, by the existence of a stock of knowledge and practice on the organization of property rights in land. Over time that system was increasingly indigenized. The feasibility of creating private property rights in land in Thailand was enhanced by the concomitant development of a provincial court system. In 1892 the Ministry of Justice was created, in 1896 the Law of Provincial Courts was promulgated, and in 1908 the Law of Courts of Justice transferred control of the provincial court system from the Ministry of Interior to the Ministry of Justice.[15] Both Thai officials and foreign experts were engaged in drafting modern civil and criminal codes. Although it has never been vigorously exploited in Thailand, a better cadastral system also gave the government an enhanced land-tax revenue base. Finally, private and social interests coincided. Members of the elite, primarily government officials, participated in the land boom and benefited from the more secure system of property rights in land. They had an incentive to supply the new system because they too would share in the pecuniary gains.

In addition to the pecuniary gains from landownership, there was another source of gain to elites in Thailand (Gehan 1987). The creation of a land-titling system allowed the government to prevent the alienation of land to foreigners. Under Thai land law only citizens may own land. Restrictions on alienation of land to foreigners were particularly important to Thai elites in the late nineteenth century, when the Thai government was largely occupied with the preservation of sovereignty.

In the case study one can see that, given the initial common-property nature of usufruct land rights and the growing incentive to exploit land resources for commercial agriculture, the existing set of decision-making arrangements generated suboptimal outcomes. The existence of the unexploited gains and resulting land disputes fed back into the system producing a series of reasonable administrative changes. At first simple and inexpensive remedies were tried. When the outcomes were still far from satisfactory, more elaborate and expensive solutions were attempted. A new system of property rights evolved and is still evolving. In this case, a system of private property rights (even if less than ideally implemented) was the solution to the problem of common-property resource management. Although manipulation of the property-rights system by elites for their private gain occurred and continues to occur, in the majority of cases the new system provided more secure rights in arable land to the party who actually cleared and cultivated it. Ownership rights that did not depend on continued use and that were more precisely defined provided cultivators with the assurances necessary to make investments in land development privately profitable. In short, the new system of property rights reduced the divergence between the private and social rates of return on land development.

An Overview

The discussion may now be briefly summarized in the framework provided by Oakerson in Chapter 3.

Resource Attributes. Arable cropland lends itself to excludability; thus the creation of boundaries marking areas for exclusive private use was not prohibitively expensive. Arable land is also divisible. Finally, at low levels of population density, much arable land may be left idle. Jointness may be maintained sequentially.

Decision-Making Arrangements. From the mid-nineteenth century on, land rights and disputes were adjudicated under operational and legislative rules imposed by the Thai government on existing usufructory rights. Both local administrative officials and the national government were involved in specifying and enforcing the rules governing land use. Over time local customary rules increasingly conformed to the national laws as interpreted through the provincial court system. The national laws, however, were also formally modified to reflect the lack of a complete cadastral survey and the long-standing Thai tradition of homesteading on unoccupied lands.

Interactions. Under the traditional usufruct system and in the environment of a largely subsistence economy with a low population density, there was limited competition in land use—in the interactions among cultivators. The usufruct system allowed the cultivator to exclude others from using land currently in use. But given the abundance of land and limited outlets for surplus production, there was full jointness or at least little rivalry in the use of wasteland.

As the property-rights system gradually evolved, individuals made use of the new government-established institutional arrangements to enhance the security and precision of their land rights. Many people, influential and otherwise, shared in the gains. Differential access to the use of the institutional arrangements did, however, affect the outcomes in terms of who obtained land rights to various tracts of land in a minority of important cases.

Outcomes. The development of more secure property rights in land did, however, underwrite increased intensification in land use, greater investments in land development (putting in bunds, or small dikes, and leveling fields to promote the use of transplant varieties instead of the broadcast planting of paddy), and the increased use of land as collateral.

At another level, that of the system as a whole, the result was an evolution of institutional arrangements, changes in the rules through which individuals interacted. The outcome of the efforts of the landowners to more securely define their rights in land was a gradual evolution of new legislative rules and operational regulations resulting in the privatization of rights in arable land.

Conclusions

From the two case studies, several generalizations concerning the dynamics of common-property management emerge. As Oakerson stresses in Chapter 3, understanding the dynamics of institutional change involves assessing the opportunities for individuals to learn from the consequences of their actions. The recursive nature of the evolution of systems is evident in both cases. An understanding of change also requires examination of the ways in which existing institutional arrangements constrain or enhance the ability of individuals to make adjustments in the decision-making arrangements. In both the Thai and the Zinder cases, existing constitutional structures required action by central government if innovations in institutional arrangements were to be made that would ameliorate problems of common-property resource management. In both cases peasant farmers in general had limited access and influence in the political system and few instrumentalities of local government or local association. Nevertheless in the Thai case the demands of landowners for innovations in the property-rights system were largely met. This appears to have been due to the fact that elite and peasant interests largely overlapped on the issue of land rights. In both cases, privatization of a common-property resource made sense for a number of reasons.

First, the costs of organizing collective management are extremely high and its effectiveness is problematic. Privatization does, however, risk inequality at the subdivision stage when control over the resource itself is allotted to particular individuals. If this is a one-time allocation, with no easy mechanisms to rectify maldistribution, inequities can pose a serious problem. It should be noted that maintaining common-property institutions in no way avoids equity problems; they are simply pushed back a step. They reappear when annual or other increments of production from the resource are harvested and distributed to users. Distribution rules specify who gets what, when, and how. The potential for inequity inherent in such regulations and practices is substantial.

Second, commons management depends on a situation of perceived scarcity; on the legal possibility (that is, legal authority) to manage a resource (or at least the lack of a legal prohibition on local efforts to manage it); and some comparative advantage sustaining common-property status for the resource rather than privatizing it (for example, prohibitively expensive fencing that makes it reasonable to hire a few guards jointly to protect the resource for everyone). Therefore, it follows that effective commons management depends on: (1) local capacity to experiment with joint management forms as production-consumption relations deteriorate and resource shortages appear;[16] and (2) low political and economic costs of collective organization to manage the commons.

Villages in the Zinder area have no authority for, and little tradition of, collective management of any kind of resource. The ethnic Hausa who inhabit this region tend to be highly individualistic in orientation, and show little interest in state-organized groups. Collective-action groups that could be readily altered to effectively manage a commons just do not currently exist. Given the existing institutional arrangements and cultural norms, the transaction cost associated with collective management in this setting are high. Much the same can be said for Thailand, where highly individualistic behavior also generally prevails. In such settings privatization may minimize transaction cost.

Third, population pressure, world or local market opportunities, and changing production technologies will influence the type of management structure local people will prefer. These trends shape the demand for new institutional arrangements.

Finally, effective decision makers must perceive that organizing the management enterprise is worthwhile, or in other words that it will benefit them in a personal manner, either directly or indirectly. Incentive compatibility—the congruence of the interests of the individual decision maker and of those affected by his decision—appears to be essential.

NOTES

The authors acknowledge the helpful comments of Jere Gilles, Margaret McKean, Elinor Ostrom, Pauline Peters, C. Ford Runge, and several referees.

1. A cadaster (from the French *cadastre*) is a public record of the extent, value, and ownership of land within a district. A cadastral survey generally involves the use of surveying equipment to define the boundaries of individual plots with precision. The effectiveness of the system depends on both the quality

of the survey and the ongoing diligence and accuracy of the record keeping. For more detail, see Williamson 1983.

2. The specific model employed here is described in more detail in Feeny 1982, 1987, 1988b, 1988c; see also Feder and Feeny 1991; Ostrom, Feeny, and Picht 1988; Ruttan and Hayami 1984; and Hayami and Ruttan 1985.

3. It should be noted that there is a long tradition in West Africa of a distinction between property rights in land and in the trees that grow on that land. In part the distinction may be a result of the fact that property rights in land were acquired through the investment of the labor necessary to clear the land and bring it under cultivation. Thus, by analogy, the person who invested his labor in cutting a tree had acquired ownership in the wood, even if he did not own the land on which it was grown.

4. Furnivall (1909) provides an example of the conflict between fallow-rotation systems and usufruct rights in lower Burma in the nineteenth century.

5. In a usufruct system of land rights, the act of selling land transfers the use rights from the original user to a new party who in the process obtains the original holder's right to exclude third parties. In many instances, it is the investments in clearing the land that are being sold. Thus, the purchase price compensates the original owner for improvements in the land.

6. The trends toward commercialization in the Thai economy over the nineteenth and twentieth centuries are discussed in Ingram 1971, Hong Lysa 1984, and Feeny 1982. Developments in the Thai property-rights system are discussed in Feeny 1982, 1988a, 1988b, 1988c, n.d. For a general discussion of the economics of property rights see Barzel 1989.

7. After 1909 the Royal Survey Department was transferred back to its original mapping duties and the rate of increase in the surveyed area plunged. The number of title deeds on file (primarily in the Central Plain) did, however, continue to increase; the average annual rate for the whole kingdom was 4.69 percent from the year 1905–1906 until 1941. The Torrens cadastral survey system was brought to Thailand by R. W. Giblin, director of the Royal Survey Department from 1901 to 1910. Giblin was a licensed surveyor trained in New South Wales, Australia, where the Torrens system was originally innovated.

8. After 1909 a number of minor changes were made in the system. Administrative procedures were changed and fees were instituted on land transfers. Restrictions were placed on the sale of public lands in 1916 and 1919 with the intent of curbing land speculation. Finally, in the year 1938–1939, a new schedule of agricultural land taxes was established.

9. See Engel 1978, 156; and Yano 1968, 853, 856).

10. Ingram 1971, 266. See also Feder et al. 1988, Feeny 1982, Johnson 1969, Hooker 1975, Gisselquist 1976, Engel 1978, Kemp 1981, Yano 1968, Chalermrath 1972, and Muscat 1990. Reasons for the incomplete coverage include the lack of a complete cadastral survey as well as the unwillingness or inability of farmers to obtain formal documentation of their land rights. The overwhelming constraint appears to have been the incomplete coverage of the cadastral survey supplied by the government.

11. Primary documents relevant to this case are found in the Thai National Archives, Sixth Reign, Ministry of Agriculture Documents 5/1–5/12. See also Feeny 1982.

12. See Engel 1978.

13. See Kunstadter, Chapman, and Sanga Sabhasri 1978, and Anan 1987.

14. Unfortunately, archival and other records provide little evidence on the individual strategies employed among the competing parties involved in disputes over land use. Some of the limited available evidence is discussed in Engel 1978 and Feeny 1982; see also Kemp 1981, Chalermrath 1972, and Yano 1968.

15. See Engel 1978, 24–29; and Tanin 1967a, 1967b.

16. In the woodstock case, the state forester lives so far away from most users that they do not consider him a reasonable source of authorization. Besides, nothing guarantees he would consider it his duty to meet a request in this sense. The national system of common woodstock management thus failed and still fails to function. In Zinder, then, illegal privatization efforts appear critical as indicators of a fundamental change in user perspective. From being producers for their own consumption only, the users in these cases have begun to become producers of wood for sale as well.

REFERENCES

By convention, Thai authors are listed alphabetically by their first name rather than last name.

Anan Ganjanapan. 1987. "Conflicting Patterns of Land Tenure among Ethnic Groups in the Highlands of Northern Thailand: The Impact of State and Market Intervention." In *Proceedings of the International Conference on Thai Studies*, Vol. 3, pt. 2, 503–11. Canberra: Australian National University.

Barzel, Yoram. 1989. *Economic Analysis of Property Rights*. New York: Cambridge University Press.

Berkes, Fikret, David Feeny, Bonnie J. McCay, and James M. Acheson. 1989. "The Benefits of the Commons." *Nature* 340:91–93.

Bromley, Daniel W. 1989. *Economic Interests and Institutions*. Oxford: Blackwell.

Chalermrath Khambanonda. 1972. *Thailand's Public Law and Policy for Conservation and Protection of Land with Special Attention to Forests and Natural Areas*. Bangkok: National Institute of Development Administration.

Chatthip Nartsupha and Suthy Prasartset, eds. 1977. *Socio-Economic Institutions and Cultural Change in Siam, 1851–1910: A Documentary Survey*. Singapore: Institute of Southeast Asian Studies.

Dhira Phantumvanit and Suthawan Sathirathai. 1988. "Thailand: Degradation and Development in a Resource-Rich Land." *Environment* 30:10–15, 30–36.

Engel, David M. 1978. *Code and Custom in a Thai Provincial Court*. Tucson: University of Arizona Press.

Feder, Gershon. 1987. "Land Ownership Security and Farm Productivity: Evidence from Thailand." *Journal of Development Studies* 24:16–30.

Feder, Gershon, and David Feeny. 1991. "Land Tenure and Property Rights: Theory and Implications for Development Policy." *World Bank Economic Review* 5: 135–53.

Feder, Gershon, and Tongroj Onchan. 1987. "Land Ownership Security and Farm Investment in Thailand." *American Journal of Agricultural Economics* 69:311–20.

Feder, Gershon, Tongroj Onchan, Yongyuth Chalamwong, and Chira Hongladarom. 1988. *Land Policies and Farm Productivity in Thailand*. Baltimore: The Johns Hopkins University Press.

Feder, Gershon, Tongroj Onchan, and Yongyuth Chalamwong. 1988. "Land Policies and Farm Performance in Thailand's Forest Reserve Areas." *Economic Development and Cultural Change* 36:483–501.

Feeny, David. 1982. *The Political Economy of Productivity: Thai Agricultural Development 1880–1975*. Vancouver: University of British Columbia Press.

———. 1987. "The Exploration of Economic Change: The Contribution of Economic History to Development Economics." In *The Future of Economic History*, ed. Alexander J. Field, 91–119. Boston: Kluwer Nijhoff.

———. 1988a. "Agricultural Expansion and Forest Depletion in Thailand, 1900–1975." In *World Deforestation in the Twentieth Century*, ed. John F. Richards and Richard Tucker, 112–43, 281–87. Durham, N.C.: Duke University Press.

———. 1988b. "The Demand for and Supply of Institutional Arrangements." In *Rethinking Institutional Analysis and Development: Issues, Choices, and Alternatives*, ed. Vincent Ostrom, David Feeny, and Hartmut Picht, 159–209. San Francisco: ICS Press.

———. 1988c. "The Development of Property Rights in Land: A Comparative Study." In *Toward a Political Economy of Development: A Rational Choice Perspective*, ed. Robert H. Bates, 272–99. Berkeley: University of California Press.

———. 1989. "The Decline of Property Rights in Man in Thailand, 1800–1913." *Journal of Economic History* 49:285–96.

———. n.d. "The Demise of Corvée and Slavery in Thailand, 1782–1913." In *Breaking the Chains: Slavery, Bondage, and Emancipation in Africa and Asia*, ed. Martin A. Klein. Madison: University of Wisconsin Press. Forthcoming.

Feeny, David, Fikret Berkes, Bonnie J. McCay, and James M. Acheson. 1990. "The 'Tragedy of the Commons' Twenty-Two Years Later." *Human Ecology* 18:1–19.

Furnivall, J. S. 1909. "Land as a Free Gift of Nature." *Economic Journal* 19:552–62.

Gehan Wijeyewardene. 1987. "Notes on Urban Land Tenure in Chiangmai." In *Proceedings of the International Conference on Thai Studies*, Vol. 2, 381–89. Canberra: Australian National University.

Gisselquist, David Phillip. 1976. "A History of Contractual Relations in a Thai Rice Growing Village." Ph.D. diss., Department of Economics, Yale University.

Hayami, Yujiro, and Vernon W. Ruttan. 1985. *Agricultural Development: An International Perspective*. Rev. Ed. Baltimore: The Johns Hopkins University Press.

Hong Lysa. 1984. *Thailand in the Nineteenth Century: Evolution of the Economy and Society*. Singapore: Institute of Southeast Asian Studies.

Hooker, M. B. 1975. *Legal Pluralism: An Introduction to Colonial and Neo-Colonial Law*. London: Oxford University Press.

Ingram, James C. 1971. *Economic Change in Thailand, 1850–1970.* 2d ed. Stanford, Calif.: Stanford University Press.

Johnson, V. Webster. 1969. "Agricultural Development in Thailand with Reference to Rural Institutions." Bangkok: Division of Land Policy, Department of Land Development. Mimeo.

Kemp, Jeremy H. 1981. "Legal and Informal Land Tenures in Thailand." *Modern Asian Studies* 15:1–23.

Kunstadter, Peter, E. C. Chapman, and Sanga Sabhasri, eds. 1978. *Farmers in the Forest: Economic Development and Marginal Agriculture in Northern Thailand.* Honolulu: University Press of Hawaii.

Medhi Krongkaew. 1985. "Agricultural Development, Rural Poverty, and Income Distribution in Thailand." *Developing Economies* 23:325–46.

Muscat, Robert J. 1990. *Thailand and the United States: Development, Security, and Foreign Aid.* New York: Columbia University Press.

National Academy of Sciences. 1983. *Agroforestry in the West African Sahel.* Washington, D.C.: National Academy Press.

Nicolas, G. 1962. "Un village bouzou du Niger: Etude d'un terroir." *Les Cahiers d'Outre-Mer* 15, no. 58:138–65.

Ostrom, Elinor. 1990. *Governing the Commons: The Evolution of Institutions for Collective Action.* New York: Cambridge University Press.

Ostrom, Vincent, David Feeny, and Hartmut Picht, eds. 1988. *Rethinking Institutional Analysis and Development: Issues, Alternatives, and Choices.* San Francisco: ICS Press.

Pelissier, P. 1980. "L'arbre dans les paysages agraires de l'Afrique Noire." In *L'Arbre en Afrique tropicale: La fonction e le signe.* Cahiers O.R.S.T.O.M., Series Sciences Humaines 17:3–4.

Ruttan, Vernon W., and Yujiro Hayami. 1984. "Towards a Theory of Induced Institutional Innovation." *Journal of Development Studies* 20:203–23.

Salifou, André. 1971. *Le Damagaram on Sultanat de Zinder au XIXᵉ Siecle.* Niamey, Niger: Centre Nigerien de Recherches en Sciences Humaines.

Siamwalla Amar, Chirmsak Pinthong, Nipon Poapongsakorn, Ploenpit Satsanguan, Prayong Nettayarak, Wanrak Mingmaneenakin, and Yuavares Tubpun. 1990. "The Thai Rural Credit System: Public Subsidies, Private Information, and Segmented Markets." *World Bank Economic Review* 4: 271–95.

Tanin Kraivixian. 1967a. "The Legal System." In Thai Bar Association, *The Administration of Justice in Thailand,* 1–10. Bangkok: Thai Bar Association.

———. 1967b. "The Judiciary and the Courts." In Thai Bar Association, *The Administration of Justice in Thailand,* 11–27. Bangkok: Thai Bar Association.

Terwiel, Barend J. 1983. *A History of Modern Thailand 1767–1942.* St. Lucia [Brisbane]: University of Queensland Press.

Thomson, James T. 1976. "Law, Legal Process, and Development at the Local Level in Hausa-speaking Niger." Ph.D. diss., Department of Political Science, Indiana University, Bloomington.

———. 1977. "Ecological Deterioration: Local-level Rule-making and Enforcement

Problems in Niger." In *Desertification: Environmental Degradation in and around Arid Lands*, ed. Michael H. Glantz, 57–79. Boulder, Colo.: Westview Press.

———. 1980. "Bois de villages (Niger): Report of an Investigation Concerning Socio-cultural and Political-economic Aspects of the First Phase of the Project and Design Recommendations for a Possible Second Phase." Report submitted to International Development Research Center, Ottawa, Canada, centre file no. 3-P-72-0093.

———. 1982. "Peasants, Rules and Woodstock Management in Zinder Department, Niger." Paper presented at the Annual Meeting of the African Studies Association, November 4–7, Washington, D.C.

———. 1983. "The Precolonial Woodstock in Sahelian West Africa: The Example of Central Niger (Damagaram, Damergu, Air)." In *Global Deforestation and the Nineteenth-Century World Economy*, ed. Richard P. Tucker and John F. Richards, 167–77. Durham, N.C.: Duke University Press.

———. 1985. "The Politics of Desertification in Marginal Environments: The Sahelian Case." In *Divesting Nature's Capital: The Political Economy of Environmental Abuse in the Third World*, ed. H. Jeffrey Leonard, 227–62. New York: Holmes & Meier.

Tongroj Onchan, ed. 1990. *A Land Policy Study*. Bangkok: Thai Development Research Institute Foundation Research Monograph no. 3.

Weber, F., and M. W. Hoskins. 1983. *Soil Conservation Technical Sheets*. Washington, D.C.: Office of International Cooperation and Development, U.S. Department of Agriculture.

Williamson, Ian P. 1983. "Cadastral Survey Techniques in Developing Countries—with Particular Reference to Thailand." Washington, D.C.: World Bank, East Asia and Pacific Projects Department.

Yano, Toru. 1968. "Land Tenure in Thailand." *Asian Survey* 8:853–63.

Yongyuth Chalamwong and Gershon Feder. 1988. "The Impact of Landownership Security: Theory and Evidence from Thailand." *World Bank Economic Review* 2:187–204.

7

Success and Failure in Marine Coastal Fisheries of Turkey

Fikret Berkes

This chapter, based on five fishery case studies chosen from the southern coasts of Turkey, explores the conditions for success and failure in common-property management. Following Ronald J. Oakerson (see Chapter 3), it focuses on the role of the technical and physical nature of the resource, the decision-making arrangements, and the behavior of the users in each case study. It explores the conditions under which common-property institutions can exist and function successfully, as opposed to conditions under which they cannot.

Four of the five case studies involve coastal, open-water fisheries, while the fifth involves a lagoon fishery. Marine resources in Turkey, except for aquaculture and lagoon fisheries, are defined in law as being open to all citizens. This is generally true also for other countries in the eastern Mediterranean. Turkish lagoon fisheries are not open to all. Lagoons are leased by the state to private operators or to cooperatives as a monopoly, as is also done in some other countries of the region such as Greece (Katsonias 1984).

There is no recent tradition of sea tenure in Turkey, and precious little literature on sea tenure in the eastern Mediterranean and the Middle East in general that would be comparable, for example, to that on East Asia and the Pacific (Ruddle and Johannes 1989). This is perhaps surprising, for evidence on sea tenure in this part of the world goes back to the ancient Sumerians (ca. 2300 B.C.), among whom "fishers were organized in guildlike organizations each with a leader . . . and joined separate groups which fished different waters"(Royce 1987, 74). Such systems still survive in the western Mediterranean. The guildlike *prud'homie* system in France (Tempier 1985) and similar communal management systems on the neighboring Mediterranean shorelines of Spain and Italy (Levieil, pers. comm. 1989) provide a time-tested code of ethics for the conduct of inshore fisheries.

The eastern Mediterranean area and the Middle East have a rich recent tradition of common-property institutions pertaining to water resources and grazing lands (Berkes and Farvar 1989; see also Chapter 10 of this book).[1] In rural Turkey, there are communal-property arrangements for water, for rangelands, and, in limited areas, for forests (Kişlalioglu and Berkes 1990). Over extensive areas, rangelands of Anatolia have been under common-property management since ancient times. Village or, in the case of Turkomans, tribal territorial rights on grazing lands are part of Turkish folklore and known to all. Grazing commons have been in decline, however, because of the settlement of migratory herders (mainly in the first half of this century) and the encroachment of agriculture into rangelands.

Nevertheless, the communal use of resources in Turkey is ubiquitous. Common-property arrangements are found with the major resource types mentioned above, and they also arise from time to time with other resources. A case in point is mountain wildflower resources, especially the *Galanthus* species, which were being depleted rapidly in the 1970s by the increase in export trade. Studies by T. Ekim and coworkers (1984) showed that the resource was holding its own only in a few areas. What these areas had in common was that the local producers were able to take collective action to establish rules and hired guards to enforce them. Such arrangements have been promoted as a promising model for the sustainable use of natural resources in Turkey in general (Kişlalioglu and Berkes 1990).

Study Areas, Methods, and Status of Fisheries

All five of the study areas are located in the southern seas of Turkey, the Aegean and the Mediterranean. These fisheries share a number of common characteristics by virtue of their location: they operate in biologically poor waters and utilize a diverse assemblage of demersal (bottom-living) species that are of limited abundance but relatively high market value. Most of these fisheries are artisanal operations that use simple fishing gear and return daily to home port.

The role of the southern seas in the overall production of Turkish fisheries is relatively minor. The Aegean region accounts for only about 3 percent of the total catch of around one-half million tons annually, and the

Mediterranean region for only about 2 percent (DPT 1985; TCZB 1982). The greatest part of the total yield is landed in the eastern Black Sea, a biologically productive area dominated by pelagic (surface-living) schooling species such as the anchovy. The Aegean and the Mediterranean are technically oligotrophic marine environments in which the low level of nutrients in the water is translated through the food web into low levels of fish productivity (Gulland 1971).

Most of the commercially utilized fish of the Aegean and the Mediterranean are demersal species. The fish fauna is highly diverse, but none of the individual species is particularly abundant. Many of them, however, have a high market value, as elsewhere in the Mediterranean. D. Charbonnier (1977) has observed that the prices for the Mediterranean fish (demersal and pelagic together) are five times higher than the average world price and, for the demersal species alone, seven times higher.

The standard small-scale operation in Turkish coastal fisheries is a two-man, 8-meter boat equipped with an inboard diesel engine of 10 to 25 horsepower; some are three-man, 10-meter boats. The standard fishing equipment is the trammel net, a gillnet-like net that is set rather than trawled and captures fish by entanglement. Longlines, or a series of baited hooks on a main line attached to a float, are also used. Both types of equipment are used in exploiting a diverse fauna of demersal species dominated by sea breams, basses, mullets, and groupers.

Larger-scale operations include trawlers, purse seiners, and beach seiners. Trawlers drag a bag-shaped net for demersal fish. In the Aegean and the Mediterranean, they average 15 to 25 meters with a crew of seven or eight. Purse seiners catch pelagic species using a net that hangs from the surface by its attached floats. The bottom of the net may be closed off like a purse when a school of fish has been surrounded. Purse seine boats average 15 meters and carry a crew of ten. Beach seiners, 10-15 meter boats with a crew of five, drag nets while anchored in shallow areas.

As may be seen from the description above, the larger-scale fisheries that operate in the Turkish Mediterranean and Aegean are really not large-scale fisheries by international standards or even by the standards of the Turkish Black Sea (Berkes and Kişlalioglu 1989). They may best be identified as medium-scale operations. Three of the fisheries in the study area consist only of small-scale operations; two consist of both small-scale and medium-scale ones.

The study area is shown in Figure 7.1. Three of the fisheries are located north of Cyprus on the eastern Mediterranean coast of Turkey and two on the southern Aegean coast. Some of the pertinent characteristics of the five fisheries are summarized in Table 7.1. The first three of the areas (Çamlik lagoon near Adana, Taşucu near Silifke, and Alanya) were chosen for the study because they were known from previous surveys to be well-

FIGURE 7.1
The Study Area, Showing the Five Fisheries

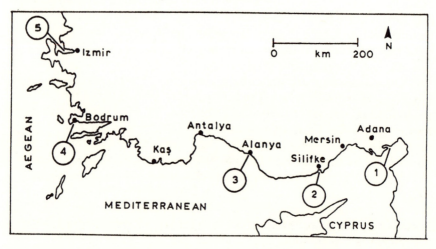

run, successful fisheries. The fourth (Bodrum) was chosen as an example of a previously successful fishery that had overcapitalized (that is, overexpanded the fleet) in the early 1970s. The fifth (Bay of Izmir) was chosen as an example of an intensive fishery in a multiple-use area adjacent to a large urban center.

In contrast to the first three fisheries, which are used by single groups of small-scale fishermen, the last two are used by medium-scale operators as well. Further, in Bodrum and the Bay of Izmir, there are relatively large groups of casual or sport fishermen; Table 7.1, however, accounts for only the registered commercial fishermen.

The data in Table 7.1 represent the situation in 1983, the main year of study. These five areas were selected from among some fifty fishing communities first investigated between 1976 and 1978. The five fisheries are not a random selection, nor are they meant to be representative of all Turkish coastal fisheries. The three "successful" cases were intermittently reinvestigated between 1985 and 1989. Information was collected through participant observation techniques, informal discussions with individuals and groups of fishermen, and more formal interviews with master fishermen, cooperative leaders, and local officials. In some cases, catch records of the cooperative were made available. (More details of the study areas and user groups may be found in Berkes 1986.)

TABLE 7.1
Description of the Five Fisheries in the Study Area, Southern Turkey, 1983

Fishery	Area used (approx. km²)	No. and types of boats	No. of registered fishermen	Cooperatives and user groups	Outcome
(1) Çamlik Lagoon	20	43 small inboard 80 nonmotorized	103	All in one co-op; 1 user group	Successful
(2) Taşucu	150	90 small inboard	140	All in one co-op; 1 user group	Successful
(3) Alanya	80	65 small inboard	100	Half in one coop; 1 user group	Successful
(4) Bodrum	(overlapping with other communities in the area)	11 trawlers 2 purse-seiners 9 bottom-seiners 100 small inboard	80 20 45 250	No active cooperatives; 6 user groups	Unsuccessful
(5) Bay of Izmir	400	27 purse-seiners 30 bottom-seiners 700 small inboard	300 150 1,400	Many cooperatives; 5 user groups	Unsuccessful

SOURCE: Author.

Use of the Oakerson Framework:
The Outcome

In this chapter, the Oakerson framework will be used diagnostically, beginning with the "outcome" and working backward to investigate the reasons behind it. It is therefore important to specify the criteria by which the outcome has been evaluated. Basically, four criteria are considered to be appropriate measures for the purposes of this work, two from the Oakerson framework—efficiency and equity—and two additional criteria—sustainability and the expression of satisfaction or dissatisfaction by the users themselves. The latter two criteria are meant to address the ecological and the social dimensions of the outcome. The last criterion may perhaps also provide a composite measure of the outcome as perceived by the fisherman.

Efficiency, defined as Pareto optimality, cannot be worked out because of lack of suitable data on individual yields and incomes in the study area. In any case, there may be serious complications in the application of the Pareto-optimality approach to resources in which there are large year-to-year variations in productivity, and in which short-term efficiency undermines long-term sustainability.

Equity, like efficiency, is difficult to calculate in this study. It can be evaluated indirectly, however, from the general conduct of the five fisheries. In the first and third areas in Table 7.1, there were explicit sharing mechanisms to ensure equity. In the second area, all fishermen had access to bank credit equivalent to U.S. $3,000 (1983 dollars) through their cooperative society. By contrast, in the last two areas, there were no mechanisms by which a certain basic fishing income or other benefits could be guaranteed.

Sustainability of the harvest is a criterion often used to evaluate the success of common-property resource use (Berkes and Farvar 1989). Together with other biological criteria (maintenance of diversity and of ecological life-support processes), measures of sustainability have been incorporated into the definition of conservation by several international agencies (IUCN/UNEP/WWF 1980, 1991). In the present study, sustainability can be estimated. There are insufficient data, however, to test fully whether any of the fisheries in the study area is truly sustainable.

Perhaps the most practical measures of outcome in the present study are the usual bioeconomic criteria of success used in fisheries science: evidence of overfishing and overcapitalization (Gulland 1974; Stevenson 1991). These criteria have the added advantage that they may be used as a proxy for efficiency and sustainability. Together with a measure of equity, as above, and an expression of satisfaction or dissatisfaction of the users themselves, these criteria should provide a suitably complete assessment of the outcome.

By these three criteria, the first three study areas—Çamlik lagoon, Taşucu, and Alanya—represent successful fisheries: As of 1983, there was no decrease in overall catches over the years, no sharp drops in the catch per unit of effort, no obvious overcrowding in the fishing area, and no indication of vessels and fishermen dropping out of the fishery. In these areas, the fishermen indicated that conflicts were for the most part resolved internally and the majority of them expressed general satisfaction with the fishery.

By contrast, the last two areas—Bodrum and the Bay of Izmir—represent unsuccessful fisheries. While there has probably been no decrease in the overall yield over the years, there has been a sharp decline in the catch per unit of fishing effort. The more valuable species have all but disappeared. There are too many fishermen and too many boats chasing too few fish. In the Bodrum area, many fishermen have become occupational pluralists, catering to tourists in the summer and fishing part-time opportunistically. The larger vessels have left Bodrum for the lack of fish. In 1983, all but one of eleven Bodrum-based trawlers operated outside the area, and one had dropped out of the fishery altogether. In the Bay of Izmir, many of the small fishermen of the area were forced to travel north to the outer bay, even though this meant much higher operating costs. The more valuable species were so scarce that it was said that a fisherman could more than recoup his daily expenses if he could catch a single good-sized specimen of *Dicentrarchus labrax* (a type of white bass) and sell it to a restaurant in Izmir. In these two areas, fishermen either talked bitterly of the conflicts or refused to talk at all. Although some expressed general satisfaction with the fishery, many said they were dissatisfied with the outcome.

Technical and Physical Attributes of the Resource

The techno-environmental attributes of the resource base are much the same in the five study areas, with a few notable exceptions. Jointness is a problem in all areas: each individual user is potentially capable of subtracting from the welfare of other users, even when fishing lawfully. Certain illegal practices (such as the use of dynamite and nets with sublegal mesh sizes) exacerbate the problem.

Excludability poses a serious problem in all of the five study areas. In general, access to a fishery is difficult to restrict. The first study area,

Çamlik lagoon, is the easiest one of the five from which to exclude outsiders because of its small size and geographical location. The next three coastal fisheries are less easy to defend because they are conducted along a stretch of the shoreline, and the fifth, Bay of Izmir, is much the same only larger.

Divisibility poses both a theoretical and a practical problem. The resource itself, the fish stock, is indivisible; it cannot be divided up among private property holders. The fishing areas, however, can be divided up by using landmarks and the usual measures of location finding among coastal fishermen, such as triangulation. The problem in dividing up the fishing grounds is that fish do not stay in one place for long. Moreover, all of the stocks fished in the study areas range beyond the actual areas harvested by the fishing communities. Each major species has a different migratory behavior, and it would not be possible to match the management area to the geographical range inhabited by the stocks.

Finally, the techno-environmental attributes of the resource may include some measure of the potential demand for it by the people who live in the area or come as tourists. On this count, there are differences among the five study areas. The Bay of Izmir fishery is near a metropolitan area of nearly 2 million, and the Çamlik lagoon fishery is only one hour from Adana (over 1 million). Both suffer from urban pressures but the Izmir fishery much more so. Bodrum (a tourist center since the early 1970s), Alanya, and Taşucu (developed in the 1980s) have all been affected by the relatively recent popularity of the southern Turkish coasts among tourists.

Decision-Making Arrangements

Rules and institutions governing fishery resource use include laws issued by the central government and operational rules instituted locally. The government of Turkey regulates fisheries through the Aquatic Resources Act no. 1380 of 1971. The restrictions and conditions provided under the act include the licensing of commercial fishermen (but not license limitation); the regulation of a minimum mesh size for nets; and the prohibition of trawling within three miles of the coast and within bays.

The Ministry of Agriculture has jurisdiction over fisheries but employs no fishery conservation officers. The provisions of the Aquatic Resources Act and its regulations, such as the three-mile limit, are enforced by the coast guard and the rural police (the gendarmerie) under the Ministry of the Interior.

Operational rules instituted locally are one of two kinds. In areas in which the fishermen belong to cooperatives, such operational rules are subject to the conditions of the charter of the local cooperative. The charter, in turn, is subject to government regulations that govern producers' cooperatives for agriculture and fish. For example, the rules on membership allow for no discrimination on an ethnic basis but do allow for residency requirements in the local community.

Other operational rules are those that exist without any reference to formal government legislation. The rule that establishes the condition for collective choice within the fishing community is willing consent. The actual operational rules that emerge by the application of this rule differ from fishery to fishery in the five study areas, even though the "general rules of the game," or the constraints that shape the management choices, are much the same. The more pertinent operational rules regarding common-property management are summarized below for each of the five study areas.

Çamlik Lagoon Fishery at Ayvalik-Haylazli

As with all lagoon fisheries, use rights are established by the lease of the lagoon from the government of Turkey. Thus, members of the cooperative, all of whom come from three neighboring villages, have exclusive and legal rights to the fish of the lagoon and the lagoon's adjacent waters. All fishermen are cooperative members, and all cooperative members are active fishermen. They protect their rights by patrolling the boundary of their fishing area and chasing off or apprehending intruders (but apparently most trespassers get away). Rules for membership are stated in the charter of the cooperative and include six months of residency in one of the three villages from which members come. The other important condition is that those earning wages from employment and those who are larger farmers (defined on the basis of income tax) are ineligible for membership. Of the five fishing areas in the study, the clearest operational rules are found in this fishery because the mechanisms for establishing use rights and membership are legally defined.

Taşucu Fishery

All fishermen are small-boat fishermen and all belong to the local cooperative. The right to fish is not restricted to membership in that cooperative, but membership has the attractive features of bank credit for members and a seasonally adjusted, year-round guaranteed price. Fishing rights of the group were, until 1983, protected by the 3-mile limit for trawlers. Small-boat fishermen from elsewhere may come into the area fished by Taşucu fishermen, but apparently do not because the adjacent areas are less heavily fished and therefore more attractive than Taşucu Bay.

Alanya Fishery

This fishery is located on the edge of a deep basin, and the inshore zone suitable for setting nets is very limited. The operational rules for the use of this zone are established on the basis of willing consent, and are organized by the community of fishermen informally, as follows.

- Each September, a list of eligible fishermen is prepared consisting of all licensed fishermen in Alanya, regardless of cooperative membership (about half were members in 1983, declining to one-third by 1989).
- Within the area normally used by Alanya fishermen, all usable fishing locations, some better than others, are named and numbered. These spots are spaced so that the net set in one does not block the fish that should be available at the spot next to it.
- Special regulations for these fishing locations are in effect from September to May, and the practice applies to the use of the large-mesh (80-millimeter) nets for bonito and large carangids (*Sarda sarda* and two species of *Lichia*).
- In September, the eligible fishermen gather in the coffee-house (in which most drink tea) and draw lots. Each boat is assigned a starting number that corresponds to a fishing site number.
- During the period September to May, each participating fisherman moves each day to the next location to the east. This gives each fisherman an equal opportunity at the best sites. The stocks are constantly migrating through the area, east to west between September and January, and reversing their migration from January to May.

These operational rules are formulated by the fishermen themselves.[2] They do, however, draw legitimacy from a broad interpretation of the Aquatic Resources Act, which states that the cooperatives have jurisdiction over "local arrangements." The rules are enforced by having each fisherman endorse the list of fishing locations. Copies of the agreement are then deposited with the mayor and the local gendarmerie. Violations are dealt with by the fishing community at large, in the coffeehouse. Violators may come under social pressure and, on occasion, threats of violence. The threat of removing the violator's name from the list, to our knowledge, has never been carried out. (The organizers concede privately that such an action would overstep the authority of the group and could not be legally enforced.)

Alanya is unusual in that there are no problems with trawlers. The coastal zone is steep and deep enough (1,000 meters deep at 1 kilometer from shore in some places) to discourage trawlers. There are no known operational rules to deal with small fishermen of adjacent communities and with the increasing numbers of spear and sport fishermen.

Bodrum Fishery

In this area, the traditional small-boat fishery collapsed after the development of a trawl fleet in the 1970s that coincided with the emergence of Bodrum as a tourism center. A local cooperative tried unsuccessfully through the 1970s to mediate between small boats and trawlers; by 1983, the cooperative was inactive. No single organization is likely to speak for all fishermen and organize the consensus necessary to establish operational rules. In 1983 there were six distinct groups of fishermen: (1) small-scale coastal fishermen; (2) larger-scale operators including trawlers and beach-seiners; (3) semiprofessionals who obtain their own fish and sell the occasional surplus; (4) large numbers of unskilled sport fishermen; (5) spear fishermen licensed as sponge fishermen but who sell fish on the open market; and (6) charter boat operators who fish to feed their clients and occasionally sell the surplus.

Bay of Izmir Fishery

This fishery differed from the Bodrum fishery by the presence of two large and active cooperatives, both based at the Izmir fish market; one represented small-scale fishermen and the other large-scale fishermen. There were also several local cooperatives within the bay area. The Bay of Izmir was similar to Bodrum with respect to the presence of several distinct groups of fishermen: (1) purse-seiners, (2) small-scale gillnetters, (3) small-scale liftnetters, (4) larger-scale beach-seiners, and (5) sport and semiprofessional fishermen from the urban metropolitan area of Izmir. Each of these groups reportedly conflicted with at least one other group, and in some instances with more than one.

There were no operational rules applicable to the bay as a whole to allocate the fish, to reduce the conflicts, or to limit crowding. There were rules, however, within each of the groups. For example, among the beach-seiners, most of whom operated in the southern part of the bay, there were numbered seining locations, allocated on the basis of first-comer's rights.

Patterns of Interaction

The five study areas are under somewhat similar constraints with respect to technical and physical attributes of the resource and decision-making arrangements for the use of the resource. Yet the outcomes are different, perhaps partly because of differences in urban and recreational demands on the resource. Alanya is different from the others because the narrowness of the continental shelf in this area restricts possible fishing sites. To explore these differences further, each of the five fisheries will be described in terms of the users' patterns of interaction.

Çamlik Lagoon Fishery

This successful fishery is run by a cooperative established in 1974 to make a bid for the lease of Çamlik lagoon, which had previously been operating under a private company. A few of the members had been employed as laborers by the company. Taking advantage of a provision under the Aquatic Resources Act to give priority to cooperatives in the leasing of lake and lagoon fisheries, the Ayvalik-Haylazli Cooperative was successful in its bid. Even though few of the members had fishing experience, they were able to run the lagoon profitably. The cooperative initially included members from a nearby town and those who held wage employment. Subsequently, the cooperative interpreted its charter more strictly and expelled members who lived elsewhere and who could not choose between fishing and wage employment. However, many of the members in 1983 were themselves part-time fishermen: some 80 percent were part-time farmers and only 20 percent full-time fishermen.

To maintain the profitability of the fishery, the cooperative has rejected requests for membership from a large village nearby. The limitation of membership enables it to capture a larger resource rent than would otherwise be possible. As compared with other fisheries, the cost of fishing is kept low by the use of rowboats. Fishermen work in groups of four, using two rowboats and one motorized vessel per group. The rowboats are towed to the fishing area, and the motor boat is then anchored, thus saving fuel. Each group owns its means of production collectively and splits the income equally. Cooperative officers take turns in accompanying the cooperative truck to the city of Adana, a large market only one hour's drive away.

Apart from the occasional problem of sales accounting (a common one with cooperatives), and aside from the discontent of those excluded from the fishery, the operation appears to be relatively trouble-free. Even though the membership is open to all residents of three villages (combined population 2,500), the organizers do not foresee a crowding problem in the near future but do anticipate increasing interference from outsiders.

Taşucu Fishery

The Taşucu Fishing Cooperative is often cited as an example of a producer's cooperative that works. There is a substantial literature on it in Turkish, including a book (Ozankaya 1976), and the head of the cooperative is somewhat of a folk hero. At the time the cooperative was established (1968), there were only two motorized fishing boats in Taşucu and five rowboats. Most of the others who made their living from fishing used dynamite. The cooperative banned dynamite-fishing and promised fishermen financial help to allow them to obtain proper means of production. In 1970, the growing cooperative confronted trawlers that operated (illegally) within Taşucu Bay, and chased them off with shotguns (ibid.). By 1971, cooperative members owned forty inboard boats and controlled their fishing area. Membership reached a peak of 180 in 1975 (ibid.), and then declined through the loss of members from adjacent communities who formed their own associations.

The history of the cooperative has been one continuous struggle against other interests and user groups. In the early 1980s, the cooperative fought a local pulp and paper mill over pollution, and sought more effective governmental enforcement of the ban on night fishing with scuba gear. Starting in 1983, the cooperative fought the exemption obtained by trawlers to conduct a "controlled" shrimp fishery within Taşucu Bay for part of the year.

The cooperative has been particularly successful as a marketing enterprise, perhaps because its leader is a successful local businessman. By operating a large freezer facility, it has been able to stabilize and control the local market and guarantee the price of fish for the producers. Further, the cooperative has been able to obtain for its members a bank credit of U.S. $3,000, which is sufficient capital for a new fisherman to buy the essential equipment. The cost of most two-man boats averages about twice that amount. Some fishermen have apparently made enough to pay off the loan in a year: U.S. $2,800 is probably a reasonable estimate of the mean annual gross income (200 fishing days per year × 10 kilograms per day × U.S. $1.40 per kilogram).

The cooperative was thus able to build up the membership, establish a strong financial position, and acquire political power. The leadership did not appear to be concerned about overcapacity and stock depletion, arguing that Taşucu Bay could support perhaps as many as 300 boats, provided that destructive practices such as trawling and night fishing with scuba were controlled.

Alanya Fishery

In the 1950s, there were only eight to ten fishermen in Alanya. First-comer's rights determined access to fishing spots. Conflicts increased through the 1960s as the number of fishermen increased. The present system of lottery and rotation first started in the late 1960s as an equitable means of conflict resolution over the limited number of productive fishing sites.

Developed by trial and error, the system is based on the principle of preventing fishermen from cutting off one another's "rightful supply of fish." This is done by spacing the fishermen sufficiently far apart to prevent interception between September and May when migratory fish dominate the harvest. The system has the support of the great majority because it optimizes production at the best fishing sites and in turn allocates these sites by lottery, with a rotation provision that ensures all fishermen an equal chance to fish these best spots.

Thirty-seven boats were on rotation in 1983 (three others were not fishing for various reasons). There were thirty-four named fishing locations, including two prime and five subprime sites. When a boat finished its turn at each of the thirty-four sites, the fishermen had the option of repairing equipment, going long-lining in deeper waters, or simply tying up for three days. After May and through the summer months, fishermen sought large and valuable members of the Sparidae family (snappers) and red mullet (*Mullus barbatus*), all nonmigratory species for which the rotation system was not deemed necessary.

All of those eligible were licensed fishermen. However, admission to membership in the fishing community probably required more than the acquisition of a valid license. A fisherman who wants to participate in the system has to know the rules of the game and the named fishing spots. (As one fisherman put it: "Suppose some guest worker comes from Germany in his Mercedes car and wants to fish, do you think we would allow him? No way.")

The organizers of the rotation system had sufficient support from the community of fishermen as a whole because the system benefited everyone except those who once monopolized the prime sites. The organizers were cooperative members, but the cooperative was not formally involved in the rotation system. Yet the organizers often cited the legal authority of cooperatives over "local arrangements" to legitimate the system. Some of the differences between Alanya and, for example, Taşucu may be due to the lack of a strong cooperative organizer and to a greater sense of individual entrepreneurship in Alanya. (Again, a fisherman: "Fixed prices as in Taşucu? Well, our fishermen in Alanya would never stand for that. We are individualists; we sell to whoever offers a better price.")

About half of the Alanya fishermen were not members and sold their catch through buyers who were able to offer a slightly better price than the cooperative ("by evading municipal taxes," according to the cooperative secretary). The nonmembers were thus preventing the cooperative from building a stronger financial base and accumulating political power. The cooperative was therefore unable to offer its members the kinds of service the Taşucu cooperative was able to give.

Bodrum and the Bay of Izmir Fisheries

Both of these fisheries were overcrowded and the stocks overexploited. In the case of Bodrum, overfishing appeared to be due to the financial success of trawlers in the early 1970s, success that attracted new entries until the cost of fishing exceeded the revenues of the fleet as a whole—a textbook example of rent dissipation in a fishery (see, for example, Gulland 1974). Most of the trawlers then abandoned the area, leaving the depleted stocks to small-boat fishermen. The spokesmen for the trawlers expressed dissatisfaction with this turn of events, not so much because the stocks had been depleted, but because the trawlers had become very restricted in their area of operation. According to trawlermen, in the 1970s the government had encouraged them to build the new vessels and had rarely enforced the 3-mile limit, much to the anger of the small fishermen. However, with tighter regulations on trawling, trawlers could no longer make a living in the Bodrum area and went to the shrimp grounds near Mersin.

Meanwhile, in Bodrum conditions had become no better for the small fishermen. The booming tourist trade resulted in higher prices for fish, but this also brought a great many part-time fishermen and charter boats into the fishery, and created apparently insurmountable problems of conflict among user groups.

A similar situation also existed in the Bay of Izmir, although the lineup of conflicting groups was somewhat different. But here the problem was not the trawlers (none were allowed in the bay). Rather the problem was the proximity of a large urban center, a lucrative market but also a source of large numbers of semiprofessional fishermen. Unlike Bodrum, the bay area did have cooperatives, but they represented only the narrow interests of various groups competing over their share of the markets.

With over 750 licensed commercial boats (see Table 7.1) and a great many semiprofessional fishermen, the area was so crowded that it was simply not possible for any group to defend a fishing area. In fact, many trammel-net fishermen found it difficult even to defend their own nets. This explains the existence of liftnet fishermen as a distinct group. The liftnet fishermen do not set and leave the net in the water to be retrieved later, but rather set and lift the net repeatedly over a wide area and look for visual evidence of such fish as the gray mullet (*Mugil cephalus*).

Cases of Success Revisited

The conditions under which a fishery conducts its business no doubt change over time. These changes may provide clues regarding the determinants of success and failure in common-property management. The three cases of success were therefore reinvestigated between 1983 and 1989 to trace changes in conditions and to identify stresses that may impinge on the fishery system. Major findings are summarized below for each of the three.

Çamlik Lagoon Fishery

The lagoon is located in the delta of the Ceyhan River. In most delta areas, the river changes its course once every few years, affecting the balance between salt and freshwater in lagoons. In the case of the Çamlik lagoon, there has been a salinization problem since the early 1980s. The rate of evaporation apparently exceeds the inflow of fresh water into the lagoon, resulting in salinity too high for fish survival in the lagoon's far reaches. Fish production has therefore been restricted to the area near the mouth of the lagoon and the adjacent coastal area. Thus, through the mid-1980s, the main stress on the fishing was of a technical-physical nature. To solve the problem, the cooperative sought government assistance to dig a canal to the Ceyhan River to dilute the lagoon.

A second line of action taken by the cooperative was to improve the utilization of the gray mullet, the major fish resource of the area. To do this, the cooperative sought biological data to determine the distribution of mullet stocks along the adjacent coast (the indivisibility problem), and tried to develop new techniques to catch the available fish more efficiently.

A third issue that preoccupied members of the cooperative was that of exclusion. Membership was limited to the residents of the three villages as before, but increasingly larger numbers of outsiders fishing illegally in the area created problems. The cooperative members appeared to tolerate the intruders as long as violations were not too blatant and there was not too much damage to the resource.

Taşucu Fishery

By far the most serious issue in the Taşucu case was the exclusion problem. Effective control by the cooperative over the fishing area, which had started in 1970, was eroded after 1983 when shrimp trawlers obtained permits to come into Taşucu Bay legally. Larger numbers of trawlers entered the area through the mid-1980s. Having lost the legal battle, Taşucu fishermen responded by modifying their fishing strategies. They stopped targeting shrimp and red mullet because these fish, the fishermen claimed, had been reduced to uneconomic levels. Many of the marginal fishermen dropped out of the fishery; some started to look for outside buyers to maximize the revenue for what little was obtainable, thus breaking the solidarity within the coop. The cooperative retaliated swiftly, starting in 1987, by expelling members who sold outside. But since these fishermen could not be excluded from the local fishery, the outcome was loss of market control, fragmentation of the fishery, and loss of the capability for strong, collective action that had been the hallmark of the Taşucu cooperative (Ozankaya 1976).

Statistics made available by the cooperative indicate that the total production by members declined from 34.3 tons in 1983 to 22.8 tons in 1987 (Table 7.2). The number of more active fishermen (defined as those selling at least 200 kilograms per year) declined marginally from 45 to 39 over the same period.

In fishery science, one of the most reliable indicators of resource depletion is the decline in the catch per unit of fishing effort (CPUE) together with a drop in overall yield. To investigate changes in CPUE from the coop records, a sample of six fishermen was chosen; all were well regarded by their peers as experienced and steady producers. The mean annual CPUE was calculated for each of the six. Results showed that the decline from 1983 to 1987 was not statistically significant (Table 7.2).

TABLE 7.2
Changes in Catch and Catch per Unit of Effort (CPUE) of Taşucu Cooperative Fishermen after Entry of Shrimp Trawlers, Starting in 1983, into Their Area

Production	1987	1986	1985	1984	1983
Total production by cooperative members (metric tons)	22.8	23.4	24.4	35.6	34.3
Number of cooperative members producing over 200 kg/yr	39	36	38	49	45
Mean annual CPUE (kg/trip)	16.6	15.1	12.8	20.3	17.5
Mean CPUE (kg/trip), Jan.–May only	6.2	6.4	10.0	14.4	20.5

SOURCE: Taşucu Fishing Cooperative landing records.

Fishermen themselves, however, claimed major declines. Since cooperative records only indicate the number of trips and not their duration, the
CPUE data used in Table 7.2 were masking the fact that, to keep
production relatively constant, fishermen were making longer trips in the
warm months and carrying an icebox (an innovation) to stay out longer.

In summary, the small-scale inshore fishermen of Taşucu were targeting species relatively unaffected by trawlers and taking longer trips to
offset the effect of open-access competition. In addition, some of them left
Taşucu bay and started long-lining in the deep waters toward Cyprus.
Some found productive grounds for deep-sea snappers and groupers.
Ironically, as the large trawlers moved inshore, the small fishermen thus
moved offshore; in the fall of 1988, some of them were landing unprecedented amounts of high-value fish from newly discovered offshore banks.

Alanya Fishery

There were two major factors of stress in Alanya, one related to technology and the other to increasing numbers of participants. The declining
numbers of snapper and increasing market demands forced a search for
new technology. By 1985, eight boats were carrying small echo-sounders.
These gave the fishermen the ability to detect rocky outcrops on the
seabed, the habitat of the snapper. The first innovators reaped good
returns; about 50 kilograms of the top snapper (two weeks' catch for
some) was all they needed to pay off the investment for the echo-sounder.

But the first innovators never did make the profits they were hoping
for. Soon many boats carried echo-sounders and then, by 1987, the
resource was depleted. Unlike the fast-growing *Lichia*, which is the
mainstay of the September–May fishery, large red snappers, as the
fishermen themselves knew, were long-lived fish and unable to withstand
an efficient fishery.[3]

Depletion of the snappers (summer fishery), which left everyone
slightly worse off, did not directly affect the rotation system. But in the
meantime, the system itself was coming under pressure, in part because
of its own past success.

From thirty-seven boats in the 1983–84 season, the fleet expanded to
forty in 1984–85, forty-three in 1985–86, and forty-six in 1986–87, reaching
sixty in 1988–89. The number of fishing locations went up by three to
thirty-seven in 1984–85, was cut back to thirty-two in 1986–87, but was
restored to thirty-seven in 1988–89 in an attempt to accommodate greater
numbers of fishermen.

Only part of this increase in boat numbers, however, was due to new
fishermen. Some of the existing fishermen were building additional boats
and entering the draw with multiple units to improve their chances of

getting a good spot. Others recruited boat-owning relatives or friends. The extra boats could always make some money in the booming tourist trade, anyway. But as more fishermen subverted the system, the more difficult it became for the others to stay honest.

The community of fishermen tried to deal with this no-win situation by tightening the rules. "The problem," one organizer said, "is not that the man owns three boats. The problem is that he wants more than his rightful share." The group decided that "if a person owns no fishing gear, he cannot enter the draw." Yet this did not quite solve the problem; as long as the person had a license to fish and some gear to enter the draw, he could not be excluded from the fishery.[4]

Conclusions

Success in the management of fishery commons in these Turkish case studies does not depend solely on the technical-physical nature of the resource, or the decision-making arrangements, or the behavior of the users, but on a combination of these. The physical nature of the resource, especially excludability (are the users of the resource able to limit the access of others?) is always a problem with common property, and perhaps more so in fisheries than in some other resource types.

Decision-making arrangements, both at the level of the central government and at the local level, are obviously also important. The case studies suggest that the crucial decision-making arrangement pertains to limiting the user pool. Fishing is a zero-sum game; jointness can only be maintained if the fishing pressure does not exceed the ability of the stock to sustain it. Since there is no license limitation in Turkish fisheries, one would expect that sooner or later there will be too many fishermen chasing too few fish. This is the prediction of the open-access theory (Stevenson 1991), and it is indeed the case in Bodrum and Bay of Izmir.

The three cases of success are exceptions; they do not fit the prediction. The Çamlik lagoon fishery is a special case in that the transfer of property rights from the state to the fishing cooperative enables the formulation of local operational rules, both to limit the access of outsiders and to regulate behavior among members. Follow-up studies indicate that the lagoon fishery is the only stable one of these three cases, despite its problems of a technical-physical nature.

The other two cases of success are unstable *because the open-access policy of the state undermines local rules to limit access and to regulate behavior*. Taşucu is a case in point: the fishery was efficient, equitable, and sustainable between 1970 and 1983 when the cooperative controlled the fishing area and regulated the conduct of the participants, all of them small-boat fishermen. This system collapsed when trawlers obtained legal rights to fish in the bay and within the 3-mile limit. (An ironic twist was added to the story when the small-scale fishermen of Taşucu were able to move with their longlines into the deep water, beyond the trawlers' capability, and make a success of it.)

The causes of instability are different in the Alanya case. The problem is the difficulty of keeping down the numbers of participants from within the community. The access of outsiders is not a major problem; there is some competition from divers but, at least, not from trawlers. Over the years, the community of fishermen produced fairly sophisticated local operational rules, but unlike the rules for Çamlik lagoon Alanya's local rules have a very weak legal basis. Yet local rules have continued to evolve, responding to the problems at hand. The fishermen use the Aquatic Resources Act as "enabling legislation" for their system concocted at the coffeehouse, but know full well that they cannot exclude anyone with a fishing license—and fishing licenses are open access. This fundamental weakness of the operational rules highlights the fragility of any community-based resource management system that is directly or indirectly, deliberately or inadvertently, undermined by the government.[5]

NOTES

I am thankful to Daniel Bromley, Wilfrido Cruz, David Feeny, Jere Gilles, Mina Kişlalioglu, Dominique Levieil, Margaret McKean, Ron Oakerson, Elinor Ostrom, and Jean-Philippe Platteau for their valuable comments. The study was supported by the Social Sciences and Humanities Research Council of Canada (SSHRC).

1. Morocco, the subject of Chapter 10, is not, of course, in the Middle East. Rather, the point is that the Moroccan *agdal* is a variant of the *hema* system in the larger Middle Eastern tradition (Gilles, pers. comm. 1985). The Middle Eastern tradition of communal property, in the case of irrigation water, was transferred by the Arabs to Spain. This *huerta* system, in turn, has given rise through Spanish influence to the *zanjera*s of the Philippines, as explained by E. Ostrom (1990).

2. The practice of allocating turns by lottery is common in fisheries in diverse parts of the world: in French Mediterranean lagoon fixed-gear fisheries under the *prud'homie* system; among the cod traps and salmon net berths of Newfoundland (Matthews and Phyne 1988); in Sri Lankan beach-seine fisheries (Alexander 1982); and in surrounding-net and seine fisheries in Dominica, West Indies (Wylie 1989).

3. Rapid-growing *Lichia* are fished in their first year. By contrast, large-sized red snappers are over ten years old; such a long-lived resource is slow to renew itself.

4. Platteau and Baland (1989, 36) analyzed and modeled a similar situation in Sri Lankan beach-seine fisheries in which local rules guaranteed equal access to all nets registered in the village but, as the number of fishing units increased, "existing participants had to construct additional nets. This was with a view to preventing the number of their turns per unit of time and their chance of participating in the flush period from declining too much."

5. This chapter is a revised and updated version of that in the 1986 National Research Council volume. The introductory and concluding sections were rewritten and a new section, "Cases of Success Revisited" was added, to update the chapter. The middle sections have been revised only slightly.

REFERENCES

Alexander, P. 1982. *Sri Lankan Fishermen: Rural Capitalism and Peasant Society*. Canberra: Australian National University.

Berkes, F. 1986. "Local-Level Management and the Commons Problem." *Marine Policy* 10:215–29.

Berkes, F., and T. Farvar. 1989. "Introduction and Overview." In *Common Property Resources: Ecology and Community-Based Sustainable Development*, ed. F. Berkes, 1–17. London: Belhaven.

Berkes, F., and M. Kişlalioglu. 1989. "A Comparative Study of Yield, Investment and Energy Use in Small-Scale Fisheries." *Fisheries Research* 7:207–24.

Charbonnier, D. 1977. "Prospects for Fisheries in the Mediterranean." *Ambio* 6: 374–76.

Devlet Planlama Teşkilati (DPT). 1985. *Beşinci Beş Yillik Kalkinma Plani. Su Ürünleri ve Su Ürünleri Sanayii. Özel Ihtisas Komisyon Raporu* (The Fifth Five-Year Plan. Aquatic Resources Expert Committee Report). Ankara: State Planning Agency.

Ekim, T., M. Koyuncu, S. Erik, A. Güner, B. Yildiz, and M. Vural. 1984. *Türkiye'nin Ekonomik Deger Taşiyan Geofitleri Üzerinde Taksonomik ve Ekolojik Araştirmalar* (Taxonomic and ecologic studies on the economically important geophite species in Turkey). Ankara: National Research Council of Turkey.

Gulland, J. A. 1971. *The Fish Resources of the Ocean. C. Mediterranean and Black Sea*. Rome: Food and Agriculture Organization.

———. 1974. *The Management of Marine Fisheries*. Seattle: University of Washington Press.

IUCN/UNEP/WWF 1980. *World Conservation Strategy: Living Resource Conservation for Sustainable Development*. Gland, Switzerland: IUCN/UNEP/WWF.

———. 1991. *Caring for the Earth: A Strategy for Sustainable Living*. Gland, Switzerland: IUCN/UNEP/WWF.

Katsonias, G. 1984. "The Messolonghi-Etolico Lagoon of Greece: Socioeconomic and Ecological Interactions of Cooperatives and Independent Fishermen." In *Management of Coastal Lagoon Fisheries*, ed. J. M. Kapetsky and G. Lasserre. FAO GFCM Studies and Reviews 61:521–28.

Kişlalioglu, M., and F. Berkes. 1990. *Ekoloji ve Çevre Bilimleri* (Ecology and environmental sciences). Istanbul: Remzi Kitabevi.

Matthews, R., and J. Phyne. 1988. "Regulating the Newfoundland Inshore Fishery." *Journal of Canadian Studies* 23:158–76.

Ostrom, E. 1990. *Governing the Commons*. Cambridge: Cambridge University Press.

Ozankaya, O. 1976. *"Kooperatif Kur, Sefaletten Kurtul": Türkiye'de Kooperatifçilik* ("Start a cooperative and escape poverty": Co-operatives in Turkey). Istanbul: Milliyet Yayinlari.

Pauly, D., and G. Murphy, eds. 1982. *Theory and Management of Tropical Fishery*. Manila: International Center for Living Aquatic Resources Management (ICLARM).

Platteau, J.-Ph., and J.-M Baland. 1989. "Income-sharing through Work-spreading Arrangements: An Economic Analysis with Special Reference to Small-Scale Fishing." *Cahiers de la Faculté des Sciences Economiques et Sociales de Namur, Serie Recherche* 91:1–45.

Royce, W.F. 1987. *Fishery Development*. New York: Academic Press.

Ruddle, K., and R. E. Johannes, eds. 1989. *Traditional Marine Resource Management in the Pacific Basin: An Anthology*. Jakarta: UNESCO.

Stevenson, G. G. 1991. *Common Property Economics: A General Theory and Land Use Applications*. Cambridge: Cambridge University Press.

Türkiye Cumhuriyeti Ziraat Bankasi (TCZB). 1982. *Su Ürünlerini Artirma ve Kredileri Yönlendirme Sempozyumu* (Symposium on fishery production and fishery investment policies). Ankara: State Agricultural Bank.

Tempier, E. 1985. *Mode de régulation de l'effort de pêche et le rôle des prud'homies de patrons-pêcheurs*. Issy-les-Moulineaux: Institut Français de Recherche pour l'Exploitation de la Mer (IFREMER).

Wylie, J. 1989. "The Law of the Streets, the Law of the Courts and the Law of the Sea in a Dominican Fishing Village." In *A Sea of Small Boats*, ed. J. Cordell. 152–76. Cambridge, Mass.: Cultural Survival, Inc.

8

Sea Tenure in Bahia, Brazil

John Cordell and
Margaret A. McKean

Property institutions—systems of rules specifying permissible and forbidden actions and the rights and obligations of individuals and groups with respect to the resources in question—are potent forces in social evolution (Bromley 1978, 1989; Runge 1986). Knowledge of the formation and functions of property systems, however, is largely confined to studies of terrestrial economies, Western countries, or legal institutions. There have been few inquiries into the nature of sea ownership or fishing rights aside from the theoretical or public policy studies and ongoing debates over the international law of the sea. Even less is known about matters of "sea rights" in the third world, or of de facto fishing-property arrangements and hereditary claims in small-boat fishing communities. Curiously, the issue of customary sea rights and laws—a paramount concern for many coastal fishing peoples—has almost never been raised by anthropologists otherwise interested in the territorial rights observed by indigenous and traditional cultures (see, for instance, Bodley 1981).

In recent years, however, ethnographers have begun to investigate the neglected domain of customary property relations in maritime fisheries and have discovered "sea tenure"—collectively managed informal territorial use rights in a range of fisheries previously regarded as unownable (Johannes 1978; Acheson 1981; Christy 1982; Cordell 1989). Sea tenure is concerned with ways in which inshore fishermen perceive, name, partition, own, and defend local sea space and resources. Western authorities have conventionally viewed coastal sea space and fishing grounds as resources to which no property rights are attached, where the "commons" are open to all comers, and fishermen engage in unrestricted competition for a limited product (Christy and Scott 1965; Crutchfield 1982; Gulland 1974). Because no single user has exclusive use rights in the resource or any right to prevent others from sharing in its exploitation (Christy and Scott 1965, 6), individual users have no incentive to restrain production (Christy 1964, 2). No consideration is given to the possibility that certain arrangements of property rights, jurisdiction, or ownership might be able to reduce resource use (Christy 1982). Where these authorities do admit the existence of cooperation in maritime communities, they see exclusively selfish motives (Muir and Muir 1982).

> It is worth noting that maritime networks for all their egalitarianism are not based on friendship. Friendship implies an emotional relationship which supersedes economic advantage. You'd give a friend the shirt off your back. That makes a friend an economic liability . . . maritime networks don't rely on trust or the emotional bonds of friendship. [Muir and Muir 1981, 77]

Moreover, the well-entrenched "culture of poverty" school of thought on Latin America construes social marginality as a foremost obstacle to any adaptive community organization or stable resource management (Oberg 1965; Lewis 1952; Varallanos 1962; compare Pearlman 1973; Lobo 1982). From this perspective, the marginal fishermen of Bahia would be especially incapable of regulating their own fishing behavior and protecting the ecology of tropical marine resources.

These conventional views fail us in two respects: first, they cannot account for the allocation of exclusive joint-use rights that we find in traditional inshore fishing regimes. Second, they fail to take into account the powerful currency of reciprocity and cooperation—even generosity—in poverty, or their mollifying effects on potentially destructive competition and capacity to assist in sustaining and regulating fisheries and other renewable resources. In fact, many maritime communities have "informal" systems of rights to resources and sea territories that are supported by unwritten laws and subtle interpersonal relationships within close-knit communities. Even if they are not evident to the outside, these arrangements are just as real, socially binding, and ecologically consequential as standard catch quotas, seasons, and selective licensing programs used by governments to manage fisheries for sustained yields. Indeed, in certain nonindustrial inshore settings they are more effective.

This chapter looks outside mainstream Euro-American definitions of fishing rights in order to document fishermen's sea tenure in shallow, nearshore waters in the province of Bahia, Brazil. Southern Bahia is one of the few tropical coasts where traditional sea tenure has been sufficiently documented for us to perceive its social logic, ecological basis, and strategic role as a resource management institution. In view of the well-known difficulties of designing and enforcing regulations in fishing, valuable lessons may be learned from traditional, "unofficial" management practices. This ethnography of Brazilian sea tenure suggests some of the benefits of studying and working to maintain local tenure and customary fishing rights in the marine commons.

Four salient features of sea tenure in peasant communities of rural Bahia are discussed:

- *Physical and technical attributes.* The environmental parameters conducive to subdivision of the fishing grounds into "closed-community" territories.
- *The decision-making arrangements.* The rules and mechanisms of collective action and group sanction that work to legitimize and uphold the tenure system.
- *The patterns of interaction.* The social contexts in which sea rights are extended, in which disputes arise, and in which conflict is resolved.
- *Outcomes.* The problems of uncontrolled coastal belt and fishery development that undermine village solidarity and break down territorial autonomy in local fishing, with detrimental impacts on the equity among fishermen and also on long-term efficiency and productivity of inshore fisheries.

Physical and Technical Attributes

Throughout the Latin American tropics are many impoverished fishing peoples who have not made the transition to modernity. Among the poorest are the fisherfolk or *beirados* ("shore dwellers") of southern Bahia in the Brazilian Northeast. Fishing for subsistence or for a small cash or supplementary income has long been a critical alternative livelihood for the poor in this region. Today's predominantly black maritime communities developed as successive generations of hinterland plantation laborers lost out in the wider economy and took refuge in the mangrove swamps that no one else had the need or stamina to exploit. These fishermen still work from dugouts, slogging through the mangroves day after day, often with little more to eat than the crab bait left over from their traps and trotlines. There is no upward mobility out of swamp fishing into the Brazilian economic mainstream. The Bahian canoe-fishing population has no stable market involvement and at times even suffers the failure of its "last-resort" fishing strategies. There is an unmistakable decline in living standards at the landward edge of the swamps where a majority of fishermen live.

In the Brazilian economic hierarchy, fishing has low visibility: in 1976, revenue from fishing was 1.31 percent of the gross national product and only 2.5 percent of total agricultural production (Morris 1979). Traditional fishermen, assumed to be primitive and inefficient, are often blamed for the low productivity of the industry. Yet Bahia's traditional marginal fishermen still land roughly 70 percent of the catch on the southern coast (Silva 1979), and thus contribute substantially to the area's internationally acclaimed cuisine, help to sustain the vital tourist industry, and seasonally stock the domestic seafood market with fresh fish. They are struggling to maintain control of their mangrove, estuarine, and coral-reef sea territories as large seafood companies, high-tech fleets, and export and inter-state markets increasingly dominate both inshore and offshore fishing in most other parts of Brazil.

The Bahian coastline is indented by estuaries, swamps, and tidewaters dotted with sedimentary and coral reefs. These comparatively sheltered waters seem conducive to marking off microhabitats for fishing claims. In addition, the proximity of fishing grounds to home ports affords the fishermen great ease in guarding their territory. Typically, the inshore fishing pattern centers around local plantation ports and provides coastal and immediate hinterland markets with fresh catches. Day-trip operations and many traditional methods (for example, the *calao*, a purse-seine) have changed remarkably little since their introduction by sixteenth-century Portuguese settlers. Fishermen on the southern Bahian coast still work mainly from sail canoes, using customary lines, nets, traps, and corrals to harvest more than 200 different species of fish and shellfish. They lay claim to extensive fishing grounds in the 1,000-kilometer strip of shallow waters between Salvador and the Abrolhos Banks (see Figure 8.1).

The *calao* is a shallow-water purse-seine, finely adapted to catching large schools of estuarine-spawning fish; it is operated by eight-man crews from dugout canoes 6 to 10 meters long. New nets may cost from U.S. $200 to $700, depending on size, quality, and elaborateness of mesh; few *calaos* are bought brand-new. They are usually inherited in various advanced states of use and have been extensively repaired. Owning such a net is a fisherman's foremost economic aspiration and a mark of high social standing. A 200-to-300-meter *calao* typically represents the investment of a fishing captain's life savings.

Purse-seining must conform to the intricate tidal changes along Bahia's estuaries and creeks that wind back into the mangrove swamps. A system of reckoning tides based on phases of the moon enables the canoe bosses (*mestres*) to monitor closely the behavior, migratory routes, and life cycles of fish (Cordell 1974). Seining and nearly all canoe fishing moves in

FIGURE 8.1
Fishing Territories of Southern Bahia

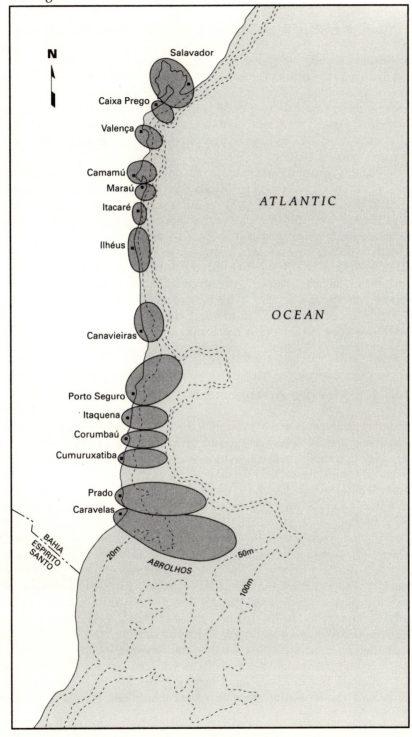

a circuit: at neap tide, fishermen concentrate along the northeastern shores; as the tide begins to rise, they move inward into the main body of the fishing grounds. At spring tide, activity shifts to the southern reaches, and finally, as the tide falls, boats move back up into the main channels. The contours of the estuary are affected by currents, so a spring tide in the inner reaches of the fishing ground is like a neap tide in the outer reaches and vice versa. The result is that fishermen can use most of their techniques every day, as long as they choose fishing spots appropriate to the day's current regime.

Favorably located water space becomes valuable, and netcasting spaces are ranked according to criteria such as ease of access during foul weather, distance from port, past production history, and so on. Because fish and fishermen alike must move from spot to spot, it is neither possible nor desirable to create physical barriers around each fishing territory, so rules must substitute for fences to exclude interlopers from each spot. The elaborate system of rules and enforcement mechanisms that has evolved then allows the fishermen to maintain considerable jointness of use of the inshore fishery as a whole. In sum, whereas in most fishing systems, including those of Bahia, the limiting condition on production is ultimately resource availability, a more immediate check on sea-tenure relations is the configuration of waterspace opportunity for purse-seines.

Decision-Making Arrangements

It is important to note at the outset that the forms of sea tenure practiced in rural Bahia are not acknowledged by any formal governmental body; in fact, they contradict national fishing codes that stipulate that Brazilian territorial waters are public property. As far as the national government is concerned, any Brazilian boat registered in a national port can move anywhere and take any amount or species of fish. Superintendencia do desenvolvimento da pesca (SUDEPE), the fisheries bureaucracy, simply does not have the capability to play a significant managerial role in fishing. The fact that Bahian and other similar fisheries in the Northeast exist outside the purview of the national fisheries administration poses critical questions for marine resource use. What happens when fishermen are left to their own devices? Are resources and fishing activities essentially unmanaged? Do local fishermen share the government's view of their resources as available to all? Is fishing destined to degenerate into what Garrett Hardin (1968) calls the "tragedy of the commons"? What happens when traditional fishing collides with modern markets and fleets that penetrate previously isolated fishing grounds?

Bahian canoe-fishing systems reveal a number of paradoxes and hidden strengths of life within the confines of marginality. Within their inshore domain, Bahia's rural fishermen, even those heavily dependent on creditors and middlemen, are their own bosses. They take advantage of the screen of geographical and cultural marginality to work unencumbered by government regulation. They are able to avoid purchasing licenses for their boats and gear or paying dues to the corrupt local fishing guilds. Instead, they market a large portion of their catch clandestinely to avoid special docking and municipal fisheries tariffs. Though they do not have to deal with national regulations and laws, they do not live in local anarchy; rather, they create, maintain, transfer, and defend an elaborate system of fishing rights outside the written law of the sea. Thus, the destitute and politically powerless fishing population of Bahia can own large stretches of shoreline sea that Brazilian law regards as open-access public property.

It is impossible to determine with any finality how and when sea tenure evolved or how canoe bosses consolidated control over premium water space in Bahian canoe fishing. There are no court records or laws to support fishermen's claims. Yet sea tenure in the form of space controlled by the community, by individuals, and by social networks has existed over the span of the oldest net bosses' memories, including their knowledge of fishing in previous generations. It is a century-old tradition at the very least. Fishing grounds range from 400 to 600 square kilometers and are restricted in size by how species are distributed close to shore, by the fact that the sail canoes (even if motorized) cannot effectively carry ice or maneuver at sea, and by the rhythm of markets in local ports and the hinterland, where consumers demand a daily supply of fresh fish.

In the northern part of the fishery around the port of Valença there are 258 traditional netcasting spots (*pesqueiros*), each accommodating a range of methods (hand lines, trotlines, set nets, traps, and seines). To prevent people using different techniques from interfering with each other, *pesqueiros* are subdivided into nonoverlapping *lanços*, or minimal water spaces as determined by fortnightly current changes, daily tide-level changes, lighting conditions during different phases of the moon, position of the *lanço* relative to the shore slope, bottom conditions, and the interactions of wind and current. Names are bestowed on the spots by fishing captains who exercise exclusive use rights over these tiny chunks of lunar-tide fishing space.

Tenure may vary from sequential netcasting claims on migratory species lasting hours or a few days to long-term private claims covering spawning grounds in brackish water, reefs, and netfishing spots defined by the lunar-tide cycle (Cordell 1974; compare Forman 1967). Relative mobility of gear and fishing craft, seasonality, microenvironmental zones, life cycles of fish, and a whole host of social variables enter into the constellation of tenure arrangements found in a given locale. Rights to fish are characteristically transmitted in limited numbers of apprenticeships, kinship, and other long-term social relations connected to the work setting.[1]

Tenure-holding units vary from loosely allied groups of fishing captains, families, or informal partnerships to extended ritual kin groupings and individual canoe fishing captains who monopolize clusters of netcasting locations. Knowledge of how to fish under this system is passed on in a limited number of apprenticeships; these may last as long as ten or fifteen years. Some apprentices never become proficient netcasting specialists and equipment owners, and consequently do not inherit rights of access to the most valued fishing grounds.

Marginal areas of the fishing grounds also include areas of essentially unclaimed sea space where new fishing spots are discovered and staked out from time to time. There is also a series of intervillage buffer zones, where rights are defined loosely, if at all. Yet even in the most marginal waters, special agreements exist for exercising well-ordered, sequential, temporary claims to netshooting areas. This system of property rights and rules has evolved slowly and only as a response to endogenous competitive pressures; there is no formal assembly of all rights holders, nor are there constitutional rules (rules for making rules) by which rights holders may convene to change the operational rules for fishing the inshore sea. Instead, existing kinship and other social relationships provide the arena in which rules are enforced.

Patterns of Interaction

Purse-seining is the occasion for much social drama. These large, encircling *calaos* are thought to be particularly deadly for the catfish, which is greatly prized locally for its flavor and tenderness, though worth relatively little on the official market. Thus, a good *calao* catch reaffirms a man's faith that God will continue to send him runs of fish. A captain can take great pride in bestowing these fish on friends and relatives, paying off debts to middlemen, and holding beer-drinking fests. A bar floor littered with broken beer bottles at dawn is a sure sign that a fishing captain has been celebrating great good fortune and skill: empty beer bottles are valued storage containers in swamp-fishing neighborhoods, and to break them is considered extravagant.

Purse-seining gives people a special opportunity to air their grievances through soap box oratory, to bestow or withhold favors, to praise or ostracize their companions, and to mobilize participants in social networks.

It is necessarily a cooperative enterprise, as many people may be involved in a single netcasting sequence—sometimes several crews of eight to ten men each—and catches are shared. Risks are great because there is often precious little time to deploy and haul a net against the tidal flow and get the fish back to market without ice at peak hours before they spoil (Cordell 1974). Purse-seining is also naturally conducive to conflict because the stakes are high relative to the catch and earning potential of other techniques. Fishermen spend many hours debating and analyzing what goes on in *calao* fishing. What is condensed here of their storytelling and fussing illustrates how sea space is named, owned, partitioned, and governed by an implicit social contract or reciprocity and an ethical code of *respeito* ("respect"); this constellation of techniques regulates access to premium netcasting locations and minimizes conflict.

Cooperation

The ethical code associated with *respeito* is much more encompassing than is superficial fishing etiquette, and far more binding on individual conscience than any government regulations could ever be. Where material wealth is scarce, debts obviously arise from reciprocal exchanges among fishermen, and the *respeito* that ensures that these debts will be honored is the measure of a person's worth. It is impossible to fish for long in a given community without receiving and showing *respeito*. People honor each other's claims because of *respeito*, which is created, bestowed, and reaffirmed through sometimes trivial and sometimes substantial acts of benevolence bordering on self-sacrifice. Fishermen need not be physically present to defend their territories or to make them real. Shoreside economic necessities continually reinforce cooperation.

Marketing fish, obtaining bait, building canoes, borrowing and lending equipment, mending nets and sails, locating crew, and acquiring information on weather and catches create opportunities to perform small favors, building up dependencies for future exchanges. Some favors up the ante: giving tows, helping someone string a trotline, or bringing special wood of the white mangrove to form crossbeams for a house. Gifts of fish, income from the catch, and shares taken filter down through the neighborhood and village networks. All these exchanges set up comfortable interdependencies that carry over into fishing and make it a distinctly social undertaking.

Perhaps the most explicit show of cooperation and *respeito* is made during the peak catfishing season in June and July. Good netfishing spaces are narrow because of tidal fluctuations, so the chance of conflict over water space is great. To relax spatial-access codes in the lunar-tide property system during this time, fishermen enter into temporary partnerships that are dissolved when the spawning runs subside. This turns out to be a very practical scheme, since catfish are liable to enter the estuary in such large schools that a single boat and crew cannot possibly catch all the available fish. If the catch is too large to fit into several boats, one crew's net is used to construct a temporary fish corral out on the tidal or reef flats. Once the main catch is delivered, more live fish are retrieved from the corral net.

Another important occasion for bestowing favors involves marketing fish. Some captains double as fish hawker-gamblers (*pataqueiros*). These people are supposed to be officially licensed by the mayor's office, but there is considerable moonlighting, and it is difficult to bring the activities of hawkers under the control of the local prefecture that oversees the operation of the fish market. Fishermen can always find black market buyers who usually pay slightly less than the going rate in the official market. But selling fish to a hawker enables one to avoid paying a weight and class-specific tax and eliminates the annoyance of going upriver into the market to unload fish. Hawkers have a clientele in mind, and they have a fairly good idea of what the demand will be for the fish available. The problem with selling to hawkers is that they seldom have cash on hand for an on-the-spot transaction. A fisherman, then, may choose to sell to a hawker on credit.

A great deal of mutual trust must accompany such transactions: selling on credit is a vote of confidence in the hawker's reputation. Another fisherman and his hawker provide an audience for the display of *respeito*. When a price is agreed on and a transaction falls through, the hawker must cover the loss himself. If the hawker fails to fulfill his end of the deal, witnesses to it can usually bring enough pressure to bear by way of gossip and verbal censure to extract the amount due.

For Bahian purse-seiners, the ultimate test and strongest demonstration of the cooperative ethic occurs in the context of godparenthood networks, with their distinctive rituals and obligations. As summer weather opens up the outermost fishing spots, those directly on the Atlantic rather than in river deltas, boats from ports upriver and in the swamp fan out to the ends of their territories, and intervillage conflicts can arise over netcasting space and schools of fish. Becoming a godparent is one strategy to gain access to new territory and to fish safely in waters of an adjoining community. The first step is to arrange to sell a catch to hawkers in neighboring territories, to make gifts of fish all around and, if the catch is good, to pay for a beer-drinking session. After initially displaying good will, the visiting captain may either volunteer or be asked to be a godparent to another fisherman's child. Such relationships are frequently established after only a brief acquaintance, and a major benefit is to confer summer fishing rights. These ongoing rights may endure for many years, reinforced by other types of cooperation.

Alternatively, a captain planning to fish close to another community's sea space will arrange to take along a crew member who has a local friend. This is a necessary precaution to ensure that his crew will receive good treatment if they have to go ashore, and to avoid the threat of competition during netcasting sequences. Some people will venture into interstitial areas to fish only when they have a network of friends or actual kin in adjoining villages.

The phenomena of becoming a godparent and establishing networks of informal contracts to ensure sea rights result in wide-ranging circles of fishermen bound by *respeito* and also account, in part, for the cooperative extension of sea tenure within a community. Canoe fishermen, purse-seiners in particular, have huge personal networks with many godparent connections that often run through a series of villages. Such ritualized extension of sea rights restores an element of flexibility in fishing opportunities where waters are otherwise exclusively used and claimed by single villages.

Another tactic is used to minimize the possibility of competitive encounters: when a captain wishes to fish in a particular spot outside the system of lunar-tide property rights, he announces his intention—including what tide level or series he will use in casting nets—several days in advance at a local bar where fishermen like to congregate. All that is required is for another fisherman to be present as a witness. To ensure the claim, the captain must follow his proclamation by going to the chosen spot the day before fishing to leave a canoe anchored with paddles sticking up in the air. This forewarns competitors that the casting space has been taken. Fishing captains go to considerable lengths to support each other in this routine, which is part of the sea-tenure politics that shore up the entire fishing system.

A cogent illustration of the honor code is the way fishermen cope with potential and actual competitive encounters while fishing the intervillage buffer zones. What often happens to create territorial conflict in unclaimed or less-fished waters is the simultaneous arrival of several boats, sometimes from different ports, to go after a sizable school of fish when the tide offers room and time for only one optimal net cast. Net bosses follow a standard procedure of drawing lots to decide who will cast first. Once an order is established, a tide marker, usually a pole stuck in the bank, dictates a sequence of netshooting rights. Not more than one tide-level change is allowed to each boat. On this basis, captains decide whether to remain. Sometimes this queuing pattern works out well, but often a boat will not close its seine and draw in the catch in the specified time. If the next boat in line begins its operations regardless, the two nets can become fouled.

Within a community's fishing grounds, where tenure privileges to lunar-tide space are clear-cut, accidents happen. Although units of netshooting space have been worked out over time so that boats can operate at a safe distance from one another, one prime casting space will occasionally overlap with another immediately upstream or downstream that belongs to a different phase of the tide cycle. In this case, fishermen may observe spatial boundaries correctly but miscalculate time boundaries. The resulting territorial infringements might appear trivial, but nonetheless have the potential to disrupt fishing operations and social relations.

Bahian fishermen take a certain amount of competition and boundary fuzziness for granted. The limits that people will tolerate depend on the extent to which potential competitors are linked by the honor code. Within these limits, which vary between individuals and social networks, people try to get away with whatever scheme will increase their fishing success. Canoes, for instance, have a way of disappearing before a critical fishing expedition and later turning up adrift on the tide. Nor is it unusual to find a fishing captain buying drinks for a competitor's crew, in hopes of getting them too drunk to leave in the time required to reach a mutually desirable fishing spot.

In any of the above situations, however, where there is a potential conflict over a fishing claim as a result of net crossing, most captains would rather act deferentially toward a competitor than force the issue. At first glance, the rationale for this ostensibly one-sided concession may appear self-defeating. However, the posture of noninterference increases a skipper's respectability, upholds the cooperative ethic, and sets up reciprocal debts of gratitude to be paid at a later date. As a captain goes out to work borderline fishing grounds, it is especially important to know who can and who cannot be trusted to stay within acceptable bounds of competition and honor the prior occupancy rule.

Failure to cooperate in these practices can be much more devastating for a fisherman than breaking a government law would be. *Respeito* is a cognitive reference point to the community conscience. It influences how fishermen evaluate each other's actions on and off the fishing grounds. It is a yardstick for measuring the justice of individual acts, especially in conflicts. Collective social pressure to conform to the ethics of fishing is reflected in the *olho do povo* ("watchfulness of the community's eye," or sense of justice), reminiscent of the forceful moral and ethical standard in Palauan fishing, "words of the lagoon" (Johannes 1981). Reputations rise and fall in terms of the *olho do povo*. The *olho do povo* determines whether territorial competition in fishing is deliberate or accidental, and whether it is antagonistic enough to require counteraction.

Conflict

Just as the community confers rewards on those who follow *respeito*, it may withdraw the benefits of exchange and reciprocity from people who consistently create conflict in fishing. The most severe gesture occurs when an entire network of fishing captains decides to deny territorial use rights to a troublemaker who does not respect their lunar-tide claims. They can do this by sabotaging equipment, disavowing the prior occupancy rule and competing fiercely for space, engaging in deliberate net crossing, or booby-trapping netcasting spaces. These strategies and withdrawal of cooperation on shore are powerful incentives for renegade fishermen to mend their ways or leave the community.

From time to time, competition within the traditional community gets out of hand and escalates into disputes, calling into play a coercive and punitive set of social controls on fishing. Most captains espouse an "eye-for-an-eye, tooth-for-a-tooth" brand of swamp justice. They recognize a danger in letting someone get away with violations of claims or codes and consider it their prerogative to redress grievances so no one will become addicted to wrongdoing.

But the backup social controls are also strictly channeled. In cases of serious rifts, certain individuals are called upon as mediators (*aconselheiros*). Were it not for the concerted efforts and personal examples set by these key individuals, the cooperative ethic might remain more symbolic than real as a binding force in social relations. Mediators are people to be emulated. They epitomize *respeito* in all they do. They are usually retired fishing captains, or in some cases fishermen's widows. These individuals take an active interest in the welfare of the fishing community and are constantly sought out for advice and to exhort fishermen to maintain *respeito* in times of controversy.

Although more or less deliberate incursions into private fishing space are a common feature of disputes, they are seldom the root cause. Conflicts of this sort usually have a long history. Mediators must be able to comprehend and soothe social relationships that have fluctuated and festered over a long period of time. Prolonged disputes resemble the legendary Appalachian feuds: they reach across several generations and are marked by vengeful acts and general hostility among coalitions of fishermen and their families and friends. Most fishermen's disputes begin with rifts onshore and carry over into fishing with its peculiar competitive possibilities. Contesting captains may try to claim each other's fishing slots by force. The victims are likely to retaliate by poaching, stealing equipment, sinking canoes, or booby-trapping fishing spots with jagged tree trunks and boulders capable of ripping an intruder's net to shreds. In extreme cases, people fight with machetes. Disputes over fishing claims frequently result from family quarrels over infidelity, wife-beating, or inheritance of assets (such as a house or fishing equipment). Once a confrontation (such as ramming a canoe) occurs on the fishing grounds, much drama in the fishing neighborhoods is bound to arise, especially if anyone is physically hurt. The heated public exchanges, threats, and counterthreats that follow surely have reverberations in subsequent fishing trips.

There is only one way to end a state of disunion among fishing captains, crews, and families once grievances have escalated to violence: the combatants must be willing to air their grievances before a mediator. To promote reconciliation, the mediator must invoke *respeito*, the cooperative ethic, as it is reflected in the *olho do povo*, and bring it to bear on individual consciences.

Thus, the way out of a dispute is not to fix blame and then to punish the wrongdoer, but to negotiate reunion (by appealing to the sense of justice) and to restore equality. A simple face-saving gesture by either one of the parties will suffice for openers. This involves humbling oneself and showing that one no longer wishes to carry a grudge. If successful, this strategy will lead to an exchange of favors or kindnesses. The conciliatory gesture may consist of a gift, perhaps a fish or a tow in from fishing in bad weather, that might otherwise seem insignificant. Through an exchange of just such small favors and concessions, fishermen are frequently able to come to terms, reestablish *respeito*, renew cooperative relations, and reaffirm the value of honor and deference in avoiding challenges over water space.

In most cases, fishermen involved in disputes not only feel justified in selective acts of reprisal, but consider themselves immune from punishment by police in nearby towns. At the request of the local sheriff, civil disorders are usually handled by state military police who have garrisons in the major seaports along the southern coast. Fishermen see little threat from these authorities, however, because they contend that their swamp neighborhoods are outside the jurisdiction of the state and local townships. They believe that their homes and fishing grounds come under the control of the Brazilian navy and federal jurisdiction.

Under Brazilian law, there is in fact such a separation in authority over land and sea, and the navy historically has been the central figure in regulating fishermen's activities and registration in professional organizations. But most of these regulations never penetrate the mangrove swamps, and fishermen's only contacts with naval authorities are with indifferent local port captains who for the most part leave fishermen alone.

Because of their peripheral social status and dissociation from government, fishermen believe that they cannot be prosecuted on land for illegal acts committed in fishing. Taking advantage of the thinness of national political and legal authority in rural coastal fishing areas, a fisherman charged with a serious crime will flee to the recesses of the swamp until things blow over, because he will be on federal territory and supposedly safe from prosecution. Accordingly, fishermen exercise their own brand of "bush" justice in the course of fishing disputes, most of which are ultimately a response to harmful acts committed on shore. This laissez-faire situation underscores the marginality of traditional swamp fishing with respect to modern Brazilian politics and the legal system, and it allows Bahian fishermen to create and enforce their own rules for sea tenure.

Outcomes

For many years, Bahia's inshore sea-tenure traditions operated smoothly. There was no evidence that coastal fisheries were being exploited in an ecologically damaging manner, an absence indicating that the practices described above were a successful arrangement for managing common-property resources. A true self-regulated fishery presumes not only that fishermen know both the limits of their resources and the impact of their equipment on resource availability, but also that they have the ability to keep their rates of exploitation in line with the productive capacity of the environment. It is doubtful that there is a traditional system anywhere that would meet this presumption. Many commercial species are trans-boundary or highly migratory, and no group of inshore fishermen can manipulate the fate of entire species over their life cycles (compare Johannes 1981).

Yet this is not to say that deliberate conservation strategies do not occur or that fishermen cannot assess the effects of their gear on resources and accordingly adjust their fishing efforts. Captains possess various means to gauge how much their production system can safely expand (Cordell 1977). Perceptions of what constitutes a "safe" number of people on fishing grounds, however, are primarily based on acceptable levels of boat crowding rather than on estimates of the reproductive reserves of fish that are necessary to sustain certain levels of production.

Resource management in purse-seining is socially diffuse and does not involve decisions by a controlling group or individual; neither does the configuration of territorial ownership control fishing. Rather, fishing is controlled by the special cooperative relationships fishermen develop with one another. Sea tenure is an extension, almost an epiphenomenon, of these personal networks. Within their sea-tenure networks, fishermen exercise controls on participation in fishing that may directly or indirectly limit the intensity of exploitation. Apprenticeships and associated channels for the recruitment and mobility of fishermen serve to limit entry to the fisheries in question, in turn curtailing fishing pressure. Although there is no evidence that tenure patterns were intentionally elaborated for conservation purposes, fishermen have species-specific knowledge of reproductive and migratory behavior and display a sophisticated and biologically well-founded perception of the natural limits to their production system.

The sea territories are collectively defensible; and only local fishermen know how to work them safely and productively on a sustained basis—two features that both discourage encroachment. Left to their own devices, local fishermen can enforce their territorial claims against competitors of similar economic means. However, since sea tenure is legitimized only by internal mechanisms like *respeito*, it can easily be subverted by the modernization of fishing technology and the expansion of markets. Traditional fishermen are extremely vulnerable to territorial displacement, loss of sea rights, and resource "piracy." All that is required to shatter the balance is for an external power to assert domain—easily done in Brazil because of national laws declaring the shore to be public property—or for a local enclave to begin using competitive technology. Local fishermen cannot cope indefinitely with entrepreneurs who have more capital or with nonresident vessels that have no respect for local customs and no need to cooperate because they will move on after they deplete local resources. At that point, the internal code among local fishermen loses its own raison d'être and breaks down; there is no longer anything for them to gain through cooperative fishing or respect of traditional authority or autonomy.

Such encroachment by inappropriate gear and nonresident boats began in the early 1970s, when nylon nets started to compete with traditional gear for identical species and water space; the consequences for traditional fishing were very destructive. We do not have the statistical data on costs and catches for different fishing methods that would be needed to evaluate the efficiency of different techniques, but we do know that overfishing of certain species and areas has occurred since 1970, and that traditional fishermen are even poorer in relative terms than they used to be. Hundreds of monofilament nylon gillnets and seines were introduced by SUDEPE, which provided loans and tax incentives for investors.[2] Affluent strangers using nylon nets were unable to coexist peacefully with the established purse-seiners, and cutthroat competition for limited netcasting spaces began in earnest. This rivalry has altered the distribution of equipment in Valença and the concentration of ownership in the different categories represented. There is a tendency for traditional nets to be abandoned in favor of secondary methods, such as mobile trotlines and fish corrals, which have a fixed seasonal location and an uncontestable exclusive or even private-tenure status. By far the greatest reduction of gear has occurred in the category of traditional natural-fiber nets. On the whole, net fishing has been in decline since 1970; but traditional purse seining, which is remarkably well adapted to estuarine fishing and to the social organization and redistributive food networks of poorer neighborhoods, has been making a slight comeback since 1976.

As a result of encroachment, rich nursery-area fisheries have been gravely damaged, and short-term speculation and overcapitalization have led to sudden overfishing of a number of native estuarine and reef species. Previous studies of the Valença Delta (see Figure 8.1) have recorded the debilitating changes in canoe-fishing society that were set in motion with the arrival of nylon gear (Cordell 1973, 1978). Since 1970, conditions have worsened in the Valença Delta and along the southern coast of Bahia, as far as the Abrolhos Archipelago. Uncontrolled exploitation of land and sea resources in the coastal zone has reached a critical intensity (compare Kottak 1983). Over the past fifteen years, investors and economic planners have targeted the southern shore for every conceivable kind of development—not just fisheries but also oil exploration, shipbuilding, tourism, lumber, agriculture, aquaculture, mining, and heavy metal processing. New roads have been built into the region, making it accessible from the large urban centers of southern Brazil and the state capital, Salvador.[3] The greatest exploitation of fisheries has been near the major cities and near shore. A critical area of actual and potential overfishing now extends from the landward range of mangrove swamps out to a depth of 50 meters, which roughly corresponds to the limits of most inshore fishing gear.

Two of the most visible and possibly destructive pressures on inshore species are the aforementioned use of monofilament nylon nets and the "pirating" of peasant fishing territories by out-of-state trawlers and long-liners. The unregulated use of nylon gear—a single vessel may set several kilometers of nets—is implicated in territorial conflicts, equipment foul-ups, and reduction of catches from traditional gear. The blockade effect of gillnets stretched across a channel may also adversely affect spawning runs. There has been a continuous escalation of trawling in waters with depths between 20 and 50 meters. Large powerboats with tiny meshed seines for shrimp kill many other demersal species. In general, modern trolling and trawling interfere with the operation of traditional methods and can irreparably damage the set gear of small-scale fishermen. Particularly during spawning runs, they compete for the same spots and species.

In Valença and other southern ports, excessive netting of major commercial varieties of finfish has produced a spillover effect on shellfish. Many local fishermen work the shellfish habitats among the mangroves, and migrants to and from cities often settle in the swamp areas to scavenge. More and more fishermen who conventionally work in the estuaries and farther offshore with large encircling and dragged nets have been forced to turn to the swamp for survival. Recent studies indicate that the intensity of foraging for some mollusks and crustacea exceeds the sustainable-yield levels (Cordell 1973; Blanco 1978). Near Valença, swamp-fishing settlements must shift frequently to achieve a satisfactory ratio of work to production from shellfish ranges. Change in these fishing communities has taken different forms and has differing effects on the economy and the power structure.

Nylon nets have been selectively introduced in parts of the delta fishing community; other parts still use traditional technology. Some communities have switched their economic dependence from the traditional power base of captains and middlemen to factory bosses, wealthy merchants, and speculators from the Salvador fish and grain markets. This new power base purchases nylon gear and canoes for a small segment of townspeople, some of whom have little or no fishing experience but are desperate enough to work at fishing for very low fixed wages. Traditional captains must be conservative with their equipment (usually representing a lifetime's investment), unlike their competitors with nylon, who can afford to precipitate spatial conflict that destroys gear. The chaotic expansion of a nylon-outfitted fishing enclave in the narrow corridor of brackish water between land and sea marks the end of an era in which marginality was the small-scale fishermen's hedge against encroachment and overexploitation of the fish.

Today in Brazil, capital is available in unprecedented amounts to fund the expansion of interstate seafood markets, and developers are reaching out with advanced technology to capture even the most residual supplies of fish and shellfish. They are diverting local food supplies, which the coastal poor have always fallen back on for subsistence in times of scarcity, to elite urban and foreign markets. Technical innovation per se is not destructive. But the way in which change proceeds does disrupt customary sea tenure and removes the informal spatial and political autonomy local groups must enjoy if they are to fish substainably and without conflict. Escalating conflict in Bahia's fisheries demonstrates that the tragedy of the commons is catalyzed when institutions break down that have supported traditional sea tenure. Indeed, traditional sea tenure seems to prevent the tragedy.

Conclusions

Both the conventional view that fisheries are invariably open-access resources and the argument that poverty inhibits constructive collective action fail to account for what we find in Bahian fishing communities before the arrival of outsiders: the successful management of inshore fisheries resources by marginal, traditional fishermen. Both theories assume that there is no relatedness or strategic interdependence among people who use resources jointly (compare Runge 1986). Both contain a certain cynicism about human nature; neither allows for community. Fishing in Brazil, if anything, indicates that cooperative sea tenure is a logical mechanism for allocating perilously scarce resources, and that poverty strengthens these incentives to cooperate all the more. Sea tenure, legitimized through *respeito* and reciprocity, is embedded in the culture; what has been all too casually deemed self-regulation in small-scale fishing (see, for example, Acheson 1981) is actually a subterranean economic system that overflows into every facet of social life.

With extended maritime jurisdiction, many countries, including Brazil, assume sweeping new powers and responsibilities for managing resources without any coherent frame of reference or forum to evaluate fishing claims, particularly traditional ones, or to define and justify new allocations of use rights. Arguments concerning the relative superiority of public or private ownership ignore the value and legitimacy of a third category, that of collective ownership. This study shows that there are practical reasons for the development of inshore tenure. Fishing productively and sustainably near shore requires regulation of access (compare Stiles 1976). Governments might support such traditional institutions by giving fishermen something approaching guarantees of exclusive community tenure and recognition of the importance of their customary, limited-entry recruitment procedures.

If Brazil and other tropical countries are to begin serious long-range management of their marine resources, they must be prepared to take into account a wide range of customary rights and claims to the sea that they do not now acknowledge. The real managerial strengths in third world coastal fisheries are indigenous, vested not in the state or its bureaucracies but in fishermen's own informal institutions, norms, and cooperative organizations.

It is difficult to convince fishery authorities that traditional sea tenure even exists in places like Bahia, much less that it is worth preserving. Fishermen's laws are nontechnical and, admittedly, somewhat intangible to the uninitiated. Sea tenure is a kind of invisible wealth, created and maintained for both material and nonmaterial ends. Yet beneath the ragged, impoverished exterior of swamp-fishing communities are rational and proven solutions to problems of sharing, partitioning, and maintaining the fishery. In a traditional context, these solutions minimize conflict and ease fishing pressure by limiting the number of people and types of boats and gear that can fish compatibly in fixed territories close to the shore. Together with fishermen's extensive ecological knowledge of the sea, the tenure arrangements are valuable resources in themselves, worthy of some type of formal protection.

Fishing is one of the few economic alternatives available to the coastal poor in Bahia and other parts of northeastern Brazil. Establishing sea tenure through their own unwritten laws helps local fishermen transcend the misfortune of being born marginal. Sea rights, in place of land rights that seem forever beyond their reach, give fishermen a group identity, honor, some sense of security, and a chance to own something in the highly class-stratified society of northeastern Brazil. Paradoxically, the marginality that keeps them poor also allows people the independence to invent and speak boldly of their "sea rights," and sometimes to sing like birds and dance as they walk.

NOTES

This research builds on Cordell's earlier fieldwork in Bahia, Brazil (Cordell 1973, 1974, 1978), but is principally based on materials collected on the southern coast of that province during an eighteen-month marine conservation survey sponsored by the World Wildlife Fund in the United States during 1982 and 1983. For assistance in preparing this study, Cordell gratefully acknowledges the support of the WWF-US and a fellowship awarded by the Social Science Research Council.

1. Studies elsewhere in northeastern Brazil (Forman 1967, 1970; Kottak 1966; Robben 1984) contain valuable clues and observations concerning the emergence of territorial systems among similar groups of small-scale fishermen.

2. For the past twenty-five years, Brazil has pursued policies of unrestricted fishery development, encouraged by a number of fiscal incentives for entrepreneurs and investors. Decreto-Lei 221/67 provided tax exemptions of 25 to 75 percent on personal income invested in fishing; it suspended both import tariffs on fisheries technology and craft and various federal taxes on catches destined for luxury internal and export seafood markets. These incentives supersede the fisheries codes (*Codigos de Pesca*) of 1938 to 1939, which contained some potentially useful, though unenforceable, management concepts (such as exclusive zones for fixed-territorial methods like fish corrals). The tax incentives remain in effect at this writing, and will probably be prolonged despite recent sobering catch statistics.

Falling catches are illustrated by changes in shrimp and several other major species. With one of the most extensive coasts in the world (nearly 8,000 kilometers) and a favored climate, Brazil ranks among the ten largest shrimp-producing countries. Its total shrimp harvest, however, after reaching a high of

129,000 tons in 1972, decreased to 79,000 tons in 1979 (Silva 1979). Exports rose somewhat during this period, from 6,783 to 7,172 tons, but per capita consumption decreased from 0.506 to 0.197 kilograms (Silva 1979), because of steep increases in the price of shrimp on the domestic market. Overall, catches in Brazil rose from 280,000 tons in 1960 to 816,000 tons in 1974 (*Annuário Estatistico do Brasil* 1976, 158). This growth was largely spurred by tax incentives (Silva 1979, 28–43). Between 1974 and 1979, the total catch only increased from 816,000 to 858,000 tons (*Annuário Estatistico do Brasil* 1981, 354–55), indicating a nationwide leveling off of production. The five principal species caught—tuna, corvina, shrimp, lobster, and sardines—have been in a state of decline since 1979 (Nascimento 1982).

3. Additional impacts on coastal fishery resources that are difficult to quantify are: stepped-up drilling and exploration by the Brazilian oil company, PETROBRAS; biocide runoff from plantations in the littoral zone; increasing landfill for highways, resorts, and other construction; and widespread extraction of coral for *cal* (lime). Dynamite is heavily employed in this mining process, and according to the coral-reef specialist Laborel (1969), who worked in Bahia, the Itaparica reefs in Salvador Bay were practically dead from the extraction of lime-rich deposits.

REFERENCES

Acheson, J. M. 1972. "Territories of the Lobstermen." *Natural History* 81:60–9.

———. 1975. "The Lobster Fiefs." *Human Ecology* 3:183–207.

———. 1981. "Anthropology of Fishing." *Annual Reviews of Anthropology* 10:275–316.

Annuário Estatistico do Brasil. 1908–. Rio de Janeiro.

Blanco, Merida. 1978. "Race and Face in Bahia." Ph.D. diss., Department of Anthropology, Stanford University, Stanford, Calif.

Bodley, J. 1981. *Victims of Progress.* Menlo Park, Calif.: Benjamin-Cummings.

Bromley, D. 1978. "Property Rules, Liability Rules, and Environmental Economics." *Journal of Economic Issues* 12:43–60.

———. 1989. *Economic Interests and Institutions: The Conceptual Foundations for Public Policy.* Oxford: Blackwell.

Christy, F. T., Jr. 1964. "The Exploitation of Common Property Natural Resource: The Maryland Oyster Industry. Ph.D. diss., University of Michigan, Ann Arbor, Mich.

———. 1982. "Territorial Use Rights in Marine Fisheries: Definitions and Conditions." FAO Technical Papers, no. 227. Rome: Food and Agriculture Organization.

Christy, F. T., Jr., and Anthony Scott. 1965. *The Common Wealth in Ocean Fisheries.* Baltimore: Johns Hopkins University Press.

Ciriacy-Wantrup, S., and R. Bishop. 1975. " 'Common Property' as a Concept in Natural Resource Policy." *Natural Resources Journal* 15 (4):713–27.

Cordell, J. C. 1973. "Modernization and Marginality." *Oceanus* 17:28–33.

———. 1974. "The Lunar-Tide Fishing Cycle in Northeastern Brazil." *Ethnology* 13:379–92.

———. 1977. "Carrying Capacity Analysis of Fixed Territorial Fishing." *Ethnology* 17:1–24.

———. 1978. "Swamp Fishing in Bahia." *Natural History*, June, 62–74.

———. 1983. "Sea Tenure and Marginality in Brazilian Fishing." Joint publication of the Latin American Studies Association, Occasional Papers in Latin American Studies, no. 6. Berkeley and Stanford, Calif.: The Association.

———. 1989. *A Sea of Small Boats.* Cultural Survival Report no. 26. Cambridge, Mass.: Cultural Survival, Inc.

Crutchfield, J. 1982. "The Economics of Fisheries Management." In *Managing Renewable Natural Resources in Developing Countries*, ed. Charles W. Howe, 5–32. Boulder, Colo.: Westview Press.

Dasgupta, P. 1982. *The Control of Resources.* Oxford: Blackwell.

Fenn, P. 1926. *The Origin of the Right of Fishery in Territorial Waters.* Cambridge: Harvard University Press. Reprinted in 1974 by Crofton, Newton, Mass.

Forman, S. 1967. "Cognition and the Catch: The Location of Fishing Spots in a Brazilian Coastal Village." *Ethnology* 6:405–26.

———. 1970. *The Raft Fishermen: Tradition and Change in the Brazilian Peasant Economy.* Bloomington: University of Indiana Press.

Gulland, J. 1974. *The Management of Marine Resources.* Seattle: University of Washington Press.

Hardin, Garrett. 1968. "The Tragedy of the Commons." *Science* 162:1243–48.

International Union for the Conservation of Nature. 1980. *The World Conservation Strategy.* Gland, Switzerland: IUCN.

Johannes, R. E. 1978. "Traditional Marine Conservation Methods in Oceania and Their Demise." *Annual Review of Ecological Systems* 9:349–64.

———. 1981. *Words of the Lagoon: Fishing and Marine Lore in the Palau District of Micronesia.* Berkeley: University of California Press.

Kottak, Conrad. 1966. "The Structure of Equality in a Brazilian Fishing Community." Ph.D. diss., Department of Anthropology, Columbia University, New York. Reissued by University Microfilms International, Ann Arbor, Mich., 1981.

———. 1983. *Assault on Paradise.* New York: Random House.

Laborel, J. 1969. "Les peuplements de Madreporaites de côtes tropicales du Brasil" (The settlement of the coral islands on the tropical Brazilian coast). *Annales de l'Université d'Abidjan (Ecologie)*: 2 (3):1–261.

Lewis, Oscar. 1952. "Urbanization without Breakdown." *Scientific Monthly* 75 (1):31–41.

Lobo, Susan. 1982. *A House of My Own: Social Organization in the Squatter Settlements of Lima, Peru.* Tucson: University of Arizona Press.

Lomnitz, Larissa. 1977. *Networks and Marginality: Life in a Mexican Shantytown.* New York: Academic Press.

McCay, Bonnie. 1978. "Systems Ecology, People Ecology, and the Anthropology of Fishing Communities." *Human Ecology* 6 (4):397–422.

———. 1989. "Sea Tenure and the Culture of the Commoners." In *A Sea of Small Boats*, ed. J. C. Cordell, 203–27. Cultural Survival Report no. 26. Cambridge, Mass.: Cultural Survival, Inc.

Morris, Michael. 1979. *International Politics and the Sea: The Case of Brazil*. Boulder, Colo.: Westview Press.

Muir, Bryce, and Margaret Muir. 1981. "Where've You Been, Stranger? Disintermediation in the Maritimes." *Coevolution Quarterly*, Summer, 74–77.

———. 1982. "Think It's Breezin' Up?" *Coevolution Quarterly*, Summer, 40–43.

Muhsam, H. 1977. "An Algebraic Theory of the Commons." In *Managing the Commons*, ed. G. Hardin and J. Baden, 34–37. San Francisco: W. H. Freeman.

Nascimento, Iracema Andrade. 1982. "Cultivo de camarão marinhos no Brasil," (Cultivation of the salt-water shrimp of Brazil). *Boletim de Pos-Graduaçao e Pesquisa* 2, no. 1:5–11. Salvador, Bahia, Brazil: Universidade Federal de Bahia.

Oberg, Kalervo. 1965. "The Marginal Peasant in Brazil." *American Anthropologist* 67:1417–27.

Pearlman, Janice. 1973. "Rio's Favelados and the Myth of Marginality." Institute of Urban and Regional Development, Working Paper no. 222. Berkeley: University of California.

Robben, A. C. 1984. "Entrepreneurs and Scale: Interactional and Institutional Constraints on the Growth of Small-Scale Enterprises in Brazil." *Anthropological Quarterly* 57 (3):125–38.

Runge, C. F. 1986. "Common Property and Collective Action in Economic Development." In National Research Council, *Proceedings of the Conference on Common Property Resource Management*, 31–60. Washington, D.C.: National Academy Press.

Silva, S. B. 1979. "Consideracoes sobre a pesca baiana no contexto da pesca Brasileira" (Considerations on Bahian fishing in the context of Brazilian fishing). *Boletim Baiano de Geografia* XII, 18, no. 11:28–45.

Stiles, Geoffrey. 1976. "The Small Maritime Community and Its Resource Management Problems." In *Marine Policy and the Coastal Community*, ed. Douglas M. Johnston, 233–54. New York: St. Martin's Press.

Varallanos, Jose. 1962. *El cholo y el Peru: Introducción al estudio sociological de un hombre y un pueblo mestizo y su destino cultural* (The cholo and Peru: Introduction to the sociological study of a man and a Mestizo community and their cultural destiny). Buenos Aires: Imprensa Lopez.

Yngresson, B. 1978. "The Atlantic Fishermen." In *The Disputing Process: Law in Ten Societies*, ed. L. Nader and H. Todd, 59–85. New York: Columbia University Press.

9

Common-Property Resource Management in South Indian Villages

Robert Wade

How do Indian villagers manage such common-pool resources as canal irrigation water and grazing lands? In one small area of South India, villages vary remarkably in the degree to which they organize themselves to undertake such management. Some are more highly organized than anything hitherto reported in the literature on (nontribal) Indian villages; others, perhaps only a few miles away, have no village-level organization at all. This chapter sets out in broad terms an explanation of that variation.

The presence or absence of village-level organization has a great deal to do with the risk of crop loss faced by many or most farmers of the village—a risk related to the ecological conditions of soil type and water scarcity. These conditions influence the demand for joint management of some common-pool resources. Within the limits of the sample studied here, it seems that some villages are organized and others are not because of variations in the demand for common-pool resource management rather than variations in the village's capacity to supply such management. This does not mean that the sorts of supply-side obstacles to collective action emphasized by the public choice theorists are irrelevant in these villages. What it means is that such obstacles as the free-rider problem have been effectively checked or bypassed by a series of ingenious institutional arrangements. To extend the argument beyond the sample, however, one needs both a theory of demand and a theory of supply to explain the presence or absence of common-property resource management institutions.

"Indian society today," says the sociologist V. R. Gaikwad, "is an

207

atomized mass, composed of individuals who are not in any organized fold except the family and the extended kin-groups which form the sub-caste" (1981, 331). Much the same has been said not just of Indian peasants, but of peasants in general. Such writers as G. Foster (1965) and S. Popkin (1979) have given great emphasis to the unimportance of the village as a focus of collective action and sentiment. This theme in the peasantry literature resonates with a theme in the "public choice" litera-ture that stresses the difficulties of voluntary collective action in any kind of society other than, perhaps, certain kinds of communes. Common sense would suggest that people who perceive a joint interest will join together to pursue this interest, and hence that a perceived common interest is a basic element in explaining collective action. The public choice theorists say that common sense is misleading. The rational individual, they say, will not voluntarily contribute to a common goal if the group is large and if he or she cannot be excluded from enjoying the benefit. The individual will, instead, seek a free ride. As a result, any collective action (in other than very small groups) that is not based on coercion or on the availability of selective incentives tends to be fragile, and to supply fewer public goods than the members would be prepared to pay for on the market—if the market were an option (Olson 1965).

Not everyone would agree that collective action and the voluntary supply of public goods must be explained only in terms of the behavior of rational, self-interested individuals. We do, after all, observe a good deal of voluntary collective action that seems on the face of it difficult to explain simply in terms of the selective benefits provided to participants (ecologi-cal lobby groups, for example; see Kimber 1981). In any case, whether or not the axiom is accepted, there remains the empirical question of the conditions under which varying types and degrees of collective action are found. Yet questions of degree and difference have been overlooked by many writers on peasantry because they have been so concerned to emphasize the difficulties of collective action.

Much of the literature on collective action and public choice has dealt with the question of what conditions propel individuals to make volun-tary financial contributions to the provision of a public good. We can turn the same kind of analysis to common-pool resource management by rephrasing the question as: Under what conditions will individuals formu-late, and agree to abide by, a rule of restrained use of common-pool resources? In this case too, as in the case of financial contributions to the provisions of a public good, there seem to be built-in incentives for the rational, self-interested individual to free ride—to cheat on the rule of restrained use while everyone else abides by it, on the assumption that others will not notice. There seems, then, to be an inner imperative for regression from abiding by the rules to unrestrained use. Certainly the literature describes many violations of rules for restrained use of common-pool resources (such as grazing, irrigation water, and trees), violations that deplete the resource. But the literature also contains many cases of local groups that have been able to agree upon the rules of restrained use and have enforced the rules by using authority from within the group rather than some authority from outside, such as government. In these cases, we can talk of a "public realm" within the group that consists of the rules and roles involved in common-pool resource management.

Indian Villages

The conventional understanding of Indian villages is that they do not have any real public realm. A number of men are usually regarded as "big men," that is, as being in some sense first in the village. But there is no clearly defined social domain or institution separate from state authority where activities of a "public" nature are carried out; no center of community management other than the bottom levels of the state apparatus itself; and no machinery for raising resources for public (village) purposes other than through state-sanctioned taxation.

My research suggests a more complex picture. I compared forty-one villages in an upland part of South India in terms of the range and strength of their public realm. Thirty-one of the villages are irrigated from a large canal system; ten are dry. A significant number of the forty-one do show a common purposefulness and ability to provide public goods and services. The arrangements are local and autonomous. They are not integrated with, initiated, or sustained by outside bodies, whether government or voluntary agencies. The scope and degree of local collective action in these villages exceeds that reported previously in the literature on Indian (nontribal) villages. On the other hand, such villages are not in a majority; most villages in my sample do fit (roughly) the "atomized mass" characterization, and only a few miles may separate a village with a substantial amount of corporate organization from others with none.

The Public Realm

The public realm consists of four main institutions:

- a village council (quite distinct from the statutory council, or *panchayat*, of local government legislation, which is moribund in all villages in my area)
- a village standing fund (distinct from local government moneys)

- a work group of village field guards, employed by the council to protect the crops from the depredations of livestock and thieves
- a work group of "common irrigators," employed by the council to distribute water through the government-run irrigation canal

The council, and through it the field guards and common irrigators, are loosely accountable to an annual meeting of all the village's cultivators. In addition to the central services of crop protection and water distribution, the council also organizes the supply of many other public goods and services, such as repairing wells, catching monkeys, donating money to help meet the cost of a new primary school or of an animal infirmary, and so on. All these services except water distribution are financed from the village standing fund, which the council administers. The fund is fed by a variety of income-raising devices that the council also administers.

Take K village as an example. It has a population of just over 3,000. Its council generally consists of nine members; the number is fixed for any one year, but varies slightly from year to year. Together they have authority to make decisions affecting all the village. The village's standing fund spends about Rs. (rupees) 10,000 a year in an economy where a male agricultural laborer gets about Rs. 4 a day outside of seasonal peaks. The standing fund pays the salaries of the field guards. Four field guards are employed full-time for most of the year, and another two to four are added near harvest time. As for those who work as common irrigators, about twelve are employed for up to two and a half months, to cover about 1,200 acres of first-season rice. At harvest time, the common irrigators, no longer needed for water, supplement the field guards, giving K a total of some twenty village-appointed men for harvest crop protection.

In the sample of thirty-one canal-irrigated villages (all in Kurnool district of Andhra Pradesh), eight have all four of the main corporate institutions—council, fund, field guards, common irrigators; eleven have some but not all; and twelve show no trace of any of them. The sample was not drawn randomly but rather with an eye to ease of access and a representative range of water supply situations, so no conclusions can be drawn from these figures about how frequent the corporate forms are in the area as a whole. But they are clearly not rare. Moreover, many dry villages have some of the same institutions. In a sample of ten, eight have field guards, six have a village council, and six have a village fund. Some of the dry villages, then, have a more clearly defined center of community management than do some of the wet villages.

Kurnool district is semiarid: its rainfall averages 620 millimeters per year in a unimodal distribution. Population density averaged 105 people per square kilometer in 1971, up from 53 in 1870. Seventy percent of the cultivated area is under food crops; only 12 percent of the gross cultivated area is irrigated. Thirty-four percent of villages were supplied with electricity in 1971. There was one tractor per one or two irrigated villages in 1980, and many fewer in rainfed villages. Most variation in real wage rates is contained within the range of 3 ± 1.5 kilograms of food grain per day. It is a poor district, and in no way atypical.

Resources and Decision-Making Arrangements

The irrigated villages have two main types of commons: grazing land and canal irrigation water. The grazing land is of two types: year-round grazing along the verges of roads and fields, as well as on the (relatively small) areas not under cultivation; and the stubble area left after the crop harvest. Both water and grazing land are commons in the sense that many people share the use of the same resource and each individual user can reduce the welfare of other users. When water is scarce, one person's use may reduce the amount available to others. When crops are still standing, grazing by one person's (mobile) animals poses risks to the owners of standing crops nearby. Privatization as a means of reducing these "externalities" (externally imposed costs) is made difficult by the nature of the resource and the technology: running water is inherently difficult to privatize, and the cost of fencing precludes privatization of the verges or the stubble.

The impetus for central control at the village level, therefore, comes from a demand for protection against the externalities of others' decision making with respect to water and grazing. In those villages that have them, the collective rules are intended to limit individualistic choice on how much care to put into shepherding one's own animals, and on when and how much water to take for one's paddy. If the rules are enforced, their effect is to assure each decision maker that others will restrain their behavior too, so that if restraint is exercised one will not be duped (Runge 1984a).

An organization is required to decide the rules and provide enforcement. If, as in these villages, enforcement is by the employment of specialized work groups, the groups must be recruited, empowered, and paid. Procedures to settle disputes must be established. These requirements are met by a village council.

The authority of the council derives largely from the wider stratification order of caste and private property, its membership being drawn from the dominant caste and the wealthier landowners of the village. However, the users of the commons do not depend on external decision makers for enforcement, and in that sense the external dimension of this arrangement is unimportant.

Cross- or subvillage units of collective action are also unimportant, a fact that in part reflects features of land tenure and canal layout. There is relatively little crossvillage landholding (a person living in one village will have little or no land within the boundaries of another), and the canals are designed so that most outlets serve the land of only one village. That subvillage units of collective action are not important partly reflects economies of scale in monitoring and enforcement, economies that are especially valuable to ensuring cost savings.

Field guards must be paid, and payment by means of a levy on each protected acre is vulnerable to free riding. The "corporate" villages are those with all or most of the corporate institutions, and to pay the field guards they have generally devised a number of ways of raising income, all of which depend on the village's acting as a unit. For example, the village council may restrict the right of access to a resource or profit opportunity, and then sell that right to an individual or small group. The money from the sale of the franchise goes to the village fund, and the individual or members of the small group profit from the difference between what they paid for the franchise and what they earn from it. The most important resource subjected to this franchise is the stubble left on the harvested area. But a variety of other resources within the village boundary may also be so treated—the council might sell the right to collect tamarind nuts, for example, or dung dropped in public places, or fish in the village tank. These constitute another category of common-pool resources in addition to those discussed above, in that they permit exclusive use by an individual; consequently, the body able to sanction that exclusion can use the resource to raise revenue. In addition, the council may raise money for the village fund by selling the franchise to a profit opportunity based on something other than natural resource use, such as the right to collect a commission on all sales of grain from the village, or the right to sell liquor. With some of these revenue-raising arrangements in place, the council is able to supply some of the more tangible public goods and services rather than just ensure a reduced risk of water scarcity or of animal damage to standing crops.

I now describe these arrangements in more detail, taking K village by way of example.

The Management of Grazing

K has a population density of 159 people per square kilometer. E. Boserup (1981) predicts that with this density one would expect to find a farming system characterized by annual cropping (at least one crop per plot per year) and multiple cropping where irrigation permits. Indeed, this is the case in K. Little waste or yearly fallow land is left; the village has no "commons" in the sense of a large area available for common grazing for a year or more. But oxen and buffalo are needed in this agriculture for traction, and they must be fed.

During the crop growing season, the animals must graze close to standing crops on the verges or on small areas of fallow, which are treated as commons. With no fencing, crop protection is accomplished through shepherding or tethering. The problem is that the incentives for careful shepherding or tethering are distinctly asymmetrical: I may not be un-happy to see my animals getting fat on your grain. The open-field system of husbandry familiar during the medieval and early modern period in Europe was a response to the same problem. But whereas the open-field system operated primarily by regulating the cropping, these Indian villagers regulate the livestock. The rationale of the field guards is to make the incentives on tethering and shepherding less asymmetrical.

The field guards patrol the village area and make sure no animal is grazing a standing crop. If they catch an animal in the act, they take it to the village pound, where it remains until its owner pays a fine. If just a few animals are involved, the fine is a flat rate per head—Rs. 2 during the day, Rs. 4 at night, with the council setting the rate. The field guards collect and keep the fine, dividing it equally among themselves so that the arrangements contain a built-in incentive for enforcement. If large num-bers of animals are involved, the council decides the fine case by case; the fine may run into hundreds of rupees in some instances. The field guards collect the fine, keep 25 percent, and hand over the balance to the standing fund. (In most villages, the owner of the damaged crop is not compen-sated.) Notice that the field guards do not enforce "stinting." The decision about how many animals to own and graze is left to each individual.

Limited year-round grazing in the village or its environs means that most of the village's grazing animals are "big" stock—oxen and buffalo needed primarily for draught power. Relatively small numbers of "small" stock—sheep and goats—are owned by villagers. However, after most of the rainfed crops are harvested in February, large areas of stubble become available for grazing. Note that all the irrigated villages have some area under rainfed crops as well, and in most irrigated villages the area under such crops is larger than the irrigated area. It would be possible for each landowner to reserve the stubble on his own land for his own animals or for others he would allow in. The owner could do so by posting guards around each field, or by fencing. However, the cost of either method of exclusion—the cost of privatizing the stubble—is very high; all the more so given that (as is commonly the case in peasant societies) any one landowner has holdings divided into a number of scattered plots

(McCloskey 1975). Accordingly, as in the open-field system of Europe, the stubble is put in common, so that private rights to the product of the land extend only to the crop, not to the crop residues.

How is this commons managed in the "corporate" villages? Recall that the village's own stock of animals is adjusted to the year-round grazing, which is much less than the grazing that becomes available after the harvest of the rainfed crops. There is thus an opportunity for the village—for a village authority—to earn revenue by renting out the village's surplus grazing. Large tracts of the district are hilly and arid, covered in scrawny scrub, and unsuitable for more than desultory cultivation of sorghum and millet. Herding sheep and goats is a major source of income for the local residents. After the harvest of the rainfed crops, they come down into the irrigated tracts seeking grazing for their livestock. The herders want the grazing and water, while the farmers want their fields manured and cleared of stubble.

The market for grazing and manure is organized in two distinct ways. In the first, a small group of herders comes to a village and bargains with the village council for exclusive access to the village's grazing.[1] The agreement states how many sheep and goats they will bring, when they will come, how long they will stay (in terms of a date before which they will not leave and a date by which they will be gone), and, most important, how much they will pay for the franchise. Once the agreement is made, that group of herders has exclusive claim to the village's grazing, and other herders can enter only as some leave. Their flocks graze over the stubble by day. By night, when the animals drop most of their manure, they are folded, flock by flock, on the plots of particular landowners, who pay them an agreed rate per head. In this way the herders as a group pay the village fund a lump sum for access to the commons and individually get back part of what they pay through the sale of manure.

The second method (used in K and other villages) is more complex. A group of herders, as before, obtains exclusive access. But instead of a group entry fee or rent, an auction is held at a regular interval (every four days in K) to decide who will have each flock on his land at night until the next auction. The auction is arranged by the village council. Half the amount of the winning bid for each flock is then paid to the herder, and half goes to the village fund.

In K, between 9,000 and 13,000 head commonly enter the village at this time. They graze the stubble on that part of the 4,000 arable acres of land that is not still growing a crop. The village fund commonly gets about Rs. 5,000 in return, in the space of about six weeks.

At the same time, the entry of such a large number of animals while some crops (mainly the irrigated ones) are still standing poses a serious risk of loss for the owners of those crops. The response is to tighten the regulation of the livestock in two ways. One is to stipulate a set of rules for both herder and landowner. The second is to appoint full-time field guards. A village's rules of grazing are read out at the first auction of every year, and may be read out again if there are infringements. They are worth giving here, because they tend to contradict the belief that Indian villages show no deliberately concerted action.

The rules for the herder are:

1. He must take the flock to the designated field by 6:30 P.M. and keep it there until 8:00 A.M.
2. He must not allow the flock to graze standing crops.
3. Half of the amount he is to be paid for the first "turn" (four nights) must be put on deposit with the council. If he leaves before four turns (sixteen nights) have been completed, he forfeits this amount to the village fund. (This structure is to discourage the herders from leaving early, before the farmers have had their fields manured and cleared of stubble.)
4. The herder must stay within the village boundary; if the farmer asks him to go to a field outside the village boundary, he must refuse.

The rules for the farmer are:

1. He must keep the flock within the village boundary. (This rule is to ensure that the farmers of the K village, rather than those of some other village, get their fields cleared of stubble. It also helps to reduce the conflict between villages, because if a farmer from K brought a flock into another village where he owned or rented lands, he might ignore that village's own implicit or explicit rules about grazing and be less subject to formal or informal sanctions.)
2. If he wishes to pay the fund or the herder in kind rather than in cash, he must make the conversion at the rate of Rs. 1.25 per measure of hybrid sorghum or Rs. 1.50 per measure of "local" sorghum (early 1980 prices).
3. He must send men to help the herder guard the flock at night, at the rate of two men per 2,000 head. If hired, the men must be paid Rs. 3.0 per night, or the equivalent in grain (to prevent the farmer from sending nonablebodied men, who could be paid less).

Such tight specification of responsibilities by the council reflects the real danger of loss to standing crops on unfenced fields. Rules of this kind, however, are not self-enforcing. Any one farmer would have an incentive to cheat by failing to provide the stipulated number of herd guards or by bringing the flock to his field outside the village boundary. So the second intensification of joint regulation is by means of village-appointed field guards to monitor observance of the rules.

Field guards must be paid a salary. It would be possible for the council to lay down a flat rate, at so much per cultivated acre, that each landowner would have to pay them. But this arrangement would be vulnerable to free riding. A farmer may delay payment indefinitely, expecting that others will not similarly delay; in this way he can continue to benefit from the general discipline of livestock that the field guards provide while not himself having to pay a part of their cost. Most villages address the free-rider problem by finding a method of raising income for the field guards' salaries that does not depend on individual contributions. The chief source of revenue is the one we have been considering, namely, the income from renting out the village's grazing. Once a village decides on this course, the amount of money that can be earned is much more than is needed to provide a guard force for the period when large numbers of outside stock are in the village. Here, then, we see the impact of the free-rider problem: in the context of field guarding it is a serious matter, and institutions are designed to avoid it by divorcing the supply of the public good from individual contributions. The bypass institutions are more costly to administer, however, and in small villages (500 people or less) farmers will often try to institute the individual payment method for meeting the field guards' salaries. Recurrent free-rider problems then tend to force villages toward a more complex arrangement like selling the franchise to the grazing.

Indeed, the "corporate" irrigated villages tend to have several sources of revenue for the standing fund, almost all of them based on the sale of franchises sanctioned by the council. One income source is the franchise to sell liquor in the village. Some villages auction the right to collect a commission on all grain sales from the village. Still others may have an irrigation "tank" (small reservoir) within their boundaries; each year the council stocks it with fish, and later in the year auctions the franchise to catch the fish, the money going to the fund. The income sources vary considerably, but the grazing franchise is the most common. With a standing fund in surplus above the field guards' salaries, the fund can then be used to provide additional public goods and services, such as those mentioned earlier.

In short, the main advantage to the farmers of organizing the sale of such franchises is that they then benefit from the supply of collective goods and services made possible by the sales. Of these, the most important is crop protection provided by the field guards, and the most important franchise (in terms of revenue) is the sale of the stubble. By organizing to control access to the village's stubble, the farmers are able to raise income for the immediate purpose of employing a work force to protect those among them whose crops would be endangered by the arrival of large numbers of free-ranging animals; the income raised, once the franchise is organized, is sufficient to provide crop protection for all the farmers for most of the year. The alternative would be for each farmer to arrange crop protection individually or among small groups of field neighbors. The village-wide arrangements allow economies of scale in monitoring and policing the grazing animals, and also save on transaction costs.[2]

The Management of Irrigation

Irrigation is the second source of conflict and possible production loss. In any irrigation system where water is scarce, there is an inherent conflict between "upstream" and "downstream" farmers. Upstream farmers have first access and their supply is relatively abundant; their water use determines how much water those downstream will get. Without the intervention of regulation and rules of restrained access, constant conflict and crop loss are likely.

The villages under study are fed from large-scale government-run irrigation canals. Paddy is the only significant first (wet) season crop, being transplanted in late July or early August, and harvested in December or January. By the end of September, the heavy rains have normally stopped, and the crop is dependent largely on canal water. The common irrigators are appointed shortly thereafter, and do the job full-time until the harvest. Their job is to allocate the scarce and fluctuating supply of canal water over the village's land; they also help procure more water for the village from the government-run supply by one means or another, such as surreptitiously blocking the outlets of higher-up villages. The irrigators are not normally employed in the second (dry) season, however, when little paddy is grown.

Two things are to be noted about this arrangement. First, the common irrigators do not influence decisions about how much land will make a claim to the irrigation water; those decisions are left in the hands of individual cultivators, as are decisions about how many animals to graze. Second, once the common irrigators are appointed, they take very important irrigation decisions out of the hands of individual farmers in the name of a village-wide authority.

Each field is entitled to be "adequately wetted"; it cannot then receive water until all the other fields beneath that outlet have received the same treatment. This is quite different, then, from the open-access, first-come-first-served rule that prevails before the common irrigators are appointed.

"Adequately wetted" is also quite different from the basic criterion of water distribution in northwest India, where canal water is constantly scarce. There, a "fixed-time-per-acre" principle is used, such that during a fixed period of the week any one field may receive whatever water is flowing in the watercourse, but cannot receive water again until its fixed time of the week comes around. The difference presumably relates to the difference in the crop-water response function for rice and all other crops.[3] If rice gets an amount of water less than its potential evapotranspiration, the falloff in yield is much more severe than for other crops. The adequately wetted rule, used in rice areas, at least ensures that each time around some fields will be saturated; whose fields they are depends simply on their position in relation to the fields that were saturated the last time around.

This difference in rules of water allocation illustrates an important supplemental factor. Whereas the fixed-time-per-acre rule is self-policing (the next farmer in line knows exactly when his turn should start), the judgment of "adequately wetted" cannot be left to each individual irrigator. Use of this criterion requires a superordinate authority to make the judgment in the common interest. We therefore find an intriguing transition: water that was previously allocated by an open-access, first-come-first-served rule becomes, after the common irrigators are appointed, allocated by a village-wide authority. Plants show a somewhat similar transition: crops are privately owned, but what is left behind after the crops are gone from the land becomes subject to the rules of the same village-wide authority. As the season progresses, water shifts from open access to common property; crops shift from private property as crops to common property as residues.

Individual irrigators who steal water—who try to influence how much water they get once the common irrigators have been appointed— are liable to be brought before the council and fined. During a drought, when the common irrigators are "spreading water like money" (to use a village phrase), the fines may run between Rs. 20 and Rs. 50 per offense; but the main penalty is the loss of reputation that results when the offender is dressed down in front of the council.

The common irrigators are paid at harvest time by means of a levy on each irrigator (so much per irrigated acre), not from the village fund. The rate is set by the council. Is this not vulnerable to free riding? The short answer is no, because the collection is made in kind, at the time of harvest—the one time of the year when every irrigator patently has no excuse to delay payment in kind. More important, however, common irrigators not paid one year can more readily damage the nonpayer the next year. The withdrawal of common irrigator services from one individual's land has more serious implications than does the withdrawal of field guarding services from the same land. So again the free-rider issue is relevant: the fact that financial free riding could be more easily punished in the irrigation case, and that if others were to follow the example the consequences of widespread free riding would be serious for a downstream free rider, means that the council does not have to extend itself to pay common irrigators from the fund as well as field guards.

The Ecological Basis of
Common-Property Rules

I have discussed how things are done in the "corporate" villages, that is, the ones that have all or most of the four corporate institutions. Although most of my detailed information comes from K village, there is in fact remarkably little variation in the principles of organization of the four key institutions from village to village, even though the institutions evolved autonomously and were not imposed from above. Many villages, however, have no corporate organization: there is no village council and no standing fund; the villages have no village-appointed field guards (though private landowners may sometimes appoint their own, occasionally coming together into small groups to do so), and no common irrigators. Here the rule of open access to irrigation water continues through the irrigation season, though informal turn sharing may develop along some watercourses. Thus uncoordinated groups of herders may enter a village's land at will (they may have the permission of the headman, for which they have paid nothing) and negotiate individually whose fields they will use to fold their flocks, and for how long each time. Often the farmer does no more than provide the herder with meals. Why the difference between the "corporate" and "noncorporate" villages?

The first point to note is that the corporate irrigated villages are located toward the tail end of irrigation distributories (roughly, the bottom one-third of the length, where typical distributories may be 5 or more miles long). Second, the corporate dry villages tend to be located in black soil rather than red soil areas. The third point is that in the semiarid tropics generally, black soil areas tend to be lower down a watershed than red soil areas. Thus irrigated villages toward the tail end of a distributory (given that distributories run from higher to lower ground) also tend to have a higher proportion of black soil areas.

Black soils are more water-retentive than red soils and permit a wider range and higher yield of rainfed crops. Black soil villages thus have a more abundant and more varied supply of stubble after the harvest of the rainfed crops. More herders want to bring their sheep and goats to graze in them. With unrestrained access, too many animals might come in, causing the soil to become excessively impacted. But also, with more herders wanting to come in, the opportunity for earning money with which to pay for field guarding (not just while the animals are at large but also through the rest of the year) is more attractive. Moreover, the risks of crop loss are higher: in the more varied cropping pattern of black soil, large areas of stubble from the early harvested crops will become available while later harvested crops are still standing. With higher risks of crop loss, the premium on being able to organize a regulation of the livestock is also higher. This provides the impetus to field guards and a sanctioning village council in the black soil areas, while the herders' willingness to pay for good black soil grazing provides a way to finance the field guards.

This causal nexus operates in all black soil villages whether irrigated or not (recall that most irrigated villages also have a large area under rainfed crops). It is then reinforced in tail-end irrigated villages by water scarcity and the consequent risk of conflict and crop loss. Of course, if the power structure of the village were such that no collective action could be sustained without the agreement of a small number of households, and if these households held all their land close to the irrigation channel, then they would have no interest in rules of access. In practice, however, holdings are typically scattered about the village area in small parcels, partly to diffuse risk and partly because of inheritance practices: a landowner with a plot close to one irrigation outlet may have another plot close to the tail end of a block fed from another outlet. This greatly helps the consensus on the need for rules and joint regulation. It may be that the degree of scattering is greater in black soil than in red soil villages, perhaps because owners wish to utilize the greater variety of soils in the black soil areas so as to spread risks. The movement of water laterally through the soil and subsoil profile is also more complex in black soil areas, so it is not always the case that land closer to the irrigation outlet is more desirable than land farther away.

Areas of rainfed cultivation higher up a distributory have more red soil than those lower on the path. Since red soil dries out sooner after the rains stop, these areas support less stubble and herders are less interested in grazing there. Also, higher-up irrigated areas tend to be under paddy in both seasons but sheep and goat manure is wanted mainly for nonpaddy, so both demand for and supply of animals and grazing is less in higher-up villages. In higher-up villages, too, the supply of canal water is more plentiful and fluctuates less.

Thus both sources of conflict and crop loss are stronger in villages lower down a watershed than in villages higher up. The evidence of my sample suggests that lower-down villages are very likely to have a differentiated public domain in which the appointment, supervision, and payment of specialized work groups are carried out, and in which rules of common-pool use are decided upon and enforced. The existence of this sort of organization does not seem to be very sensitive to variations in the standard sociological variables, such as caste structure, factions, and the like. Common need—or demand— seems to be an almost sufficient condition, in contrast to the argument of the public choice literature. Free-rider problems remain, and they do shape the organization of the supply of public goods; but they do not generally destroy it.

At the same time, my evidence also questions the common generalization that irrigation per se induces a more clearly defined pattern of community management. Some of the dry villages have more corporate organization than any of the abundantly irrigated villages. The social response is not to irrigation per se, but to risk of conflict and crop loss. Where water is abundant, that risk is small.

What about the effects of the rules of restrained access on resource use? This question turns out to be exceedingly difficult to answer, in particular because of the difficulty of finding pairs of villages that have similar ecological conditions but dissimilar corporate institutions (meaning, essentially, that one has such an institution and the other does not). All one can say with some confidence is that both production and equity are higher in the villages with these rules and institutions than they would have been in those same villages in the absence of the rules and institutions. Whether the current levels of provision of public goods and services are in some sense "optimal," given the transaction and enforcement costs of the village-level institutions, is a question that must be raised, but that my data cannot answer.

My explanation for presence and absence uses a simple combination of individual interests joined with variations in ecological risk. I say that where there are substantial individual benefits from joint action, that action is likely to be forthcoming. This is not to say that the free-rider problem, the temptation for self-interested individuals to go for immediate gain, is minor. The need to respond to the free-rider problem has a basic effect on the organizational design. We have seen how it affects the amount of revenue the council must raise by means other than individual contributions. But we also noted that the council has developed formidable mechanisms for enforcing the rules, precisely for the purpose of convincing individuals that other people will probably abide by the rules, so that if they too abide by the rules they will not be the loser. These expectations come not only from the enforcement mechanisms. They come also from the social composition of the council, an elite body with no pretense at "representation," which draws upon the power and prestige of its individual members to bolster its legitimacy in the resource management sphere. Finally, they come from the length of time that the council and its rules have been operating, which is, in all these villages, several decades at least.

An assumption of methodological individualism is therefore used to explain why certain resource management rules have emerged in some villages but not in others. That is to say, I do not think a sense of obligatory group membership, or a belief in "cooperation" as a desirable way to live, are important factors. There are no grounds for thinking that general social norms of solidarity and cooperation vary among the villages in the study area. On the other hand, the rules and institutions I have tried to explain are distinctly "second-order," not first-order; they presuppose a wider and more fundamental set of rules and norms making for a general pattern of social order. I do not believe that these first-order rules and institutions can be explained in the same sort of terms, as the result of earlier rounds of individual maximizing (Field 1984).

Lessons for Organizational Design

Suppose local common-interest groups—"water users' associations" or other kinds of normal rural cooperatives—are to be deliberately induced by an outside authority? What design principles does this study of autonomously evolved groups suggest? The first is that, in the south Indian context at least, villagers are likely to follow joint rules and arrangements only to achieve intensely felt needs that could not be met by individual responses (Johnston and Clark 1982). These needs are likely to be concerned primarily with the defense of production (avoidance of crop or animal loss), secondarily with the enhancement of income, and finally (and a long stretch from the first two), with education, nutrition, health, and civic consciousness. The opportunities for avoiding losses or making income gains by collective action will only be taken if the losses or gains are large. This is the significance of the fact that, in the irrigated villages in my sample, corporate organization to manage common property is found, with hardly any exceptions, only toward the tail ends of distributaries, where resources are most scarce.

The second principle is that the generation of authority (that is, of the right to decide for others) is likely to be problematic within such common-interest organizations, and that if the organization is to be sustained it should draw on existing structures of authority. In practice, this means that the council will be dominated by the local elite, which is a disturbing conclusion for democrats and egalitarians. Would it not be better to prescribe a representational rule, a majority vote, or both for selection of decision makers?

If the experience of these Indian villages is a guide, the answer is no. One reason is that such rules carry little legitimacy in the eyes of the powerful. But more importantly, the robustness of the organization depends on its councillors' all having a substantial private interest in seeing that it works; and for the kinds of functions we are considering here, that interest is greater the larger a person's landholding (assuming that landholdings are typically in scattered parcels). By including on the council only those who have a substantial private interest in seeing that the collective good is provided, the council itself comes close to becoming a modified version of M. Olson's "privileged group" (1965, 50): the minimum coalition whose members find it in their private interest to bear the transaction costs of organizing others to share in the costs of providing the collective good. This effect is then greatly reinforced by the greater power of the elite councilors versus the mass of the population: the tendency of the nonelite to cheat, hoping that because of large numbers no one else will notice, can be checked by sanctions contained in the wider order of property and stratification. Without these wider sanctions, the formal penalty mechanism would in all likelihood constitute an inadequate barrier to cheating. This is a point that the public choice literature tends to overlook because it assumes a context of free and equal individuals.

One specific implication is that, where water users' associations are to be deliberately fostered, the village rather than the water unit is likely to be a more viable unit of organization. The attempt to induce irrigators who depend on one canal outlet to form a water users' association (an outlet-based group) is likely to be fragile if such a group has not already been mobilized for other purposes. It will simply not contain enough authority. Yet many programs for irrigation improvement in India assume that the "natural" unit organization is the outlet.

If the elite run the organization, will the organization not become another instrument of exploitation? That it does not become so in these Indian villages reflects the third basic principle: the council is concerned only with benefits or costs that cannot be privatized. It is not involved in input supply other than water. It is not involved in settling disputes unrelated to husbandry or water. It does not try to compensate the owner of animal-damaged crops using the fine levied upon the animal owner, for that would generate conflict about privatizable value. In K village, the one time the council tried to intervene in the allocation of privatizable goods—namely, in allocating rationed sugar from the state—the conflicts over who got it became so strong that the organization almost ceased to function. The council eventually resolved that henceforth it should have nothing to do with rationed sugar. All the activities it is involved in (with this one temporary exception) have a strong public character, and most also have important externalities.

But the restrictions on scope go much further. Several kinds of decisions with important externalities do not involve the council: notably, each village household's decision about how many livestock to hold, and each farming household's decision about how much paddy area to plant. In other words, the council is not involved in "stinting" (for which see Runge's discussion of the prisoner's dilemma in Chapter 2) or in restricting claims to irrigation water. To become involved in such issues would evidently require the council to wield a great deal more authority than it does at present. The implicit rule of selective involvement within the set of issues with strong externalities may be: Do not become involved in households' investment decisions, even in ones with strong externalities; but do organize ways of mitigating the externalities generated by those investment decisions.

The fourth principle is that the council will add on other, less vital functions only as it becomes completely accepted in the performance of the vital functions. In all the study villages, the less essential things (well repairing, monkey catching, and so on) are only done by a village-wide organization when that organization also does the core tasks of field guarding and common irrigating; but only a few of those organized to do the essentials also do many of the less essential tasks.

The fifth principle is to keep the techniques of calculation and control simple. When the councils intervene to mitigate the externalities, with respect to livestock and paddy, of households' investment decisions, they do so by using rules that are simple, easily monitored, and consistent with general notions of equal treatment. They would probably withdraw from any involvement where this principle could not be met. At the same time, however, all the councils have some procedures for record keeping and accountability, so as to "institutionalize suspicion," in Ronald Dore's phrase (1971). The procedures only make sense on the assumption that the treasurer, for example, might have stolen some funds. But it is in the interests of the treasurer, as well as the contributors, to follow procedures that would tend to expose his stealing. In this way, the suspicion that the treasurer might have stolen is given regular, accepted expression. In these Indian villages, the annual general meeting of all cultivators to discuss the forthcoming season, ratify the new council, and receive nominations for field guards is a simple technique of this kind. So also is the rather simple kind of record keeping on standing fund income and expenditure, which is read out at the general meeting. Meetings of the council are held in the open, and anyone who passes by can listen in.

Governments and voluntary agencies can perhaps help to promote local collective action by measures that reduce the transaction costs of establishing and operating arrangements such as those described here. Enabling legislation, permitting devolution of limited fiscal powers to local communities under specified conditions, would be one step. Another is to promote knowledge among farmers of the various sorts of arrangements that have been autonomously designed. Any more active promotional measures should be targeted at areas where there is a good chance that farmers will respond—areas that can be identified by means of the kind of analysis illustrated here.

Conclusions

I have examined spatial variation in common-pool management within an area of south India small enough for technology, tastes, and general social norms to be constant, while resources, notably soil and water, are varied. The central conclusion is that village-wide institutions are only likely to be formed and sustained when the risks of loss are relatively high; but within the limits of the sample, the chances that such institutions will exist in the relatively high-risk situations are good. That is, the relationship between risk and social response seems to be an almost sufficient one (risk and social organization are almost always related to one another in the predicted way). The conclusion is thus in line with the argument of several economists who have written about induced institutional innovation, such as R. Coase (1960), Y. Hayami and V. W. Ruttan (1971), and D. C. North and R. P. Thomas (1973), and who have tended to argue that when the benefits of institutional change exceed the costs, change will occur.

The limits of the sample, however, are very narrow. Wider testing will almost certainly show that the relationship between risk and social organization is affected by numerous contingent conditions, variations in which will cause the relationship between risk and social organization to vary also. The variable most likely to have an important effect here is power. In these villages, it is very important that the most powerful households tend also to have scattered holdings, which gives them an interest in what happens over the whole village area. What the councils do is certainly in the interests of the elite, but the fact of scattered holdings helps to ensure that the councils' actions also promote the common interest of landowners.

Such factors as the government's workable authority in the countryside might also be important: where the irrigation agency is more effective at spreading water scarcity evenly down a distributory, there would be a less close relationship between village location and corporate organization. I suspect that the contingencies are not so strong within India as to make the occurrence of this type of corporate organization rare. Indeed, I suspect that much more autonomous local group organization for resource management exists in the Indian countryside than is generally thought. In the general case, one has to recognize that risk reduction is only one kind of benefit. Other benefits in other situations may also create a demand for collective arrangements.

Finally, I wonder whether we can learn something about the conditions for the original formation of the state from the study of autonomous local group organization. We see in these Indian villages a clear example of how in some circumstances individuals can agree to assure mutual cooperation via mutual coercion (with some individuals more coerced than others). If, with some political theorists, we look upon the state as based on a conjunction of contract and coercion, and if we think of the first states as constituting a relatively advanced stage of evolution of a public realm in local communities, we might then draw on an understanding of how the conjunction of contract and coercion is sustained in these Indian villages today for insights about how it emerged in stateless agricultural communities.

NOTES

This chapter is based on *Village Republics: Economic Conditions for Collective Action in South India*, Cambridge University Press, 1988. It has benefited from the editorial suggestions of David Feeny.

1. I know little about how the herder groups are organized. At the start of the stubble grazing, K normally admits a group of eight to ten herders, each with a flock ranging from 800 to 4,000 head. Some come from as far as 50 miles away, but most live within 30 miles. About half the herders who come in one year will have come the previous year.

2. There might also be benefits to the farmers from the bilateral monopoly in bargaining with the herders (a point I owe to David Feeny). But such benefits are checked by the herders' mobility: they can decide to go to other villages without controlled access. The quality of the grazing and the availability of water matter more to the herders, however, than their net payment per head of livestock. In K's auctions of 1980, the price paid by farmers per head of stock per night averaged Rs. 0.038, of which half went to the herder; this represented the herder's net profit, because he did not pay to come into the village.

3. Rice is the main irrigated crop in the area of my study, but it has not until recently been grown in the northwest.

4. The first test would be how well the argument made here fits with accounts of the evolution of states in south India itself. My argument seems to be consistent with Stein's account (1980) of the formation of the "peasant state" in medieval south India.

REFERENCES

Ault, W. 1973. *Open-Field Farming in Medieval England: A Study of Village Bylaws.* London: Allen and Unwin.

Boserup, E. 1981. *Population and Technology.* Oxford: Blackwell.

Coase, R. 1960. "The Problem of Social Cost." *Journal of Law and Economics* 3 (Oct.):1–44.

Dore, R. 1971. "Modern Cooperatives in Traditional Communities." In *Two Blades of Grass,* ed. P. Worsley. Manchester, England: Manchester University Press.

Dore, R., and Z. Mars, eds. 1981. *Community Development: Comparative Case Studies in India, the Republic of Korea, Mexico and Tanzania.* London: Croom Helm.

Field, A. J. 1984. "Microeconomics, Norms, and Rationality." *Economic Development and Cultural Change.*

Foster, G. 1965. "Peasant Society and the Image of Limited Good." *American Anthropologist* 67.

Gaikwad, V. R. 1981. "Community Development in India." In *Community Development: Comparative Case Studies in India, the Republic of Korea, Mexico and Tanzania,* ed. R. Dore and Z. Mars.

Hayami, Y., and V. W. Ruttan. 1971. *Agricultural Development: An International Perspective.* Baltimore: The Johns Hopkins University Press.

Johnston, B., and W. C. Clark. 1982. "Organization Programs: Institutional Structures and Managerial Procedures." In *Redesigning Rural Development: A Strategic Perspective,* ed. B. Johnston and W. C. Clark. Baltimore: The Johns Hopkins University Press.

Kimber, R. 1981. "Collective Action and the Fallacy of the Liberal Fallacy." *World Politics* 32.

McCloskey, D. 1975. "The Persistence of English Common Fields." In *European Peasants and Their Markets: Essays in Agrarian Economic History,* ed. W. Parker and E. Jones. Princeton, N.J.: Princeton University Press.

North, D. C., and R. P. Thomas. 1973. *The Rise of the Western World: A New Economic History.* Cambridge: Cambridge University Press.

Olson, M. 1965. *The Logic of Collective Action.* Cambridge, Mass.: Harvard University Press.

Parker, W., and E. Jones, eds. 1975. *European Peasants and Their Markets: Essays in Agrarian Economic History.* Princeton, N.J.: Princeton University Press.

Popkin, S. 1979. *The Rational Peasant: The Political Economy of Rural Society in Vietnam.* Berkeley: University of California Press.

Runge, C. F. 1984a. "Institutions and the Free Rider: The Assurance Problem in Collective Action." *Journal of Politics* 46:154–81.

―――. 1984b. "The Innovation of Rules and the Structure of Incentives in Open Access Resources." Staff Papers Series (Sept.), Department of Agricultural and Applied Economics, University of Minnesota, St. Paul, Minn.

Stein, B. 1980. *Peasant State and Society in South India*. Delhi: Oxford University Press.

Wade, Robert. 1988. *Village Republics: Economic Conditions for Collective Action in South India*. Cambridge: Cambridge University Press.

Worsley, P., ed. 1971. *Two Blades of Grass*. Manchester, England: Manchester University Press.

10

Oukaimedene, Morocco:
A High Mountain *Agdal*

Jere L. Gilles, Abdellah Hammoudi, and Mohamed Mahdi

About one-fifth of the world's surface is currently threatened by deser-tification (McGuire 1978). Most of this land is now used for grazing domesticated animals. If wide-scale environmental deterioration is to be prevented, the management of world rangelands must be improved, but to date virtually every attempt to manage third world rangelands has failed. Setbacks have been so frequent that agencies that fund develop-ment programs have begun to consider pastoral development too risky for further investment (Little 1983).

In large part, the failure of pastoral development programs can be traced to a failure to understand the complexity of traditional pastoral systems. Planners often assume that the seemingly primitive techniques used by pastoralists were unproductive and poorly adapted to semiarid environments. Closer examination of these production systems reveals, however, that they are as productive as modern ranching systems in North America and Australia.

The failure of most government-sponsored range management pro-grams and the relative efficiency of traditional pastoral systems suggest that indigenous approaches to pasture management can be used to protect the world's fragile rangelands. One of the few successful government-sponsored programs of this type is based on such an approach (Draz 1983). The Syrian government and the Food and Agriculture Organization (FA0) were able to create pastoral development cooperatives based upon a traditional system of pasture reserves, or *hemas*. While it may not be possible to manage rangelands with the *hema* system everywhere, the

Syrian experience illustrates the importance of understanding traditional range management systems (Eighmy and Ghanem 1982).[1]

An indigenous system of range management, known as the *agdal* system, survives in many remote parts of Morocco. An *agdal* may be defined as a "collective pasture with rigid, fixed opening and closing dates" (Hart 1981), or as any grassy area whether collectively or privately owned from which grazing animals are excluded (Geist and Gregg 1984).[2] The focus of this chapter is the collectively managed *agdal* with collectively defined opening and closing dates. Such *agdals* exist at many levels of society; some are shared by members of a single hamlet, others by groups of villages, and still others by whole "tribes." The *agdal* of Oukaimedene described here is shared by two sedentary tribes, the Ourika and the Rhiraya.

The Oukaimedene *agdal* is located in the western High Atlas Mountains about 60 kilometers from Marrakech (see Figure 10.1). A stable institution dating from the seventeenth century, it is notably free from the high degree of conflict surrounding most pastures in the central High Atlas such as Talmest, the site of "an annual brawl which occurs as regularly as clockwork, one which neither the French nor the Moroccan government since independence in 1956 has been able to solve" (Hart 1981, 7). The stability of the Oukaimedene *agdal* gives us an opportunity to identify the elements of an appropriate range management system.

Berber Social Organization

Before we can discuss the use of Oukaimedene by the Rhiraya and Ourika tribes, it is necessary to have some understanding of the social organization of Berber society. It is a society that turns on a notion of segmentation associated with ties of solidarity within groups and among allied groups, and also with serious conflict between groups and between alliances (Hammoudi 1974). Kinship (real or mythical) is the organizing principle of segmentary groups.

The basic building block of society is the household (*takat*), which may include more than fifty members. Households in turn belong to lineages, or groups of households with a common ancestor. Villages (*douars*) may contain more than one lineage, and often share a common ancestor. Lineages belong to *fractions*. In some cases, the lineages of a *fraction* share a common ancestor and the *fraction* is similar to the "clans" in other societies. Other *fractions* may be confederations of nonrelated lineages that are united by ancient political and military alliances. A tribe is composed of *fractions* that may share common ancestors or may be long-standing

FIGURE 10.1
Location of the Rhiraya Territory and Oukaimedene *Agdal*

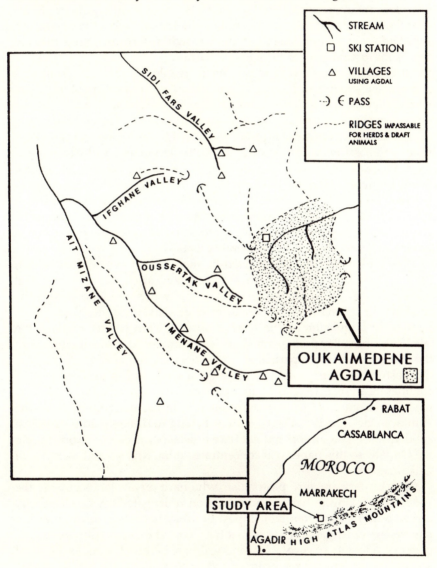

confederations of unrelated *fractions*. The Rhiraya and the Ourika are confederated groups.

Berber society, particularly in settled regions such as that of the Rhiraya drainage area, is also organized on a territorial basis: steep mountain valleys create natural social units. In the past, valleys or groups of valleys were politically united under chieftains. Today, the village is a social unit that controls water and pasture rights. Territorial units may cut across the boundaries of lineages or *fractions*.

For our purposes, it is important to remember that each unit in a segmentary group can be in conflict with other units at a similar level. Each valley in the Rhiraya territory can be viewed as a unit because villages in them share water resources and territory and often have to rely upon each other for mutual protection. At the same time, conflicts over water and pastures within a valley can be quite intense, and villages may form alliances (*leffs*) with outside groups to protect themselves against their neighbors. Conflict is likely within any unit of Berber society— between households in a lineage, between lineages in a village, between villages in a valley, or between tribes in a confederation. Subunits in conflict will generally unite, however, to respond to threats from outside groups. This is the classic segmentary pattern.

The Oukaimedene *agdal* is used by members of two confederations, the Ourika and Rhiraya, which are organized along both kinship and territorial lines. With the exception of a few watchmen who protect the property in a small ski station located at Oukaimedene, there is no permanent population on the *agdal*. Before the French came to ski in the late 1930s, the valley probably had no year-round residents. Although both the Ourika and Rhiraya participate in the opening ceremonies of the *agdal*, the pasture is clearly divided between the two tribes, and each tribe confines its animals to one of Oukaimedene's two watersheds. At present, the "Ourika side" of Oukaimedene has 115 corrals and shelters, while the "Rhiraya side" has 195. The two tribes belong to different administrative subdivisions. The authors did not have official permission to work among the Ourika, so this paper will concentrate on the Rhiraya and their use of Oukaimedene.

The Rhiraya are agro-pastoralists who have private lands outside the *agdal*. They cultivate barley and wheat on unirrigated terraces carefully carved out of steep mountain slopes. But they have developed an elaborate system of irrigated terraces that has allowed them to cultivate maize, potatoes, a variety of vegetables, and walnuts; in recent years, orchards of apples and cherries have been added. The stark beauty of the rocky canyons and of the carefully manicured terraces attracts hikers and mountaineers from throughout North Africa and Europe, and one has the impression that every possible resource is being exploited. The reality, allocate the surplus savings of the rich industrialised countries in a manner as could avoid the generalised problems of debt default, not only in the LDCs but also in the industrial economies (recall the stock market crash of 1987 and the S & L débâcle of the US economy). The reason behind is a general tendency for global growth rates in real output to lag behind the growth in financial liabilities and debt.

The standard guidelines of the macro-economic stabilisation package also tend to influence the author's emphasis on 'fiscal discipline' as one of the three major factors behind the relative success of the debtor countries in terms of GDP growth (pp.104–8). Cooper, however, departs from the conventional notion of 'fiscal-tightness' as a desirable goal. The idea, however, remains ambiguous in absence of adequate specifications of the requisite discipline.

Similar tendencies for following a beaten track come up with the off-quoted 'Dutch Disease' syndrome (p.46–7) which, according to the author, may prevail when an export boom spills over to the domestic non-traded goods sector an augmented demand for which may shift domestic resources away from the production of traded goods. It is not clear why the author does not consider the logical possibility that unutilised resources in the economy could be put to use to match the additional demand for non-traded goods, without affecting production in the traded goods sector. Similarly the author leans on the fiscal merits of an 'inflation tax' ruling out its regressive effects (pp.64–9), an outcome which can only be true if the income of the poor is always indexed.

Gaps in analysis as above, however, do not rob the merit of this very significant contribution on debt and adjustment experiences, both in terms of analysis and policy prescriptions. Touching the rather grey area of international capital flights Cooper recommends, as supplements to stricter controls from developing country governments, a closer surveillance of private banks in the advanced economies by their own governments. If implemented, the step would mark a radical departure from the passive attitude of private bank operations as currently prevail. Finally, consistent to the central thesis in the book which in essence is typically Keynesian, Cooper warns the reader of the 'costs of world disinflation', not only for the LDCs but also for the industrialised countries (pp.134–5).

In a short compass Richard Cooper has sought to address the central issues on debt and adjustments, from a viewpoint which departs from the neo-classical paradigm. The book deserves a readership that is much broader than the narrow range of specialists in economics.

SUNANDA SEN
Centre for Economic Studies and Planning,
Jawaharlal Nehru University, New Delhi

Making the Commons Work: Theory, Practice and Policy. Edited by Daniel W. Bromley. *San Francisco, CA: ICS Press*, 1992. Pp.xii + 339. $44.95 and $14.95. ISBN 1 55815 198 2 and 217 2.

Since the 1985 Annapolis panel on Common Property Resource Management in the Developing Countries (organised by the US National Academy of Science) there has been a wealth of literature generated on the commons and local

institutions that protect and govern them, of which *Making the Commons Work* is the latest example. These have been produced individually and collaboratively by a range of mainly North American academics from the disciplines of anthropology, economics, political science, biology and ecology, among others.

The editor, Daniel Bromley, succinctly summarises the book's main themes as well as the other essays in his introduction. Bromley argues convincingly, in common with the book's other authors, that the 'Tragedy of the Commons' thesis, which stresses that individuals will 'free ride' on and destroy common resources, confuses what Bromley terms common pool and open access resources. The latter are resources where there is no collective or other management of a resource and are therefore open to all, while the former are resources that are controlled and protected collectively, often by local groups who manage the resource in such a way as to exclude potential free riders. It is the latter type of situation with which most of the chapters in the book are concerned.

An interesting feature of the book is that almost all of the chapters follow a common methodological typology, set by Ronald Oakerson in chapter three. Oakerson suggests examining first the physical attributes of a resource, then decision making arrangements around it, patterns of interaction within these, and finally the outcome of these arrangements and interactions. It is to the credit of the editor that as most of the authors follow this typology they make their overall argument more accessible, plausible and coherent.

After Oakerson, there follows eight chapters of case studies from throughout the developing world. Margaret McKean provides a fascinating account of the management of traditional common lands in Japan, and Bruce Campbell and Ricardo Godoy's comparative analysis of commonfield agriculture in the Andes and medieval England is equally interesting. The essay by James Thomson, David Feeny and Oakerson, comparing management of natural resources in Thailand and Niger, and an exploratory piece by Piers Blaikie, Adam Pain and John Harriss on Tamil Nadu, give examples of situations where there are no effective local management institutions. Fikret Berkes writes persuasively about the success of small co-operatives in coastal fisheries in Turkey, and Cordell and McKean, in an excellent contribution, make visible the customary collective ownership by poor fishermen of sea tenure rights in Brazil. There is also a piece by Robert Wade on the organisation of village councils in Andhra Pradesh for the regulation of grazing and irrigation there. The book ends with a speculative essay on methodology by Feeny, and a thoughtful concluding and synthesising chapter by Ostrom on why local organisations work.

There can be little doubt reading this and companion volumes by the same authors (all of which are referenced in the chapter by Feeny) that there is considerable organisation within villages throughout the developing world concerning the management of a wide variety of common resources. But a central question that is not answered in this book is: Who gets organised? The attack by its authors on the Tragedy of the Commons thesis is partly based on the concept of excludability. There is, however, little analysis of who makes up the appropriator organisations and who is excluded from them. It is only in a footnote to the chapter by Blaikie *et al*, that we learn that the councils Wade describes in Andhra Pradesh: '. . . are essentially institutions of the dominant Reddy caste community . . . poor and low-ranking people are not participants in the institutions' (p.263, fn2). Blaikie *at al*, themselves comment: 'That bureaucratic regulation of CPRs is of particular concern in CPR-dependent villages, for this regulation is often subject to manipulation by local power to the disadvantage of poorer people' (p.262). Similarly, in her chapter on Japan, McKean informs the reader that in some villages '. . . the proportion of disenfranchised tenants, household servants, and outcastes without rights of access to the commons might exceed 50 per cent of the total population' (p.74). What this 50 per cent of the population then did to meet its needs is not made clear. In the same way, while the chapter by Campbell and Godoy mentions inequality and exclusion, it does not deal with them in any detail, in particular how the poor might have been excluded from the benefits of the commons. There is a further gap in the book's analysis, which is a failure to discuss questions of gender. It seems that almost all of the local organisations referred to are run by men. Several of the chapters appear to be saying that better-off village men can organise to control resources; but what if in the course of this organisation to protect a resource poor women are excluded?

The failure to address this question comes from a focus of the authors on institutions rather than the whole local 'community'. In this sense it has much in common with the recent literature on irrigation organisations. Future work on common pool resources could fruitfully examine conflicts between rich and poor villagers and men and women over resources which groups with differing interests attempt to control and access. The Third Common Property Conference in Washington in 1992 on 'Inequality and the Commons' was a first step in this direction, and it would be interesting to see an edited version of some of the papers from the conference dealing with this theme.

TONY BECK
Institute of Asian Research,
University of British Columbia

Factory Daughters: Gender, Household Dynamics, and Rural Industrialisation in Java. By Diane Lauren Wolf. *Berkeley, Los Angeles, CA and Oxford: University of California Press*, 1992. Pp.xv + 323. $38. ISBN 0 520 07072 0

Wolf's account of the implications of industrialisation and opportunities for factory work in Rural Java is timely and important for two reasons. First, it bridges a gap between the different literatures which have separately been concerned with different but related aspects of industrialisation: the effects of industrialisation on households and intra-household relations; the effects of multinational factories and the new international division of labour on third world industrialisation; and the economic organisation of peasant and rural households in the Third World. And secondly, it deconstructs the ahistorical notion of women which has dominated much of the discussion in this area. Instead it looks at the different perspectives of mothers/wives/daughters both as different generations, and as the women themselves move through their life cycles.

Most accounts of changes within the rural economy focus on agrarian change and ignore the ever increasing growth of factory and other industrial production within rural areas. Wolf urges the necessity to prise the analysis of intra-household dynamics and decision-making from the grasp of agricultural economics which, she demonstrates, reduces complex and contradictory processes to interactions between depersonalised contestants. Wolf's detailed empirically-

tremely elegant discussion of 'economic retrenchments' (Chapter 2) and the lessons (Chapter 3) for the developing countries. The book concludes with extensive discussions on the 'lingering problem of debt', specially its origin (Chapter 4) and the proposed solutions (Chapter 5).

The main contribution of this new work on developing country debt lies in the pointer it has provided against an uncritical acceptance of the allocational efficiency arguments in the standard stabilisation and structural adjustment policies. Sharing his convictions with other post-Keynesians, Professor Cooper points at the potential output losses in the debt-ridden developing economies which experience shortfalls in the flow of net aid or export earnings since these initiate a pace of structural adjustments with switches of resources from the non-traded to the traded goods sector. The author's disbelief in a cost-less transition from one point to another along the production possibility curve of a typical developing country can be viewed as a warning signal to policy-makers, not only with the consequent unemployment of productive resources (including labour) but also with the probable terms of trade losses as might result from efforts on their part to push exports in a stagnant international market. Cooper can visualise quite clearly that '. . . in the worst circumstance, labour and capital will become idle in the non-traded sector and will not be absorbed in the export-sector' (p.53). Problems get even more compounded as the debtor country is compelled to cut back its absorption, causing a second round contraction of the output of non-traded goods.

In another major departure from the precepts of the Structural Adjustment Loan (SAL) packages for economic reform, Cooper rejects a strait-jacketed approach to currency depreciation, especially by large doses, as a remedy for payments deficits. Using his own argument of the sixties that the timing and pace of currency depreciations are important in determining their effects on the balance of payments of the developing nations, Professor Cooper advocates a 'relatively steady or only slowly changing real exchange rate . . . large and erratic movements (in which) can be highly disturbing both to a country's external account and to its domestic economy (p.112).

Attention is also drawn to the potential instabilities inherent in the domestic economy with uncertain movements in the real exchange rate, causing political tension because of the redistributional effects of devaluation and an inflated debt servicing liability in terms of local currency as are faced by the economy. In reality '. . . steadiness in the real exchange rate has a strong influence on the stability of the economic environment in which business enterprises must make their marketing and investment decisions. A highly variable real exchange rate is likely to discourage efforts to develop new export markets' (pp.103–4).

A conscious move to distance the arguments from the market efficiency norms advocated in the neo-classical literature does not, surprisingly enough, keep the remaining analysis in the book out of the traps which have their origin in both liberal ideology and also in the economic diplomacy preached by the industrialised countries. Cooper has no illusions that '. . . contrary to widespread assumptions, there are no villains in the piece' (p.138). The entire problem of developing country debt, as he sees it, was due to 'mistakes' and 'violation of expectations' (p.131) not only in the developing but also in the advanced economy. The author fails to recognise that the inadequacies of the international economic environment hardly allows the international capital market to however, is that even with extensive terracing, less than 10 percent of the territory can be used for crops; most of it is steeply sloped, and many areas are denuded of vegetation. Nonetheless, the valleys inhabited by the Rhiraya are heavily populated for such a marginal region—the average density is 55 persons per square kilometer (Chami 1982). The population of the Rhiraya is estimated at about 36,000 persons or about 2,800 households (ibid.), but only a small proportion of the Rhiraya tribe actually bring their animals to Oukaimedene. While all members of the tribe have some "right" to place their animals on the *agdal*, the physical and social constraints outlined below prevent most of them from doing so.

Physical and Technical Attributes of the *Agdal*

The *agdal* of Oukaimedene is located in the highest part of the western High Atlas mountains abut 16 kilometers from Jebel Toubkal, the highest peak in North Africa. Oukaimedene's elevation varies from 2,600 meters at its lower end to 3,260 meters atop Jebel Oukaimedene. Oukaimedene itself is a treeless valley, 4.5 kilometers long and 4 kilometers wide at its broadest point, divided into two watersheds separated by a low grass-covered mountain. These watersheds meet at the end of the valley at the entrance of a narrow gorge. With the exception of the granite cliffs of Angour and Jebel Oukaimedene, the valley is characterized by steep grass-covered slopes. A strip (1,000 meters long and 150 meters at its widest point) of naturally subirrigated pastures runs along the valley floor; the peaty soil is rich in organic matter, moistened by underground seepage, and capable of supporting plants that can be cut for hay and reserved for cattle. A number of small permanent springs are scattered throughout the valley; herders have built stone corrals and stone huts or shelters next to these sources of water. Ascending from the valley floor, the mountain slopes have fine-textured soils in their lower reaches and coarse alluvium in higher areas. The rainfed slopes provide pasture for sheep and goats.

Detailed climatic data on the *agdal* do not exist. The average minimum winter temperatures for December, January, and February are approximately −3°C. Precipitation is estimated to be 500 to 600 millimeters per year, most of it in winter and early spring, with virtually no rainfall during the months of June and July. The usually heavy snowpack at Oukaimedene precludes grazing during winter months, but is sufficient to permit alpine skiing.

The *agdal* is only one of the forage resources used by the people of the region. The local population classifies its pastoral resources into five components: (1) *asif* or streambanks, (2) *adrar* or mountain, (3) *l'rabit* or forest, (4) *uta* or plain, and (5) *agdal* or closed reserve. The streambanks are the focus of economic activity, since they provide both the arable land and sources of crop residues, hay, and pasture for cattle. The mountain slopes are common grazing lands (especially for sheep and goats), generally used by people from one village. Although the forest is legally state property from which the state is entitled to exclude people, local groups still manage to exercise their traditional usufruct rights. The plains are the territory of other groups, but many Rhiraya have reciprocal arrangements that permit them to graze their animals on the plains during winter months.

The streambanks and the mountain slopes are the most important forage resources because they comprise the majority of any village's land and can be used throughout the year. Nonetheless, the *agdal's* pastures are highly coveted because they provide high-quality forage at a time when grass is in short supply everywhere else.

The use of the *agdal* is affected by climate, technology, the distance between Oukaimedene and one's village, family size, the size and composition of the family's herd, and the family's eligibility to use an overnight shelter on the *agdal*. Thus, while a fairly large group of people are theoretically entitled to the area, the factors just mentioned sharply reduce the number of families who can in fact make profitable use of the land. Oukaimedene's elevation prevents it from being a permanent settlement, given traditional technology and housing. The growing season is too short for most subsistence crops, and even though the majority of the *agdal's* area is desirable pasture for sheep and goats, the winters are too severe to permit year-round pasturing. High elevation and low temperature prevent goats from using the pasture except in the hottest months of the summer, as these animals are more sensitive to cold than are sheep or cattle. Sheep are more resistent to cold, so they can utilize the *agdal* for several months, but even they are forced to leave when the heavy snows arrive. Forage suitable for cattle is limited to the small subirrigated portions of the *agdal*, and because so many cattle are taken to the *agdal*, the area can provide them with adequate food for only two to four weeks.

The remoteness of the *agdal* from village settlements also affects its utilization. Two to three hours are needed to herd animals to the *agdal* from the nearest villages, and up to two days from more distant hamlets. Only those who have successfully negotiated for the right of transit may cross the territory of other groups that lie between their own village and the *agdal*. The *agdal* is too remote to permit herds to move back and forth between pastures and the village on a daily basis, so herders must remain with their animals on the *agdal* overnight. Considerable amounts of time and labor must be devoted to ferrying supplies between the villages and the *agdal*, so a family using the *agdal* must have enough labor to simultaneously maintain households in the village, care for the herd at Oukaimedene, and go back and forth with supplies for the shepherds on the *agdal*. Finally, in order to maximize the quantity of hay available to the cattle, families find it necessary to harvest hay from the subirrigated areas of the *agdal* rather than allow the cattle to roam loose and trample their own food. Thus only families with labor to spare are able to make use of the *agdal* for feeding their cattle. This is a burden for most families, as the average number of animals per household is quite small, yet it is also a necessary one, as virtually all families have cattle and therefore value the *agdal*'s usefulness as a cattle pasture. Nearly every family in the region owns one or two head of cattle, but herds of over five cattle are quite rare. Many families also own goats, but a substantial minority do not, and even fewer have sheep.

Because of the low nighttime temperatures and the importance of corralling one's herd for the night, Oukaimedene is effectively available only to those who have access to shelters or camps there. Moreover, since most shelters are located in the sites favored with a source of water and a hay meadow for cattle, eligibility to use a shelter is also crucial in obtaining access to the *agdal*'s resources. Shelters and corrals are owned by individual families, so someone wishing to use the *agdal* must belong to a group that regularly uses it and thus exercises its usufruct rights, and must either own his own shelter or enter into a cooperative arrangement with someone who does.

The characteristics of jointness, excludability, and indivisibility described in Chapter 3 by Ronald J. Oakerson apply differently to each part of the *agdal* and to different groups of users. The hay meadows on the subirrigated portions of the *agdal* are small enough and valuable enough to make division into individual fields feasible—as with the land at lower elevations—but the isolation of the *agdal* from human settlements makes the enforcement of private property rights utterly impractical. Families and even villages simply cannot afford to post guards on the meadows year-round to ensure that the proper people and animals are using the proper piece of land. However, a collective agreement to close the *agdal* completely can be enforced even without such on-the-scene monitors. Grazing animals and intruders can easily be detected—though their identity and precise location cannot be pinpointed—from a distance of several kilometers, and the fact that they are violating the closure of the *agdal* is instantly apparent. Thus the Rhiraya maintain jointness of use of the hay meadows, as well as of the other resources of the *agdal*, through collective regulation.

The dry uplands of the *agdal* are extensive, but have a relatively low productive value per unit of area. Individual appropriation of such lands is neither technically feasible nor desirable (Gilles and Jamtgaard 1981). The costs of dividing land among hundreds of coowners and maintaining so many boundaries would exceed the benefits derived from owning pasture privately, given the small number of animals held by each family. Collective ownership is beneficial because it spreads the risks inherent in extracting resources from a relatively fragile and often-changing ecosystem; it also allows individual households to change the size and composition of their herds without worrying about whether their particular private pasture is suited in a particular year for the herd they happen to have that year. Yet the total number of animals brought to the *agdal* each year could easily destroy its pastures if grazing were uncontrolled, so collective regulation is needed to maintain jointness of use for the tribe as a whole.

The remote location of Oukaimedene, on the frontier of several rival Berber groups and closer to the territory of the Ourika tribe than of the Rhiraya tribe, also encourages collective management of the *agdal*. When the Ourika and Rhiraya tribes established the *agdal* at Oukaimedene, the possibility of bloody confrontations among users and raids by rivals dictated that herders band together for mutual protection to use the *agdal*. A group of shepherds from a single village would be too vulnerable to attack. The result was alliances among villages.

Decision-Making Arrangements

The Oukaimedene *agdal* is closed to grazing from March 15 until August 10. According to tradition, these dates (and other institutions surrounding the use of Oukaimedene) were created by a Muslim saint who lived in the late seventeenth or early eighteenth century: Sidi Fars, patron saint of the Rhiraya tribe.[3] The *agdal* itself is considered to be holy ground "belonging" to Sidi Fars.

A day or two before the August opening date, family members with mule loads of personal effects arrive at the *agdal*, but herds do not enter the valley until about seven in the morning of August 10. Some family members precede those driving the herds to repair the rock shelters and corrals where they and their animals will pass the nights. The Rhirayas who use the *agdal* come from villages in the five valleys of the Rhiraya area that possess corrals and shelters; they are therefore the principal users of the pasture. These valleys, in the order of their distance from Oukaimedene, are Oussertak, Imenane, Ifghane, Aït Mizane, and Sidi Fars.

Herds from the most distant locations arrive the night of August 9 and camp near the passes that open into the pasture. In earlier times the regulations concerning order of entry were more complex, specifying the sequence by household. There is still a definite order of entry, with people from Oussertak beginning and those from other valleys following. Cattle enter the *agdal* first, followed by herds of sheep and goats.

Immediately after the opening, the principal activity is hay cutting in the subirrigated meadows. All members of the family participate: women and children do most of the cutting and men transport the hay to the camps. Among rights holders, hay is cut on a first-come-first-served basis, so that those families with the largest labor force harvest the most hay. Cattle, mules, and horses could be left to graze in the hay meadows, but people prefer to cut as much of the choicest grass as quickly as possible to reserve it for their dairy cows. Rules require that this hay be consumed at Oukaimedene and not be transported back to the village, preventing anyone from cutting more hay than the animals can consume while they are on the *agdal*. Cutting the hay by hand produces a larger hay crop than if the animals graze directly and trample part of the grass underfoot. It thus prolongs the period of time that the *agdal* is useful as pasture. Sheep and goats are not permitted to graze the meadows but instead graze the mountain slopes adjacent to them.

Following the opening of the *agdal*, groups of women from specific valleys and villages participate in ceremonies at various springs and other sacred spots. On the first Friday after the opening of the *agdal*, the festival of the spring of Sidi Fars takes place. Young men and women from both the Ourika and Rhiraya groups hold a dance adjacent to the spring, which is protected by a small shelter and is visited by women who want to receive the blessings of Sidi Fars. Money collected at this time is used to compensate one of the herders for an animal that will be sacrificed at the *zaouia* (shrine of Sidi Fars and lodge of his disciples). Two weeks after the opening of the *agdal*, another celebration marks the departure of most of the people and animals.

Patterns of Interaction

In principle, all members of the Rhiraya group have the right to graze their animals at Oukaimedene once the pasture is opened. It is clear, however, that not everyone exercises this right. To use the *agdal*, one needs access to a campsite with a shelter and a corral for the animals, located near a hay meadow and a source of drinking water. Although exact population figures for the Rhiraya are not available, even conservative estimates indicate that no more than 16 percent of the Rhiraya households actually have camps at Oukaimedene. The total number of families using the *agdal* is substantially higher than the number of campsites because other families place their animals in the care of a neighbor or relative. In 1983, for example, all of the families residing in the Oussertak Valley sent some

animals to the *agdal*; those without camps of their own added their
animals to the herds that their relatives took to camps on the *agdal*. The
campsites used by households from the five valleys of the Rhiraya are
shown in Table 10.1 by valley of origin, with the closest first.

Several points are worth noting about the relative size and distance
from the *agdal* of the various valleys of the Rhiraya tribe. First, families
from the relatively nearby valleys of Oussertak and Imenane, with 72
percent of all of the shelters on the *agdal*, prevail among Rhiraya families
who actually maintain corrals and shelters there. This is quite understandable, since such families face the lowest transport costs for using the *agdal*.
Similarly, there seems to be a rough association between proximity to the
agdal and the likelihood that a family will go to the trouble of maintaining
a shelter there, doubtless also because of transport costs. However, the
households from the three villages that send animals to the *agdal* from the
most distant valley of Sidi Fars deviate from this rule somewhat by
maintaining a larger presence on the *agdal* than their distance from it
would appear to warrant.

The existence of a convenient modern road traversing part of the
distance between the valley of Sidi Fars and Oukaimedene reduces the
effective distance and associated transport costs for families from Sidi
Fars. But religious factors also give extra benefits to the Sidi Fars families
who use the *agdal*: the fact that they claim to be the servants or direct
descendants of Saint Sidi Fars gives these households, along with those
from Oussertak and Ifghane (who claim to be protectors of the saint) what
we can call "senior rights" (extended or full rights) to the *agdal*. As we will
see below, they may graze their animals anywhere on the *agdal* and are
entitled to stay longer than the families from Imenane or Aït Mizane.
These extra benefits from using the *agdal* presumably make its use
worthwhile even for families who face somewhat higher costs. The claim
by some families from the valley of Sidi Fars to direct descent from the
saint, as well as their right to command a "gift" (a payment or a tax) from
all other Rhiraya households that use the *agdal*, may also be important in
reinforcing their rights of access to the *agdal*. The Oussertak, who live
closest to the *agdal* and could conceivably exclude all others from the *agdal*
if they chose to, legitimize their own access to it by their affiliation with
Sidi Fars. They are therefore in no position to deny similar access to other
groups able to claim connections with the saint.

The various ethnic divisions of the Rhiraya have access to different
springs and hay meadows. Shelters and corrals are located in proximity to
these resources in campgrounds or clusters known as *azib*s. There are
three main Rhiraya *azib*s: Dou Fatfira *azib* (approximately ninety camps),
occupied mostly by households from the valleys of Oussertak and
Ifghane; Assif n'Aït Irene *azib* (approximately seventy camps), occupied

TABLE 10.1

Use of *Agdal* Camps by Valley of Origin, Rhiraya Households
(percentages are rounded)

Valley	Number of camps	Percentage of all camps on *Agdal*	Percentage of households owning camps from each valley
Oussertak[a]	56	29	66
Imenane	83	43	22
Ifghane[a]	27	14	38
Aït Mizane	7	4	5
Sidi Fars[a,b]	22	11	22[c]/10[d]
Total	195	101%	16%

a. Protectors and retainers of Saint Sidi Fars.
b. Direct descendants of Saint Sidi Fars.
c. Of households from the three villages in the valley that send animals to the *Agdal*.
d. Of households from all nine villages in the valley of Sidi Fars.
SOURCE: Authors.

primarily by families from Imenane and Aït Mizane; and Imine Taghya *azib* (approximately twenty camps), occupied by herders from Sidi Fars. Within each of these larger areas, there are smaller groups of camps adjacent to particular hay meadows or watering sites, often occupied by people from a single village.

People from the valleys of Oussertak, Ifghane, and Sidi Fars have more extensive rights than those from Imenane and Aït Mizane. Senior rights holders are allowed to cut hay in the large meadow just below the sacred spring of Sidi Fars and to graze their animals in the well-irrigated areas nearby. Junior rights holders (whose rights are limited but not necessarily any more recent in origin) must put their campsites above the spring and graze their animals in this drier, less-favored, upper zone of the watershed. They also leave Oukaimedene soon after the festival that takes place on the fifteenth day after the opening of the *agdal*, after which time the senior rights holders may then allow their herds to graze the upland areas vacated by the junior rights holders. Shepherds from Oussertak may stay until snowfall or until the pastures are exhausted. They may also return in late February to pasture their sheep in years when the snowfall is light.

These two classes of users disagree with each other over the rules concerning the exact time of departure from the *agdal*. Such disagreements probably reflect fluctuations in the power of various groups. The senior rights holders, claiming to be protectors and descendants of Saint Sidi

Fars, argue that the others are required to leave the *agdal* after the fifteenth day—that is, immediately after the closing ceremony—and that the senior rights holders generously allow the others to extend their stay for another few days until the grass supply runs out. In contrast, the junior rights holders argue that there is no difference at all in their rights and that they are not expected to leave on the fifteenth day, but that within a few days of that time the grass for their herds is exhausted anyway and it makes no sense to stay longer. In fact, once a substantial number of people leave the *agdal*, the camaraderie and the temporary traveling marketplace for bread and supplies evaporate, and the attraction of remaining on the *agdal* declines even for those who insist that they are entitled to stay. Moreover, the grass supply diminishes and the weather becomes more severe.

Ethnic identity not only creates a hierarchy of rights among users but is also important in extending right to new users and denying rights to others. Reciprocal arrangements through relatives permit people without camps to use the camps of others or to construct a new corral and shelter adjacent to those of their kinsmen—as long as the kinsmen or others with camps in the same *azib* do not object. Those with objections can take them to the *jmaa*, the council of people with corrals in a particular *azib*. Wherever there is a collective resource, a council composed of one adult male per household that is empowered to enforce the rules and resolve conflicts among users can be established. All members of a council are theoretically equal, although representatives from rich families usually have considerable power. Nonetheless, a learned or articulate representative from a poor family occasionally can be persuasive and influence council decisions. Members of a community normally oppose the effort by an "outsider"—say, a member of a village that has no *azib*—who attempts to construct a camp. The council is also likely to deny permission to use water points or to build corrals even to other members of the Rhiraya who theoretically have the right to use the *agdal*.

Rights to a corral and shelter can be maintained only through regular use. In a real sense, the only title one can have to a camp is the historic fact that one's family has always come to Oukaimedene and used its corrals and shelters. We know that villages that do not currently use the *agdal* used it in the past and possessed corrals and camps there. Informants from the villages of Imlil and Aremd in the Aït Mizane Valley could point out their former corral sites, though no physical evidence remains. If a family fails to use its camp, others slowly pilfer the rocks from the stone walls of the unused corrals. The theft is hardly noticeable at first, but the corrals may literally disappear in a few years' time. Those who build new corrals and encounter no objections can eventually claim that the silent compliance of their fellows confers permission. Thus actual use over the years determines the ebb and flow of rights to the *agdal*.

Finally, particular and idiosyncratic circumstances have given many people rights to corrals that are not located in the *azib* "belonging" to their community or valley. A substantial number of households from the valleys of Sidi Fars and Imenane have corrals and shelters in the Dou Fatfira *azib*, which is otherwise limited to households from the Oussertak Valley. The Dou Fatfira *azib* is particularly desirable because it is adjacent to the largest hay meadow and is close to a modern ski resort that provides some temporary winter employment. Some families may have acquired rights there when the original sites of their camps were leveled to make way for the ski resort and ski lift. Other people may have constructed shelters to live in while they worked at the resort, expanding these later to include corrals. Still others may have "inherited" rights from in-laws. Recently, however, this proliferation of camps at Dou Fatfira has been stopped. Although the Oussertak insist that they still have the right to construct new corrals there, the Moroccan government has forbidden the construction of new camps.

People from other tribes and from communities not possessing *azib*s in the *agdal* may still use it by asking or buying permission from a "friend" to share the friend's corral. Such transactions require approval by the council of users. Many people at Oukaimedene have been allowed such reciprocal grazing arrangements, but "strangers" are often denied permission and asked to leave. The council determines who is able to construct and occupy the corrals and *azib*s, and deals with objections raised by users to others' efforts to construct new corrals. The council functions on the basis of consensus, and Moroccan government authorities normally will respect and enforce a consensual decision.

Such councils may levy fines and exclude intruders from the *agdal*, but the major sanctions against illegal use of the *agdal* appear to be supernatural. Because Saint Sidi Fars or his spirit supposedly watches over the pasture, those who violate the rules are expected to become the victims of natural disasters and disease. Similarly, the councils at Oukaimedene cannot easily alter the fundamental rules of use as long as these are believed to be the sacred heritage handed down by Saint Sidi Fars. The opening and closing dates for the *agdal*, supposedly set over two centuries ago by Sidi Fars, are universally observed and not easily amended. Other rules not as closely associated with Sidi Fars are stretched or their very existence debated.

Outcomes and Equity

As a resource management system, the *agdal* of Oukaimedene is a reasonable success. Even an untrained eye can detect the difference between the quality of pastures at Oukaimedene and pastures beyond the *agdal*'s boundaries. Several desirable forage species that exist at Oukai-medene have disappeared entirely in adjacent valleys. The August open-ing date appears to ensure that most of the major forage species have time to produce seed before they are grazed.

Yet resource conservation is probably not the main reason for the creation of Oukaimedene or other *agdals*. Equity among various user groups was probably the main motivation. Without regulation at Ou-kaimedene, the people from Oussertak could easily use the resources of the whole pasture each year before other groups could get there. Similarly, without regulation of grazing by sheep and goats, the meadows would not produce hay for cattle. Since virtually all families in the tribe own cattle, but the poor generally lack sheep or goats, these constraints on sheep and goats actually favor the poorer families. Similarly, since the race to harvest hay favors families with large amounts of labor relative to the number of cows they possess, the regulations on grazing that maximize hay produc-tion also protect the poor families, which have the largest numbers of people and the smallest numbers of cattle.

Conclusions

If everyone with rights to use Oukaimedene were actually to exercise them, Oukaimedene would be devoid of vegetation. The survival of the *agdal* is due largely to a combination of technical and social factors. First, the *agdal*'s isolation and distance from villages make its use extremely costly for shepherds from the Aït Mizane and Sidi Fars valleys, so that only large, relatively rich households from these valleys can profit from it. As a result, a larger proportion of families from nearby valleys use the pasture than of those from distant valleys. In addition to the technical prohibitions on use, there are sociopolitical constraints. In order to have access to hay and drinking water, a person must either belong to a village that has maintained usufruct rights to corrals and campsites, or have a relative in such a village. An individual from a village not possessing an *azib* will have difficulty establishing a camp. The problems of group membership and the physical characteristics of the *agdal* serve to limit the number of rights holders who actually use the pasture.

We studied the Oukaimedene *agdal* in order to understand this pasture management institution and its implications for resource conser-vation in Morocco and elsewhere. The closing of the *agdal* preserves plant cover and protects some desirable forage species. In order to discuss the implications of this study for resource management in general, we must first describe some of the differences between Oukaimedene and other *agdal*s.

The first reason for the stability at Oukaimedene is the sacred nature of the *agdal* as the land of Saint Sidi Fars. Many Moroccan *agdal*s are similarly sacred, but others are primarily secular institutions. In the latter, where the rules are entirely in the hands of the community of users, attempts to change the rules and conflicts over these attempts frequently occur. The poor often try to privatize land suitable for cultivation or hay production, or the groups that live closest to an *agdal* may reduce the access of more distant users (Bourbouze 1982; Geist and Greg 1984). The councils overseeing the use of *agdal*s are consensual bodies that cease to operate in the context of nonnegotiable conflicts, which were traditionally settled by force of arms, but today invite government intervention. In such cases, the state may impose an arbitrary solution that is inevitably unacceptable to some, freezing a conflict in place without permitting the emergence of the new consensus that is essential to the functioning of group decision making.

Another factor that may contribute to the stability of the *agdal* at Oukaimedene is, oddly enough, the presence of a ski resort. The ski season coincides with the period when it is impossible to use Oukaimedene for pasturing, so in one sense skiing is a complementary resource use. Conflicts in land use do exist, however: a ski slope may be an excellent pasture, but stone corrals and shelters are dangerous obstacles to skiers. In addition, there may be conflict over water. Some land that is not now subirrigated has peaty soils, indicating that they were once moist. The large well that serves as the water supply for the ski resort may have altered the hydrology of the lower part of the *agdal* and thus reduced the size of hay meadows. Thus further expansion of the resort would threaten the pastoral users of the *agdal* and would not necessarily benefit any of them.[4]

How then does this potential conflict affect the stability of the *agdal*? Berber society, as we have seen, is segmentary, made up of tribes that are conglomerates of many smaller groups (*fractions*, *sous-fractions*, villages, lineages, and extended households), among which conflict is frequent. Traditionally, the various components of society were held together by the need for allies in case of conflict with other groups. But the arrival of the French protectorate at the beginning of the twentieth century reduced intergroup conflict—at least at the intertribal level—and thereby reduced the social significance of tribes and similar large groups. Supravillage organizations still have some importance, however, because the boundaries of administrative units in rural areas still largely coincide with the territory of a tribe or a *fraction*. Conflict at lower levels, among lineages and villages, still continues, so such groups continue to have a high degree of solidarity. In the case of Oukaimedene, the external threat posed by resort development may contribute to the solidarity of those who use the *agdal* and thus to the *agdal's* ecological stability.

The Oukaimedene *agdal* illustrates some management principles for communal pastures. There are many ways to manage a rangeland—through rest, rotation, deferment, and control over the timing and intensity of grazing. The case of Oukaimedene suggests that deferment is a desirable approach. If a pasture is visible to users, and if unfavorable weather conditions end the grazing period, it is relatively easy to set opening and closing dates. After a deferment period is set, constant evaluation of pasture quality is not required, and the rights concerning use of the pasture can also be quite flexible. Thus, those without rights may use the pasture occasionally, as the Rhiraya will sometimes graze lands belonging to other groups.

A possible barrier to the extension of these traditional institutions for resource management is the fragility of the councils that govern them. These councils are largely consensual bodies that depend on a certain degree of group solidarity. As society changes, Berber groups become increasingly differentiated and it becomes difficult for the councils to operate, particularly when the central government claims a superior right to decide questions of resource use. Today, an "injured" minority that objects to a decision of the council may appeal to government authorities, who will sometimes contravene council decisions that are not accepted by all, and who will even ignore unanimous decisions that interfere with the central government's plans for development. Such intervention can only undermine further the legitimacy of local institutions, legitimacy that is already a serious problem because the local councils' decisions have no legal status and are only advisory. The fact that council decisions have no official recognition makes it likely that the councils will be supplanted by the state in regions where economic development is a high priority. If the *agdal* concept is to be used as the basis for rangeland conservation in Morocco, the legal status of the *agdal* councils must be clarified and strengthened.

NOTES

The order of authorship is alphabetical and does not indicate degree of contribution. Field research was begun in the summer of 1983 by Mohamed Mahdi under the direction of Abdellah Hammoudi and Jere Gilles and continued till the fall of 1986. Beginning in June of 1984, Lloyd Mendes joined the team to conduct range and animal husbandry research. Research on the Oukaimedene *agdal* was in part sponsored by the Small Ruminant Collaborative Research Program, U.S. Agency for International Development grant no. DSAN/VII-G-0049.

1. Eighmy and Ghanem (1982) have called into question the utility of the *hema* system. They imply that the success of efforts in Syria may be due to unique local conditions.

2. The origins of the word *agdal* are obscure. David Hart (1981) defines an *"agudal"* (plural, *igudlan*) as "collective pasture with rigid, fixed opening and closing dates." This is normally what is meant when the word *agdal* is used in the anthropological literature. Although this is the sense of the word that is most of interest to us here, this is not the only one. *Agdal* (or *agudal*) is more often used as a verb to denote the exclusion of grazing animals from a piece of pastureland. Geist and Gregg (1984) note that during the season when pasturing is permitted on an *agdal*, there is no *agdal*. A second sense of the word used among traditional agropastoralists of the western and central High Atlas is that of a meadow or a prairie. In the Rhiraya Valley and in adjacent areas, small private hay meadows are also given the name *agdal*. Thus the word *agdal* can be the act of exclusion or a particular place, and its use in everyday speech seems to combine both of these.

3. Muslim holy men played an important role in maintaining the structure of Berber society. Successful ones (saints) founded religious lodges (*zaouia*) that were houses of learning and places of mediation for various Berber groups. These lodges were generally located between the territories of tribes or *fractions*. One way in which land could be made open to two conflicting groups was to make it sacred land "belonging" to a saint—like the Oukaimedene *agdal*.

4. The only way that those using the *agdal* might benefit from the expansion of the resort would be if the site of their corrals and shelters could be developed for the construction of a ski chalet.

REFERENCES

Bourbouze, A. 1982. "Déplacements des troupeaux et utilization des parcours dans le Haut Atlas Central." *Production Pastorale et Société* 10:34–45.

Breman, H., and C. de Wit. 1983. "Rangeland Productivity and Exploitation in the Sahel." *Science* 221:1341–47.

Chami, M. 1982. *Productions animales et systèmes alimentaires des troupeaux du Haut Atlas Central*. Mémoire du Troisième Cycle. Rabat: Institut Agronomique et Vétérinaire Hassan II.

Couvreur, G. 1968. "La vie pastorale dans le Haut Atlas Central." *Revue Géographique du Maroc* 13:3–54.

Draz, O. 1983. "The Syrian Arab Republic: Rangeland Conservation and Development." *World Animal Review* 47:2–14.

Eighmy, L. J., and Y. S. Ghanem. 1982. "Prospects for Traditional Subsistence Systems in the Arabian Peninsula." *Culture and Agriculture* 16:10–5.

Geist, A., and G. Gregg. 1984. "Tinguerf/Aït Dadd Ou Ali: Observations of an 'Agudalled' Pastureland." Report prepared for the Food and Agriculture

Organization (FAO) of the United Nations, Rabat, and the range management project of Utah State University sponsored by USAID. In the FAO Archives, Rabat.

Gellner, Ernest. 1969. *Saints of the Atlas.* London: Weidenfeld and Nicolson.

Gilles, J. L., and K. Jamtgaard. 1981. "Overgrazing in Pastoral Areas: The Commons Reconsidered." *Sociologia Ruralis* 21:129–41.

Hammoudi, A. 1974. "Segmentarité, stratification sociale, pouvoir politique et sainteté: réflexions sur les thèses de Gellner." *Hesperis Talmuda* 15:147–79.

Hart, D. 1981. "Dadda 'Atta and His Forty Grandsons: The Social Organization of the Aït Atta of Southern Morocco." Boulder, Colo.: Westview Press.

Hyder, D. H., ed. 1978. *Proceedings of the First International Rangelands Congress.* Denver, Colo.: Society for Range Management.

Little, P. D. 1983. "Businessmen and Part-Time Pastoralists: Some Factors Affecting Drought and Overgrazing in Baringo District, Kenya." Paper presented at the 149th meeting of the American Association for the Advancement of Science, May 26-31, Detroit, Mich.

McGuire, J. R. 1978. "Rangelands, Fulfilling the Premise through Planning." In *Proceedings of the First International Rangelands Congress,* ed. D. H. Hyder, 2–3. Denver, Colo.: Society for Range Management.

11

The Management and Use of Common-Property Resources in Tamil Nadu, India

Piers Blaikie, John Harriss, and Adam Pain

Tamil Nadu is the state at the southeastern tip of the Indian peninsula. It is traversed from the higher west to the coast by several major river valleys where the cultivation of irrigated rice predominates. The intervening plateaus also have some irrigated agriculture, dependent upon water stored in surface reservoirs and groundwater, as well as dry cultivation of millets, sorghum, pulses, and oilseeds. Both the valleys and the plateaus have been relatively intensively cultivated over a long historical period. Common-property resources play some part in agricultural systems throughout the state, the most important of them being surface water and groundwater for irrigation. These have been the object of some other recent studies, however, and our research has been focused rather upon land-based resources: principally fuel, fodder, and grazing, but also construction timber, green manure, and a variety of minor forest products with domestic, craft, or sometimes industrial uses.

All of these products may be obtained, subject to environmental conditions, from one or another of the types of publicly owned land that are defined as such by the systems of land and forest administration, and sometimes also from private land (see Figure 11.1). The system of land administration has its roots in the precolonial period but was further developed as a major instrument of British rule, with the objective of maximizing the appropriation of land revenue. Thus the "commons" of Tamil Nadu are now those lands defined under this system as: (1) *poromboke*, or "lands incapable of cultivation or set apart for public or communal purposes" (including, sometimes, public grazing lands), which are not

FIGURE 11.1

Common-Property Resources (CPRs) Mentioned in This Chapter

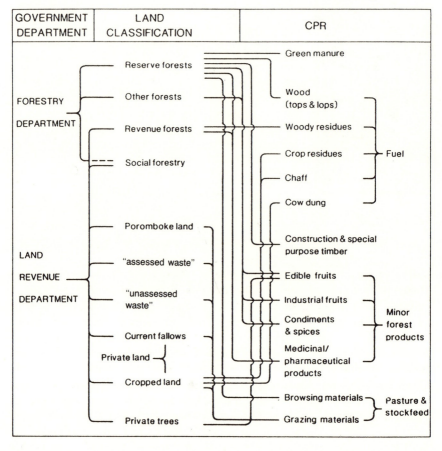

GOVERNMENT DEPARTMENT	LAND CLASSIFICATION	CPR

generally liable for revenue; (2) "waste," which may be either "assessed waste" (that is, "cultivable lands which have been left uncultivated, lands relinquished by cultivators, and lands bought in by government in revenue sales"), or "unassessed waste" (that is, "lands to which no classification or assessment has been assigned because they are considered unfit for cultivation");[1] and (3) areas designated under the terms of the forest act as either "reserve forests" or "revenue forests."

Poromboke and assessed and unassessed waste land fall within village boundaries and are nominally "village lands," while forests are usually outside village limits. None of the lands covered by these official categories should be encroached upon for settlement or cultivation; if they are, then official penalties may be applied. Fuel, fodder, and other products available on *poromboke* and waste lands may be freely collected, except in the case of designated trees or bushes (such as palmyra palms or tamarind trees), the rights to which are in the control of the local administration and are usually auctioned annually. These products may also be available from designated forests, in which case rights to collect or cut are under the control of the forest department of the state government. In addition, fuel and fodder may sometimes be obtained quite freely from private land, where there are generally accepted common rights, for example, to dig up the stumps and roots of harvested plants for fuel, to graze animals after harvest, or to cut grass from field edges.

There is a problem in clearly labeling the various resources available and the exact property rights attached to each. *Poromboke* and waste land, for example, are designated as village land and, as such, would seem to be land on which the resources are common property. In many cases, however, *poromboke* and waste land are used by persons outside the village too, particularly when they are in large tracts or abut roads or other settlements, in which case they are "open-access" resources. But in the majority of cases, users of the *poromboke* and waste lands close by a village tend to be the villagers themselves. Also, within any one territory, a variety of property rights are attached to specific resources, as Figure 11.1 makes plain. A sandalwood tree in a reserved forest, for example, is treated as state property, while the grass around it is a common-property resource for which users pay the state. Thus the unambiguous label is threatened by "illegal" use. At what point does poaching turn state property into an open-access resource?

Official data on the areas of land covered by these official categories give us a measure, though an imprecise one, of the availability of commons in different parts of the state, and of the extent to which they are being depleted. The official land utilization data, shown in Table 11.1, give

TABLE 11.1
Changes in Land-Use Patterns Relevant to Common-Property Resources, Tamil Nadu, 1961–1962, 1969–1970, and 1981–1982 (percentage of geographical area)

	Forest			Culturable waste			Permanent pasture		
Year	61/62	69/70	81/82	61/62	69/70	81/82	61/62	69/70	81/82
Percentage	14.5	15.5	15.6	5.3	4.1	2.6	2.8	1.7	1.2

SOURCE: Government of Tamil Nadu, Ministry of Agriculture, *Season and Crop Reports.*

only an imprecise measure because the categories employed may lump together both public and private land. It is fair to assume, however, that the major share of the areas of "forest," "culturable waste" (the sum of assessed and unassessed waste), and "permanent pasture" shown in the data is under public ownership, and that any changes in extent that are recorded are likely to include changes in this "public" area. These figures suggest, then, that while the forest area has remained constant over the last twenty-one years, the areas of culturable waste and of permanent pasture have undergone a general, steady decline.

Field investigations at the village level show that there is a good deal of diversity in the importance of common-property resources (CPRs) in the economy. But it seems that we may broadly distinguish in terms of both area and potential benefits between "CPR-limited" and "CPR-dependent" villages. In villages in areas of old, established, and quite intensive cultivation, CPRs may in fact be of rather marginal importance, where there is no frontier of "waste" land that can be encroached upon for cultivation—apart perhaps from limited areas of tank foreshores (gently sloping land at the edge of an irrigation tank, exposed during the dry season). Cattle are largely stall-fed with crop residues and even purchased feeds, and grazing on public or common lands is of secondary importance; fuel includes dung cakes made from the manure of privately owned cattle, thorn bush twigs cut on privately owned land, and even purchased firewood (only very poor people collect fuel on *poromboke* land). Soil fertility depends upon purchased inorganic fertilizers, and even organic manures are purchased from outside; few, if any, minor products supply food or raw materials, apart from the roots of some cacti that are famine food. These can be termed CPR-limited villages.

In contrast with these circumstances are those of villages in more marginal environments such as the hilly areas of Dharmapuri and Salem districts and in the western areas of the state. Here, a "frontier" of waste still exists and offers livelihood possibilities even for poor people. Fuel and fodder are extensively obtained from the commons by all classes of people, and soil fertility may be closely bound up with the numbers of livestock that can be maintained. These CPR-dependent villages are often situated in the west of the state, where forest still covers a significant percentage of the land area.

Physical and Technical Attributes

Tamil Nadu has a wide range of vegetative formations reflecting a diversity of rainfall patterns. This vegetation provides the productive base for CPRs. Although the area of natural vegetation has decreased both quantitatively and qualitatively, the government of Tamil Nadu had listed 1,219 species in the area in 1983, the majority of which are used for one purpose or another (for a detailed list, see Blaikie, Harriss, and Pain 1985).

The physical and technical qualities of these CPRs can be considered in terms of their jointness of supply, excludability, and indivisibility (see Oakerson in Chapter 3 of this book). We will discuss them under the two broad headings of timber and fuel, on the one hand, and grazing resources, on the other (although for many purposes there is no need to distinguish between them). With regard to jointness of supply of these CPRs, clearly they all can be used by a number of people simultaneously, and that use can subtract from the per capita benefit. There are important methodological issues here, however, since use is not necessarily harmful to productivity. There is evidence, in fact, that under certain circumstances limited degradation of, for example, climax to secondary vegetation can actually lead to enhancement of productivity. Indeed, continued use of many biological resources is the key to sustained productivity.

Data on the production and productivity of CPRs is very scarce. Livestock, for example, obtain fodder supplies from crop residues, grazing on village common lands (*poromboke* and tank foreshores) and from browsing in reserved forests. The relative importance of these various sources is quite variable over space and time, and the intensification of rice production has evidently alleviated problems of fodder supply in some areas. Nevertheless, fodder and browse resources from forests constitute a major source of supply for cattle in western Tamil Nadu, but (as with fuel species) data on natural browse species, on actual and potential productivity, and on carrying capacity of browse areas are almost entirely absent. Thus, precise statements on actual or potential supply and benefits cannot be made. If we knew the sustainable yield of browse species, we could make a determination of what the grazing limits could be. In that case, however, one would have to accept a trade-off between fodder and fuel supplies, since maximizing the one would reduce production of the other.

The excludability of CPRs is an issue that is constantly at the center of contradiction between the rural population and government departments. It is physically feasible to fence off forests, but also very expensive. It is estimated that fencing social forestry plantations doubles the costs of establishment (Karnataka State Forestry Department, pers. comm. 1985). In addition, fences are difficult to guard and are easily cut. It is extremely difficult to guard and to exclude users from small forests entirely surrounded by rural populations. For *poromboke* land and other major grazing resources, exclusion of nonlocals (those from outside the village) might be quite easy through recognition. In practice, however, little effort is made to exclude outsiders from village *poromboke*. If a village decided to stint on the *poromboke* land, it would be fairly easy for people to identify free riders although not necessarily to exclude them, since effective exclusion is a matter of political power as well as of the physical characteristics of the CPR itself. This point underlines the difficulty of clearly labeling the type of property rights attached to each resource.

There is another aspect of excludability that depends upon the location of the CPR in relation to potential users. The friction of distance derives from relative location and not from the technical attributes of the CPR, but it is an important aspect. Development of the road system even to the remote parts of Tamil Nadu has opened up many forest products to commercial pressures. Pappanaickenpatti (a village in Salem district) has developed a substantial local export industry in green manure for paddy and in curry leaves from the curry leaf plant (*Murraya koenigi*); the former is transported to the Salem district, the latter to the markets of Madras over 100 miles away. The new road to the village laid in the last decade has made this business possible, and has made most CPRs in Tamil Nadu accessible to commercial exploitation.

The physical attributes to CPRs in Tamil Nadu can be summarized, therefore, as broadly accessible and nonexcludable, subject to relatively high subtractibility and divisibility, and with a clear set of boundaries.

Decision-Making Arrangements

Decision-making arrangements regulating the use of CPRs in Tamil Nadu have these characteristics: first, the development of institutions for collective choice within the groups involved with these commons is very restricted indeed; second, there is extensive bureaucratic control under rules that are partial and often unclear, and that leave a great deal to the discretion of field officers in matters of enforcement; and third, following from these features, the arrangements are highly susceptible to manipulation by those with local power.

Conditions of Collective Choice

Few local institutions regulate choices over the use of CPRs in Tamil Nadu. In some instances, purely local, community-level councils, committees, or informal groups, such as those described by R. Chambers (1977), in North Arcot district, act to regulate surface irrigation. A tradition of *kudi-maramut*, or locally organized collective work in the maintenance of irrigation structures, can also be found to a limited extent in some parts (Harriss 1982, 72–76). But these instances are exceptional and they relate to irrigation water. We know of no such institutions or arrangements for the management of the resources of *poromboke* and designated waste lands or of forests.

Tamil Nadu, like other Indian states, has a history of local institutions (*panchayats*) with juridical powers (for the resolution of disputes) and executive authority (for decisions over certain matters in the public realm, such as temple affairs and village religious ceremonies). (We refer here to village and caste *panchayats* rather than to the officially constituted *panchayat*, the lowest level of organization in the system of democratic local government adopted in India in the 1950s and 1960s.) The *panchayats* still exist (see Harriss 1982, 227–33), but there is little, if any, evidence that they have been instruments for the management of resources such as waste land and forest, at least over the last 200 years. They may be used, however, to resolve disputes such as those arising from quarrels over grazing.

The effectiveness of such local dispute resolution and decision making depends upon local power structures, in which the dominance that is exercised by a particular caste group and the capacity of that caste group for taking collective action, are factors of crucial importance. In circumstances where dominance is disputed among different groups or where the dominant caste group is itself divided by strong factional rivalries, collective action may be compromised. G. Djurfeldt and S. Lindberg (1975, 125) record an instance of effective action by locally dominant cultivators to prevent encroachment on *poromboke* lands used for grazing, while P. Hill (1982, 131) documents a case in which common grazing lands have been encroached upon by richer households. What happens to common lands in a particular village area is likely to depend upon the specific interests and politics of richer and more powerful people. Such effective choice as exists with regard to CPRs in the highly stratified rural society of Tamil Nadu is unlikely to involve the entire village population. It will involve the richer, more powerful households and will usually reflect their interests. The mass of rural people may or may not derive some benefit from their action.[2]

The official *panchayats* have assumed some responsibility for the management of some CPRs. Palmyra and tamarind trees, growing on tank bunds (containing banks) or at roadsides, thorn bushes used as fuel, and certain green manure plants all are treated as public property. Rights to the use of these plants were handed over to the village *panchayats*, which in turn auctioned them and put the money earned into *panchayat* funds. Though the village *panchayats* have been in abeyance in Tamil Nadu since 1975, it is still said by villagers and by officials that the *panchayat* controls the use of these resources. At present, in practice, use rights are auctioned by a local official and the proceeds go into official coffers. It is significant, though, that the *panchayat* should still be referred to: there is a strong belief in the power and endurance of popular institutions of local self-government even when these institutions no longer exist. This belief perhaps helps to legitimate state interventions. Under both the village *panchayats* and the current arrangements, there is evidence that relatively wealthy or powerful people have been able to obtain rights to CPR produce at very low rates in auctions, and to sell this produce for a substantial profit.

In sum, the use of CPRs consisting of fuel, fodder, and other produce from *poromboke*, waste, and forest lands is subject to a high degree of personal discretion—and individuals are generally able to act on the basis of personal discretion in matters of common concern. This discretion, however, is limited mainly by bureaucratically enforced controls that can be manipulated, to one degree or another, by each individual who encounters them. Fieldwork showed a number of corroborated accounts of bribery: bribes are considered necessary when users want to gain access to resources to which the state has laid claim, or when they need to extricate themselves from the consequences of being caught. There were reported to be considerable variations between individual officials at all levels, however, as well as between the way in which the administration operated at the village, district, and state levels.

Individuals adversely affected by others may turn to local, unofficial *panchayats* to adjudicate disputes, or they may find remedies through the law and the local bureaucracy. All these institutions are susceptible to influence by those holding local power. In any event, the extent to which collective decisions are taken at all is very restricted, and both this and the degree to which such decisions are binding depend upon the local power structure, especially on the politics of the dominant caste. Powerful individuals both in the village and in the bureaucracy have extensive powers of veto.

Operational Rules

In circumstances such as those just described, the operational rules affecting CPR use exist on two levels. On the one hand, bureaucratic rules regulate access to and use of *poromboke* and waste lands and their products; these are enforced by the revenue department while rules regarding officially designated forests are enforced by the forest department. The former include a scale of fines that should be levied in cases of cultivation of *poromboke*; the latter, such rules as giving rights to collect fallen wood, but not to cut standing trees.

On the other hand, informal rules arise from the nature of the local power structure and the interactions of people with the bureaucracy. Thus the revenue and forest departments are empowered to enforce rules that, in principle, prevent partitioning of CPRs and establish strong boundary lines. Local officials of the revenue department should prevent encroachment upon the *poromboke* lands and regulate the use of designated waste, while forest officers should control access to the forests. In practice, these rules can be bent systematically in favor of the relatively rich and powerful, for whom the fines imposed by the bureaucracy or the bribes paid to local officials for turning a blind eye on infringements may be treated as acceptable "costs of production." For the officials concerned, on the other hand, these payments are part of a kind of bureaucratic rent.

External Arrangements

Our account thus far has emphasized the crucial importance of external arrangements in decision making over CPRs in Tamil Nadu. The commons is actually defined by bureaucratic categorization of land as *poromboke*, or as "waste," or as "forest" (which is then really "state" land and not local "commons"); its boundaries are defined bureaucratically and may or may not correspond to a division based upon vegetational zoning. Rules about access and use are laid down in the standing orders of the departments concerned.

The arrangements in force are mainly bureaucratic, with both highly centralized rule making and, in practice, a great deal of discretion for field officers, given the extreme difficulty of supervising their activity very closely. Petty corruption is endemic. But there are also arrangements at other levels, as, for example, with the recent establishment of village social forestry committees that supposedly encourage participation in the management of social forestry plantations. These committees have only been in existence for a few years, and it is still difficult to assess their impact. The limited information we have suggests that they are often "paper" organizations characterized by indifference and ignorance on the part of the majority of their members. There is no reason to suppose that they will be any more effective as instruments of participation and collective decision making than are the village *panchayat*s. Their power to make rules is seriously limited. The forestry department can and does coerce villagers to accept social forestry projects on their foreshores (Centre for Research, Extension and IRD 1984). The village-level social forestry worker is responsible to the forestry department and not the village; the department selects the species to be planted and the dates when cutting is permitted, and the produce is auctioned off at its wish. Thus the villagers cannot choose who will use the CPRs or decide upon how the products will be used.

Conclusion

In this sphere, as in others in south Indian villages, it seems that the long-standing attempt by the state to exercise close supervision over land use has actively discouraged collective choice and action at the local level (on this in general, see Washbrook 1976). Utilization of CPRs such as fodder and fuel is in principle extensively controlled by the local officials of several government departments. In practice, the system is subject to manipulation by those with local power and generally works in their favor.

Patterns of Interaction

The foregoing account of decision-making arrangements for the management of CPRs implies that the consequent patterns of interaction are of two types: those between people and the state with its various functionaries; and those among people who themselves use the CPRs in the village. Since collective choice in the management of CPRs has been reduced to a minimum, the dominant set of interactions concerns the direct users and the state or, more specifically, the state land revenue and forestry departments.

Although these two sets of interactions are distinct, they are often closely related in the way CPRs are actually used. Any group of would-be users of CPRs is heterogeneous in its economic, social, and political resources. Users usually compete for CPRs, and competition among individual households for CPRs is encouraged by the lack of institutions at the local level (or any other level) to manage the commons in a cooperative way. Each household thus competes against the others and against the state, and in this interaction the notion of access is crucial.

Access to CPRs has many dimensions. It implies that the would-be user has sufficient labor to use the resource (this is particularly important for fuel collection and grazing). It also implies that the potential user has spatial proximity to the resource and either the funds to purchase access from state officials (the payment of bureaucratic rent) or sufficient political power and coercion to gain access without paying. Such power usually is the result of land ownership and facilitates dealing with official regulations over CPRs and with other competing households who are also direct users of the CPR. Thus, the users' access position largely determines their choice of strategy to obtain CPRs, and therefore the pattern of interactions among users themselves, and between users and the state.

The first and most common interaction between users and the state is the "legitimate" use of CPRs. This involves the removal of dead wood from both revenue and reserved forests, which is permitted for certain forests by official regulations. In addition, tribal peoples are given special dispensation to graze sheep and cattle (but not goats) in reserved forests. Others pay grazing fees, and there is no restriction on the number of cattle to be grazed. Stock may graze on waste and *poromboke* lands. As we shall see in the next section, the outcome of legitimate use of CPRs alone (leaving aside the "illegitimate" use to be discussed below) has led to extreme pressure on some CPRs, notably grazing land and in some places fuel and construction timber (on the situation in India generally with regard to this point, refer to Government of India 1984). It is not the central contention of this chapter that the illegal use of CPRs is necessarily the main culprit in the physical decline of many of them, although illegal action certainly is an additional use of CPRs and, as such, contributes to their overuse. Illegal use also highlights the contradiction between would-be users and the state (which makes most of the rules).

Patterns of interaction involving illegal use of CPRs are of two major types: (1) instances when the illegal use constitutes overuse or overextraction by an individual of a common resource over and above the limits set by the state; and (2) cases when the illegal use involves a theft of state property (such as sandalwood). The two major resources that are most often overextracted are fuelwood and grazing land for goats, both of which are found on revenue and reserved forests. Those who collect fodder and fuelwood are frequently caught by forest guards; if the wood they have collected is found to have been cut green, the guards will impound their sickles. A fine of Rs. 5 is common in such circumstances.

The case of theft of state property of timbers (such as sandalwood) is of a different order, since it is so valuable (up to about U.S. $10 per kilo of grade one timber) that it has long since ceased to be a CPR; rather, it is a much-prized commodity to which the state has laid claim. A few private individuals, often backed by considerable capital and equipment, do mount raids on these trees. The revenue collected by the forest department from this source is so much greater than from all others in certain forest divisions in western Tamil Nadu that much of the resources of staff and transport are committed to protect and harvest sandalwood. This undoubtedly diverts personnel from guarding less valuable resources such as small wood for fuel and species used for construction purposes.

Bamboo is not such a severe case, although it is valuable enough commercially to provide the forest department with considerable revenue. It is also used by local artisans for weaving winnowing fans and mats, so that forest guards often fine artisans not only at the site but also when they attempt to sell the finished product at the market.

It is difficult to assess how much of the fines levied by forest guards finds its way to the official revenues of the department, and how much is appropriated by employees as "bureaucratic rent." But widely corroborated accounts of bribery abound. Villagers informally arrange an annual bribe to local forest guards to facilitate the grazing of goats, for example, by a capitation "fee" of about Rs. 5 per goat-owning family (which in one village provided a sum of some Rs. 600, or U.S. $50, handed over annually). Similarly, artisans using bamboo arrange an annual bribe. In one village, the collection of green manure from the more productive reserve forests attracts a standardized charge of Rs. 80 of which Rs. 36 is an unreceipted fine to forest guards. The forest guards (and perhaps forest rangers, too) have an informal organization for dividing this rent among themselves and for collecting it in a variety of ways. One tribal village, well endowed with reserve forest, has forest guards who arrive two or three times a year with a truck, make a spot check on fuelwood stocks of households, and confiscate and remove any timber that they believe was cut green. The value of a truckload is estimated to be at least Rs. 1,000.

The other main type of interaction between state and user is the privatization of CPRs through encroachment. Successful encroachment on *poromboke* and other common lands (such as uncultivated waste lands) depends upon the access position of the individual encroacher, with regard both to other villagers and to the bureaucracy of the land revenue department. Individuals of widely differing access positions encroach upon *poromboke* land. Landless and near-landless households are perhaps the most numerous, but their position is threatened by powerful "big-men" and speculators from outside the village who employ strong-arm tactics to evict less powerful people. Sometimes, indeed, they use the law to have them removed and then evade the law themselves through bribery to take over the land and register it in their own names. Such was the case in Pappanaikenpatti, where the village *munsif* (headman) had evicted tribal encroachers from land to which he subsequently gained title right (*patta*). There is therefore a long-drawn-out process of de facto occupation of *poromboke* land, including annual fines for illegal privatization that may go on for many years, and finally change of revenue classification to *patta* land. Revenue records, then, inevitably lag behind the true extent of encroachment. Encroachment clearly has been going on for a very long time, so that opportunities for further encroachment are generally limited. Local revenue records show that most of the encroachment takes place on land designated as *poromboke*, cultivable waste, permanent pastures, and other grazing lands, and only to a very limited extent on land under the jurisdiction of the forest department.

Turning to the interactions among individuals in the use of CPRs, it will by now be plain that there is very little cooperation in the management of commons that have been taken over by the state. Competition rather than free riding is the dominant relationship in CPR use. The intensity of competition among users is a function of the supply of CPRs and the demand for them, on the one hand, and of the lack of legitimacy of the rules governing the resources, on the other. The state makes the rules but enforces them arbitrarily (from the local users' point of view), so that their legitimacy is low.

To summarize the principal patterns of interaction: the chief actors are users and state functionaries, backed by the law that, in official terms, clearly demarcates and sanctions categories of rights and restrictions. The arena of local management and interaction is thereby drastically limited, and is characterized by individualistic patterns of use and competition among users who have differing qualifications for gaining access.

Outcomes

Political Economy

The outcomes of the political economy of Tamil Nadu can be summarized in seven major points as shown in the following discussion.

It will already be clear that the state has taken control of virtually all lands on which common-property resources are to be found. The social forestry program, as it is currently conceived, is merely an extension of the state's control and a further restriction upon the use of common-property resources. At the local level, too, no institutions take a major part in managing these resources. In sum:

1. *The state seeks to regulate most CPRs in Tamil Nadu.*

The outcome of CPR management in Tamil Nadu cannot be analyzed properly without reference to changes in the ownership and productivity of private-property resources (PPRs). Here there has been a steady reduction in the average size of landholdings, and a considerable degree of differentiation among rural households has existed for a long time. Some farmers have managed to increase both the size and productivity of their farms; others have been reduced to the status of either landless laborers or submarginal farmers and have been pushed onto the economic fringes of cultivation. Their situation sometimes finds spatial expression in that they illegally squat on *poromboke* land and barren wastes, and may be forced to cut and sell firewood to eke out a living. These people are also marginalized in the sense that they cannot usually invest in productive assets and so tend to lose land to more adventurous, unscrupulous, and wealthy people. For the most part, encroachment on CPRs is the result of population pressure within a society with a highly skewed distribution of power. The exception is encroached-on land that is irrigable and attracts speculative purchase by wealthier people. Greatly increased pressure on CPRs has led to rising costs to users whose travel and collective time have increased; users may also be paying more for bribes and fines.

Other changes in PPRs also affect the use of CPRs, these come about as a result of irrigation. When an extra one or two crops a year are produced, crop residues for feeding livestock and for fuel are more plentiful. In Tamil Nadu, the double-cropped area has generally increased, especially as a result of the expansion of groundwater irrigation (see the data in Kurien 1980). At the same time, paddy cultivation may create a demand for green manure, which is usually obtained from forests where these are accessible. Thus:

2. *Marginalization of poorer rural people has led to increased use of CPRs and encroachment on them through illegal squatting.*

3. *Increases in irrigated area have tended to ease the shortage of pastures on common land, but may also have increased the demand for green manure, particularly near forests.*

In the areas of Tamil Nadu that were studied, there is a notable exception to an encroachment pattern that seems widespread throughout India, namely, the unauthorized collection of fuelwood. There is little evidence of a serious shortage of fuel in Tamil Nadu. There are at least three reasons for this. First, there are a fair number of woody residues from tree crops (for example palmyra and coconut palm), and annual crops (such as cotton, cassava, and sorghum) that are not readily recyclable through the agricultural system via composting, but that are still suitable for burning as fuel. Second, there is not an appreciable cold season (as in central or northern India). Third, opportunistic thorn bushes (such as various species of *Lantana*) grow rapidly and freely on *poromboke* land on roadsides, tank foreshores, and elsewhere, and provide an adequate source of fuel in many areas. In eastern districts, *Prosopis juliflora* provides fuel, since it is rarely browsed by goats, and it both coppices well and grows fast. This finding is different from that of N. S. Jodha (1987), who found quite acute shortages of fuel in the drier areas of western India, where dung is burned as a substitute for wood. In Tamil Nadu, dung is burned in areas far from any available forest but not universally. Thus, we may summarize our fourth outcome:

4. *There is not yet a widespread nor severe shortage of combustible fuel.*

Increased pressure on grazing is undoubtedly severe, however, and is reflected in reduced numbers of livestock (see Table 11.2). The views of individual owners of cattle, buffalo, and small stock also support this view. The extension of government-sponsored social forestry onto tank foreshores clearly exacerbates the pressure on remaining land. Thus:

5. *There is severe pressure on grazing land, and this is partly associated with a decline in the numbers of cattle.*

TABLE 11.2
Changes in Livestock Population, Tamil Nadu, 1961–1982

	1961	1974	1982	% change 1961–1982
Buffalo	2,594,271	2,853,252	3,212,224	+ 23
Bovines	13,420,174	10,572,378	10,365,500	− 23
Sheep	7,159,956	6,392,821	5,536,514	− 23
Goats	3,428,847	3,954,477	5,246,192	+ 53
Total	26,603,248	23,772,928	24,360,430	− 8

SOURCE: Government of India, *Census of India*, 1961, 1971, 1982 (provisional).

Other forest products both for commercial exploitation and for subsistence have also become scarce or unavailable altogether. Exploitation of those that have commercial possibilities (such as gall nuts and curry leaves) has increasingly been organized by contractors who have successfully bid for the rights sold by the forestry or the land revenue department. Medicinal herbs, wild roots, honey, and relishes have long since disappeared from both the forests and the minds of those who use the forest (curry leaves are the one exception here). Thus:

6. *Most minor forest products have ceased to be CPRs, either because they have been overused to the point of extinction or because they have been commercialized and taken out of the realm of CPRs for local use.*

Turning now to the overall extent of land on which CPRs are or were exploited, we can see from Table 11.1 that encroachment onto *poromboke* land and unassessed and assessed waste land has reduced the area of common land to a very small proportion of the whole. While the remaining *poromboke* and waste land is dwarfed by land held in reserve and revenue forests, it remains the only land that could conceivably be managed by a committee of users. Thus:

7. *The area of village lands from which CPRs are obtained has been diminishing over a long period, and has left very little common land under the control of the village.*

Environment

It is difficult to be precise about the efficiency of use of CPRs in Tamil Nadu because of the general dearth of accurate physical information on their potential and actual levels of productivity. Further, if one considers the interactions among different CPR products, such as browse or grazing and fuel, obtained from the same common lands, data on how productivity of the one will affect productivity of the other do not exist.

Statements of biological efficiency that concern themselves solely with aggregate productivity or vegetative material are meaningless without recourse to exact information on human needs and on whether in fact fuel or grazing products are or should be more significant. This is not to suggest, of course, that there is no compatibility of use among different CPR products. But one must recognize the limitations of simply using physical data in a vacuum.

Verbal reports and some physical evidence do suggest that overall usage rates of CPRs has led to a depletion of resources. Productivity has actually increased in one case where tank foreshores were planted with *Acacia nilotica* (babul) under social forestry schemes; this has not necessarily enhanced common benefits, however.

There are differences among villages in the higher west of Tamil Nadu and those on the eastern plain. The Kalrayan Hills in Salem district surrounding the village of Pappanaickenpatti still support a diversity of flora in a well-structured community, which hardly indicates severe environmental pressure (see the detailed analysis in Blaikie, Harriss, and Pain 1985). In the neighboring district of Dharmapuri on the common lands of Arakasanahalli, this vegetation cover is largely gone and the lands are covered by the opportunistic *Lantana* species and thickets of heavily coppiced *Albizia amara*. But despite the fact that the vegetation is degraded, the village does not suffer from problems of fuel supply. On the other hand, in Dusi, a predominantly paddy village in North Arcot district, the remaining 21.56 acres of common grazing lands support no standing timber, and although there is full grass cover, the species composition is such that productivity is low and little benefit is derived by anyone using these lands for grazing. But the fuel situation in Dusi has actually improved over the last decade with the spread of the thorn bush *P. juliflora*, and the village is almost self-sufficient in its fuel requirements.

In general, production from village grazing lands is minimal, but this has probably been the case for some decades. There is no doubt that many of the forests and their various products are degraded or exploited beyond their natural rate of sustainability, and the overexploitation of bamboo has been well documented.

Livelihoods

CPRs are of varying importance as sources of food, fodder, fuel, manure, and minor products; these products, in turn, are the basis for livelihoods in villages in different parts of Tamil Nadu (see our earlier remarks on "CPR-limited" and "CPR-dependent" villages). The bureaucratic regulation of CPRs is of particular concern in CPR-dependent villages, for this regulation is often subject to manipulation by local power to the disadvantage of poorer people.

But in both CPR-dependent and CPR-limited village economies, CPRs present livelihood opportunities that are either not pursued or that are inefficiently pursued from the point of view of poor people's welfare. In the latter category, we would include the current use of tank beds and foreshores for so-called social forestry projects; there is often no benefit at all to local people and particularly none to the rural poor, given that they find neither employment nor resources of use to them in the social forestry plantations. In the former category, we would include the possible uses of marginal lands (classified as waste) for forestry conducted by poor people for their own benefit.

Clearly, the mobilization of opportunities like these is subject to difficulties that should not be underestimated. These are circumstances in which the powerful and wealthy have been able to take advantage systematically of the confusing layering of rights and enforcement, so that considerable inequalities in access to common resources has resulted. Any fresh interventions by the state are likely to be susceptible to manipulation by local power holders. The point is that opportunities for the production of livelihoods do still exist, and that the means for exploring them are not available under the current system of management by a bureaucracy imbued with an ethic of regulation and control.

NOTES

The research on which this chapter is based was essentially of an exploration kind. The authors undertook field research together in the state of Tamil Nadu in September 1984, when they collected secondary data and made studies of six villages, three of them in an area of intensive irrigated agriculture in the North Arcot district. Thereafter, Adam Pain undertook an additional six weeks of field work, including some ecological analysis, in the same villages.

1. These definitions are quoted from Sundararaja 1933.

2. Wade (1988) makes this point with regard to some villages in Andhra Pradesh that display an unusual degree of corporateness. The councils in these villages, with their common funds—used to pay the field guards and common irrigators whom they employ—are essentially institutions of the dominant Reddy caste community. It may be that in this case low-caste, landless people do derive benefits from the existence of these institutions because of the higher levels of economic activity that they are instrumental in bringing about. But poor and low-ranking people are not participants in the institutions. Wade's study describes institutions concerned with collective choice that are certainly unusual in India,

and his account in the end emphasizes just how exceptional the circumstances are that seem to explain the existence of corporate activity in this case.

REFERENCES

Blaikie, P., J. Harriss, and A. Pain. 1985. *Public Policy and the Utilization of Common Property Resources in Tamil Nadu, India.* A report for Economic and Social Committee for Overseas Research (ESCOR). Norwich, England. Overseas Development Administration, School of Development Studies, University of East Anglia.

Blaikie, P. M., and H. C. Brookfield, eds. 1987. *Land Degradation and Society.* London: Methuen.

Centre for Research, Extension and IRD. 1984. *People and Social Forestry: Case Studies in Cooperation and Conflict.* Gandhigram, Maduari district, Tamil Nadu, India: Gandhigram Rural Institute.

Chambers, R. 1977. "Men and Water: The Organization and Operation of Irrigation." In *Green Revolution?*, ed. B. H. Farmer, 340–63. London: Macmillan.

Djurfeldt, G., and S. Lindberg. 1975. *Behind Poverty: The Social Formation in a Tamil Village.* London: Curzon Press.

Farmer, B. H., ed. 1977. *Green Revolution?* London: Macmillan.

Government of India. 1984. *Report of the Review Committee on Rights and Access to Forest Areas.* New Delhi: Government of India.

Government of Tamil Nadu. 1983. *List of More Common Plants of Tamil Nadu and Their Uses.* Madras: Statistics and Planning Cell, Office of the Chief Conservator of Forests.

Harriss, J. 1982. *Capitalism and Peasant Farming: Agrarian Structure and Ideology in Northern Tamil Nadu.* Bombay: Oxford University Press.

Hill, P. 1982. *Dry Grain Farming Families.* Cambridge: Cambridge University Press.

Jodha, N. S. 1987. "Common Property Resources and Environmental Decline in Western India." In *Land Degradation and Society*, ed. P. M. Blaikie and H. C. Brookfield. London: Methuen.

Kurien, C. T. 1980. "Dynamics of Rural Transformation: A Case Study of Tamil Nadu." *Economics and Political Weekly* 15:365–90.

Sundararaja, I. 1933. *Land Tenures of the Madras Presidency.* Madras: The Law Press.

Wade, R. 1988. *Village Republics: Economic Conditions for Collective Action in South India.* Cambridge: Cambridge University Press.

Washbrook, D. 1976. *The Emergence of Provincial Politics: The Madras Presidency, 1870–1920.* Cambridge: Cambridge University Press.

PART 3

Toward a Theory of the Commons

12

Where Do We Go from Here? Implications for the Research Agenda

David Feeny

The Annapolis conference in 1985 was both symbolic of and instrumental in the advancement and consolidation of our analytical and empirical knowledge of the issues surrounding the development, evolution, performance, and survival of institutional arrangements for the management of common-property resources. A number of prominent works on common property and collective action have been published since the mid-1980s.[1] These and other works provide syntheses and interpretations of the results of the renewed research interest in the commons. Quite naturally and appropriately these works focus on assessments of what has been learned, how the issues should be analyzed and understood, identification of important hypotheses for testing, and what the next steps in the research agenda should be. Daniel Bromley in Chapter 1 and Elinor Ostrom in Chapter 13 of this book provide additional important assessments.

The focus in this paper is instead on methodology. In addition to identifying important topics and hypotheses, recent work on the commons also provides an important set of implications concerning the means by which additional research should be conducted. These implications, which apply to a wide variety of theoretical approaches, will be discussed in this chapter.

The chapter is written from two perspectives. First, it is concerned with the methodologies used by the scholarly community for describing and understanding common-property resources and their management. Second, it considers methodologies for the generation of knowledge for direct use in the formulation of policy. These two processes overlap and interact.

Research is needed both to formulate hypotheses and to subject them to a variety of tests. The results of inquiry will contribute to intellectual development in a number of areas including theories of collective action, social choice, and an understanding of human societies, especially in the setting of less-developed countries. Improved social science knowledge in the field of institutional analysis has the potential to improve institutional design. One model of policy intervention requires an understanding of how things work as a prerequisite to informed and productive interventions to affect performance. Although there are other viable approaches to policy formulation, improved institutional design has been a long-run goal of much of the recent inquiry on the management of common-property resources.

The Annapolis conference was organized around the presentation and discussion of a diverse set of high-quality case studies of common-property resource management. The cases represented a variety of resource types and regions and, in order to capture the synergy of a comparative approach, were presented in a common taxonomic framework (see Oakerson in Chapter 3 of this book). Similarly, most of the other recent contributions to the literature on the commons have been case studies, collections of case studies, or comparative collections of case studies. Given the prominence of these approaches it is important to explore the methodological advantages and disadvantages of case-study and other approaches for future research. To provide an overview, a number of studies dealing with the management of common-property resources or closely related issues have been arbitrarily classified by study design (see Table 12.1). Although the table divides studies according to their major purposes, in fact virtually all studies contain elements of each major purpose. The distinction between retrospective and prospective refers to whether the data were collected after the event or as events unfolded. The intent in Table 12.1 is not to provide an exhaustive list of examples. Instead the intent is only to provide an illustration of each type of study design. The advantages and disadvantages of each approach will be discussed.

Case-Study Approaches

Studies of common-property resource management by social scientists, historians, biologists, and human ecologists have largely relied upon natural experiments to generate observations about the behavior of natural

TABLE 12.1
Examples of Studies on the Management of Common-Property Resources, Classified by Research Design

Primary purpose of study	Case-study approach					Laboratory experiment	Field experiment
	Retrospective data collection		Prospective data collection				
	Single case	Comparative	Single case	Comparative			
Description or inductive hypothesis generation	Kisangani 1986	Campbell & Godoy (Chapter 5)	Blaikie, Harriss, & Pain (Chapter 11)	Arnold & Campbell 1986		—	—
Hypothesis testing	McKean (Chapter 4)	Thomson, Feeny, & Oakerson (Chapter 6)	Wynne 1986	Hayami & Kikuchi 1981		Isaac, McCue, & Plott 1985	—

SOURCE: Chapter 12 references and this book.

and human systems and the interactions among and within them. Given the logistical, ethical, and conceptual problems associated with experiments involving human subjects, natural experiments will quite appropriately continue to be the stock-in-trade for scholars interested in the issues surrounding common-property resources. Case-study approaches include a variety of studies.

First, there are case studies by design, in which scholars collect information expressly for the purpose of investigating common-property resource management. Many of the chapters in this book, including those by John Cordell and Margaret McKean (Chapter 8), and McKean (Chapter 4) fit this category. Second, there are the serendipitous case studies—situations in which the scholar was investigating one topic but in the process generated case study materials for another as well. Third, there are the comparative case-study approaches such as Chapter 5 by Bruce Campbell and Ricardo Godoy, Chapter 9 by Robert Wade, and Chapter 7 by Fikret Berkes.

The advantages of prospective case studies designed to take advantage of on-going natural experiments are illustrated by the work of Yujiro Hayami and Masao Kikuchi (1981). They were able to collect data on the situation before major changes occurred and to document the effects of exogenous demographic and technological changes on the choice of institutional arrangements for organizing harvest operations. The prospective design allowed them to obtain data on the variables they felt were of key importance. Retrospective data collection, in contrast, does not in general permit the investigator to design data collection instruments and decide on the types of information to be recorded.

Traditional harvest labor contracts found in many areas in both Java and the Philippines involved the payment of a share of the harvest to harvest workers. Access to such employment opportunities was open to all members of the village. Rights for residual gleaning on harvested fields accompanied the rights in some cases. The effects of population growth and technological change have challenged these harvest labor arrangements. Population growth has resulted in a downward pressure on real wages, which have declined in some areas. When this has occurred, the real wage implied by the traditional share arrangement—rates like one-eighth of the crop that the person harvested—has exceeded the prevailing local wage. Hayami and Kikuchi provide detailed village-level evidence on the former equilibrium between real wages in equivalent units of rice per day, the implied wage associated with the traditional harvest share arrangements, and the growing disequilibrium between them. Another important source of disequilibrium in some areas has been the effects of adopting modern rice varieties that produce higher yields in response to fertilizer. The result has again meant that the traditional share of the harvest exceeds the local wage.

Three types of new institutional arrangements have evolved in response to the pressures of demographic and technological change. In villages characterized by less inequality in holdings and more community cohesion, traditional share-wage arrangements have been preserved. In some cases the share has been lowered; in others, the arrangements have been modified so that access to harvest employment is now open only to those who provide unremunerated weeding labor earlier in the season. Another development has been the hiring of workers from outside the village through labor contractors. Outsiders have no traditional right of access to the share-wage contracts and thus are more willing to work for wages (and thus also require more direct supervision). These arrangements emerged when the local community was unable to agree upon a change in the rate or conditions of employment for the share wage. Finally, in villages characterized by greater inequality in landholdings and topography conducive to the use of machines, the harvest operations have begun to be mechanized. Thus existing institutional arrangements, characteristics of the community, and changes in relative prices generated by demographic and technological changes have all interacted to affect the emergence of new arrangements.

The usefulness of case-study materials collected for other purposes for crude hypothesis testing is illustrated by Robert H. Bates (1983). Bates conducted a study in which Human Relations Area File materials on precolonial African states were coded and used to test neocontractarian and neo-Marxian ideas concerning the emergence and growth of centralized states. Several themes emerged. The benefits of the state in providing institutional arrangements and enforcement were indeed positively related to the existence and size of centralized states. An important mechanism in the amelioration of free riding in organizing such collective action was the use of coercion. Although this enabled the state to more readily provide a public good, it also conferred on the state the ability to coerce contributions even when performance was poor. The tension between the benefits and potential abuses of using the state to solve collective-action problems is also reflected in Chapter 6 of this book (by Thomson, Feeny, and Oakerson; compare Kisangani 1986).

Case studies may be used to generate hypotheses inductively, as Elinor Ostrom (1986) shows when she examines the hypotheses generated by the body of case studies and discussion at the Annapolis conference. Alternatively, the case-study material may be used to test hypotheses derived from theory or from previous inductive exercises. Chapters 6 and 9 of this book provide examples of the latter (see also E. Ostrom 1990; Tang 1991).

The use of case-study materials to test hypotheses is also illustrated by several studies that examine the effects of group size on the performance of institutions managing common-property resources. The analytical literature on collective action and the case-study materials highlight group size as a factor that affects the ability of the group to manage a common-property resource. The intuition is obvious. If a group is smaller, all other things being equal, it should be less costly for members of the group to recognize each other and so easier for the group to detect rule infractions by group members and entry into the commons by nongroup users. The cost of decision making and coordination of activities should similarly be related to group size. Four factors have already been mentioned: cost of intragroup enforcement, cost of extragroup exclusion, cost of decision making, and cost of coordination. (The per capita benefits of cooperation are assumed in these mental experiments to be held constant as group size varies.) The costs involved for each of these activities is affected by more than group size and in particular responds to the costs of transportation and communication, which in turn depend in part upon the available technology. Thus it is not surprising that unequivocal generalizations do not emerge from a quick review of the case studies.

Yet the case studies do include information corroborating our intuition. The three "successful" cases discussed by Berkes (Chapter 7) were located in bays exploited by from 100 to 140 registered fishing units; the numbers of units in the bays in which failures occurred were twice to ten times as large. All four factors appear to be relevant in the cases discussed by Berkes.

Similar results are reported by Kari Bullock and John Baden (1977) in their discussion of the operation of Hutterite communes. Group sizes of 60 to 150 have promoted successful communal operations in such settings. Victor S. Doherty and N. S. Jodha (1979; compare Doherty 1982), like Doherty, Senen M. Miranda, and Jacob Kampen (1982) also highlight the importance of group size in the successful operation of tank irrigation schemes in semiarid areas in South Asia. (Similar evidence for aquaculture in Panama is found in Molnar, Schwartz, and Lovshin 1985.)

A standard methodological argument is that some framework underlies all case studies—that the investigator has a model that identifies key variables and suggests the kinds of information that are relevant and important. The argument is that the efficiency of such approaches can be enhanced by making the framework explicit; an explicit treatment will clarify thought as well as communication. The use of a common taxonomic framework at the Annapolis conference reflects this methodological argument.

Historical Approaches

Historical studies are examples of the case-study approach with retrospective data collection based on natural experiments drawn from the past. Yet because the focus is on the analysis of the development, evolution, survival, and performance of institutional arrangements associated with the management of common-property resources, and because these are processes that take place over time, historical studies are likely to be a particularly rich source of information for generating and testing hypotheses. Studies of economic history have been a primary vehicle for the development and testing of crude models of institutional change (see for instance Hayami and Ruttan 1985; North 1981; Feeny 1982, 1987). Such studies have reiterated a point made in Chapter 3 by Oakerson, namely, that outcomes depend on more than endowments, technology, and preferences; institutions also matter (see also Solow 1985; Field 1984; Feeny 1987, 1988b; Feder and Feeny 1991; Field 1991; Gardner and E. Ostrom 1991; Langlois 1986a, 1986b; E. Ostrom, 1990; V. Ostrom, Feeny, and Picht 1988; Rosenberg and Birdzell 1986; Smith 1991).

Historical studies, too, provide grist for the mill of inductive hypothesis generation. A number of them have focused on the emergence and evolution of systems of property rights and provide material relevant to the analysis of common-property resource management.[2] More directly relevant are the studies in which Gary Libecap and Steven Wiggins (1984, 1985; compare Wiggins and Libecap 1985) investigate the choice of institutional arrangements for the exploitation of common pools of oil in Texas and Oklahoma (1926–1935), Texas, Oklahoma, and Wyoming (1948–1975), and Texas and New Mexico (1950s to the 1970s). Under an 1889 Pennsylvania Supreme Court ruling, rights to oil were defined according to "rule of capture"; that is, oil was defined as private property only after it was brought to the surface. This assignment of property rights created incentives to drill more wells than necessary and to pump oil to the surface more rapidly. The extra drilling and more rapid pumping lowered the rate of return on the pool of oil, dissipating the economic rents (the difference between the price at which the resource can be sold and the cost of extracting the resource). An alternative assignment of property rights is unitization of the pool of oil, or the creation of property rights in the entire pool when the oil is still underground. Under unitization, there is little incentive for excessive drilling or pumping.

Libecap and Wiggins found that, in spite of the large gains that could have been realized by adopting unitization to prevent the dissipation of rents, unitization was in fact infrequently employed. The effects of rule of capture could also have been ameliorated through lease consolidation and the prorationing of field output among oil firms. Even though unitization was more effective in preventing the dissipation of rents, the high cost of contracting among firms often led, instead, to the prorationing option. The cost of contracting was also affected by high and asymmetric information costs. The historical samples provide quantitative information with which Libecap and Wiggins tested their models of contracting and the effects of state and federal regulations on the choice of institutional arrangement. The results demonstrate that the availability of enforcement by the state has a major effect on contract choice and the pattern of exploitation of the resource.[3] Clearly historical studies have much to offer.

Prospective Data Collection

A major drawback of historical studies is that the scholar is left with little choice about the kinds of information that may be used. Just because the chosen framework of analysis suggests that data on certain variables should be collected, the historical record will not necessarily comply. Although earnest archival work, parsimonious modeling that makes minimal data demands, creativity, and good luck can sometimes overcome the drawbacks, the limitations are still very real.

One solution is "prospective" data collection. (Prospective designs include studies in which the investigator is a participant observer or observer participant.) In this case the scholar deliberately collects the information that the analytical framework suggests is important. Thus Hayami and Kikuchi (1981) were able to collect data on events as they unfolded. This approach is also reflected in the work of J. E. M. Arnold and Gabriel Campbell (1986). Their work is notable in that the project in which they are involved explicitly includes provisions for baseline measurement and ongoing monitoring of conditions in the study areas. Thus more powerful inferences about the effects of introducing new institutional arrangements may be drawn.

It is unfortunate that baseline measurement and ongoing performance monitoring are not routine components of most major development projects. A great deal of valuable information on the effects of the intervention is thus lost and the period of costly trial-and-error learning is prolonged. The chief advantage of formal research is not that the investigators are more intelligent than the subjects of the study but that the structure of the research design allows more valid conclusions to be drawn more quickly. Through study design, information is in a sense multiplied.

The development of longitudinal data on management systems for common-property resources represents an important task for the research agenda. With baseline measures and ongoing monitoring, more valid information can be derived from examining the effects of deliberate interventions on and exogenous shocks to such systems (Campbell 1969; Hilborn 1987).

Laboratory Experiments

The management of common-property resources involves complex interactions among human agents. Modeling such behavior is difficult. A wide variety of quite different results concerning the equilibria of such behavior systems may be obtained by varying any of a number of key assumptions. Clearly the theorist is in need of guidance about the plausible range of and values of key variables—stylized facts. In order to improve theory, a means for testing the predictions of theory is crucial. Yet because of the size, complexity, and interactive nature of such systems, natural experiments are difficult to interpret and hence provide only crude tests. Data from uncontrolled natural experiments derived from prospective data collection will increase the efficiency of the tests but are unlikely to overcome the problem fully.

One solution is to conduct controlled experiments that allow for more direct and unambiguous tests of the predictions of theory. Two major approaches are possible. First, there are small laboratory experiments in which naturally occurring situations are re-created. To borrow from the clinical epidemiology literature, such experiments can be used to demonstrate efficacy—that something works under ideal circumstances (see Sackett, Haynes, and Tugwell 1985). Second, there are field experiments— the effectiveness or management trial that determines if something works (or how well it works) under more realistic field conditions.

Laboratory experiments are becoming increasingly popular in a number of social science disciplines. A growing body of experimental economics studies (see for instance Roth 1988; Smith 1987, 1991; Hoffman and Spitzer 1985; Plott 1982) highlights the importance of institutional arrangements. The outcome in market experiments is systematically affected by the institutional arrangements of the market, as when posted-price markets are compared with double auction markets or sealed-bid first-price with second-price ones.

More directly relevant to the analysis of common-property resource management are a number of experiments designed to test major propositions in game theory and public-goods theory. For instance, R. Mark Isaac, Kenneth F. McCue, and Charles R. Plott (1985) found that although initial voluntary contributions for the provision of a public good were substantial (but below the optimal level), in successive periods free-riding behavior became more evident.[4] After five periods the level of voluntary contributions was low, but still greater than zero; in other words, free riding was less than complete. (Similar evidence is found in Kim and Walker 1984.) They also found that individuals with high personal payoffs from the provision of the public good contributed more than those with low personal payoffs.[5] Further, allowing for communication among experimental subjects—and thus more closely imitating the natural environment in which most common-property resources are managed—did increase the level of contributions moderately, although the optimal level was still not achieved.[6]

Another example of the laboratory experimental approach is the fisheries work of Charles D. Samuelson and David M. Messick (1986). They found that subjects were more willing to vote for controls on the harvesting of the resource in situations characterized by overuse than in situations characterized by the optimal rate of exploitation; the net benefits from choosing an alternative arrangement affected its choice (see also Messick and Brewer 1983; Isaac, Walker, and Thomas 1984; Messick et al. 1983; and Samuelson et al. 1984). Again in an experimental context, R. C. Cass and J. J. Edney (1978) demonstrate that providing up-to-date information on the condition of the resource and granting private usufruct territorial rights of exploitation both move the rate of exploitation closer to the optimal level (see also Allison and Messick 1985; Hoffman and Spitzer 1986; Messick and McClelland 1983). Even though some of the abovementioned studies contain methodological flaws, they do demonstrate that it is possible to explore the issues of common-property resource management in laboratory experiments and lay a foundation for further research.

Aside from contributing to the testing and refinement of theory, the laboratory experimental approach should also be an efficacious strategy for initial practical tests of institutional designs (Goodman 1987; Harrison et al. 1987; Hoffman and Spitzer 1985; Plott 1983). Imagine a situation in which a variety of natural-experiment studies suggest that a certain institutional arrangement appears to be an effective means of resource management in a number of settings. A simple experiment may then be devised to test that hypothesis. If the arrangement works in a controlled and simplified environment it may be worth considering; if it fails, then it is likely that it can be discarded. If it cannot work under ideal conditions, it is unlikely to work in the field. The argument here is that we are less concerned with rejecting a true hypothesis (Type II error) than with failing to reject a false one (Type I error).

The application of laboratory experimental methods in institutional design and public policy is illustrated by investigations of methods for allocating airport landing rights (see Grether, Isaac, and Plott 1979, 1981).

On the basis of their experimental results they predicted that the methods used by the Civil Aeronautics Board could lead to deadlocks (which they subsequently did) and suggested that they be replaced by sealed-bid auctions. Similar exercises have been conducted by J. T. Hong and C. R. Plott (1982) to investigate the effects of proposed requirements for posted prices on Mississippi river barges, and by J. S. Banks, D. P. Porter, and Plott (1985) to assess various cost-sharing formulas for determining equitable and efficient user charges for space-orbiting laboratories. Finally, gambling experiments have been used to elicit information on the risk preferences of farmers in less-developed countries for crop choices and new technologies (see for instance, Binswanger 1980, 1981; Grisley and Kellogg 1983; Quizon, Binswanger, and Machina 1984; Sillers 1980; Walker 1981).

The Field Experiment Approach

The power of the laboratory experimental approach is also its weakness. The exercises that it generates provide a means to test simple hypotheses. Yet the controlled nature of the environment, in which at most only one of a few treatment variables is allowed to vary at a time, makes the method less capable of capturing the complex interactions and feedbacks that we believe are characteristic of naturally occurring situations.[7] Applied research in the agricultural and biomedical sciences attests to numerous cases in which new techniques that worked under ideal circumstances failed to perform under realistic field conditions. Thus laboratory experiments complement rather than substitute both for uncontrolled natural-experiment studies and for controlled field experiments.

There are indeed serious drawbacks to a reliance on natural experiments, even with prospective data collection. In the context of institutional design such a method is likely to be organized around a pilot or demonstration project. A number of biases typically accompany this type of endeavor. Although they may not all operate in a given circumstance—occasionally, the researcher or evaluator may be fortunate in that they all run in the same direction—such biases reduce the validity of the results. In part the issue is one of "internal validity," or being able to construct a sound explanation of what was observed in a particular circumstance, and "external validity," the ability to generalize from the experience.

Pilot-project sites are often selected on the basis of their relatively favorable initial conditions, such as the presence of a particularly committed or able provincial governor, or the proximity to a regional university with conscientious investigators. Even if these biases in favor of success are not operative, bureaucratic reputations and the reputations of donor agencies are generally involved, and consciously or unconsciously investigators may be biased toward finding evidence of success. In the context of local public administration in less-developed countries, the supposed clients of the project have often learned that it is wise to tell government officials what they want to hear. These natural biases in favor of declaring the intervention a success are not merely a figment of the armchair methodologist's imagination. H. S. Sacks, R. C. Chalmers, and H. Smith (1982; see also Campbell 1969; Sacks, Chalmers, and Smith 1983) examined fifty controlled trials of six different medical therapies and compared them with fifty-six studies of the same treatments in which inferior designs were used. Whereas 79 per cent of the studies using inferior designs found the therapy better than the control regimen, only 20 per cent of the controlled trials agreed. Similar results were obtained by John S. Sinclair (1966). He found that 85 per cent of uncontrolled studies investigating various treatments for respiratory distress syndrome concluded that the treatments were effective. When the same treatments were investigated in controlled studies, only one-half were found to be effective.

Although a great deal can be learned from pilot studies, especially well-designed prospective ones, a formidable barrier to their external validity is the lack of randomization in the selection of the study site. Frequently it is government officials who decide on the location of projects. For instance, Robert E. Evenson found that the location of public health facilities in rural areas in the Philippines was systematically related to the health status of the local population. Even if policy makers randomly chose sites for projects, self-selection by clients could bias the results. Although there are statistical techniques involving simultaneous equation systems to ameliorate such biases, the solution is generally less than complete.

Yet the situation for systems of common-property resource management is even more complex. Such systems are multidimensional and interactive. Similar conditions apply in the aeronautical, agricultural, and biomedical sciences. While a richer theory of the fundamental mechanisms is being developed, researchers have also sought to bypass the crudeness of their theory by using simple but powerful experimental approaches. Such techniques have been especially valuable in the agricultural and biomedical sciences, where natural variability and location specificity are important. The analogy in the context of common-property resources is clear. Many of these resources involve biological systems, so that the human management system interacts with the natural variability. One of the important lessons of the literature on agricultural technologies is their location specificity: a generic innovation must frequently be adapted to specific local conditions (see for instance Griliches 1957; Hayami and Ruttan 1985; see also McEvoy 1986, 1988). In the case of common-property resources the location specificity includes not only the ecological adaptation but also the institutional context.

A solution pursued in the agricultural and biomedical sciences has been the field experiment, or randomized controlled trial. In the design, sites (or subjects) to receive the intervention are randomly selected and the outcomes compared to those obtained in randomly assigned control sites (or subjects). Both the experimental and the control groups are prospectively monitored and assessed with the same procedures and measures. When properly designed and executed such experiments provide powerful and valid evidence on the realistic effectiveness of the intervention. They avoid most of the biases associated with uncontrolled studies. These advantages come, however, at a considerable cost. The experiments are difficult to organize and execute. The methodological problems that arise when the unit of randomization is a whole community rather than an individual are not fully understood. Yet there have been successful large-scale field experiments concerning institutional arrangements.[8] For logistical purposes one might want the experimental and control communities to be reasonably contiguous so that they share the same ecological and economic environments. Yet proximity may also lead to contamination, in which the intervention diffuses from the experimental to the control group.

There are additional problems. To be feasible such experiments need to be completed within a reasonable time frame. Yet in the common-property resource context, the natural variability over time, or the biological nature of the resource (slow-growing trees for instance), may make experiments of short duration less valuable.

Such reservations need to be kept in mind. Furthermore there are ethical considerations. The experimental group receives an intervention for which the evidence on the effectiveness of the intervention is less than conclusive. But what is the current standard of performance—the alternative? At present governments and donors routinely initiate projects for which the evidence of effectiveness is far from unequivocal. Thus human experimentation is already part of the scene. What is particularly troubling is that the inherent exposure to risk is seldom compensated for by even minimal care to insure that as much as possible can be learned from the experience. Routine use of the baseline measurement and monitoring previously discussed would in part address this problem. If people are being subjected to experiments through policy initiatives, why not design such experiments properly so that valid information can be more efficiently derived from the experience? Agricultural scientists are reluctant to release a new variety that has not previously been subjected to rigorous randomized field trials. Several jurisdictions require similar testing before a new drug may be introduced. Yet policymakers and institutional designers in the social sciences appear to be quite content to do so, even though the underlying models upon which the intervention is based may be less well developed and validated than the biological models upon which the agricultural scientist bases a new design.[9]

The argument is not that all policy initiatives should be tested in this fashion. The alternative to not doing any such testing is to continue to rely on more costly forms of trial and error. If new programs were to include a few field experiments, at least the potential for improvement in the future would be enhanced. Better yet, if the field experimental approach became more common, large commitments of resources in the future could be based on rigorous prior demonstration of effectiveness in the field (Campbell 1969; for a similar argument in the context of health technology assessment, see Feeny, Guyatt, and Tugwell 1986).

The role for field experiments should be only a modest one, however, even if on a trial basis it proves successful. Such methods will not be feasible in many situations and are not well suited to answering questions for which long-term follow-up is necessary; other prospective study designs are more appropriate in that context. Nevertheless, field experiments could be an important contribution to the testing and refinement of institutional design.

Performance Measures

The effectiveness of the experimental and nonexperimental studies on management of common-property resources would be improved if operational measures of performance were developed and validated. Such methodological development could be incorporated into the designs of studies with prospective data collection.[10]

The challenge is formidable. It is generally easier to focus on process variables (for instance, existence or lack thereof of a user-group organization) than outcomes. Yet if proper management contributes to the livelihood and quality of life of persons engaged in exploiting the resource base, that contribution becomes a source of valuation for the management system. A problem arises in that many other factors also affect such broad outcome measures, necessitating either laborious data collection and an analytical framework to isolate the effects of the management system, or a shift to more narrowly focused performance measures. Both conceptual and field studies will be needed to develop such measures and relate them to more basic valuations such as the welfare of human agents. Performance for the current generation may often be enhanced, but at a cost to future generations. Thus in a broader context a means to quantify such trade-offs may be needed. Similarly, performance for a particular group of users or potential users may be enhanced at the expense of others.

Although the wider ramifications of any particular operational measure of performance must be appreciated, there is still a need for practical tools. To be useful such tools will have to meet a number of methodological standards. First, they must pass tests of intra- and interobserver reliability. The same person viewing the same system at two points in time should arrive at essentially the same score. Different but contemporaneous observers at the same time, each unaware of the other's valuation, should have answers in close agreement. A useful measure should also be applicable in a number of institutional settings, for instance, in open-access, communal property, state-property, and private-property regimes.

Reproducible and reliable measures may not be valid, however. The operational measure must be linked to measures of more fundamental interest in a meaningful way. Validation may be demonstrated by showing that the operational measure that has been obtained inexpensively is highly correlated with an accepted and previously validated measure—the "gold standard." For instance if a measure of irrigation system performance is shown to be closely related to crop yields, and if movements in crop yields have been shown to correspond to movements in household incomes, and again if household incomes closely correspond to consumption of goods, services, and leisure, then the validity of the operational measure may be established. Data demonstrating the chain of correspondences are costly to collect. If such a correspondence can be demonstrated within at least several studies, then a more inexpensively implemented performance measure that focuses on an intermediate outcome may be validated.

In addition to being reproducible and valid, a useful outcome or performance measure should be responsive. The measure must be able to capture change, if it in fact has occurred, while providing stable scores for situations in which there has been no change.

If reproducible, valid, and responsive performance measures were to be developed, they could then be used as outcome measures for field experiments, project evaluation, routine monitoring of performance, and prospective data collection for both research and public administration purposes. Success on a number of fronts will in part depend on developing improved performance measurement.

Setting Research Priorities

The methods discussed above are among the appropriate ones for investigating the issues surrounding the management of common-property resources. Clearly, there is a need for better theory. The development and testing of theory also needs to be better informed by a variety of historical and contemporary empirical studies, complemented by experiments and prospective data collection. Progress will be made on a number of fronts, utilizing the comparative advantages of different investigators.

Fruitful hypotheses for testing as well as some attractive analytical approaches have been discussed elsewhere in this book (see, for instance, Chapters 1, 2, 3, 6, and 13). Another set of considerations also applies. In the context of performing applied research and testing the effectiveness of particular institutional arrangements, the relationships among the social and physical sciences are also relevant. The successful management of common-property resources depends in part on basic knowledge of the natural environment. Traditional indigenous systems often bring the culmination of generations of learning to bear in making management decisions (see Berkes 1989; McKean in Chapter 4). Although such knowledge is often at least somewhat idiosyncratic and may not generalize to other settings, it is nonetheless extremely valuable. If the knowledge has been retained, it should be preserved and tapped in resource management. For intervention in such systems to improve outcomes, it will need to incorporate incentives for the knowledgeable to share their information. (The problem is highlighted in a related context by Wynne 1986.) The source of knowledge of the technical and physical operation of the resource system may, however, be extralocal. In situations in which a solid foundation of ecological studies has been laid, interventions incorporating such knowledge and then focusing on the institutional arrangements may have an even greater potential to improve performance.

In contrast, if the indigenous knowledge base in the physical sciences is weak and if folk knowledge has been lost, it may be premature to focus on the innovation of new institutional arrangements. Clearly, the institutional arrangements and the technical and physical characteristics of the resource system interact. Perhaps technical knowledge is not prior, but in the absence of such knowledge it is difficult to determine whether failure was due to a lack of technical knowledge or to an institutional failure. In such circumstances it may be advisable to focus initially on the physical science knowledge base.

Common-property resources arise in particular physical and institutional contexts. Meaningful research on them—or interventions concerned with them—requires location-specific knowledge of both types. As in the case of agricultural research (see Hayami and Ruttan 1985; Evenson and Kislev 1975), creation of an indigenous capacity to perform research and design institutions will be crucial. Even if the principles of resource management are universal, appropriate technologies for each setting require local craftsmanship. The international agricultural research centers and their linkages to national research systems in less-developed countries have accelerated the transfer of agricultural technologies that are economically and ecologically adapted. A similar model may be applied to common-property resource management. As in the agricultural case, organizing multidisciplinary teams of researchers in mission-oriented establishments devoted to particular resources or problems is likely to be a productive applied research and development strategy.

Final Remarks

The issues are important and timely. The Annapolis conference and activities like it represent important accomplishments. There is a body of reasonable theory upon which to build. The existing stock of empirical knowledge is rich and diverse. Thanks to taxonomic frameworks (see, for instance, Oakerson in Chapter 3; Berkes et al. 1989; or Feeny et al. 1990), the cost of interdisciplinary communication has been reduced, allowing for mutual gains. An array of research methodologies has the potential to make important contributions in studies that exploit the advantages of each methodology while hopefully neutralizing its disadvantages. Major challenges loom in the development of performance measures and application of experimental methods. The results will contribute to better social science. The results also have the potential to improve human welfare through improved institutional design.

NOTES

The views expressed in the paper are personal ones. The author acknowledges the helpful comments of J. E. M. Arnold, Fikret Berkes, Daniel W. Bromley, R. Brian Haynes, Robert Hunt, Jonathan Lomas, Margaret McKean, Stuart Mestelman, Ronald J. Oakerson, Elinor Ostrom, Pauline Peters, Mark Sproule-Jones, and several referees.

1. National Research Council 1986; Berkes et al. 1989; E. Ostrom 1988, 1990; Bromley 1989; Wade 1987; McCay and Acheson 1987; Berkes 1989; Karpoff 1987; Larson and Bromley 1990; McEvoy 1986, 1988; Oakerson 1988; Fenoaltea 1988; Fortmann and Bruce 1988; Boyd and Richerson 1988, 1989; Buck 1989; Wilson 1990; Feeny et al. 1990.

2. See for instance Allen 1991; Anderson and Hill 1975; Dennen 1976; Feder and Tongroj 1987; Feder 1987; Feder et al. 1988; Feder, Tongroj, Yongyuth 1988; Feeny 1982, 1988a, 1988b, 1988c, 1989; Fenoaltea 1988; La Croix and Roumasset 1990; Libecap 1978, 1986; McEvoy 1986, 1988; North 1981; North and Thomas 1973; Rosenthal 1990; Roumasset and LaCroix 1988; and Umbeck 1977.

3. Blomquist and E. Ostrom (1985) also provide a historical study with quantitative hypothesis testing in their examination of the evolution of arrangements for the management of water in southern California.

4. Other experimental studies on the provision of public goods and related issues involving collective action include Alfano and Marwell 1980; Banks, Plott, and Porter 1988; Gardner, E. Ostrom, and Walker 1990; Guttman 1986; Harrison and Hirshleifer 1989; Isaac and Walker 1988a, 1988b; Isaac, Walker, and Thomas 1984; Kim and Walker 1984; Marwell and Ames 1979, 1980, 1981; Schneider and Pommerehne 1981; Smith 1980; and Walker, Gardner, and E. Ostrom 1990.

5. This result may correspond to the observation that major landowners in Wade's villages (see Chapter 9; Wade 1987) played a major role in organizing the communally operated irrigation and grazing systems. Mestelman and Feeny (1988) provide results suggesting that ideology ameliorates free riding but does not overcome it. Experimental results also indicating that cultural norms, ideas of fairness, or ideology affect the extent of free-riding behavior include Alfano and Marwell 1980; Andreoni 1988; Brann and Foddy 1987; Harrison et al. 1987; Hoffman and Spitzer 1986; Marwell and Ames 1979, 1981; Palfrey and Rosenthal 1988; Roth 1988; and Smith 1991.

6. Braver and Wilson (1986), Brechner (1977), Dawes, McTavish, and Shaklee (1977), Edney and Harper (1978), Isaac and Walker (1988a), Jerdee and Rosen (1974), Jorgenson and Papciak (1981), Liebrand (1984), Schwartz-Shea and Simmons (1990), and Wilson (1985) also conclude, on the basis of experimental results, that communication among subjects affects the management of a common-property resource (see also Dawes 1980).

7. The role of complex interactions in motivating field experiments in the development of industrial technologies is discussed by Rosenberg (1982a, 1982b).

8. The RAND Health Insurance Study is one example; see for instance Newhouse 1974, Manning et al. 1984, and Manning et al. 1987. Arguments for controlled experiments are also found in Campbell 1969, Doherty and Jodha 1979, and Hunt 1979.

9. The point is made in the context of public policy discussions concerning the organization of police services in E. Ostrom 1975.

10. For a similar argument in the context of health care planning in less-developed countries see Evans, Hall, and Warford 1981.

REFERENCES

Alfano, F., and Gerald Marwell. 1980. "Experiments on the Provision of Public Goods III: Non-Divisibility and Free Riding in 'Real' Groups." *Social Psychology Quarterly* 43:300–309.

Allen, Douglas W. 1991. "Homesteading and Property Rights; or, 'How the West Was Really Won.'" *Journal of Law and Economics* 34:1–23.

Allison, S. T., and D. M. Messick. 1985. "Effects of Experience on Performance in a Replenishable Resource Trap." *Journal of Personality and Social Psychology* 49:943–48.

Anderson, T. L., and P. J. Hill. 1975. "The Evolution of Property Rights: A Study of the American West." *Journal of Law and Economics* 18:163–79.

Andreoni, James. 1988. "Why Free Ride? Strategies and Learning in Public Goods Experiments." *Journal of Public Economics* 37:291–304.

Arnold, J. E. M., and Gabriel Campbell. 1986. "Collective Management of Hill Forests in Nepal: The Community Forestry and Development Project." In National Research Council, *Proceedings of the Conference on Common Property Resource Management*, 425–54. Washington, D.C.: National Academy Press.

Banks, J. S., D. P. Porter, and C. R. Plott. 1985. "Public Goods Pricing Mechanisms: Experimental Analysis for Space Station Pricing Policies." Paper presented at the Allied Social Science Associations Meeting, December 28–30, New York.

Banks, Jeffrey S., Charles R. Plott, and David P. Porter. 1988. "An Experimental Analysis of Unanimity in Public Goods Provision Mechanisms." *Review of Economic Studies* 55:301–22.

Bates, Robert H. 1983. "The Centralization of African Societies." In *Essays on the Political Economy of Rural Africa*, ed. Robert Bates, 21–58. London: Cambridge University Press.

Berkes, Fikret, ed. 1989. *Common Property Resources: Ecology and Community-Based Sustainable Development*. London: Belhaven Press.

Berkes, F., D. Feeny, B. J. McCay, and J. M. Acheson. 1989. "The Benefits of the Commons." *Nature* 340:91–93.

Binswanger, H. P. 1980. "Attitudes toward Risk: Experimental Measures in Rural India." *American Journal of Agricultural Economics* 62:395–407.

Binswanger, H. P. 1981. "Attitudes toward Risk: Theoretical Implications of an Experiment in Rural India." *Economic Journal* 91:867–90.

Blomquist, William, and Elinor Ostrom. 1985. "Institutional Capacity and the Resolution of a Commons Dilemma." *Policy Studies Review* 5:383–93.

Boyd, Robert, and Peter J. Richerson. 1988. "The Evolution of Reciprocity in Sizeable Groups." *Journal of Theoretical Biology* 132:337–56.

———. 1989. "The Evolution of Indirect Reciprocity." *Social Networks* 11:213–36.

Brann, Peter, and Margaret Foddy. 1987. "Trust and the Consumption of a Deteriorating Common Resource." *Journal of Conflict Resolution* 31:615–30.

Braver, Sanford L., and L. A. Wilson II. 1986. "Choices in Social Dilemmas: Effects of Communication within Subgroups." *Journal of Conflict Resolution* 30:51–62.

Brechner, K. C. 1977. "An Experimental Analysis of Social Traps." *Journal of Experimental Social Psychology* 13:552–64.

Bromley, Daniel W. 1989. *Economic Interests and Institutions*. Oxford: Blackwell.

Buck, Susan J. 1989. "Cultural Theory and Management of Common Property Resources." *Human Ecology* 17:101–16.

Bullock, Kari, and John Baden. 1977. "Communes and the Logic of the Commons." In *Managing the Commons*, ed. Garrett Hardin and John Baden, 182–99. San Francisco: Freeman.

Campbell, Donald T. 1969. "Reforms as Experiments." *American Psychologist* 24:409–29.

Cass, R. C., and J. J. Edney. 1978. "The Commons Dilemma: A Simulation Testing the Effects of Resource Visibility and Territorial Division." *Human Ecology* 6:371–86.

Dawes, R. M. 1980. "Social Dilemmas." *Annual Review of Psychology* 3:1169–93.

Dawes, R. M., J. McTavish, and H. Shaklee. 1977. "Behavior, Communication, and Assumptions about Other People's Behavior in a Commons Dilemma Situation." *Journal of Personality and Social Psychology* 35:1–11.

Dennen, R. T. 1976. "Cattlemen's Associations and Property Rights in Land in the American West." *Explorations in Economic History* 13:423–36.

Doherty, Victor S. 1982. "Tank Irrigation in Crosscultural Perspective." International Crops Research Institute for the Semi-Arid Tropics, Economic Program Progress Report no. 36. Hyderbad, India.

Doherty, Victor S., and N. S. Jodha. 1979. "Conditions for Group Action among Farmers." In *Group Farming in Asia*, ed. John Wong, 207–23. Singapore: Singapore University Press.

Doherty, Victor S., Senen M. Miranda, and Jacob Kampen. 1982. "Social Organization and Small Watershed Development." In *The Role of Anthropologists and Other Social Scientists in Interdisciplinary Teams Developed Improved Food Production Technology*, 9–24. Laguna, Philippines: International Rice Research Institute.

Edney, J. J., and C. S. Harper. 1978. "The Effects of Information in a Resource Management Problem: A Social Trap Analog." *Human Ecology* 6:387–95.

Evans, John R., Karen L. Hall, and Jeremy Warford, 1981. "Health Care in the Developing World: Problems of Scarcity and Choice." *New England Journal of Medicine* 305:1117–27.

Evenson, Robert E., and Yoav Kislev. 1975. *Agricultural Research and Productivity.* New Haven, Conn.: Yale University Press.

Feder, Gershon. 1987. "Land Ownership Security and Farm Productivity: Evidence from Thailand." *Journal of Development Studies* 24:16–30.

Feder, Gershon, and David Feeny. 1991. "Land Tenure and Property Rights: Theory and Implications for Development Policy." *World Bank Economic Review* 5: 135–53.

Feder, Gershon, and Tongroj Onchan. 1987. "Land Ownership Security and Farm Investment in Thailand." *American Journal of Agricultural Economics* 69:311–20.

Feder, Gershon, Tongroj Onchan, Yongyuth Chalamwong, and Chira Hongladarom. 1988. *Land Policies and Farm Productivity in Thailand*. Baltimore: The Johns Hopkins University Press.

Feder, Gershon, Tongroj Onchan, and Yongyuth Chalamwong. 1988. "Land Policies and Farm Performance in Thailand's Forest Reserve Areas." *Economic Development and Cultural Change* 36:483–501.

Feeny, David. 1982. *The Political Economy of Productivity: Thai Agricultural Development 1880–1975*. Vancouver: University of British Columbia Press.

———. 1987. "The Exploration of Economic Change: The Contribution of Economic History to Development Economics." In *The Future of Economic History*, ed. Alexander J. Field, 91–119. Boston: Kluwer Nijhoff.

————. 1988a. "Agricultural Expansion and Forest Depletion in Thailand, 1900–1975." In *World Deforestation in the Twentieth Century*, ed. John F. Richards and Richard Tucker, 112–43, 281–87. Durham, N.C.: Duke University Press.

————. 1988b. "The Demand for and Supply of Institutional Arrangements." In *Rethinking Institutional Analysis and Development: Issues, Alternatives, and Choices*, ed. Vincent Ostrom, David Feeny, and Hartmut Picht, 159–209. San Francisco: ICS Press.

————. 1988c. "The Development of Property Rights in Land: A Comparative Study." In *Toward a Political Economy of Development: A Rationalist Perspective*, ed. Robert H. Bates, 272–99. Berkeley and Los Angeles: University of California Press.

————. 1989. "The Decline of Property Rights in Man in Thailand, 1800–1913." *Journal of Economic History* 49:285–96.

Feeny, David, Fikret Berkes, Bonnie J. McCay, and James M. Acheson. 1990. "The Tragedy of the Commons: Twenty-Two Years Later." *Human Ecology* 18:1–19.

Feeny, David, Gordon H. Guyatt, and Peter Tugwell, eds. 1986. *Health Technology: Effectiveness, Efficiency, and Public Policy*. Montreal: Institute for Research on Public Policy.

Fenoaltea, Stefano. 1988. "Transaction Costs, Whig History, and the Common Fields." *Politics and Society* 16:171–240.

Field, Alexander J. 1984. "Microeconomics, Norms, and Rationality." *Economic Development and Cultural Change* 32:683–711.

Field, Alexander J. 1991. "Do Legal Systems Matter?" *Explorations in Economic History* 28:1–35.

Fortmann, L, and J. W. Bruce, eds. 1988. *Whose Trees? Proprietary Dimensions of Forestry*. Boulder, Colo.: Westview Press.

Gardner, Roy, and Elinor Ostrom. 1991. "Rules and Games." *Public Choice* 70:121–49.

Gardner, Roy, Elinor Ostrom, and James Walker. 1990. "The Nature of Common-Pool Resource Problems." *Rationality and Society* 2:335–58.

Goodman, Paul S. 1987. "Experiments, Institutional Arrangements, and Organizational Design." Paper presented at the Symposium on Knowledge and Institutional Change, November 13, University of Minnesota.

Grether, David M., R. Mark Isaac, and Charles R. Plott. 1979. "Alternative Methods of Allocating Airport Slots: Performance and Evaluation." Pasadena, Calif.: Polinomics Research Laboratories.

————. 1981. "The Allocation of Landing Rights by Unanimity among Competitors." *American Economic Review* 71:166–71.

Griliches, Zvi. 1957. "Hybrid Corn: An Exploration in the Economics of Technological Change." *Econometrica* 25:501–22.

Grisley, William, and Earl D. Kellogg. 1983. "Farmers' Subjective Probabilities in Northern Thailand: An Elicitation Analysis." *American Journal of Agricultural Economics* 65:74–82.

Guttman, Joel M. 1986. "Matching Behavior and Collective Action: Some Experimental Evidence." *Journal of Economic Behavior and Organization* 7:171–98.

Harrison, Glenn W., and Jack Hirshleifer. 1989. "An Experimental Evaluation of Weakest Link/Best Shot Models of Public Goods." *Journal of Political Economy* 97:201–25.

Harrison, Glenn W., Elizabeth Hoffman, E.E. Rutstrom, and Matthew Spitzer. 1987. "Coasian Solutions to the Externality Problem in Experimental Markets." *Economic Journal* 97:388–402.

Hayami, Yujiro, and Masao Kikuchi. 1981. *Asian Village Economy at the Crossroads: An Economic Approach to Institutional Change.* Tokyo: University of Tokyo Press.

Hayami, Yujiro, and Vernon W. Ruttan. 1985. *Agricultural Development: An International Perspective.* Rev. ed. Baltimore: The Johns Hopkins University Press.

Hilborn, Ray. 1987. "Living with Uncertainty in Resource Management." *North American Journal of Fisheries Management* 7:1–5.

Hoffman, Elizabeth, and Matthew L. Spitzer. 1985. "Experimental Law and Economics: An Introduction." *Columbia Law Review* 85:991–1036.

———. 1986. "Experimental Tests of the Coase Theorem with Large Bargaining Groups." *Journal of Legal Studies* 15:149–71.

Hong, J. T., and C. R. Plott. 1982. "Rate Filing Policies for Inland Water Transportation: An Experimental Approach." *Bell Journal of Economics* 13:1–19.

Hunt, Robert C. 1979. "The Comparative Method and the Study of Irrigation Social Organization." In Cornell Rural Sociology Bulletin Series, Bulletin no. 97, 45–46. Department of Rural Sociology, Cornell University.

Isaac, R. Mark, Kenneth F. McCue, and Charles R. Plott. 1985. "Public Good Provision in an Experimental Environment." *Journal of Public Economics* 26: 51–74.

Isaac, R. Mark, and James M. Walker, 1988a. "Communication and Free-Riding Behavior: The Voluntary Contribution Mechanism." *Economic Inquiry* 26:585–608.

———. 1988b. "Group Size Effects in Public Goods Provision: The Voluntary Contribution Mechanism." *Quarterly Journal of Economics* 103 (1):179–200.

Isaac, Mark. R., James M. Walker, and Susan H. Thomas. 1984. "Divergent Evidence on Free Riding: An Experimental Examination of Possible Explanations." *Public Choice* 43:113–49.

Jerdee, T. H., and B. Rosen. 1974. "Effects of the Opportunity to Communicate and Visibility of Individual Decisions on Behavior in the Common Interest." *Journal of Applied Psychology* 59:712–16.

Jorgenson, D. O., and A. S. Papciak. 1981. "The Effects of Communication, Resource Feedback, and Identifiability on Behavior in a Simulated Commons." *Journal of Experimental Social Psychology* 17:373–85.

Karpoff, Jonathan M. 1987. "Suboptimal Controls in Common Resource Management: The Case of the Fishery." *Journal of Political Economy* 95:179–94.

Kim, Oliver, and Mark Walker. 1984. "The Free Rider Problem: Experimental Evidence." *Public Choice* 43:3–24.

Kisangani, Emizet. 1986. "A Social Dilemma in a Less Developed Country: The Massacre of Loxodonta Africana in Zaire." In National Research Council, *Proceedings of the Conference on Common Property Resource Management,* 137–60. Washington, D.C.: National Academy Press.

La Croix, Sumner, and James Roumasset. 1990. "The Evolution of Private Property in Nineteenth-Century Hawaii." *Journal of Economic History* 50:829–52.

Langlois, Richard N. 1986a. "The New Institutional Economics: An Introductory Essay." In *Economics as a Process: Essays in the New Institutional Economics*, ed. Richard N. Langlois, 1–25. Cambridge: Cambridge University Press.

———. 1986b. "Rationality, Institutions, and Explanation." In *Economics as a Process: Essays in the New Institutional Economics*, ed. Richard N. Langlois, 225–55. Cambridge: Cambridge University Press.

Larson, Bruce A., and Daniel W. Bromley. 1990. "Property Rights, Externalities, and Resource Degradation: Locating the Tragedy." *Journal of Development Economics* 33:235–62.

Libecap, G. D. 1978. "Economic Variables and the Development of Law: The Case of Western Mineral Rights." *Journal of Economic History* 38:338–62.

———. 1986. "Property Rights in Economic History: Implications for Research." *Explorations in Economic History* 23:227–52.

Libecap, G. D., and S. N. Wiggins. 1984. "Contractual Response to the Common Pool: Prorationing of Crude Oil Production." *American Economic Review* 74:87–98.

———. 1985. "The Influence of Private Contractual Failure on Regulation: The Case of Oil Field Unitization." *Journal of Political Economy* 93:690–714.

Liebrand, Wim B. G. 1984. "The Effect of Social Motives, Communication and Group Size on Behaviour in an N-person Multi-Stage Mixed-Motive Game." *European Journal of Social Psychology* 14:239–64.

McCay, Bonnie J., and James M. Acheson, eds. 1987. *The Question of the Commons: The Culture and Ecology of Communal Resources*. Tucson: University of Arizona Press.

McEvoy, Arthur F. 1986. *The Fisherman's Problem: Ecology and Law in California Fisheries, 1850–1980*. Cambridge: Cambridge University Press.

———. 1988. "Toward an Interactive Theory of Nature and Culture: Ecology, Production, and Cognition in the California Fishing Industry." In *The Ends of the Earth: Perspectives on Modern Environmental History*, ed. Donald Worster, 211–29. New York: Cambridge University Press.

Manning, Willard G., Arleen Leibowitz, George A. Goldberg, William H. Rogers, and Joseph P. Newhouse. 1984. "A Controlled Trial of the Effect of Prepaid Group Practices on Use of Services." *New England Journal of Medicine* 310:1505–10.

Manning, Willard G., Joseph P. Newhouse, Naihua Duan, Emmett B. Keeler, Arleen Leibowitz, and Susan M. Marquis. 1987. "Health Insurance and the Demand for Medical Care: Evidence from a Randomized Experiment." *American Economic Review* 77:251–77.

Marwell, Gerald, and Ruth E. Ames. 1979. "Experiments on the Provision of Public Goods I: Resources, Interest, Group Size, and the Free Rider Problem." *American Journal of Sociology* 84:1335–60.

———. 1980. "Experiments on the Provision of Public Goods II: Provision Points, Stakes, Experience, and the Free Rider Problem." *American Journal of Sociology* 85:926–37.

————. 1981. "Economists Free Ride, Does Anyone Else?! Experiments on the Provision of Public Goods, IV." *Journal of Public Economics* 15:295–310.

Messick, D. M., and M. B. Brewer. 1983. "Solving Social Dilemmas: A Review." *Review of Personality and Social Psychology* 4:11–43.

Messick, D. M., and C. L. McClelland. 1983. "Social Traps and Temporal Traps." *Personality and Social Psychology Bulletin* 9:105–10.

Messick, D. M., H. Wilke, M. B. Brewer, R. M. Kramer, P. E. Zembke, and L. Lui. 1983. "Individual Adaptations and Structural Change as Solutions to Social Dilemmas." *Journal of Personality and Social Psychology* 44:292–309.

Mestelman, Stuart, and David Feeny. 1988. "Does Ideology Matter?: Anecdotal Experimental Evidence on the Voluntary Provision of Public Goods." *Public Choice* 57:281–86.

Molnar, Joseph J., Norman B. Schwartz, and Leonard L. Lovshin. 1985. "Integrated Aquacultural Development: Sociological Issues in the Cooperative Management of Community Fishponds." *Sociologia Ruralis* 27:61–80.

National Research Council. 1986. *Proceedings of the Conference on Common Property Resource Management*. Washington, D.C.: National Academy Press.

Newhouse, Joseph R. 1974. "A Design for a Health Insurance Experiment." *Inquiry* 11:5–27.

North, Douglass C. 1981. *Structure and Change in Economic History*. New York: Norton.

North, Douglass C., and R. P. Thomas. 1973. *The Rise of the Western World: A New Economic History*. Cambridge: Cambridge University Press.

Oakerson, Ronald J. 1988. "Reciprocity: A Bottom-Up View of Political Development." In *Rethinking Institutional Analysis and Development: Issues, Alternatives, and Choices*, ed. Vincent Ostrom, David Feeny, and Hartmut Picht, 141–58. San Francisco: ICS Press.

Ostrom, Elinor. 1975. "On Righteousness, Evidence, and Reform: The Policy Story." *Urban Affairs Quarterly* 10:464–86.

————. 1986. "Issues of Definition and Theory: Some Conclusions and Hypotheses." In National Research Council, *Proceedings of the Conference on Common Property Resource Management*, 599–616. Washington, D.C.: National Academy Press.

————. 1988. "Institutional Arrangements and the Commons Dilemma." In *Rethinking Institutional Analysis and Development: Issues, Alternatives, and Choices*, ed. Vincent Ostrom, David Feeny, and Hartmut Picht, 101–39. San Francisco: ICS Press.

————. 1990. *Governing the Commons: The Evolution of Institutions for Collective Action*. New York: Cambridge University Press.

Ostrom, Vincent, David Feeny, and Hartmut Picht, eds. 1988. *Rethinking Institutional Analysis and Development: Issues, Alternatives, and Choices*. San Francisco: ICS Press.

Palfrey, Thomas R., and Howard Rosenthal. 1988. "Private Incentives in Social Dilemmas: The Effects of Incomplete Information and Altruism." *Journal of Public Economics* 35:309–32.

Plott, Charles R. 1982. "Industrial Organization Theory and Experimental Economics." *Journal of Economic Literature* 20:1485–1527.

————. 1983. "Externalities and Corrective Policies in Experimental Markets." *Economic Journal* 93:106–27.

Quizon, Jaime B., Hans P. Binswanger, and Mark J. Machina. 1984. "Attitudes toward Risk: Further Remarks." *Economic Journal* 94:144–48.

Rosenberg, N. 1982a. "How Exogenous is Science?" Chapter 7 in *Inside the Black Box: Technology and Economics*, 141–59. Cambridge: Cambridge University Press.

————. 1982b. "Learning by Using." Chapter 6 in *Inside the Black Box: Technology and Economics*, 120–40. Cambridge: Cambridge University Press.

Rosenberg, Nathan, and L. E. Birdzell, Jr. 1986. *How the West Grew Rich: The Economic Transformation of the Industrial World*. New York: Basic Books.

Rosenthal, Jean-Laurant. 1990. "The Development of Irrigation in Provence, 1700–1860: The French Revolution and Economic Growth." *Journal of Economic History* 50:615–38.

Roth, Alvin E. 1988. "Laboratory Experimentation in Economics: A Methodological Overview." *Economic Journal* 98:974–1031.

Roumasset, James, and Sumner J. La Croix. 1988. "The Coevolution of Property Rights and Political Order: An Illustration from Nineteenth-Century Hawaii." In *Rethinking Institutional Analysis and Development: Issues, Alternatives, and Choices*, ed. Vincent Ostrom, David Feeny, and Hartmut Picht, 315–36. San Francisco: ICS Press.

Sackett, David L., R. Brian Haynes, and Peter Tugwell. 1985. *Clinical Epidemiology: A Basic Science for Clinical Medicine*. Boston: Little, Brown.

Sacks, Henry S., Thomas C. Chalmers, and Harry Smith. 1982. "Randomized versus Historical Controls for Clinical Trials." *American Journal of Medicine* 72:233–40.

————. 1983. "Sensitivity and Specificity of Clinical Trials." *Archives of Internal Medicine* 143:753–55.

Samuelson, C. D., D. M. Messick, C. G. Rutte, and H. Wilke. 1984. "Individual and Structural Solutions to Resource Dilemmas in Two Cultures." *Journal of Personality and Social Psychology* 47:94–104.

Samuelson, Charles D., and David M. Messick. 1986. "Alternative Structural Solutions to Resource Dilemmas." *Organizational Behavior and Human Decision Processes* 37:139–55.

Schneider, Friedrick, and Werner W. Pommerehne. 1981. "Free Riding and Collective Action: An Experiment in Public Microeconomics." *Quarterly Journal of Economics* 96:689–704.

Schwartz-Shea, Peregrine, and Randy T. Simmons. 1990. "The Layered Prisoner's Dilemma: Ingroup versus Macro-Efficiency." *Public Choice* 65:61–83.

Sillers, D. A. 1980. "Measuring Risk Preferences of Rice Farmers in Nueve Ecija, Philippines: An Experimental Approach." Ph.D. diss., Department of Economics, Yale University.

Sinclair, John S. 1966. "Prevention and Treatment of Respiratory Distress Syndrome." *Pediatric Clinics of North America* 13:711–30.

Smith, Vernon L. 1980. "Experiments with a Decentralized Mechanism for Public Goods Decisions." *American Economic Review* 70:584–99.

———. 1987. "Experimental Methods in Economics." In *The New Palgrave: A Dictionary of Economics*, ed. John Eatwell, Murray Milgate, and Peter Newman, 241–49. Vol. 2. London: Macmillan.

Smith, Vernon L. 1991. "Rational Choice: The Contrast between Economics and Psychology." *Journal of Political Economy* 99:877–97.

Solow, Robert M. 1985. "Economics History and Economics." *American Economic Review* 75:328–31.

Tang, Shui Yan. 1991. "Institutional Arrangements and the Management of Common-Pool Resources." *Public Administration Review* 51:42–51.

Umbeck, J. 1977. "The California Gold Rush: A Study of Emerging Property Rights." *Explorations in Economic History* 14:197–226.

Wade, Robert. 1987. *Village Republics: Economic Conditions for Collective Action.* Cambridge: Cambridge University Press.

Walker, James M., Roy Gardner, and Elinor Ostrom. 1990. "Rent Dissipation in a Limited-Access Common-Pool Resource: Experimental Evidence." *Journal of Environmental Economics and Management* 19:203–11.

Walker, T. S. 1981. "Risk and Adoption of Hybrid Maize in El Salvador." *Food Research Institute Studies* 18:59–88.

Wiggins, S. N., and G. D. Libecap. 1985. "Oil Field Unitization: Contractual Failure in the Presence of Imperfect Information." *American Economic Review* 75:368–85.

Wilson, James A. 1990. "Fishing for Knowledge." *Land Economics* 66:12–29.

Wilson, Rick K. 1985. "Constraints on Social Dilemmas: An Institutional Approach." *Annals of Operations Research* 2:183–200.

Wynne, Susan. 1986. "Information Problems Involved in Partitioning the Cultivation Commons." In National Research Council, *Proceedings of the Conference on Common Property Resource Management*, 359–89. Washington, D.C.: National Academy Press.

13

The Rudiments of a Theory of the Origins, Survival, and Performance of Common-Property Institutions

Elinor Ostrom

In the opening paragraphs of this book, Dan Bromley reminds us that there is "no such thing as a common property *resource*; there are only resources controlled and managed as common property, or as state property, or as private property" (Chapter 1). Bromley (ibid.) stresses the confusion created when "resources over which *no property rights* have been recognized" are casually referred to as "common-property resources" rather than as "open-access" resources (compare Ciriacy-Wantrup and Bishop 1975). A clear prediction can be made in situations where no one has a property right related to the flow of benefits from a resource. If the benefits are greater than the costs of obtaining them, open-access resources will be overexploited and may well be destroyed. When property rights exist—whether private property, state property, or common property—overexploitation and destruction depend on how well the property-rights regime copes with problems of allocating the costs and benefits of managing and governing a particular resource. In other words, property rights defining who has access, how much can be harvested, who can manage, and how rights are transferred are a necessary but not sufficient condition for avoiding overexploitation of a resource (see Schlager and E. Ostrom 1992).

The authors of the empirical chapters in this book have heeded Bromley's advice. They have not presumed that all resources used jointly by multiple individuals are open-access resources. Instead, they have attempted to explore how decision-making arrangements—to use the general concept of Ronald J. Oakerson's framework—affect "who decides what in relation to whom" (Oakerson in Chapter 3). This effort to describe the decision-making arrangements that are operational, rather than presuming the absence of any authority relationships, has produced a rich set of cases describing successful indigenous, resource-management regimes as well as less successful ones.

The effort summarized in this book has brought together the work of anthropologists, biologists, economists, ecologists, political scientists, sociologists, and members of other disciplines. Anyone committed to interdisciplinary scholarship knows how difficult communication is when members of just two disciplines attempt to combine their skills. When members of more than half a dozen attempt to learn from each other, the problems of communication and cumulation are several orders of magnitude greater.

The success of this difficult enterprise is largely attributable to the goodwill and the substantial knowledge, skills, and hard work of the participants. A major contributing factor, in addition, has been the conceptual generality and organization brought to this effort by the framework presented by Oakerson in Chapter 3. By identifying a common set of concepts and how these are thought to be related, Oakerson helped authors focus on the same set of conceptual variables and their relationships when they presented their empirical case studies. Without this common framework, it is hard to imagine how any cumulation could have been derived from this effort. By the time of the Annapolis conference, the case authors had already participated in workshops where they discussed the framework and its significance for organizing their case materials; they had also distributed their papers in advance of the conference (see Feeny 1986). It was thus possible to aim for and achieve a higher level of theoretical synthesis.

At the conference, I attempted to note and discuss with participants any propositions made concerning particular variables that could be associated with the establishment of coordinated or organized strategies for managing common-pool resources. This chapter represents my effort to draw on these inductive hypotheses as the foundation for the development of a more general theory. Given my own background, it is not surprising to find that the type of theory I present has a close family resemblance to the work of political economists interested in the effect of institutional arrangements (see, for example, Bates 1983; Brennan and Buchanan 1985; Buchanan and Tullock 1962; North 1981; V. Ostrom 1987; V. Ostrom, Feeny, and Picht 1988; Williamson 1985). This chapter is, however, a blend of my own efforts to understand how institutional arrangements affect individuals' incentives and behavior as well as the variables that the case authors identified as being important now that they had organized their analyses using a common framework.

The next section of this chapter is an effort to refine the part of the Oakerson framework that refers to the technical and physical attributes of the resource. Most of the resources discussed by case authors are common-pool resources. If one is to understand how various types of decision-making arrangements affect patterns of interactions and outcomes, it is important to ascertain in what ways common-pool resources resemble other types of "difficult" environments—such as public goods—and in what ways these environments are different.

The third section focuses on how "the tragedy of the commons" is avoided in many of the cases presented in this volume. Since those who harvest from common-pool resources—the appropriators—organize themselves in at least a minimal way in all cases where common-property institutions are associated with successful management, the next question explored is how to explain the origin of appropriator organizations. The broad conceptual categories of the framework are now broken into their component parts and related theoretically. This leads to a discussion of the conditions that may serve to prevent the emergence of some form of organization where the tragedy of the commons is not avoided. The last two theoretical sections develop propositions related to the survival and performance of organizations for governing and managing common-pool resources.

The conclusion of this chapter is in two parts. First, a brief review is presented of recent efforts to refine, extend, and test this theory. Second, I give a summary of the type of policies that donors and governments of developing countries could adopt that is consistent with this initial theory.

Common-Pool Resources

To understand the opportunities and constraints that individuals using a property-rights regime face, one also needs to distinguish among types of resources. Common-pool resources (CPRs) are natural or man-made resources sufficiently large that it is costly to exclude users from obtaining subtractable resource-units. Two criteria are used to define a CPR: (1) the cost of achieving physical exclusion from the resource; and (2) the presence of subtractable resource-units (Gardner, E. Ostrom, and Walker 1990).

For relatively small CPRs, a single family or small production unit may be technically able to enclose the entire resource and exclude others at a low cost. For large and amorphous resources, such as ocean fisheries or the radio spectrum, it is extremely difficult, both technically and economically, to exclude potential beneficiaries from obtaining benefits from them. The cost of exclusion is affected by the size and type of the resource system's natural boundaries and the technology available to enclose them (fences, markers, electronic passwords and decoders, and so on). Entry and exit rules also affect the operational patterns of exclusion, but they must be tailored to the particular attributes of specific types of resources within a cultural and historical setting.

The definition of a CPR distinguishes between the *flow of resource-units* and the *resource system* producing the flow (Blomquist and E. Ostrom 1985). "Resource-units" are what individuals produce or appropriate from a resource system. Examples of resource-units include: fish harvested from a fishery, the animals fed on a grazing plot, and wood or other usable plants harvested from a forest. Subtractability is a characteristic of the resource-unit appropriated from a CPR. The fish harvested by one boat are not there for someone else. Jointness of use is, however, a characteristic of the "resource system." More than a single boat can harvest fish simultaneously on the same fishing grounds. More than one family production unit can graze animals on a commons, or harvest a variety of forest products from a forest.

Failure to make this distinction between the subtractability of the resource-units and the jointness of the resource system has contributed to past confusion about the attributes of common-pool resources. Common-pool resources and collective (or public) goods share one major attribute and differ in regard to a second. The relatively high cost of achieving physical exclusion is an attribute of both collective goods and CPRs. The theoretical literature focusing specifically on the problem of free riders is relevant to the analysis of both collective goods and CPRs because the problem of free riding stems entirely from the difficulties of excluding beneficiaries from resources.

Collective goods and CPRs differ, however, in regard to jointness of consumption. Consumption units of collective goods are consumed without subtracting from the quantity available to others, while consumption units of CPRs are consumed subtractively. The "crowding effect" or "overuse" problem of CPRs does not occur in regard to the use of such collective goods as a weather forecast or national defense.

The subtractability of the resource-unit leads to the possibility of approaching the limit of the number of resource-units produced by a CPR. When the CPR is a man-made structure, such as a bridge, approaching the limit of the number of vehicles that can simultaneously use the bridge leads to congestion. When the CPR is a biological resource, such as a fishery or a forest area, approaching the limit of resource-units increases the costs of harvesting for all but may also destroy the resource. If the human demands made on a CPR are considerably lower than the quantity of resource units available, many individuals can simultaneously use the CPR without adversely affecting each other or the long-run yield.

How Is the Tragedy Avoided?

If a relatively large number of individuals make high demands on a single CPR, do not communicate with one another, and act independently taking only their own expected return into account, the "tragedy of the commons" (G. Hardin 1968) is likely to occur. The "tragedy" may take the simple form of overexploitation or the more complex form of destruction. Many of the cases in this book illustrate situations in which individuals *do* talk with one another about the long-run condition of their shared resource and take account of one another's actions when deciding on their own. If we are to move beyond the work of Hardin, we need to begin to specify the conditions that are conducive to the emergence of coordinated, rather than independent, actions by the individual users of a CPR.

In the following discussion, the set of individuals who withdraw resource-units from a CPR will be referred to as the "appropriators" of a CPR (Plott and Meyer 1975). Appropriators may live in or near by a CPR or far away and travel to the resource to harvest resource-units. They may remain latent and unorganized, or they may begin to discuss their problems with one another, recognize some commonly accepted rules for who has access to the CPR under what conditions, and develop some mechanisms for conflict resolution about it. The forum for discussion and decision may be a local gathering place, a village council, or any other place where the users of the same CPR congregate from time to time to discuss their common problems.

Because organizational arrangements frequently emerge from the patterns of behavior that are informally agreed upon over long periods of time, it is difficult to determine when user groups are latent and when they are organized. The following definition of an appropriator organization (AO) provides demarcation criteria. A set of appropriators is considered to be organized whenever it shares common understandings about:

- who is and is not a member
- the type of access to a CPR conveyed by membership or other grounds for such rights (the rights, duties, liberties, and exposures of different individuals, for example)
- how decisions will be made that affect the development of coordinated strategies for appropriating from or providing for a CPR
- how conflicts over these patterns will be resolved

AOs vary from relatively informal, meeting occasionally for appropriators to discuss how their individual strategies affect one another, to formal organizations with written rules clearly specifying mutual rights and duties and procedures for making binding decisions on all members. An AO could be a village governed by local oligarchs or by open democratic processes. An AO may also be a unit of local government where members of the local community select their own representatives and pass discretionary legislation about the use of the CPR and other matters.[1] But a unit of local government that is primarily an administrative district of a central government is not included within the meaning of the term "appropriator organization."

When an AO is created by individuals who are able to make sustained claims to exclude others from access and appropriation from their resource in external courts and administrative bodies, the organization is more stable. Examples of AOs organized by appropriators with less than full ownership rights are illustrated, however, in situations such as those described by John Cordell and Margaret McKean in Chapter 8 of this book. Many of these AOs have been rather ingenious in their efforts to control the CPRs on which their members' livelihood depends. Given the external legal orders in which they find themselves, they are exposed to greater uncertainty than if they could gain proprietorship rights in those external forums.

Examples of long-run success in managing CPRs subject to high levels of use, such as the Japanese villages described by McKean in Chapter 4, involve the establishment of an AO meeting the criteria stated above (see E. Ostrom 1990). This leads me to conjecture that the development of an AO is a second necessary *but not sufficient* condition for avoiding the tragedy of the commons through the actions of local appropriators themselves.[2]

Given the importance of AOs, we need to examine the factors associated with the emergence of some form of organization. It is obvious from the cases in this book that organizations do not always emerge whenever they are needed. Three of the five fishing villages studied by Fikret Berkes, for example, did not have an AO (see Chapter 7). Many of the neighboring villages to the one described by Robert Wade (Chapter 9) did not have an AO either. Consequently, we need to examine the conditions that are conducive to the emergence of such an organization. At the Annapolis conference several participants helped to identify a set of variables that appeared to affect the likelihood of the origin of one or more AOs related to a common-pool resource.[3] These variables relate to attributes of the CPR, to the relationships between use and supply, and to attributes of the appropriators. The variables discussed at the Annapolis conference are reproduced in Table 13.1.

TABLE 13.1

Variables Mentioned by Case Authors as Being Associated with the Emergence of Appropriator Organizations

A. Variables Related to the Resource
   1. *Size.* The boundaries of the CPR are sufficiently small, given the transportation and communication technology available, that appropriators can develop accurate knowledge of external boundaries and internal microenvironments.
   2. *Clear-cut boundaries.* The boundaries of the CPR are sufficiently distinct that appropriators can develop accurate knowledge of the external boundaries.
   3. *Indicators of CPR conditions.* Reliable indicators of the condition of the CPR can be obtained as a result of regular use.
B. Variables Related to the Relationship between Demand and Supply
   1. *Scarcity.* The amount of resource-units extracted from the CPR is sufficiently high that users are aware that their withdrawal patterns are interdependent.
   2. *Asset structure.* The legal claims that some members of a group can sustain are sufficiently large that they are motivated to pay a major share of the initial organizational costs of creating or restructuring an organization.
C. Variables Related to the Appropriators
   1. *Size.* The number of appropriators is sufficiently small that the costs of communication and decision making are relatively low.
   2. *Residence.* Appropriators permanently reside near or "in" the CPR.
   3. *Degree of Homogeneity.* Appropriators are not strongly divided by:
      (a) natural boundaries
      (b) different, conflictual use patterns
      (c) different perceptions of the risks of long-term extraction from the CPR
      (d) cultural antagonisms
      (e) substantially different exposures to risk (as upstream differ from downstream users).
   4. *Existing organization.* The appropriators have some prior experience with at least minimal levels of organization through:
      (a) the presence of a general purpose organizational structure, such as a village council or a cooperative organization
      (b) the presence of a specialized organizational structure related to this resource without prior management responsibilities, such as a boating club
      (c) the presence of nearby organizations that have helped others to solve similar CPR management problems.
   5. *Ownership status.* The rights that appropriators have to access, use, and potentially, to the exclusion of others, are sustainable and certain.
   6. *Degree of centralization.* The appropriators are not prevented from exercising local initiative by a centralized government.

NOTE: CPR stands for "common-pool resource."
SOURCE: Author.

Toward the Rudiments of a Theory of the Origins of Appropriator Organizations

This is a long list of variables. Many of them do play an important role in specific cases, but such a list is too unwieldy to allow for further theory development and testing. To develop a theory of the emergence of some form of user organization, we need to develop a smaller set of key variables.

In this effort, we can also draw on previous theoretical work related to the theory of constitutional choice.[4] An AO can be conceptualized as a small polity constituted by appropriators for the purpose of gaining a joint benefit (the regulation of the CPR). A central assumption of the theory of constitutional choice is that the costs of decision making involved in arriving at a set of coordinated strategies for the members of a collectivity are greater than the costs of decision making involved when each and every person is free to adopt his or her own independent strategy. In deciding whether or not to create a new polity—in our case a new AO—it is presumed necessary for individuals to examine not only the expected benefits to be derived from the coordinated strategies of the collectivity, but also the expected costs in time and resources devoted to decision making and the expected, potential deprivations imposed on individuals by the polity itself.

A general proposition of the theory of constitutional choice is that a group of individuals will constitute a new polity when the perceived benefits to be gained from the enterprise are greater than the total estimated decision-making costs of the enterprise using a particular set of rules (Buchanan and Tullock 1962). By thinking in a more general fashion about the list of variables shown in Table 13.1, the same general proposition can be made regarding the emergence of an AO. AOs do not emerge unless the perceived benefits of organization exceed the perceived cost of organization.

If a CPR is a valuable resource worth the costs of managing it, the *perception* that benefits exceed costs is more likely to arise when participants have relatively full and accurate information about: (1) the physical structure of a resource, (2) the past actions of other appropriators, (3) the relationship of demand to yield, (4) the benefits and costs of various actions and outcomes impinging on different individuals and firms, and (5) the likelihood that other participants will keep promises. The specific variables in Table 13.1 can be viewed as variables that enhance the information that individuals possess about both the benefits and the costs of constituting a new organization. With this view of how these variables are important to the emergence of AOs, we can now make the following more general propositions:

Individuals will tend to switch from independent strategies for exploiting a CPR to more costly, coordinated strategies when they share a common understanding that:

1. Continuance of their independent strategies will seriously harm an important resource for their survival.

2. Coordinated strategies exist that effectively reduce the risk of serious harm to the CPR.

3. Most of the other appropriators from the CPR can be counted on to change strategies if they promise to do so.

4. The cost of decision making about future coordinated strategies is less than the benefits to be derived from the adoption of coordinated strategies.

Let us now discuss how these general propositions are related to the specific variables in Table 13.1.

Common Understanding of the Problem

Whether appropriators share a common understanding that continuing independent strategies will seriously harm a resource important for their survival depends on the size and performance of the resource itself and on their own actions. Drawing on Table 13.1, we can say that if the resource is relatively small (A1), the boundaries are easy to determine (A2), and reliable indicators of its conditions are present (A3), appropriators can begin to develop a consistent understanding of the amount and value of the yield of the CPR. Users need relatively good information about the amount of the yield or reliable and sensitive indicators about the condition of the CPR. How fast this type of information is obtained and synthesized depends heavily on the type of resource involved and the level of scientific knowledge used (Gilles and Jamtgaard 1981).

If appropriators live in a small community (C1) near to the CPR (C2), they will have a relatively accurate picture of each other's withdrawal practices.[5] Further, open communication about the problems they face, as well as about potential solutions, is enhanced when users live in a small community. This is consistent with a major finding from the research of scholars who have constructed commons laboratory experiments on commons situations. When communication is unconstrained in laboratory CPRs, participants are far more likely to devise joint strategies that achieve higher joint outcomes than when communication is constrained (see Wilson 1985; E. Ostrom and Walker 1991; and the review of laboratory experimentation by Feeny in Chapter 12 of this book).

As users come to recognize through communication that demands are close to or are exceeding the yield (B1), then one can expect that they will share an understanding that continuance of their independent strategies will seriously harm the CPR. This recognition is not sufficient for a change from individual to coordinated strategies. The users must also place a high value on the CPR itself in terms of their own economic and social survival.

Common Understanding of Alternatives for Coordination

Appropriators must be able to conceptualize the possibility of alternative strategies that might avoid this harm. The capacity to think about alternative coordinated strategies is affected by the prior experience that users have had with other forms of local organization (C4a and C4b in Table 13.1), knowledge about the experiences of other groups trying to solve similar problems (C4c), the certainty of their own status as owners (C5), and a capacity to take local initiative (C6). One would expect appropriators with little or no common experience with or knowledge of successful efforts to achieve coordinated strategies to have greater difficulties in developing strategies to manage a CPR.

Common Perception of Mutual Trust and Reciprocity

Participants need assurance that if they change to more costly, coordinated strategies, others will do likewise. This is the central argument in the work of Oakerson (Chapter 3; Oakerson 1988) and C. Ford Runge (Chapter 2; Runge 1981, 1984), who stress how important the assurance of mutual promise keeping is in solving CPR problems. Given the structure of the commons dilemma as it is frequently modeled, this is the problem that each individual must be assured that he or she will not be the "sucker" who adopts the most costly coordinated strategies (that is, cooperates) while others yield to their "temptation" not to cooperate and continue their own practices. Assurance may also be obtained through reliance on formal police, formal surveillance and investigations, and formal courts. Use of formal legal methods to gain assurance is costly, however, and appropriators can reduce the costs of assurance dramatically if they are willing to develop relationships of trust and reciprocity among themselves (R. McKean 1975).

Mutual trust has been conceptualized as an asset that individuals build over time by engaging in mutually beneficial transactions that cannot be consummated in an immediate quid pro quo exchange (see Breton and Wintrobe 1982; see also Posner 1980). Perceptions concerning the likelihood that other users will follow an agreed-upon coordinated strategy are affected by all of the factors related to the group (C1, C2, C3a,

C3b, C3c, C3d, C3e) and to prior experience with local organization (C4a, C4b, and C4c).

Common Perceptions That Decision-Making Costs Do Not Exceed Benefits

Users would also need to share an expectation that the costs of future decision making about coordinated strategies will not exceed the benefits to be derived from the use of coordinated strategies. Expectations about decision-making costs are affected by all of the characteristics of a group and by its prior experience of and knowledge about organizational arrangements. Almost all theories of organization posit that decision-making costs rise with the size of the group making decisions (C1 in Table 13.1). One would expect that the greater the homogeneity of the group, the lower the costs of arriving at decisions. Decision-making costs are also lowered if some individuals are willing and able to undertake entrepreneurial efforts to get organized or to persuade an existing organization to include the CPR within its frame of interest (Olson 1965).

When the Tragedy Is Not Avoided

By focusing on the conditions necessary for the emergence of coordinated strategies to use a CPR, the four propositions developed above also help to explain why so many CPRs have been destroyed or are suffering severe problems of degradation. One can reverse the direction of the propositions in the following shortened version:

> Appropriators will continue independent strategies for exploiting a CPR unless they share a common understanding and perception of: (1) the nature of the problem, (2) the alternatives for coordination available to them, (3) the likelihood of mutual trust and reciprocity, and (4) expected decision-making costs as being less than the benefits to be derived.

Given this statement of the problem, one understands why individuals continue independent strategies for exploiting many CPRs. Unless creative efforts are expended to create large-scale user-group organizations, independent, exploitative strategies are a dominant strategy for all participants. Problems of controlling ocean fisheries, migratory wildlife, and international air pollution are several orders of difficulty greater than localized common-pool problems such as managing grazing lands, irrigation projects, inshore fisheries, and the like.

The general principles involved in solving large-scale CPR problems are similar to those involved in dealing with smaller resource systems. The processes of gaining a common understanding and devising workable coordinated strategies are, however, far more difficult and costly for large-scale common-pool problems. Institutional designs relying on nested structures of smaller organizations within larger organizations are most likely needed (see Coward 1980; Bendor and Mookerjee 1985). The development of such structures, when the resource crosses jurisdictional boundaries (or, even worse, exists outside all jurisdictional boundaries), is costly and difficult.

On the Survival of Appropriator Organizations

The creation of an organization and the development of coordinated strategies for using a common-pool resource are no guarantee that an organization can survive over time. Many efforts to achieve coordinated strategies have collapsed after a few years. Initial perceptions of the nature of the problem, the alternatives for coordination, the likelihood of mutual trust, and the costs of decision making may be altered by experience. Is it possible to posit the variables that may be conducive to the survival of an AO, once it has emerged through the slow accretion of common understandings or has been consciously designed by individuals trying to solve a specific problem? I think it is.

Six general propositions can be stated as a means of summarizing the more specific variables discussed at the Annapolis conference.

An appropriator organization is more likely to survive if:

1. The organization devises a small set of simple rules related to access and use patterns agreed to by appropriators.
2. The enforcement of these rules is shared by all appropriators, supplemented by some "official" observers and enforcers.
3. The organization is constituted with internally adaptive mechanisms.
4. The appropriators from the CPR are able to sustain legal claims as owners of the CPR.
5. The organization is nested in a set of larger organizations in which it is perceived as legitimate.
6. The organization is not subjected to rapid exogenous change.

Let us discuss each of these propositions in turn.

A Small Set of Simple Rules

The development of a small set of simple rules agreed to by appropriators has many survival advantages. The key advantage is that participants can remember the rules and transmit them to new participants over time. The constraints that social systems use to structure behavior—rules, that is— are constraints only to the extent that humans can understand what is and is not allowed and can transmit this information over time (see V. Ostrom 1980, 1985; E. Ostrom 1986). To the extent that rules are backed up by physical constraints (for example, fences or governing devices on motors), it is easier for individuals to follow a rule without actually knowing it and to be sure that behavior is in conformance with rules. Most rules, however, are constraints only in so far as humans learn them, follow them almost automatically, tell others about them, and know when others are or are not following them.

The fewer the rules used to organize activities (relative to the complexity of the activities), the more likely that individuals can understand, remember, and follow them. Further, the fewer and less ambiguous the rules are, the higher will be the agreement among all participants about what is and what is not an infraction. At the Annapolis conference we discussed the multiple functions of the simple rule "You must live locally to use this system."[6] Following this rule

- is easy because the rule is extremely easy to learn, remember, and transmit
- enhances the local knowledge that appropriators have about the resource
- enhances the possibility for reciprocity and trust among participants because they have a higher probability of knowing one another and engaging in other transactions
- reduces decision-making costs about who can or cannot use the system
- reduces enforcement costs since a stranger will be obvious to most participants

An unchanging rule that a grazing commons will be open for use between the same dates every year (and closed otherwise) is a low-cost rule for coordinating the behavior of large numbers of appropriators who may live miles apart during much of a year (see Gilles, Hammoudi and Mahdi in Chapter 10 of this book). Assigning a single individual in a residential community the responsibility for announcing the dates for opening and closing of a commons is, as McKean points out in Chapter 4, a more flexible and equally clear rule of access, but may be difficult to use when appropriators live far apart without modern modes of communication.

Dual Enforcement

That the rules of an AO are enforced by the appropriators themselves backed up by some "official" enforcers also appears to be an important condition for survival. The long-serving village institutions described by McKean in this volume illustrate this clearly. One or two participants simply forgetting to follow the rule without anyone saying anything can be the beginning of the end. Once some participants unconsciously (or consciously) forget to follow the rules, and no one says or does anything to them, others observe the lack of sanctions and are less inclined to follow the rules themselves.

Dual enforcement is a mutually reinforcing process. No AO can hire enough guards to see all the boundaries of a CPR and all of the activities of users. Users are the effective "public eyes" (Jacobs 1961) that cover more of the territory than official guards could ever see. If users know, understand, and have agreed to a simple set of rules, and if they use social sanctions against one another for rule infractions of various kinds, there is a higher probability that a rule infraction will not go unnoticed and unsanctioned. Further, if social sanctions are backed up by official guards, this helps everyone remember the rules and gives the social sanctions more weight.

Internally Adaptive Mechanisms

Two aspects of adaptability were discussed at Annapolis. The first had to do with the capacity of an AO to use multiple decision rules and to relate these to different types of problems. Many conference participants articulated a need for at least three types of authority rules that would

- create a *position for a single individual* who is authorized to make decisions for the AO related to important and rapidly changing conditions
- create a *council* (either representative or a full assembly) where major problems can be discussed, general rules formulated (particularly those related to distribution and problems of equity), and penalties assessed
- rely on *broad consensus and/or formal rules* requiring extraordinary majorities for deciding on actions that may involve considerable sacrifice or penalties

This implies that even though AO rules should be as simple and as few as possible, the governance structure of an organization should be relatively complex if it is to survive over a long time period.

The second aspect of adaptability has to do with the capacity of an AO to change its own structure over time. An organization that can change its own rules regarding membership, access to and use of the CPR, collection of information, and the incentives and sanctions to be used, has a higher probability of being able to survive in a changing environment than one that must continue to use the same rules for internal organization over time. This aspect of adaptability is closely related to what W. Ross Ashby (1956) has referred to as "ultrastability."

Ownership

For survival, participants at the Annapolis conference argued that those who are the users of a CPR should also be its owners. While cases such as the one described by Cordell and McKean illustrate instances where individuals with few claims to property rights have developed rather ingenious ways to manage a CPR, the same cases also illustrate the marginal character of these AOs. While the swamp fishermen view each other as "coowners" of the resource, outsiders perceive them as having no legal claims to it. Conflicts among residential users can be worked out *within* their own de facto legal framework. Conflicts between residential users and "outsiders" cannot be worked out locally and must be settled within a de jure legal system. In Chapter 1, Bromley stresses the problems involved when only de facto ownership is exercised by participants.

Nesting of an AO in a Larger System

A fifth proposition has to do with the nesting of an AO within a set of larger organizations and authorities for dealing with problems beyond the boundaries of the AO. This is particularly critical when the CPR itself is large and AOs are organized around subparts. Thus, if those on a tertiary channel of a large irrigation system organize an AO to keep their channels clear and to regulate the opening of valves, they also need to be able to communicate effectively with the operators of the headwaters from time to time (see Uphoff 1985, 1986).

Nesting of organizational arrangements in federated structures of various kinds may also enable participants to cope with holdout problems more effectively in *large* groups. Once an AO grows large, informal sanctioning among members becomes more difficult. Building a larger organization from smaller units, however, enables participants to monitor and impose informal sanctions on each other within a smaller organization. If a member organization begins to lag behind, on the other hand, the larger organization can stimulate conformance.

Even when a particular AO is effectively organized to deal with the internal problems of a CPR, many events from outside the system can affect the CPR's operation. Local appropriators need mechanisms for effective communication with larger organizations to cope with these problems. External organizations or authorities can provide essential inputs to the decision making undertaken at the AO level. Examples include scientific information, capital fund-raising, modern technological training (where this is really needed), and supplemental conflict resolution mechanisms (available when the AO cannot resolve its own conflicts successfully).

Lack of Simultaneous Exogenous Changes

An AO is more likely to survive over time if it is fortunate enough not to have to cope with many, simultaneous changes in such key exogenous variables as population, technology, number of appropriators, external demands, and relationship to central authorities. As Bromley points out in Chapter 1, all large changes in exogenous variables threaten the capacity of individuals to learn about the change fast enough to make adaptive responses. The faster and greater the amount of the change, the higher the probability that an AO cannot respond rapidly enough.

Is Survival Sufficient?

Simple survival of an AO is not a sufficient condition for effective performance.[7] The survival of an AO over a long time leads one to presume that the AO is doing something well. The key question is *what* is it doing well? For some AOs, the answer may be that the *only* thing they are doing well is surviving. Unless AOs are in highly competitive environments that tend to eliminate the inefficient and inequitable ones, we cannot presume that those that survive are performing well. If AOs were firms in a highly competitive market, the theory of market processes would enable us to infer that survivors use efficient, long-term strategies—even though the survivors may not have selected these strategies consciously (Alchian 1950).

Some AOs have extraordinary powers not available to private firms in a competitive market. These powers enable such AOs to survive even though performing poorly. AOs that can enforce membership and contributions to collective actions (for example, if they have public powers to coerce and sanction) can survive even when most of their members do not evaluate them as performing efficiently or equitably. It is even possible for a long-surviving AO to generate more costs than benefits. The latter can occur when membership is coerced and the costs of exit are high. Many AOs organized in the public sector can coerce membership, and exit may involve extraordinary costs. Consequently, it is especially important not to presume that surviving local governments automatically perform well.

AOs established and maintained primarily through voluntary agreement and operating over a long time period without full governmental powers are most likely to generate more benefits than they impose costs. It is hard to imagine how strictly voluntary AOs could survive unless net benefits are positive. In a strictly voluntary association, members can leave the AO at any point they perceive costs of participation to exceed benefits. Yet a positive benefit-cost ratio is not equivalent to high performance.

What Is Good Performance for an AO?

Oakerson's framework (see Chapter 3) includes two criteria that could be used to evaluate the outcomes of user interactions related to the CPR: efficiency and equity. The first aspect of efficiency mentioned by Oakerson is whether appropriators have achieved an *optimal rate of use*. A less rigorous efficiency criterion is that appropriators are not exceeding the sustainable yield. A second aspect of efficiency has to do with the difference between the *benefits* resulting from the operation of an AO and the *decision-making* and *potential deprivation costs* of the AO. A minimal efficiency criterion is that this difference is positive. A comparative efficiency criterion can be used to explore whether the difference between the benefits and costs of an AO in one setting is as large or larger than that of another AO in a similar setting. Two questions are involved in using the criterion of equity: (1) Is the distribution of the costs roughly similar to the distribution of benefits? (2) Are there patterns of redistribution that appropriators wish to achieve at this level of organization?

At the Annapolis meetings several conditions—in addition to those identified as conducive to emergence and to survival—were found to enhance the performance of AOs in governing and managing CPRs. One set of conditions is concerned with the "match" of the membership of the AO and that of the appropriators. A second involves the relationship between the incidence of benefits and the incidence of costs derived from the operation of the AO. A third factor is the knowledge generated by appropriators about the CPR and about user preferences, benefits, and costs. While these might possibly be stated in propositional form, my understanding of what is involved is not yet sufficient for me to do so, and I will simply discuss each of these conditions in turn.

The Match of Membership of the AO and the Appropriators

A key factor that affects the long-run performance of organizational arrangements is whether organizations can be established and maintained whose boundaries are roughly coterminous with those of the CPR and its appropriators. This is definitely not easy to accomplish in natural settings.[8] Most communities are simultaneously concerned with many types of problems. The boundaries most relevant for managing a particular CPR may not be the same as those most relevant for managing another CPR or some types of pure collective goods. Even if we assume a considerable amount of discretion in establishing AOs, it is unlikely that the boundaries of any private or public AO will exactly match those of a particular resource system. In governmental systems, where jurisdictional boundaries are firmly established from the center and citizens are discouraged from establishing local organizations with quasi-public powers, the likelihood of even a rough match between the most relevant organizational arrangement and the CPR is low.

Mismatches can take two forms. The first form involves the case where an AO is *considerably larger* than the CPR in territory or number of appropriators. A possible outcome of this mismatch is total indifference by the larger unit to the problems of regulating the CPR. In the eventuality that appropriators were effectively represented in a democratic process in the larger unit, poor performance could still be predicted. Individuals living outside the boundaries of the CPR would have little or no information about what was happening in the CPR and would certainly not want to pay taxes to support its activities.

A second type of mismatch would occur if the organization attempting to regulate the CPR were *substantially smaller* than the CPR in territory or number of appropriators. If an AO could gain the cooperation of only a small subset of those actually using a CPR, this small subset would be the only one contributing to the regulatory program. Those who did not cooperate by changing their withdrawal patterns or through contributions to support investments in the CPR would gain substantially without contributing their fair share. If the number of noncooperators were large, those who initially might be willing to cooperate might not be willing to cooperate over the long run. While a mismatch of the first type is likely to result in an *overinvestment* in collective activities and projects, a mismatch of the second type is likely to result in an *underinvestment*. We must be careful, however, to examine *operational* patterns of relationships before presuming a mismatch. While no single, formal organizational unit may exist with similar boundaries, informal arrangements among organizations may enable appropriators to develop effective, informal organizational arrangements that roughly match the boundaries of a CPR.

The Relationship between the Incidence of Benefits and Costs

A second consideration is how rules distribute costs and benefits. Many of the simple rules adopted as a means of long-term survival are not optimal rules in the sense of maximal efficiency. J. Roumasset (1985), for example, points out that the simple rule used on many long-surviving irrigation systems of allocating water based on the amount of land owned can lead to inefficiency. If the system is large, the cost of getting water to parcels at the end of the system is much higher than getting it to those at the head of the system. The rule allocating water has to be looked at, however, in relation to the rule requiring labor or other inputs. When farmers are required to invest substantial quantities of their own labor to maintain irrigation systems, rules relating the amount of labor required to the amount of water received are relatively typical (Tang 1992). Thus a rule that is inefficient when used to allocate water on a system where no inputs are required, may be quite efficient when used to allocate water on a system where substantial inputs are required based on the same formula as water allocations (see also Bromley, Taylor, and Parker 1980 for a discussion of equitable distributions).

The Type of Knowledge Generated

It is conceivable that individuals might organize an AO that survived for some time without detailed information about the characteristics of the CPR and use patterns. It is inconceivable, however, that such an AO could perform efficiently or equitably without such information. Without detailed knowledge about the yield patterns of the CPR, rules that reduce the quantity of use-units that participants are allowed to withdraw may be more or less stringent than needed to manage the CPR efficiently. Even when appropriators are able to obtain relatively reliable information about the characteristics of their CPR, they may not obtain valid information about the actual use patterns of various appropriators over time. Appropriators are not motivated to reveal the full extent of their use since such information may lead others to try to limit their activities. Unless the CPR is small and easy to understand, and each user can easily monitor the use patterns of others, obtaining accurate information is far from a trivial problem.

Some of the technical knowledge needed about the physical structure of a CPR may be provided by larger public or private agencies that provide experts to map the CPR and describe its yield patterns. A key question, however, is whether this information is made available to the appropriators themselves or only to central agencies who are not involved in the day-to-day operation of the CPR system. It is a common practice of donor agencies to make technical reports to the bureaus of central governments and not to the appropriators themselves. Institutional arrangements used in developed countries, such as those of a "watermaster" associated with equity courts, provide technical information about the CPR and about use patterns to all participants (see Blomquist and E. Ostrom 1985), but such arrangements are used infrequently in the developing world.

Conflict can be an important feedback mechanism for the participants in an AO about how past efforts (or projected future efforts) affect the interests and behaviors of different participants. AOs vary in the extent to which they use conflict creatively for gaining information about problems perceived by different participants. If conflict is suppressed, key information about the effects of past actions is lost. If conflict is encouraged, valuable resources are spent in potentially harmful disputes. Thus, the development of effective conflict resolution mechanisms within an AO is also an important aspect of its capacity to achieve efficient and equitable performance.

Conclusion

The rudiments of a theory of the origins, survival, and performance of organizations to manage common-pool resources have now been presented. The theory represents an effort to integrate the findings of specific case authors and the speculations made at the Annapolis conference, where the chapters of this book were intensively discussed, with a broad political-economic approach to the study of institutions. Since the first draft of this chapter was circulated, a number of important books have been or will soon be published that contain still further empirical support for the propositions of the theory just sketched (Ascher and Healy 1990; Berkes 1989; Fortmann and Bruce 1988; Marshak 1987; McCay and Acheson 1987; E. Ostrom, 1990; E. Ostrom, Gardner, and Walker n.d.; V. Ostrom, Feeny, and Picht 1988; Pinkerton 1989; Wade 1986). A major bibliography has also been published (Martin 1992). In all of the cases described in these works, overexploitation of common-pool resources occurred when open access prevailed either because no set of individuals had property rights or because state property was treated as open-access property. Appropriator organizations were able in many instances—but not all—to manage CPRs effectively. Where AOs failed to develop, did not survive, or performed inadequately, it would appear that one or more of the variables identified above was responsible.

Obviously, much more work is needed to make this rudimentary theory more rigorous and to test its implications precisely rather than generally. Many scholars are engaged in this effort as an International Association for the Study of Common Property has now been established (its first international meeting was scheduled for the fall of 1990 at Duke University and the second for the fall of 1991 at the University of Manitoba). In several works published at about the same time, some of the propositions presented above were developed by a more formal method or given a more precise empirical test (see Gardner and E. Ostrom 1991; Weissing and E. Ostrom 1991; Walker, Gardner, and E. Ostrom 1991; Tang 1992; E. Ostrom 1990, 1992). It is an exciting time to be participating in an evolving interdisciplinary effort to understand how institutional arrangements affect the capacity of individuals to engage in self-governance and self-management of common-pool resources.

These theoretical and empirical efforts translate into policy proposals. At the Annapolis conference, for example, participants strongly articulated a view of the type of policies that donors and governments of developing countries should adopt to be consistent with our evolving understanding. The participants recommended to donors and policymakers in developing countries that they abandon current presumptions that local rules and customs were lacking for most common-pool resource systems. Instead, the participants urged that the burden of proof should rest with donors and policymakers to demonstrate the absence of local customs and rules before intervening to impose external ones. The advice in a nutshell was:

1. If a people have lived in close relationship with a relatively small common-pool resource system over a long period of time, they have probably evolved some system to limit and regulate use patterns.
2. Before one imposes new rules on local systems, inquiries should be made to determine if some rules and customs do not already exist.
3. If some customs and rules do exist, study these carefully in order to understand how they affect use patterns over time.
4. Propose new rules only after you have convinced yourself that either no rules and customs exist, or the rules and customs that do exist are not effective in achieving regulation or produce substantial inefficiency, inequity, or both; and you are thoroughly familiar with the configuration

of institutions in existence that may affect how new rules operate in practice.

5. Maintaining and enforcing new rules depends upon people finding those rules to be an acceptable way of ordering their relationships with one another as a community.

6. New rules cannot vary dramatically from the existing repertoire of rules in use or they will exist only on paper and not in the minds of those who must understand the rules to make them work.

We can hope that this message will be heard.

NOTES

The author is appreciative of the support given her research by the Decentralization: Finance and Management Project sponsored by the Office of Rural and Institutional Development of the Bureau for Science and Technology (S&T/RD) of the U.S. Agency for International Development (AID) and the National Science Foundation (grant no. SES 8619498). Useful comments have been made on earlier drafts of the chapter by John Baden, Christi Barbour, Fikret Berkes, William Blomquist, Peter Bogason, Daniel Bromley, David Feeny, Garrett Hardin, Bonnie McCay, Vincent Ostrom, Roger Parks, Pauline Peters, Jeanne Schaaf, Robert Wade, York Willbern, Rick Wilson, and James Wunsch.

1. See Bromley, Taylor, and Parker 1980 for a review of literature about irrigation associations in many different third world countries. Most irrigation associations would be covered by the concept of an appropriator organization.

2. The first necessary but not sufficient condition for avoiding the tragedy of the commons is the establishment of property rights limiting who can use, how much can be withdrawn, who can manage, and how rights are transferred.

3. The variables listed in Table 13.1 were mentioned by participants as being important as either enhancing or hindering efforts to achieve organized coordination of some sort. None of them were identified as necessary and sufficient conditions either for *or* against the emergence of an AO. Cultural divisions are not, for example, a sufficient condition for not achieving organization. Many successful AOs include membership that crosses ethnic and linguistic barriers. On the other hand, when individuals from cultural traditions that are deeply suspicious of and antagonistic to one another try to solve CPR problems, they have more to overcome in developing mutual trust than when a set of individuals all come from the same cultural background (see discussion in Bromley, Taylor, and Parker 1980).

4. See Buchanan and Tullock 1962 for an important general theory of constitutional choice and V. Ostrom and E. Ostrom 1977 and E. Ostrom 1989 for earlier efforts to apply the theory of constitutional choice to the analysis of CPRs (see also V. Ostrom 1982, 1986; Roumasset 1985).

5. See Berkes and Kişlalioglu 1989 for an analysis of the relative efficiency and equity of small-scale fisheries and a summary of literature on the evolution of community-based resource management systems.

6. Several of the cases in this book use this rule including those by McKean (Chapter 4), Campbell and Godoy (Chapter 5), Berkes (Chapter 7), Cordell and McKean (Chapter 8), and Wade (Chapter 9).

7. Several recent analyses have stressed the importance of *not* equating survival and optimality (see, for example, Binger and Hoffman 1989; March and Olsen 1989).

8. I do wish to stress that there are many forms of organization that accomplish this rough correspondence. Wade (1986) has shown how local organization based on a *village* structure in India is able to encompass most of the affected irrigators even though the organization is not based on the irrigation channel.

REFERENCES

Advisory Commission on Intergovernmental Relations. 1987. *The Organization of Local Public Economies*. Washington, D.C.: The Commission. (Written by Ronald J. Oakerson.)

Alchian, Armen A. 1950. "Uncertainty, Evolution, and Economic Theory." *Journal of Political Economy* 58 (June):211–21.

Ascher, William, and Robert Healy. 1990. *Natural Resource Policymaking: A Framework for Developing Countries*. Durham, N.C.: Duke University Press.

Ashby, W. Ross. 1956. *An Introduction to Cybernetics*. New York: Wiley.

Bates, Robert H. 1983. *Essays on the Political Economy of Rural Africa*. London: Cambridge University Press.

Bendor, Jonathan and Dilip Mookherjee. 1985. "Institutional Structure and the Logic of Ongoing Collective Action." Working paper, School of Business, Stanford University, Stanford, Calif.

Berkes, Fikret. 1989. *Common Property Resources, Ecology and Community-Based Sustainable Development*. London: Belhaven Press.

Berkes, Fikret, and Mina Kişlalioglu. 1989. "A Comparative Study of Yield, Investment and Energy Use in Small-Scale Fisheries: Some Considerations for Resource Planning." *Fisheries Research* 7:207–24.

Binger, Brian R., and Elizabeth Hoffman. 1989. "Institutional Persistence and Change: The Question of Efficiency." *Journal of Institutional and Theoretical Economics* 145:67–85.

Blomquist, William, and Elinor Ostrom. 1985. "Institutional Capacity and the Resolution of a Commons Dilemma." *Policy Studies Review* 5 (2):383–93.

Brennan, Geoffrey, and James Buchanan. 1985. *The Reason of Rules*. Cambridge: Cambridge University Press.

Breton, Albert, and Ronald Wintrobe. 1982. *The Logic of Bureaucratic Conduct*. Cambridge: Cambridge University Press.

Bromley, Daniel W. 1984. "Property Rights and Economic Incentives in Resource and Environmental Systems." Agricultural Economics Staff Paper Series, no. 231. Department of Agricultural Economics, University of Wisconsin, Madison.

Bromley, Daniel W., Donald C. Taylor, and Donald E. Parker. 1980. "Water Reform and Economic Development: Institutional Aspects of Water Management in the Developing Countries." Economic Development and Cultural Change 28 (2):365–87.

Buchanan, James, and Gordon Tullock. 1962. The Calculus of Consent. Ann Arbor: University of Michigan Press.

Ciriacy-Wantrup, S. V., and Richard C. Bishop. 1975. " 'Common Property' as a Concept in Natural Resource Policy." Natural Resources Journal 15:713–27.

Coward, E. W., Jr. 1980. Irrigation and Agricultural Development in Asia: Perspectives from Social Sciences. Ithaca, N.Y.: Cornell University Press.

Feeny, David H. 1986. "Conference on Common Property Resource Management: An Introduction." In National Research Council, Proceedings of the Conference on Common Property Resource Management, 7–11. Washington, D.C.: National Academy Press.

Fortmann, Louise, and John W. Bruce, eds. 1988. Whose Trees? Proprietary Dimensions of Forestry. Boulder, Colo.: Westview Press.

Gardner, Roy, and Elinor Ostrom. 1991. "Rules and Games." Public Choice 70 (2):121–49.

Gardner, Roy, Elinor Ostrom, and James Walker. 1990. "The Nature of Common-Pool Resource Problems." Rationality and Society 2:335–58.

Gilles, Jere L., and Keith Jamtgaard. 1981. "Overgrazing in Pastoral Areas: The Commons Reconsidered." Sociologia Ruralis 21 (Sept.):129–41.

Hardin, Garrett. 1968. "The Tragedy of the Commons." Science 162 (Dec.):1343–48.

Hardin, Russell. 1982. Collective Action. Baltimore: The Johns Hopkins University Press.

Holt, Sidney J., and Lee M. Talbot. 1978. New Principles for the Conservation of Wild Living Resources. Wildlife Monographs no. 59. Washington, D.C.: Wildlife Society.

Jacobs, Jane. 1961. The Death and Life of Great American Cities. New York: Random House.

Kiser, Larry L., and Elinor Ostrom. 1982. "The Three Worlds of Action. A Meta-Theoretical Synthesis of Institutional Approaches." In Strategies of Political Inquiry, ed. E. Ostrom, 179–222. Beverly Hills, Calif.: Sage.

March, James G., and Johan P. Olsen. 1989. Rediscovering Institutions: The Organizational Basis of Politics. New York: Free Press.

Marshak, Patricia. 1987. "Uncommon History." In Uncommon Property: The Fishing and Fish Processing Industries in British Columbia, ed. Patricia Marshak, Neil Guppy, and John McMullan, 353–59. Toronto: Methuen.

Martin, Fenton. 1992. Common Pool Resources and Collective Action: A Bibliography. Vol. 2. Bloomington: Indiana University, Workshop in Political Theory and Policy Analysis.

McCay, Bonnie J., and James M. Acheson. 1987. *The Question of the Commons: The Culture and Ecology of Communal Resources.* Tucson: University of Arizona Press.

McKean, Roland. 1975. "Economics of Trust, Altruism, and Corporate Responsibility." In *Altruism, Morality, and Economic Theory,* ed. Edmund S. Phelps, 29–44. New York: Russel Sage Foundation.

North, Douglass C. 1981. *Structure and Change in Economic History.* New York: Norton.

Oakerson, Ronald J. 1988. "Reciprocity: A Bottom-Up View of Political Development." In *Rethinking Institutional Analysis and Development: Issues, Alternatives, and Choices,* ed. Vincent Ostrom, David Feeny, and Hartmut Picht, 408-35. San Francisco, Calif.: ICS Press.

Olson, Mancur. 1965. *The Logic of Collective Action.* Cambridge, Mass.: Harvard University Press.

Ostrom, Elinor. 1986. "An Agenda for the Study of Institutions." *Public Choice* 48: 3–25.

———. 1989. "Microconstitutional Change in a Multiconstitutional Political System." *Rationality and Society* 1 (1):11–50.

———. 1990. *Governing the Commons: The Evolution of Institutions for Collective Action.* Cambridge: Cambridge University Press.

———. 1992. *Crafting Institutions for Self-Governing Irrigation Systems.* San Francisco: ICS Press.

Ostrom, Elinor, and James Walker. 1991. "Communication in a Commons: Cooperation Without External Enforcement." In *Laboratory Research in Political Economy,* ed. Thomas R. Palfrey, 287–322. Ann Arbor: University of Michigan Press.

Ostrom, Elinor, Roy Gardner, and James Walker. n.d. *Rules, Games, and Common-Pool Resources.* Ann Arbor: University of Michigan Press, forthcoming.

Ostrom, Vincent. 1980. "Artisanship and Artifact." *Public Administration Review* 40 (4):309–17.

———. 1982. "A Forgotten Tradition: The Constitutional Level of Analysis." In *Missing Elements in Political Inquiry: Logic and Levels of Analysis,* ed. Judith A. Gillespie and Dina A. Zinnes, 237–52. Beverly Hills, Calif.: Sage.

———. 1985. "The Constitution of Order in Human Societies: Conceptualizing the Nature and Magnitude of the Task in Institutional Analysis and Development." Paper presented at International Political Science Association meetings, July 15–20, Paris.

———. 1986. "Constitutional Considerations with Particular Reference to Federal Systems." In *Guidance, Control and Evaluation in the Public Sector,* ed. F. X. Kaufmann, G. Majone, and V. Ostrom, 111–25. Berlin and New York: de Gruyter.

———. 1987. *The Political Theory of a Compound Republic: Designing the American Experiment.* Rev. ed. Lincoln: University of Nebraska Press.

Ostrom, Vincent, David Feeny, and Hartmut Picht, eds. 1988. *Rethinking Institutional Analysis and Development: Issues, Alternatives, and Choices.* San Francisco: ICS Press.

Ostrom, Vincent, and Elinor Ostrom. 1977. "A Theory for Institutional Analysis of Common Pool Problems." In *Managing the Commons*, ed. Garrett Hardin and John Baden, 157–72. San Francisco, Calif.: Freeman.

Pinkerton, Evelyn, ed. 1989. *Co-operative Management of Local Fisheries: New Directions for Improved Management and Community Development*. Vancouver: University of British Columbia Press.

Plott, Charles R., and Robert A. Meyer. 1975. "The Technology of Public Goods, Externalities, and the Exclusion Principle." In *Economic Analysis of Environmental Problems*, ed. E. S. Mills, 65–94. New York: Columbia University Press.

Posner, Richard A. 1980. "A Theory of Primitive Society with Special Reference to Law." *Journal of Law and Economics* 23 (April):1–54.

Roumasset, James. 1985. "Constitutional Choice for Common Property Management: The Case of Irrigation Associations." Paper prepared for National Academy of Sciences Workshop on Common Property Resource Management in Developing Countries, April 21–26, in Annapolis, Maryland.

Runge, C. Ford. 1981. "Common Property Externalities: Isolation, Assurance, and Resource Depletion in a Traditional Grazing Context." *American Journal of Agricultural Economics* 63 (Nov.):595–606.

———. 1984. "Strategic Interdependence in Models of Property Rights." *American Journal of Agricultural Economics* 66 (Dec.):807–13.

Schlager, Edella, and Elinor Ostrom. 1992. "Property-Rights Regimes and Natural Resources: A Conceptual Analysis." *Land Economics*, August.

Shepsle, Kenneth, and Barry Weingast. 1984. "Legislative Politics and Budget Outcomes." In *Federal Budget Policy in the 1980s*, ed. G. Mills and J. Palmer, 343–67. Washington, D.C.: Urban Institute Press.

Tang, Shui Yan. 1992. *Institutions and Collective Action: Self-Governance in Irrigation*. San Francisco: ICS Press.

Uphoff, Norman. 1985. "People's Participation in Water Management: Gal Oya, Sri Lanka." In *Public Participation in Development Planning and Management*, ed. J. C. Garcia-Zamor, 131–78. Boulder, Colo.: Westview Press.

———. 1986. *Getting the Process Right: Improving Irrigation Water Management with Farmer Participation*. Boulder, Colo.: Westview Press.

Wade, Robert. 1986. *Peasants and Politics*. Cambridge: Cambridge University Press.

Walker, James, Roy Gardner, and Elinor Ostrom. 1991. "Rent Dissipation and Balanced Deviation Disequilibrium in Common Pool Resources: Experimental Evidence." In *Game Equilibrium Models II: Methods, Morals, and Markets*, ed. Reinhard Selten, 337–67. Berlin: Springer-Verlag.

Weissing, Franz, and Elinor Ostrom. 1991. "Irrigation Institutions and the Games Irrigators Play: Rule Enforcement without Guards." In *Game Equilibrium Models II: Methods, Morals, and Markets*, ed. Reinhard Selten, 188–262. Berlin: Springer-Verlag.

Williamson, Oliver E. 1985. *The Economic Institutions of Capitalism: Firms, Markets, Relational Contracting*. New York: Free Press.

Wilson, Rick K. 1985. "Constraints on Social Dilemmas: An Institutional Approach." *Annals of Operational Research* 2:183–200.

Index

About the Contributors

Fikret Berkes

Fikret Berkes is professor and director of the Natural Resources Institute at the University of Manitoba, Winnipeg, Canada. He is the editor of *Common Property Resources: Ecology and Community-Based Sustainable Development* (1989) and has written some thirty papers on the management of fisheries and other common resources. Trained in marine ecology, he has investigated the relationship between resources and society in a variety of geographical settings: the Canadian subarctic, the Great Lakes, Turkey, and the Caribbean. His research focuses on the evolution and persistence of sustainable resource-use practices in small-scale, community-based fisheries.

Piers Blaikie

Piers Blaikie is a professor at the School of Development Studies, University of East Anglia, Norwich, England. He has worked principally in India and Nepal but also in Kenya, Zimbabwe, Uganda, Lesotho, and Morocco. His publications include *Family Planning in India* (1975), *Nepal in Crisis* (1980), *Political Economy of Soil Erosion in Developing Countries* (1985), *Land Degradation and Society* (1987), and *AIDS in Africa: Its Present and Future Impact* (1992).

Daniel W. Bromley

Daniel W. Bromley is acting director of the Institute for Environmental Studies and Anderson-Bascom Professor in the Department of Agricultural Economics, University of Wisconsin-Madison. He is also an associate fellow of the London Environmental Economics Center, University College, London. Bromley has published extensively on the subjects of public decision making, natural resource economics, and economic development. His recent books include *Economic Interests and Institutions: The Conceptual Foundations of Public Policy* (1989), *Environment and Economy: Property Rights and Public Policy* (1991), and *The Social Response to Environmental Risk: Public Policy in an Age of Uncertainty* (1992), which he coedited with Kathleen Segerson. He has been editor of the journal *Land Economics* since 1974.

Bruce M. S. Campbell

Bruce M. S. Campbell studied and taught historical geography before transferring to the Department of Economic and Social History at the Queen's University of Belfast, where he has been a lecturer since 1989. His primary research interest is the agrarian history of thirteenth- and fourteenth-century England, upon which he has published extensively. He was awarded the 1984 Arthur H. Cole Prize of the American Economic History Association for his essay "Arable Productivity in Medieval England: Some Evidence from Norfolk" in *The Journal of Economic History*. He has recently edited *Before the Black Death: Studies in the "Crisis" of the Early Fourteenth Century* (1991) and, with Mark Overton, *Land, Labour and Livestock: Historical Studies in European Agricultural Productivity* (1991). He is currently codirector of the research projects "Feeding the City II" (a study of London's impact upon agriculture and land use in its hinterland in the fourteenth century) and "The Geography of Seignorial Land-Ownership and Land-Use, 1270–1349."

John Cordell

John Cordell is founder of the Ethnographic Institute in Berkeley, California, a nonprofit organization focusing on development anthropology and educational media. He received his doctorate in anthropology from Stanford University in 1973 and has held teaching and research positions at the Woods Hole Oceanographic Institution, The International Center for Medical Research in Cali, Colombia, the Department of Genetics at Stanford Medical Center, and the University of California at Berkeley. He is the editor of *A Sea of Small Boats* (1989) and has written widely on traditional fisheries and marine resource management, tropical human ecology, and medical anthropology.

David Feeny

David Feeny is a professor in the departments of Economics and of Clinical Epidemiology and Biostatistics at McMaster University, Hamilton, Ontario. He has been a visiting faculty member at Northeastern University, Yale University, and the University of California, Berkeley. Working in economic history and development, Feeny has done pioneering research on the economics of institutional change and, in particular, the evolution of property rights. He has published extensively on agricultural development, collective action, institutional change, property rights in man, land, and forests, and the economy of Thailand. Among his recent books is *Rethinking Institutional Analysis and Development: Issues, Alternatives, and Choices*, coedited with Vincent Ostrom and Hartmut Picht (1988). Feeny also maintains an active research program in health economics, working on methods for the assessment of health-care technologies, health-related quality of life, and the economic evaluation of health-care services.

Jere L. Gilles

Jere L. Gilles is Associate Professor of Rural Sociology at the University of Missouri-Columbia. He received a Ph.D. in development sociology from Cornell University and was a doctoral research intern in the Water Management Program at the East-West Center in Honolulu, Hawaii. Gilles has studied irrigation management in Chad and North America and arid-lands resource management in Morocco and Peru. His current research projects are in Bolivia and in Kenya; the former project examines resource management strategies in drought-prone areas and the latter examines the institutional constraints to veterinary vaccine utilization in Africa. His research in North America examines the relationship between the organization of agriculture and community well-being. In 1990–1991 Gilles was a member of the Winrock study team asked by the Consultative Group on International Agricultural Research system to assess the future of animal agriculture. He is a past chair of the Rural Sociological Society's Sociology of Agriculture Research Group and its committee on Eastern Europe and the Soviet Union.

Ricardo A. Godoy

Ricardo A. Godoy received a Ph.D. in social anthropology from Columbia University and studied public policy administration at the John Fitzgerald Kennedy School of Government, Harvard University. His major area of interest is governance problems of natural resources. He worked in Bolivia on mining and in Indonesia on tree crops and minor forest products. He has also researched agricultural issues in Nicaragua and has recently completed a book with Mario De Franco on structural adjustment and cultural barriers to growth. He is a lecturer in the Department of Anthropology, Harvard University, and a research associate at the Harvard Institute for International Development.

John Harriss

John Harriss is program director in Development Studies at the London School of Economics and a member of the Department of Anthropology. He has wide experience in both rural and urban field research in South Asia and is the author of *Capitalism and Peasant Farming* (1982).

Margaret A. McKean

Margaret A. McKean is a member of the Department of Political Science at Duke University. A specialist in Japan's environmental politics and author of *Environmental Protest and Citizen Politics in Japan* (1981), she has long been interested in the management of common lands in Japan and in "tragedy of the commons" problems and the political economy of environmental issues in general. Her work on the Japanese commons is part of a forthcoming study, "The Common Good in Uncommonly Bad Times: Japan's Experience with Collective Choice under Scarcity," on the Japanese experience at cooperating to solve collective-choice problems under conditions of unusually severe resource scarcity. She was an original member of the National Academy of Sciences Panel on Common Property Resource Management and a founding member of the International Association for the Study of Common Property.

Ronald J. Oakerson

Ronald J. Oakerson is professor of political science at Houghton College. Formerly, he was a senior member of the research faculty at Indiana University, where he was associated with the Workshop in Political Theory and Policy Analysis. He was an original member of the National Academy of Sciences Panel on Common Property Resource Management and a founding member of the governing board of the International Association for the Study of Common Property. Oakerson currently is undertaking research for the U.S. Agency for International Development and its "Decentralization: Finance and Management" project on economic liberalization and the reform of agricultural cooperatives in Cameroon. In addition, he serves on the National Rural Studies Committee sponsored by W. K. Kellogg Foundation, and has published widely on American local government.

Elinor Ostrom

Elinor Ostrom is Arthur F. Bentley Professor of Political Science and codirector of the Workshop in Political Theory and Policy Analysis at Indiana University. Her major academic interest is in the field of institutional analysis and design—the study of how rules-in-use affect the incentives facing individuals in particular settings, their behavior, and consequent outcomes. She has studied institutional arrangements related to metropolitan governance and natural resources in both the United States and the Third World. She was recently elected a Fellow of the American Academy of Arts and Sciences. Her books include *Governing the Commons: The Evolution of Institutions for Collective Action* (1990); *Crafting Institutions for Self-Governing Irrigation Systems* (1992); *Local Government in the United States* (with Vincent Ostrom and Robert Bish, 1988); *Strategies of Political Inquiry* (1982), and *Patterns of Metropolitan Policing* (with Roger B. Parks and Gordon P. Whitaker, 1978).

Adam Pain

Adam Pain, an agricultural scientist and geneticist by background, was a lecturer in Natural Resources at the School of Development Studies, University of East Anglia, from 1976 to 1987. During that time he undertook research in Sri Lanka and India in agricultural research, natural resource management, and research policy. From 1987 to 1991 he was team leader of the regional Land and Water Management Research Project, based in Botswana, operating under the auspices of SADCC, the organization of the Front Line States. He is currently a Visiting Fellow at the School of Development Studies, University of East Anglia, Norwich.

C. Ford Runge

C. Ford Runge is a professor in the Department of Agricultural and Applied Economics at the University of Minnesota, where he also holds appointments in the Hubert H. Humphrey Institute of Public Affairs and the Department of Forest Resources. He was a member of the National Academy of Sciences Steering Committee on Common Property, and has been a Science and Diplomacy Fellow of the American Association for the Advancement of Science, working in the U.S. Agency for International Development on food aid and trade issues. During 1991, he studied European trade reform and environmental policy as a Fulbright Research Fellow, visiting at the universities of Padova (Italy) and Dijon (France). His publications include four books, most recently *Reforming Farm Policy: Toward a National Agenda* (1992), coauthored with Willard W. Cochrane. He has also written a wide range of articles concentrating on agricultural trade and natural resources policy, with particular emphasis on the links from agriculture to environmental quality.

James T. Thomson

James T. Thomson, a specialist in institutional analysis and design, has a background in political science. For the past twenty-five years, much of his applied research has addressed problems in common pool resource governance and management. He has conducted long- and short-term research in Niger, Burkina Faso, Mali, and Nepal on local and national institutional arrangements for the governance and management of wood-stock, watershed, pasture, and fisheries resources. His principal intellectual and practical concern is identifying options to make national constitutions and laws more amenable to the management efforts of common-property regimes. Thomson served as a member of the National Academy of Sciences Steering Committee that organized the 1985 Conference on Common Property Resource Management. He is a managing associate at Associates in Rural Development, Inc., an American consulting firm.

Robert Wade

Robert Wade, a Fellow of the Institute for Development Studies at the University of Sussex, has written extensively on the problems of resource management in the developing world. In addition to his appointment at Sussex, Wade has taught at the Woodrow Wilson School in Princeton, N.J.; Duke University; the University of California at San Diego; and Victoria

University in New Zealand. He is currently a visiting professor of government and international management at the Sloan School of Management, Massachusetts Institute of Technology. Two of his recent books are *Governing the Market: Economic Theory and the Role of Government in East Asian Industrialization* (1990) and *Village Republics: Economic Conditions for Collective Action in South India* (1988).